GERMANY
Rejoins the Powers

GERMANY
Rejoins the Powers

Mass Opinion, Interest Groups, and Elites
in Contemporary German Foreign Policy

By
KARL W. DEUTSCH
and
LEWIS J. EDINGER

OCTAGON BOOKS

A DIVISION OF FARRAR, STRAUS AND GIROUX

New York   1973

Reprinted 1973
by special arrangement with Stanford University Press

OCTAGON BOOKS
A Division of Farrar, Straus & Giroux, Inc.
19 Union Square West
New York, N. Y. 10003

Library of Congress Cataloging in Publication Data

Deutsch, Karl Wolfgang, 1912-
    Germany rejoins the powers.

    Reprint of the ed. published by Stanford University Press, Stanford, Calif.

    Bibliography: p. 293-
    1. Germany (Federal Republic, 1949-   )—Foreign relations.
    2. Public opinion—Germany (Federal Republic, 1949-   )
    I. Edinger, Lewis Joachim, 1922-   joint author. II. Title.
[DD259.4.D46 1973]   327.43   73-4236
ISBN 0-374-92137-7

Printed in USA by
Thomson-Shore, Inc.
Dexter, Michigan

To

Ruth Deutsch and Hanni Edinger

Preface

This book represents an exploration. Its subject deserves deeper, longer, and more thorough study than it has received here. For such a study, it can at best be a prelude, or a sample of some of the salient problems to be treated.

In the meantime, this sketch attempts to do two things. In its substance, it tries to give a brief summary of some of the main background conditions of German foreign policy making. These include the major new political institutions, the main changes in public opinion, and the major parties and interest groups and their alignments. They also include the composition of the new elite—the persons and groups that are making foreign policy in the German Federal Republic. Accordingly the book tries to analyze a sample of this new elite, and it describes some recent examples of its policy-making processes in operation.

Since much of the literature about prewar Germany, both the Weimar Republic and the Nazi dictatorship, has little direct relevance to present-day German problems and actions—and since a resurgent Germany looms ever larger in European and world politics, and not least in the foreign policy of the United States—a brief summary of some of the basic facts about the new German foreign policies and their makers may perhaps not be unwelcome to the student of international relations, and to the citizen who is interested in the uncertain prospects of war and peace and the shifting alignments of world power.

The second aim of this book lies in the realm of method. In recent decades, traditional political science has developed in vigorous intellectual interchange with other social science. Out of this cooperation has come a lively interest in the study of actual political behavior, in interest groups and elites, in public opinion, and in the more deep-lying political attitudes that bear on the problems of personality and the question of national character. To understand politics will always require the description of institutions, but it also requires an appreciation of their functioning in living interplay with more informal aspects of political practice. Both the descriptive and the functional approach to the study of politics gain from comparison—the comparison of their respective findings for the same country, and the comparison of such findings among different countries. The first kind of comparisons has been developed to a considerable extent in many studies of the making of foreign policy in the United States. The second kind of comparisons—that between different countries—is just beginning. The current revival among American political scientists of an interest in comparative politics promises well for its prospects. A set of basic questions have been suggested, and research approaches have begun to emerge, which might tell us a good deal about the policies and politics of a foreign country to which we might apply them.

Germany has seemed to us a reasonable test case for finding out what some of these methods of research and analysis can do at their present stage of development. It is a country of obvious and growing interest to students of world politics, and it is one of the few major countries on which there is available a fairly large amount of published data, ranging from a highly articulate press to scholarly studies, and from opinion polls to surveys of political parties and pressure groups, and to biographical data on many of her leaders. On almost any country, a superficial sketch could be written after a few weeks' visit, or a thorough scholarly work after many years' research. To think and decide intelligently about problems of foreign policy requires deeper knowledge than the journalistic sketch, but it requires information that can be put together here and now; it cannot wait for the ultimate verdict of the historian. How much knowledge and understanding, we thus must ask, can we extract from available data with limited resources and within a limited time? This is one of the tests—though not the only one—of our contemporary methods of political analysis; and they are applied here to the case of the German Federal Republic—within severe limits of resources and time.

Certainly this book does not pretend to do anything more. If it should have brought to the attention of its readers some of the information available on postwar German foreign policy, if it should have ordered it for their more thoughtful exploration, and if it should provoke the undertaking of more thorough studies, it will have fulfilled its purpose.

Once the limitations of this book are accepted, we must still face a more specific problem of method. To what extent, if any, should opinion poll data be trusted, and to what extent, if any, should they be accepted as relevant for political research?

The second question has been settled in part by time and practice. Poll data have been used in recent years to good effect in a number of political studies.[1] The case for the limited but significant trustworthiness of particular polls has been argued in a number of publications, and the technical conditions for competent sampling have been discussed in an extensive

[1] See, e.g., the well-known works of Gabriel Almond, *The American People and Foreign Policy*; William Buchanan and Hadley Cantril, *How Nations See Each Other*; Raymond Aron and Daniel Lerner, *France Defeats EDC* (New York, Praeger, 1956) ; Wolfgang Hirsch-Weber and Klaus Schütz, *Wähler und Gewählte: Eine Untersuchung der Bundestagswahlen 1953*; and Hans Speier and W. Phillips Davison, eds., *West German Leadership and Foreign Policy*.

literature.[2] The upshot of this discussion has been to establish the reliability of competently conducted polls, within reasonably well-known limits of accuracy, such as plus or minus 4 per cent. These limits may not be sufficient to forecast the outcome of a close election, but they seem adequate to indicate in many cases the existence and distribution of particular opinions, and the approximate strength and direction of trends over time. In the case of Germany, predictions from pre-election polls have been close to the actual votes cast.[3] Poll organizations and poll results have been used extensively by public and private agencies in Germany and the United States.[4]

In the present study, however, we have tried to do more than just cite opinion polls. We have tried to cross-examine them. We have compared the results of different polls, asking the same or very similar questions of different samples of Germans at different times. We have gone a step further and have compared the results of questions that were differently worded, or that even dealt overtly with different subjects, but that involved the same underlying attitude. In such cases it became possible not only to check the consistency of the answers and the attitudes which they indicated, but also the consistency of the trends of change, the strength and persistence of variant and minority attitudes, and the relationship of hard cores of intense opinion holders to the numbers of those who shared their views to a more moderate extent.

Without the availability of extensive collections of German opinion data, this type of analysis would have been impossible. Once carried out, however, the cross-examination of poll results has led us to think that truth is found not in one poll but at best in many, and that ordinarily it is not found even in many poll results but in the relationships between them.

A word should be added about the elite analysis which we have carried out. Data about individual holders of elite positions quickly become dated.

2 For examples and references to particular studies, see, e.g., Herbert Hyman, *Survey Design and Analysis* (Glencoe, Illinois, Free Press, 1955) ; the issues of the *Public Opinion Quarterly* and the well-known collections edited by Bernard Berelson and Morris Janowitz, *Reader in Public Opinion and Communication* (enlarged ed., Glencoe, Free Press, 1953) ; Daniel Katz *et al., Public Opinion and Propaganda* (New York, Dryden Press, 1954) ; H. D. Lasswell, Daniel Lerner, and C. E. Rothwell, *The Comparative Study of Elites: An Introduction and Bibliography* (Stanford, Calif., Stanford University Press, 1952) ; Paul Lazarsfeld and Morris Rosenberg, *The Language of Social Research* (Glencoe, Free Press, 1955) ; Wilbur Schramm, *Mass Communications* (Urbana, University of Illinois Press, 1949), etc. For a recent discussion by a historian, see Robert A. Kann, "Public Opinion Research: A Contribution to Historial Method," *Political Science Quarterly*, September 1958, pp. 374–96. For examples of German discussions of the subject, see Elisabeth Noelle Neumann and Erich Peter Neumann, *Jahrbuch der öffentlichen Meinung, 1957* (Allensbach am Bodensee, Institut für Demoskopie, 1957), pp. x–xvii (henceforth cited as *Jahrbuch II*), and Hirsch-Weber and Schütz, *Wähler und Gewählte*, pp. 299–309, 413–30.

3 Cf. Hirsch-Weber and Schültz, *Wähler und Gewählte*, p. 430; *Jahrbuch II*, p. xii.

4 These agencies include the Adenauer government, the United States Department of State, of Defense, of Agriculture, and of the Treasury, the RAND Corporation, the Office of the United States High Commissioner for Germany, and many others.

x   *Preface*

Many of the available published details about the elite members of 1954 and 1956 were history by 1958. But even history would have its value, and the statistical composition of elites changes much more slowly than do the holders of almost any particular office. If new incumbents have succeeded to key positions since we surveyed the elite concerned, they were likely to be drawn from the same pool of elite members; and if further changes should occur after this book goes to press, most of the new leaders still will be apt to come from the same kind of groups, and to be the same kind of people, that made up the German foreign policy elite of the mid-1950's.

In time, no doubt, this, too, will change; but in the near future at least the changes in elite composition are not likely to be radical or rapid. The largest changes that seem clearly indicated are those caused by age and retirement, and at least a hint of the composition of the younger age groups in the elites that will succeed the older men can already be found in the elite data given in this book.

In the present study, we have not used elite samples but elite inventories. We have studied all the incumbents of 250 key positions in the German foreign policy process, about whom information was available. To this we have added a broader inventory of over 500 incumbents of elite positions in German politics, and we have compared these with further data about the composition of the entire Parliament—the *Bundestag* —of 1953–57. The composition of elites of this size is not quickly altered short of drastic political and social change. In the absence of such major upheavals, the broad data collected for the mid-1950's may well retain their general relevance for some time to come.

In any case we have viewed the role of the elite only as one factor among others in the making of German foreign policy. Some of these other factors may indeed change more rapidly than the recruitment of the elite, and sometimes they may carry greater weight. Domestic popular opinion, the actions of particular national leaders, and the changing policies of other states all may produce larger changes in the German foreign policy of the future.

To facilitate references, a chronology of relevant political events, compiled by Mr. Richard A. Merritt, has been appended at the end of the book.

In carrying on this exploration, we have benefited in regard to either substance or method from the advice and criticism of many persons, including Gabriel Almond, Gordon A. Craig, Leo Gross, Harold Guetzkow, Ernst B. Haas, Stuart Hughes, Nobutaka Ike, Morris Janowitz, John H. Kautsky, Leonard Krieger, Wilfred Malenbaum, Sigmund Neumann, I. Richard Savage, Bruce L. Smith, Fred Sondermann, Hans Speier, and Robert Triffin. We are grateful, too, for information on several points of fact to members of the German foreign service, and in particular to Consul General Werner von Holleben and Consul Gerhard Lang of the German Consulate General at Boston. None of these, of course, bears any responsibility for the opinions of the authors, nor for the weaknesses and short-comings of the book that has resulted.

Thanks are also due to Roy C. Macridis, editor, and Prentice-Hall, Inc., publishers, of *Foreign Policy in World Politics*, in which an earlier version of some sections of this study has appeared.

For research support, we are indebted to the Center for Advanced Study in the Behavioral Sciences, to the Carnegie Corporation, and to the Ford Foundation; for additional assistance to the All-University Research Fund and the Bureau of Social and Political Research, both of Michigan State University; for research assistance, to Mr. Douglas Chalmers, Mrs. Elizabeth Darrah, Miss Lois Ernstoff, Miss Barbara Hanna, Mr. Richard L. Merritt, Mrs. Ruth Ohlin, and Mr. Bruce Russett; and for unusual helpfulness in regard to books and documents, to the librarians of Stanford University, Yale University, the Center for Advanced Study in the Behavioral Sciences, and the Hoover Institution on War, Revolution and Peace.

KARL W. DEUTSCH
LEWIS J. EDINGER

Yale University
Michigan State University
June 1959

Contents

PART IV

PROSPECTS AND PERSPECTIVES

APPENDIXES

Tables

GERMANY
Rejoins the Powers

Who makes German foreign policy:
The elite concept and its limits

In April 1945, the United States Third Army liberated the vast Nazi concentration camp at Buchenwald, with its thousands of prisoners from all over Europe. When the half-starved prisoners arranged a ceremony to celebrate their liberation and to commemorate the tens of thousands who had perished in the camp, they insisted that the German inmates among them should stand in a place of honor. No other group of foreigners had acquired a more thorough experience of some of the worst and some of the best of Germany. Their verdict was clear, and it deserves to be remembered.[1]

Germany—A Crucial Member of the Democratic World

As the heroism and the helpfulness of the German opponents of Hitler had been remembered by these non-German prisoners, so the sincerity and depth of conviction of many of the democratic elements in Germany today must be remembered by all friends of freedom. And just as the German prisoners seemed indispensable to their fellow inmates at the moment of liberation, so a democratic German people has remained indispensable to the consolidation of democracy and peace in Europe.

Germany is a vitally needed member in the community of democratic nations. Her moral and political weakness would leave all of us weaker. Her illnesses cannot but threaten us. Her moral and spiritual recovery, even more than her political and economic revival, is raising hopes in the entire democratic world.

We cannot think about Germany without a sense of sympathy, of compassion for her tragedies, of warm affection of all that is lovable in her culture and her people. But in politics, sympathy must not demand illusions. A doctor's sympathy for a patient should not be permitted to blunt the accuracy of his diagnosis. Only open-eyed and realistic understanding can help both the German people and the democratic world to work out their common problems.

For better or for worse, the authors of this book are committed to the

---

[1] Similar judgments were recorded by non-German survivors from other German concentration camps. See, e.g., Ed. Hoornik, *Dooden Hardenking in Dachau*, n.d., n.p. (1946).

search for truth. Less than three decades ago, German democracy crumbled, and German culture and the German people drifted to destruction, with vast suffering for themselves and for their neighbors. We shall try to identify the influences in Germany which are now working against a recurrence of this tragedy. But where we found evidence of trends or conditions working for instability and another possible catastrophe, we have tried to name them.

Conflicting Perspectives and the Need for Evidence

We have not been able to accept, therefore, the sweeping but conflicting views of Germany put forward by some distinguished observers. The last United States High Commissioner to Germany and first Ambassador to the Federal Republic, James B. Conant, has stated his position very clearly:

> The spirit of free Germany, today, is the spirit of a people who have turned their back on the Nazi past. . . . Anything that is said or done to stir up German suspicions about American intentions in Europe or American suspicions about Germany vis-à-vis the Soviets is a blow against the solidarity of NATO; conversely, anything that can be done to quiet such suspicions will strengthen the defense of our freedom.[2]

An opposite view has been put forcefully by Drew Middleton, for many years the chief correspondent of *The New York Times* in Germany, when he quoted an unidentified diplomat as saying:

> The [United States] State Department has oversold itself on Germany . . . It has refused to contemplate anything but German loyalty to the alliance. Consequently, it is unwilling to see what may happen . . . American diplomacy . . . has a blind spot on Bonn . . . That peculiar German combination of xenophobia and nationalism is emerging again . . . Only the character of Chancellor Adenauer and the hopes of some progress toward a settlement at the summit keep them in line now . . . The new generation of West German politicians . . . resentful of . . . United States guidance [sees Germany as exploiting its position] as the strongest power between the United States and the Soviet Union.[3]

Serious students of international affairs cannot escape the responsibility for considering the evidence as to how much truth, if any, either of these views may contain, and no consideration of short-run political expediency can absolve them from this task. When the Royal Society put the words *nullius in verba*—"on the words of no man"—on its seal, the event marked a milestone in the rise of science of seventeenth-century England, for it marked a shift to reliance on evidence and away from reliance on authority. In the perilous politics of the mid-twentieth century

---

[2] *Germany and Freedom* (Cambridge, Harvard University Press, 1958), pp. 10, 109.
[3] *The New York Times*, April 7, 1958.

we cannot escape asking the hard questions and seeking empirical evidence to answer them.

What kind of country is Germany today? What images and ideas what influences and what groups determine her actions among nations? How free are her government and people to shape their conduct in world affairs? What political, economic, and military burdens can the present fabric of German society and German democratic institutions safely bear? What would be the most likely German responses to an international crisis?

Seeking Evidence: Where, When, and How

In the non-Communist world, Germany has been represented by the German Federal Republic, which is the authorized political spokesman for 53 million Germans—about 51 million in Western Germany and over 2 million in West Berlin. It is not clear to what extent, if any, politics in the Federal Republic reflect or parallel the opinions of the nearly 18 million Germans under Soviet rule—about 17 million in the German Democratic Republic and over 1 million in East Berlin. All major parties in the Federal Republic claim to represent also adherents in the Soviet zone, who would vote for them if given the chance in a free all-German election. This claim, however, remains to be put to the test.

In the present study, "Germany" will mean the German Federal Republic. Our questions about the character and prospects of German politics and German foreign policy will be answered in terms of the evidence available from the Federal Republic, and they will have to be read with the reservations appropriate to the limitations which this fact implies.

The time span for our study is short. In the spring of 1945, the German empire of Adolf Hitler went down to shattering defeat. Only in 1949 was a national German government established again, at least for Western Germany. Yet less than ten years later, at the beginning of 1959, this truncated German Federal Republic had emerged as the leading Western European power on the Continent, and as one of the leading members of the North Atlantic Treaty Organization. The West German Republic's economic prosperity was conspicuous; her government was considered stable; her international prestige was high and still rising; and her power and responsibilities in world politics seemed certain to grow still more in the future.

Our earlier questions can be restated in the light of this record of rapid change. What forces and processes had shaped German foreign policy during those years of economic recovery and political transformation? Which of these influences were temporary, and which seemed likely to be enduring? Above all, how would domestic political influences continue to shape in the future the goals of German foreign policy and the use of German power? Would German strength in Western Europe be employed in response to a single political will, formed by the new German political system—or would it become circumscribed or even paralyzed by domestic divisions? What would be the expectable capabilities and limitations of German foreign policy making, as distinct from the expanding material resources of the country?

No answers to such questions are apt to be final, or even satisfactory, in advance of the event, yet much can be learned in their pursuit. Before we go out in search of substantive answers, however, we must turn our attention to a preliminary question: What are the main influences that are likely to shape decisions about foreign policy in any modern country, and particularly in Western Germany? How we answer this question will indicate our general approach to the study of politics; it will determine our schedule of inquiry and hence much of the shape of this book.

Seven Views of the Foreign Policy Process

There are seven popular views about the influences most predominant in shaping foreign policy. Though these may be employed in combination, they are best described separately. To sketch thus each in stark outline will mean to present it inevitably simplified and overstated, but recognizable in essentials.

According to the first view, foreign policy decisions are made at bottom by a few strong men; if we can identify those leaders of outstanding ability and will—let us say, the Bismarcks and the Adenauers—then we shall understand policies of their countries,

The second view stresses not men but institutions, that is, the persistent pattern of interplay among certain jobs or roles in a system of government. Policy is seen here as something made by the flow of communications among particular officeholders, such as presidents, ministers, and the like, and among the officers and members of certain legislative bodies, according to the rules of constitutional and bureaucratic procedure, with only secondary regard to the personalities and preferences of the actual incumbents of these offices at any particulor time.

A third view centers its attention not on individuals or offices but on an "elite," that is, on some limited collective body of influential persons and their close associates, such as an aristocracy or a body of high-ranking bureaucrats. The climate of opinion prevailing in this group, their shared beliefs and expectations, their greater or lesser openness to the entry of new members or to the consideration of new problems or ideas—these are held to be most nearly decisive for the foreign policy pursued by the county where this elite collectively holds sway.

A fourth view denies the assumption of considerable homogeneity of outlook and unity of action among the influential, which the elite theories imply. On the contrary, it seems political decisions mainly as the outcome of a struggle or bargaining process among formally or informally organized special interest groups, each of which has some internal cohesion, and usually also some stable internal elite or leadership, but which is largely alienated from most other interest groups. Each group is thus relatively isolated from all competing groups, somewhat as a pin on the board of a pinball machine is isolated from the other pins; and the outcome of the political process may be determined by the push of the strongest group, or the one most strategically located, or it may be some resultant of their interplay which could not be foreseen from the point of view of any one group.

A fifth view is skeptical of the power of either individuals, institutions, elites, or interest groups to determine foreign policy, except in secondary details. Rather, this view insists that the main lines of foreign policy in any country are determined by a set of overriding and relatively persistent national interests which can be easily discerned by competent members of the government as well as by the better-informed sections of the public. These national interests are seen as fairly specific, such as the protection of a certain boundary, the recovery of some territory, the gaining of an outlet to the sea, or the prevention of an alliance between several potentially unfriendly neighbors. Being both specific and readily discernible, they will fix the limits within which any reasonable national foreign policy will have to operate.

A sixth view doubts that the foreign policies of states are always, or even often, reasonable. It stresses the importance of accepted ideologies or myths, held either in elite circles or in the country at large. These beliefs about external reality, or about desirable ways of acting, rather than any verifiable facts about the foreign situation, are then held to determine the foreign policy which a country will pursue. A set of such popularly held memories, beliefs, and values, including accepted ways of perceiving threats from abroad and of responding to them, is often included in such terms as "national culture" or "national character"; and this national character, rather than any national interest, is seen as decisive in foreign policy matters.

A seventh and last view in our enumeration would deny that anything inside a country below the first rank of military powers—and hence anything inside the present German Federal Republic—could significantly alter the main lines of its foreign policy. These lines are thought to depend almost entirely on the international situation shaped by the rivalry of two or three superpowers. The conflicts and commitments of these giants, such as the United States and the Soviet Union—and still, perhaps, the United Kingdom—then create international pressures and limitations to which, it is thought, German foreign policy has had to conform with very little chance for effective maneuver.

To apply all these viewpoints properly to the foreign policy-making processes in the German Federal Republic would require a different and far longer book than the one presented here. We shall not say very much about the first point, the influence of individuals, nor about the last, the full extent of international pressures. Our chapter about political and legal institutions will limit itself to the minimum of information required for the understanding of those aspects of foreign policy making that are our main concern.

The Focus of This Study: The Interplay of Mass Opinion and Elites

This main concern is with the role of interest groups and elites, in the broader context of popular political opinion and participation. We do not view interest groups and elites as sovereign molders of the destinies of the rest of the population. On the contrary, we propose to study their behavior as it is influenced by, and limited by, the general political climate, the national character and political culture, in short, by the actual and potential behavior of the non-elite who comprise the great majority of the inhabitants of Western Germany. What policies are likely to meet with their support, or at least not to disturb their acquiescence? At what point would political support be lost, or opposition be aroused? When polls show that a majority of elite opinion favors one course of action while a majority of voters persistently favors another, what kind of foreign policy decision or compromise is likely to emerge?

To seek an answer to these questions we shall begin with an exploration of the basic political images, values, and beliefs held among the German people at large. Many of these images are derived from history as transmitted by schools, press, and literature; others are based on personal memories from childhood or adult life, or on word-of-mouth accounts. All of them are part of contemporary German political culture, and many of them are attested not only from literary sources but from interview data and repeated opinion polls. Together, these facts of past history and present opinion form the essential setting within which interest groups and elites must operate, and which sets the basic goals and major limits to the policy-making process.

I
POLICY IMAGES
IN POPULAR OPINION

CHAPTER 1

What Germans expect: Historical memories and present aspirations

In all countries, the making of foreign policy is influenced by the legacy of the past. Not only among the small groups of influential persons but also among the broad masses of the voters, memories of the past help to shape the images of what foreign policy is and what it could be—what tasks any present or future foreign policy could accomplish, what persons and institutions should accomplish them, and by what methods. People turn to memories for answers to their basic questions: "Who are we?" "What do others expect of us?" and "What should we expect of ourselves?" In all countries, memories thus fashion expectations. Everywhere they influence the interplay between foreign policy and the continuing process of national self-perception and self-definition. In Germany, however, these historical memories are in some respects more self-contradictory than in any other large country.

Memories of Greatness and Disaster

From the tenth to the thirteenth century, the medieval German Empire was the leading power of Europe and claimed the symbolic and, at times, the actual leadership of Western Christendom. For another three centuries, from the thirteenth century to the sixteenth, German princes and cities, German knights, and German merchants were predominant in Central and Eastern Europe without finding serious rivals. Generations of German school children have had impressed upon them these three centuries of universal greatness, and the six centuries of unchallenged German predominance in Central Europe; but they have been given a far less clear picture of the processes that were at work in the centuries of decline and catastrophe that followed.

By the sixteenth century, Germany had had no effective central government for almost three hundred years. Until that time it had run no serious risk of foreign military invasion; a Mongolian attack on Silesia in 1241 was beaten off mainly by local forces. With the rise of more effectively organized states in Western Europe after 1500, however, this situation changed. France, at times allied with Sweden, fought the Spanish and Austrian empires on German soil for almost two centuries, leaving the

country divided into a multitude of independent states. The political frag-
mentation of Germany was made far deeper by the religious cleavages of
the early sixteenth century, which left the German people approximately
two-thirds Protestant and one-third Catholic.

In the same period, the routes of world trade shifted away from Central Europe to the Atlantic coast and the ocean lanes to the countries overseas. These economic processes were subtle and anonymous, but their results were ominous and conspicuous, like the decline of a patient who is
weakened by a serious disease of which he remains ignorant. The world
seemed to turn cold and hostile toward Germany. Many of the prosperous
German cities declined while French and English trade centers increased
in size and influence. These unfavorable developments left the German
middle class economically and culturally backward, as well as politically
weak and lacking in self-reliance, at a time when the middle classes in the
West were becoming more prosperous and self-reliant.

Throughout the sixteenth and seventeenth centuries, German states,
German cities, and German politics remained on the whole petty; no effective economic or political centers for the entire area developed. Yet
German books and pamphlets, German merchants and craftsmen, preach-
ers and soldiers all moved among the communities where German was
spoken. A new concept "Germany" (*Deutschland*) came into use, and a
vague notion spread that the Germans were a single people with some sort
of common identity, some common destiny, and some common need for
safety and prestige.

Early in the seventeenth century, when economic decline and political
frustration had become well established on the German scene, the full force
of political catastrophe struck. About one-third of the German people
perished in the Thirty Years' War, from 1618 to 1648, a war waged essen-
tially by foreign countries for reasons of European power politics, with no
significant result for the German people other than suffering and devasta-
tion. During the rest of the seventeenth century and throughout the eighteenth, Germany remained a battlefield of foreign power; many of the
famous battles of the War of the Spanish Succession, the Seven Years'
War, and the Napoleonic Wars were fought on German soil. From the experiences of these two centuries Germans acquired an image of Germany
as the "land of the middle," helplessly exposed to attacks, surrounded by
hostile powers, and condemned to be the perpetual victim of foreign ag-
gressors because of her own lack of unity, organization, and concentrated
military power.

The Split in the Political Tradition

By the end of the eighteenth century, two major patterns of response to
this situation had become widespread. One was to accept the political and
religious division of the country, and the military impotence of its various

petty states. Resigned to view politics as hostile and evil—as Martin Luther had pictured it—some Germans felt free to concentrate their energies on diligent craftsmanship, in economic activity, and, perhaps most important of all, in the arts and sciences. Scientists like Leibnitz, composers like Bach and Handel, often served petty princes or foreign courts; in their imagination they often saw themselves living in a republic of arts and letters, working for the good of mankind. By the end of the century, the court of the tiny duchy of Saxe-Weimar, with its galaxy of literary talent headed by Goethe and Schiller, became a symbol for this style of life. The educated Germans appeared here to others and still more to themselves as a people of poets and thinkers, supported by an obedient peasantry and administered by petty princes and their enlightened bureaucrats, with no major national needs for political organization, let alone for any common foreign policy.

A contrasting but related pattern of response developed in the state of Brandenburg-Prussia: if politics was evil, force and cunning were its only realistic methods. This view stressed the strengthening of the state as the only organization that could safeguard the survival of the individual in a world of enemies. To make this state ever larger, stronger, more efficient, and more disciplined seemed the only way to ensure a minimum of security and dignity for its population. The subjects of the king of Prussia might at least live in a state of law, with an orderly administration and some security against the whims of foreign powers. Political passivity and military assertiveness—Potsdam, the down of the Prussian soldier kings, and Weimar, the town of the German poets—thus became two opposite and equally one-sided symbols of the German response to Germany's predicament.

In the course of the nineteenth century, these two German traditions were in part fused by the German industrial revolution and the German political unification movement, which culminated in 1871 in the establishment of a united German Empire under Prussian leadership. A new political and social system developed between 1815 and 1870 and linked much of the German intellectual and literary heritage to the Prussian tradition of widespread public education and instruction. The German intellectuals of the generation that reached maturity after 1809 and experienced the closing phases of the Napoleonic Wars, on the other hand, were becoming far more receptive to nationalism and far more impressed with the need for national political power. It was not only memories of Napoleon, however, that made national military power seem ever more important; it was above all the growth of German industry and commerce, which created a whole series of conflicts with Germany's neighbors—disputes with the Netherlands about the shipping tolls on the lower Rhine, with Denmark about the duchies of Schleswig and Holstein, and hence about the territory of the future Kiel Canal. Only military power seemed likely to prevent endless frustrations in these conflicts and to resolve them in accordance with what were considered German needs.

During the nineteenth century, especially after 1848, the German middle class and the German liberal parties turned increasingly to an alliance with their own princes, with the aristocracy and the military castes of Germany, and in particular to an alliance with the Prussian state. Bismarck's policy of "blood and iron," which accomplished the reunification of Germany in three wars between 1864 and 1871, ultimately won the overwhelming support of the German intellectuals and the German middle class, as well as of most of the German people. The coming of the railroads and the triumph of industrialization and urbanization fell into the same decades as these triumphs of power politics, and Bismarck's empire was credited for all.

To this day, Bismarck's popularity has remained outstanding. In October 1956, 31 per cent of a cross-section of German adults said that among great men Bismarck had done most for Germany; more than six years earlier, in January 1950, 35 per cent of a similar cross-section of voters had given the same answer.[1] No other German historical figure even approaches this popularity. In popular memory, the empire that Bismarck founded, and that endured from 1871 to 1918, lives on as a golden age. Of a cross-section of German adults polled in October 1951, 45 per cent identified this empire as the period in which they felt Germany had been best off.[2]

The Legacy of Two World Wars

But memories of Bismarck's empire are by no means all idyllic. They include memories of the rivalries of international power politics in the age of imperialism, and images of the envy and resentment of foreign countries at German commercial and political successes; they include the beginning of the themes of a German bid for "living space," for a "place in the sun." They recall the double image of the empire-building and colony-owning Western powers, such as France and England—countries seen as models whom the Germans should imitate and from whom they had to learn how to get on in the world, and at the same time as envious enemies ready to encircle Germany and destroy her. By 1914, a very large number of Germans saw themselves engaged at one and the same time in a bitterly competitive struggle for world power and a desperate defensive effort for national survival; and they welcomed the seemingly clear-cut state of open war as a long-awaited release from the tensions and frustrations of the prewar years. The outbreak of World War I was thus accepted with enthusi-

[1] Elisabeth Noelle Neumann and Erich Peter Neumann, *Jahrbuch der öffentlichen Meinung, 1947–1955* (Allensbach am Bodensee, Verlag für Demoskopie, 1956), p. 132; and, by the same authors and publishers, *Jahrbuch der öffentlichen Meinung, 1957* (Allensbach, 1957), p. 141. These sources will be cited hereafter as *Jahrbuch I* and *Jahrbuch II*, respectively. All data are for samples of the adult population, i.e., above eighteen years, unless otherwise indicated.

[2] *Jahrbuch I*, p. 126.

asm; some three million poems celebrated the event within the first nine months of the war.[3] At the beginning, volunteers for combat duty were numerous; and the fighting morale of front-line troops remained high almost to the end. Even after 1918, with about 2.8 million German lives lost,[4] many Germans refused to accept the fact of defeat; about one-quarter of the German voters continued to support parties which insisted that with better home front morale the war would have been won.

Some of these memories of an inevitable power struggle against foreign envy and hostility were revived and reinforced by the impact of the great economic depression that hit Germany in 1929 and by early 1933 had produced six million unemployed, almost one-third of the industrial labor force. The images of a hostile international environment; the image of a German empire, similar to what the British Empire was considered to be like, as a solution to Germany's difficulties; the image of a desperate bid for "living space" and a place among the leading imperial nations of the world —all these played their part among the appeals on which the Hitler movement rose to power.

The Nazi dictatorship had mass support which is well remembered to this day. At the beginning of the Nazi terror, in the elections of March 1933, as many as 43 per cent of the German voters supported Hitler's National Socialist party, and another 8 per cent supported Hitler's close allies in matters of foreign policy at that time, the German Nationalist party. Fifteen years later in October 1948, 41 per cent of a cross-section of German voters recalled that they had approved of the Nazi seizure of power in 1933.[5] In the same month, 57 per cent agreed that National Socialism was a good idea which had been badly carried out.[6] Eight years later, in July 1956, nearly one-half of a sample of young men said that National Socialism had been "a good idea," either without qualification (16 per cent) or "in part" (33 per cent). Less than one-fourth remembered it as "a bad idea," while 29 per cent gave no opinion.[7]

The German defeat in World War II, so much more shattering than the World War I defeat, is vividly remembered. It is estimated that this war cost 5.6 million German lives—a loss that would correspond proportionately to nearly 12 million lives for the United States.[8] Postwar German

---

[3] Ernst Volkmann, "Einführung," in *Deutsche Dichtung im Weltkrieg, 1914–1918.* (Reihe Politische Dichtung, Vol. VIII) Leipzig, Reclam, 1934, pp. 11–12.

[4] Max Graf Montgelas, "Militärische und politische Geschichte des Weltkrieges," in Walter Goetz, ed., *Propyläen-Weltgeschichte*, Vol. X, *Das Zeitalter des Imperialismus, 1890–1933*, p. 458.

[5] *Jahrbuch I*, p. 133.

[6] *Ibid.*, p. 134.

[7] *Jahrbuch II*, p. 149; sample of 1,000 young men born 1929–39.

[8] Losses are estimated by the German authorities at 3.8 million in the armed forces; 0.5 million civilian dead caused by air and land action, and 1.3 million resulting from flight, expulsion, and deportation among the German population of the Eastern territories. Letter from Gerhard Lang, Consul of the Federal Republic of Germany, Boston, May 13, 1958; hereafter cited as "Lang letter."

literature is full of works that recall the sufferings of that time; poems evoke its scenes of horror and pain. Children in other countries are missing much, says a child in a poem by Hermann Mostar, published in 1947: they have no ruined houses to play in, and their dolls do not have wounds. Photographs of the burning German cities in the great fire raids of 1943 and 1944 have been edited in the form of art books. Even more than the Thirty Years' War and World War I, the memory of World War II lives on as a major traumatic experience in German literature and culture.[9]

The testimony of the poets and writers is borne out by the opinion polls. Four Germans out of every five in a cross-section of the adult population interviewed in October 1948 remembered aerial bombardments or fire at the front; almost one in four dreamed still of these experiences; about one out of every six reported these dreams as exciting, terrifying, frequent, or intense.[10] Of a sample of young men in March 1952, more than one-half remembered the loss of loved persons in the war, and intense hunger in the postwar years; more than two out of five remembered heavy aerial bombardments.[11] When asked in 1951 to identify the worst period for Germany in the twentieth century, however, about seven Germans out of ten named the first three postwar years, 1945–48; only about one in ten named the war years, 1939–45, and another one in ten named the years 1949–51.[12]

Mingled with the memories of horror are memories of power and some reviving hopes for its return. In June 1954 the belief that Germany would become once again "one of the most powerful nations in the world" was expressed by 38 per cent. By September 1955, however, this had dropped to 25 per cent, while expressions of disbelief rose from 41 to 48 per cent.[13]

Compared with the glories and terrors of two world wars, the civilian interlude of the Weimar Republic between 1918 and 1932 is remembered as relatively colorless. Fewer than one-tenth of Germans interviewed in October 1951 remembered it as the best period for Germany in the twentieth century; one month later a somewhat smaller percentage named it as the worst.[14]

---

[9] Cf. many of the poems collected in such anthologies as *Ergriffenes Dasein: Deutsche Lyrik 1900–1950* (Munich-Ebenhausen, Langewiesche-Brandt, 1953) ; *Jahrhundertmitte: Deutsche Gedichte der Gegenwart* (Wiesbaden, Inselverlag, 1955) ; *De Profundis* (Munich, Desch, 1947) ; such works as Ernst Wiechert, *Totenmesse* (Munich, Desch, 1947) ; Hermann Mostar, *Einfache Lieder* (Frankfurt, Knecht, 1947) ; and such well-known prose writings as Heinrich Böll, *Haus ohne Hüter* (KölnBerlin, Kiepenheuer and Witsch, 1954) ; Ernst Wiechert, *Der Totenwald* (Zurich, Rascher, 1947) ; Hans Helmut Kirst, *Nullachtfünfzehn bis zum Ende* (Munich, Desch, 1954) ; etc. For the growing interest of historians in the general concept of trauma—the impact of a shattering experience on the long-run psychology of a group or society—see William L. Langer, "The Next Assignment," *American Historical Review*, 63:2 (January 1958), 291.

[10] *Jahrbuch I*, p. 9.

[11] *Ibid.*, p. 23.

[12] *Ibid.*, p. 125.

[13] *Ibid.*, p. 125; *Jahrbuch II*, p. 139.

[14] *Ibid.*, p. 125–26.

The legacy of German history is thus profoundly ambiguous as a background for future German foreign policy decisions. It includes memories that counsel fear of remaining weak in a world of ruthless foreign interests, but it is also rich in memories of suffering and defeat following upon reckless bids for world power. It is rich in memories of success in fields requiring economic, technical, or scientific performance; but it lacks any impressive memories of sustained political gains following upon nonagressive foreign policies and upon peaceful development of democratic and constitutional practice. Dictatorship and war are remembered by perhaps three-fifths of the German people as terrible failures; but democracy and peaceful international relations are not at all widely remembered as successes. This store of memories is likely to limit the proportion of the hard core of German voters who will support a consistent and firm commitment to democracy and to wholehearted cooperation with the Western powers. But historical memories also influence German attitudes on foreign policy in other ways.

The Underdeveloped Traditions of Empiricism and Equality: Two Muted Themes in German Culture

The German tradition combines somewhat uneasily the steady diligence and skill of the medieval craftsman with the admiration for the military prowess and apparent romantic daring of the medieval knight, while the mercantile traditions of empiricism, rationality, adaptability, and ease of compromise seem markedly underrepresented.[15] To be sure, there are memories of the mercantile glory of the medieval Hanseatic towns, but they have left no popular heroes, no models for imitation, in German literature or folklore. In popular memory, the romantic figures of the pirates Klaus Störtebecker and Godeke Michels have remained more prominent than the mayors of the cities on whose commerce they preyed.

German culture thus offers its members two quite different roles for imitation: on the one hand the obedient, dependable craftsman, and on the other, the bold, romantic knight and his intellectual cousin, the daring, demonic magician. German literature abounds in these two contrasting types, from Hans Sachs and Walter von Stolzing in Richard Wagner's *Meistersinger* to Serenus Zeitblom and Adrian Leverkühn in Thomas Mann's *Doktor Faustus*. Skilled workers are expected to assimilate to the behavior of steadfast masters of a craft; intellectuals are expected to behave as painstaking craftsmen in the classical type of German university research, but may also embark on bold, romantic flights of the philosophic,

---

[15] Cf. Joseph A. Schumpeter, "Das soziale Antlitz des Deutschen Reiches," in *Aufsätze zur Soziologie*, p. 215; and Talcott Parsons, "Democracy and Social Structure in Pre-Nazi Germany," and "The Problem of Controlled Institutional Change," in *Essays in Sociological Theory*, pp. 104–23 and pp. 238–74.

scientific, or political imagination—often with fruitful results in the fields of fundamentals. But since the two behavior patterns are so different and stem from such divergent social roots, the transition from one to the other is often difficult, abrupt, or precarious. There are no easy intermediate ways of behaving; commitment to one style of acting persists for a time even under strain, but may be followed by a sharp break and swing to the other extreme.

Perhaps something similar is characteristic of the style of many German political commitments. They appear remarkably stable and are held for long times; they are not modified easily or in small steps; but when their ties snap, the new recommitments may be radically different: within five years, from 1928 to 1933, important sections of German opinion shifted from supporting the cautious policies of Gustav Stresemann to the reckless policies of Adolf Hitler.

This shift was only one of many dramatic shifts in the history of German foreign policy. Present-day German voters include millions who shifted in their domestic political allegiance from monarchy to republic to the Nazi dictatorship and most recently to the Federal Republic; and who shifted in their international sympathies from hatred of the West in World War I to the rapprochement of the Locarno period in the 1920's; to renewed war against the West in 1939 and to acceptance of the Nazi-Soviet pact of 1939–41; to all-out war against Russia in 1941–45; and now to a pro-Western course. The history of Prussian and German foreign policy records the famous "reversal of alliances" of 1756, in which Frederick II of Prussia changed from an ally into an enemy of France; the Convention of Tauroggen of 1812 which ushered in the subsequent shift of Prussia from grudging alliance with Napoleon to an alliance with Russia against him; the shift from a Prussian-Austrian alliance in 1864 to the Prussian-Austrian War of 1866, and back to a German-Austrian alliance in the 1870's; the shift from Bismarck's pro-Russian and pro-English policies to the policies of his successors that culminated in the War of 1914; and once again the Nazi-Soviet pact of 1939–41. These reorientations were more dramatic than many of the policy changes in other Western countries; they were not gradual but rapid and sweeping; they took many contemporaries by surprise, but they were accepted by German opinion.

Another aspect of the German political tradition is perhaps related to this relative lack of appreciation of the merchant's calling. Commerce often involves sober and yet imaginative trading with equals; it demands skillful negotiations with one's peers, without expecting or conceding any element of superiority or greater authority on either side. This tradition and these skills have been relatively weak in German culture and in German politics, where the word "compromise" long has savored of weakness and lack of principle; and in the popular perception of foreign policy, this bias may have been reinforced by the peculiarities of Germany's historical and geographical position.

Throughout much of her history, Germany has been a country without equals. One or more of her Western neighbors have usually appeared to her as wealthier, more powerful, and more highly respected in the world. Her Eastern neighbors, on the other hand, the Poles, Czechs, Hungarians, Russians, and Baltic peoples, have usually been looked down upon by Germans as inferior—in wealth, technology, civilization, or military power. Englishmen, Frenchmen, and Americans had to live for centuries with other peoples whom they could neither dominate nor accept as superior to themselves; much of their foreign policy thus had to deal with equals. By contrast, after the thirteenth century, the German people never had a state quite large enough or advanced enough to dominate all their neighbors, or to sustain a bid for world leadership.[16] Yet Germany never seemed to them quite small enough to accept the role of a small country. In the nineteenth and twentieth centuries, in particular, Germans have often looked upon Switzerland with a peculiar ambivalence. They have envied the Swiss their self-respect, their constitutional stability, their prosperity and solid level of culture, and their freedom from world-shaking political ambitions; and yet they have at times felt intensely irritated by what seemed to them an inglorious preference for mediocrity in politics.

The German people cannot see themselves as a small nation, but just now they cannot act as a great one, and they have no clear image as to how a middle power should behave. Deeply uncertain of their general role in the international politics of our age, they have found it easier to view their tasks not in terms of any one great conception, but in terms of a series of smaller and more specific objectives.

---

[16] In contrast to Germany, Italy between 1871 and 1957 had longer periods where her status approximated more nearly to equality, first vis-à-vis Austria-Hungary and later vis-à-vis France. The persistent Italian demands for parity with France at the naval conferences between the world wars may illustrate the point.

CHAPTER 2

A nation seeks a role: Popular views of foreign policy objectives

Perhaps even more than the people of any other large nation, Germans view their foreign policy in terms of their own collective status and prestige in the world at large. They expect it not only to procure material advantages and maintain peace, but to contribute to the world's respect for the Germans and thus indirectly to bolster German self-respect. One out of every three Germans interviewed in a survey in July 1952 believed that the Germans were unpopular in the world at large; and one out of six believed that they were unpopular because of their good qualities, particularly their ability. On the other hand, one German in eight believed that it was their bad qualities—their loudness, lack of adaptability, and intolerance—that made the Germans unpopular abroad.[1] In May 1955 the same question was put somewhat differently: "One often hears that the Germans are unpopular in the world; what do you think is the reason?" Only 14 per cent of the respondents denied German unpopularity, while 70 per cent took it for granted. Forty-five per cent blamed the negative qualities of the German people, but 25 per cent asserted that it was their positive qualities which made them unpopular. One German out of four in this sample—a higher proportion than in 1952—thus saw the German people surrounded by an envious or hostile world.[2]

One of the largest world powers and one of the smallest, the United States and Switzerland, are among the countries most admired; 8 per cent of the persons in a survey in July 1954 said they would like most of all to live in the United States, another 7 per cent picked Switzerland, and another 8 per cent scattered their preferences over the rest of Europe.[3] In November 1953, a cross-section of young people between fifteen and twenty-four years old were asked whether the Germans could learn anything from other peoples, and if so, from what people. Almost two-thirds of the youngsters answered that Germany could indeed learn from others; 23 per cent then named as model the United States, 10 per cent England, 7 per cent Switzerland, 5 per cent France, 3 per cent Sweden; the rest were scattered.[4]

[1] *Jahrbuch I*, p. 125.
[2] *Jahrbuch II*, p. 138.
[3] *Jahrbuch I*, p. 20.
[4] Karl-Georg von Stackelberg, ed., *Jugend zwischen 15 und 24: Eine Untersuchung zur Situation der Deutschen Jugend im Bundesgebiet*, p. 87.

Attitudes Toward the United States

Germany today is a country in search of friends, just as she is a country in search of herself. Clearly, the political friendship that is most popular in Germany today is her friendship with the United States. In June 1952, and again in January 1956, about three-fifths of Germans interviewed in polls felt that the United States was well disposed toward cooperation with Germany; in 1952, only 29 per cent made the same assumption about England, and only 12 per cent about France.[5]

As for Germany, a strong but declining majority of respondents favored close cooperation with the United States, but only a smaller number—by 1956 a minority—favored such a policy toward England and France.[6]

To questions requiring a decision between "East" and "West," or between cooperation with the United States and cooperation with Russia, more than three-fifths of the persons interviewed in surveys between 1950 and 1954 answered consistently in favor of cooperation with the United States.[7] The victory of Chancellor Adenauer and the CDU in the national elections of September 1957 was considered a popular endorsement of his policy of continuing cooperation with the United States, which had been stressed in the campaign.

To some extent, however, this is a marriage of convenience. Many Germans remember close alliances in their history, mainly since 1810, in which Germany was the senior partner, and they remember the far more cold-blooded policies of Frederick II and Bismarck in making use of temporary alliances with stronger powers.[8] When a cross-section of Germans were asked in July 1953 to say what they did and did not like about Americans, only 29 per cent gave predominantly favorable answers, another 29 per cent made predominantly unfavorable comments, and 42 per cent were neutral or ambivalent or gave no opinion. In January of the same year, only one-quarter of the respondents to a poll wanted Americans to withdraw from Europe, while 57 per cent wanted them to stay.[9] In July 1956, almost the same proportion of Germans considered

---

[5] *Jahrbuch I*, p. 331.

[6] For Close cooperation with:	March 1953 Per Cent	September 1954 Per Cent	April 1956 Political Cooperation Per Cent	April 1956 Economic Cooperation Per Cent
United States	83	78	69	69
England	62	58	49	39
France	55	46	43	34

Jahrbuch I, p. 331; *Jahrbuch II*, p. 338. In 1954, 3 per cent opposed close cooperation with the United States, 7 per cent with England, and 14 per cent with France; about three-fifths opposed cooperation with Russia or Poland, and two-fifths opposed cooperation with Israel. *Jahrbuch I, loc. cit.*

[7] *Jahrbuch I*, p. 332.

[8] "Historically, German soldiers have not taken to the idea of collaboration on equal terms with other forces." Gordon A. Craig, *NATO and the New German Army*, pp. 16–17.

[9] *Jahrbuch I*, p. 333.

the presence of Allied occupation troops either a "welcome protection" (11 per cent) or "an inevitable necessity" (45 per cent). In November 1956, after the Russian intervention in the Hungarian uprising, the number of Germans who welcomed Allied troops as protection rose to 24 per cent, while the number accepting them as necessary remained unchanged.[10]

Despite this 12 per cent shift after the Hungarian crisis, the desire of many Germans for continuing American friendship and protection seems to some extent independent of the level of American-Soviet tensions. Thus, in December 1953, a majority of the respondents (51 per cent) thought it would be best for Germany if Americans and Russians would cooperate in the future; 28 per cent thought it would be best for Germany if they did not cooperate, and 21 per cent did not know.[11] Similarly, there is no clear evidence that the temporary relaxation of international tensions after the Geneva Conference of 1955, and the earlier decline of fears of imminent war, did anything to reduce American popularity or pro-Western sympathies in Germany. In January 1958, the Gallup Poll reported that 81 per cent of respondents in Bonn favored a meeting between President Eisenhower and the Soviet leader, M. Nikita Khrushchev. Only 8 per cent were opposed, and only 11 per cent were undecided. This German response in favor of top-level United States-Soviet negotiations was considerably higher than that expressed in similar polls reported from nine other capitals, including those of leading neutral countries.[12] Cooperation with the United States appears thus solidly anchored in German public opinion, at least for the time being; but much of the long-range nature of this cooperation remains yet to be worked out.

The Appeal of Neutralism

In particular, a majority of German voters would like to combine American military protection and friendship with the advantages of neutralism. In March 1955, almost three Germans out of four expressed unequivocally hostile attitudes toward Communism, and 96 per cent of the respondents to a poll in August 1956 were sure that living conditions were more favorable in the Federal Republic than in the Communist-ruled Eastern Zone of Germany.[13] Yet neutrality appears to many to be a prudent policy for Germany, if not for themselves. In the early days of the Korean war, in July 1950, only 26 per cent described their own

---

[10] Typescript summary of poll results on German ideologies and politics, spring 1957, from EMNID Institute, Bielefeld, p. 5, henceforth cited as "Ideologies." The authors are indebted to EMNID for the communication of these data.

[11] *Jahrbuch I*, p. 333.

[12] The rank order of per cent of respondents supporting such American-Soviet negotiations was Bonn 81, Athens 71, New Delhi 69, Paris 64, Copenhagen 61, Toronto 59, Stockholm 58, Vienna 55, Washington and Chicago 54, London 51. *U.S. News and World Report,* January 10, 1958, p. 17.

[13] "Ideologies," pp. 1, 15.

attitude in the East-West conflict as neutral, but a year later, in August 1951, as many as 60 per cent chose neutrality between Americans and Russians as the best policy for Germany, and in June 1956 again 54 per cent preferred neutrality to "being on good terms with the Americans" (38 per cent) or "being on good terms with the Russians" (4 per cent).[14]

To some extent, popular images of the relative strength of the United States and the Soviet Union play a part in these alignments. In August 1953, when asked which of these two countries they expected to be more powerful than the other "fifty years from now," 32 per cent picked the United States, 11 per cent picked Russia, and 57 per cent either expected them to be equally strong (9 per cent) or were undecided (48 per cent).[15]

Later, the proportion seems to have shifted somewhat toward an increasing appreciation of Soviet strength. When asked which side they considered "stronger at the moment, the Americans and the West or the Russians and the East," 41 per cent chose the West in August 1955, but this proportion slipped to 33 per cent in August 1956, while those who saw Russia as currently stronger increased from 12 per cent in 1955 to 23 per cent in 1956. To the immediately following question, "and which side will be stronger five years from now?" 34 per cent chose the West in 1955, but only 26 per cent held to this view in August 1956; Russia and the East were chosen by 19 per cent in 1955 and 27 per cent—a slightly larger number than picked the Western side —in 1956. In both years, 47 per cent either expected both sides to be equally strong (37 per cent and 39 per cent, respectively) or were undecided (10 per cent and 8 per cent, respectively).[16] These shifts in German opinon occurred before the Soviet claims of possessing intercontinental rocket weapons and the widely publicized launching of two earth satellites by the USSR in 1957, and the news of a partial economic recession in the United States in early 1958—a series of events likely to some extent to reinforce this trend. Despite the moderate changes in their estimates of the strength of the two great power blocs, however, the great majority of Germans have continued to reject Communism and to consider themselves a part of the Western world.

Thus, policy makers can count on popular approval in their efforts to maintain a general climate of friendly relations with the United States, but they must be careful not to arouse fears of dangerous commitments which could unite a majority of voters against them. At the same time,

[14] *Jahrbuch I*, p. 332; "Ideologies," p. 10. Earlier, in December 1955, only 29 per cent explicitly endorsed neutrality, but another 28 per cent said "Don't know," while 43 per cent preferred siding with "the Western powers." (In the earlier polls, only 8–10 per cent had said "Don't know.") *Jahrbuch II*, p. 338.
[15] *Jahrbuch I*, p. 333.
[16] "Ideologies," p. 3.

politicians who prefer a closer approach to neutrality in international affairs must be careful not to arouse fears of a loss of American friendship. So long as the Western alliance appears to the German voters as primarily defensive and peaceful, these two attitudes can be reconciled. A considerable amount of agreement on basic foreign policy orientations has, in fact, developed among the major parties and among the great majority of the electorate. If, however, new and major tangible commitments should be demanded from Germany by her allies, or if the international situation should approach the brink of war, much of this consensus might disintegrate.

This reading of German attitudes does not support the widespread theory that German friendship for the United States grows stronger in periods of intensified cold war between West and East, while German neutralism grows whenever cold war tensions lessen. Rather, it seems plausible that excessive neglect of German needs as well as excessive demands for German military contributions could strain Germany's ties to the West, and that the best conditions for the popularity of German-American friendship may lie somewhere in the middle, with just enough international tension to keep the West responsive to German wishes, but not enough to demand any major German sacrifices for the Western cause. On these terms, continued German mass support of pro-Western policies seems fairly likely; but on stiffer terms it might not be wise to count on it.

National Reunification and the Eastern Territories

Other foreign policy aims on which there is a great deal of popular agreement stem directly from Germany's defeat and partition in World War II.

First of all, Germany after her defeat in 1945 was an exhausted, partly destroyed, and very hungry country, occupied by four foreign powers. Since no central government was set up for Western Germany until 1949, the task of providing a minimum of food and shelter fell to the occupying powers, and to new German local and provincial governments which were set up under their supervision. When a federal government for Western Germany was established, its first and basic long-range task appeared to be the gradual regaining of national independence. Up to a point, this goal of independence had precedence in the minds of voters over all other goals. More than two-thirds of all respondents, and more than three-quarters of the men, said in August 1949 that they were "ready to devote all their strength to making Germany once again self-supporting and independent, politically and economically."[17] This goal seems to hold precedence even over the goals of maintain-

---

[17] *Jahrbuch I*, p. 125.

ing friendship with the United States and regaining a respected position among the Western powers, a position equal eventually at least to that of France and the United Kingdom. The fact that the Adenauer government was able to pursue all these goals at the same time between 1949 and 1957 contributed much to its strength.

Other foreign policy goals also arose directly from the German postwar situation. First of these, in the minds of most West German voters, is the reunification of Eastern and Western Germany, substantially on the basis of the political and social institutions that now prevail in the German Federal Republic. Next to this, there is the question of the more than ten million Germans expelled from Eastern Europe, and from the former German territories east of the Oder and Neisse rivers which came under Polish or Russian administration after 1945. Many of these expellees want to regain their former lands, properties, and social positions; about one-half seem willing to settle there again; and their aspirations have the approval, mild or strong, of many German voters. Regaining particularly the former German Oder-Neisse territories, including coal-rich Silesia, has thus become a long-range task expected from German foreign policy. Four-fifths of the West Germans polled in March 1951 declared that Germany should not rest content with the present Polish-German frontier, but in August 1953 only 12 per cent were willing to risk a war on these grounds.[18] Only about one native of West Germany in twenty-five, and only one expellee or refugee in two, now appear interested in moving to the Oder-Neisse territories, if these should become available.[19]

There are clear signs that the majority in favor of Western-style reunification of Eastern and Western Germany is, if anything, still larger, but here again a large majority would reject war as an instrument for this policy. When asked in September 1956 which they considered "more urgent, the unification of the Eastern and Western zones of Germany or a European unification," nearly three-quarters put German reunification first.[20] Earlier, in April 1952, three-quarters of the respondents said they would not renounce the German claim of the Oder-Neisse territories even if by doing so they could buy the early reunion of Eastern and Western Germany. Nearly 70 per cent of respondents reaffirmed

[18] *Jahrbuch I*, p. 313.

[19] Among respondents to an EMNID Institute poll in September 1956, about 14 per cent said they would be willing to migrate to the Oder-Neisse territories, if this should become possible. This group consisted of approximately 9 per cent expellees from these territories, about 1 per cent expellees from other regions, another 1 per cent refugees from the Communist-ruled German Democratic Republic, and about 3 per cent natives of Western Germany. The 11 per cent expellees and refugees correspond to less than one-half of the proportion of expellees and refugees in the adult population. From data in Göttinger Arbeitskreis (Herbert Kraus and Karl O. Kurth), *Deutschlands Ostproblem: Eine Untersuchung der Beziehungen des deutschen Volkes zu seinen östlichen Nachbarn* (Würzburg, Holzner Verlag, 1957), pp. 178–79, 204–5.

[20] "Ideologies," p. 9.

this view in two polls in June and August 1955. Chancellor Adenauer they said, should not renounce the German claim to these territories, even if the Russians should offer in exchange reunification and free elections in East Germany.[21]

This contrasts with the willingness of a significant proportion of voters—38 per cent in June 1955, 31 per cent in August, and 36 per cent in December 1955—to purchase reunification at the price of renouncing all military ties to the West. Only 32, 31, and 31 per cent, respectively, opposed this bargain, while 30, 38, and 33 per cent respectively, were undecided or had no opinion. A stiffer price, renunciation of any German army, as well as of any Western alliance, still seemed acceptable to 31 per cent in June 1955, and among respondents eighteen to twenty-nine years old, the proportion was 33 per cent. In December 1955 the promise of reunification thus added another 7 per cent to the 29 per cent who favored neutrality in any case.[22]

Reunification continued to appeal to youth. Almost three-quarters of the young people between fifteen and twenty-four years old who were polled in November 1955 saw "the most urgent future task for us Germans" in the field of foreign policy. Highest-ranking among specific tasks mentioned was the reunification of Germany, which was put first by 47 per cent; this was followed by "making sure of peace" (22 per cent) and "European understanding" (7 per cent); only 1 per cent named "rearmament."[23]

For reunification, a plurality was willing to make tangible sacrifices. In a poll in 1953, 41 per cent endorsed the proposal that Germany pay to the Soviet Union an indemnity of 3 billion DM, equivalent to over $700 million, in exchange for reunification.[24]

The Fear of War

The fact seems to be, judging from many poll results, that a majority of Germans hold firmly to these foreign policy objectives in the abstract, but would be unwilling to fight for any of them. Asked in February 1955 whether Germans should fight in a case of defending Europe against an armed Soviet attack, only 38 per cent favored armed resistance; 34 per cent said that above all war should be avoided, and 28 per cent were undecided.[25] By April 1956, the proportion of adherents of armed resistance declined to 35 per cent, and by June 1956 it was

[21] *Jahrbuch I*, p. 317; *Jahrbuch II*, p. 323.

[22] *Jahrbuch II*, pp. 323–24, 338.

[23] Rolf Fröhner, *Wie stark sind die Halbstarken? Dritte Emnid Untersuchung zur Situation der deutschen Jugend*, p. 316.

[24] *Jahrbuch I*, p. 317. Opposed were 34 per cent, and 25 per cent were undecided. By contrast, the proposal to pay to Israel an indemnity in the same amount, for the Jewish survivors of Nazi persecution, was supported by only 11 per cent in a poll in 1952. *Ibid.*, p. 131.

[25] *Jahrbuch I*, p. 348.

down to 26 per cent.[26] More than two-fifths had felt in February 1955 that in case of war the West would win in the end.[27] Two months earlier, in December 1954, only 24 per cent had felt that in the event of war the United States and the Western European countries could prevent the Russians from overrunning Western Europe. By April 1956, only 18 per cent still expressed such confidence.[28] More than three out of every five Germans polled in March 1952 felt that Germany would be a battlefield in any war between Russia and the United States, and that the German people would be the losers; by June 1954, 71 per cent felt threatened by atomic weapons.[29]

Not surprisingly, atomic weapons are unpopular. The proportion of respondents opposed to having the United States use atomic and hydrogen weapons to defend Germany against a non-atomic Soviet attack was 60 per cent in April 1954, and rose to 65 per cent by September 1955, while those agreeing to such a course fell from 22 to 15 per cent.[30] In February 1958, the installation of launching platforms for atomic rocket weapons in the Federal Republic was opposed by 81 per cent, while only 15 per cent approved. The proposal to equip the German forces with such weapons was somewhat less unpopular, with 71 per cent opposed and 21 per cent in favor.[31]

German public opinion seems thus largely united in disliking and distrusting Communism and Communist governments; in fearing and rejecting war; in seeking at least economic and political equality with such other Western powers as France and the United Kingdom; and in desiring to remain friends with the United States. Subject to these overriding beliefs, large majorities wish for eventual national reunification and, less urgently, for the recovery of former German territories in the East. In the third rank of possible foreign policy goals, smaller but still appreciable majorities desire German participation in some form of a United Europe.

The Sympathies for Western European Union

In September 1955, more than two-thirds of Germans polled said they would vote in favor of forming a United States of Europe; almost three-fifths in the same poll considered the formation of a United States of Europe a practical possibility; only 17 per cent thought it impossible.

---

[26] The proportion of undecided rose to 31 per cent in April and to 38 per cent in June, while the number of those who mainly wanted to avoid war remained unchanged in April and rose to 36 per cent in June. *Jahrbuch II*, p. 360.

[27] *Jahrbuch I*, p. 351.

[28] *Jahrbuch I*, p. 351; *Jahrbuch II*, p. 364.

[29] *Jahrbuch I*, pp. 362, 357.

[30] Hans Speier, *German Rearmament and Atomic War*, p. 253.

[31] EMNID poll, cited in Lang letter, 1958. An earlier poll in March 1956 showed 49 per cent opposed to all "nuclear weapons" (including presumably, artillery) for the German army. *Jahrbuch II*, p. 298.

Majorities in favor of a European union were above 70 per cent among the better educated, from the equivalent of high school graduation (*Mittlere Reife*) up; among those in clerical and professional occupations; and among those with monthly earnings above 400 DM (about $100), representing roughly the economic top 40 per cent of the population.[32] This favorable attitude seems to have persisted. By December 1956, the proportion of those willing to vote for a United States of Europe has risen to 75 per cent, with only 5 per cent opposed.[33]

People were more evenly divided, however, when asked to choose between European union and national independence. In September 1956, when asked to choose between two "solutions for the future: the rebuilding of Germany as a completely independent national state with its own customs frontiers, or Germany as an equal member of a European union," a bare majority of 51 per cent chose membership in a European union, while 43 per cent preferred an independent national state.[34]

The favorable attitude toward European integration is subject, however, to two qualifications: though not necessarily impractical, European union seems remote; and it must not take away from Germany the sovereign right of ultimate decision. Only 34 per cent of Germans questioned in December 1956 believed that they would live to see the Western European countries unite to form the United States of Europe; and of those polled in September 1955 only between 25 per cent and 32 per cent, depending on the wording of the question, were willing to concede to a European parliament the right of ultimate decision in questions touching important German interests, while between 42 per cent and 46 per cent insisted that ultimate decisions must remain with the national parliament or government of Germany.[35] There the matter seems to have remained. In January 1957, after the dramatic Hungarian revolt, 47 per cent of German respondents to a poll felt that European cooperation toward some unification had neither improved nor delcined; 21 per cent saw an improvement, but another 20 per cent believed they saw a decline.[36]

More specific institutions of European cooperation did not become popular foreign policy goals. The number of those endorsing the ratification of the European Coal and Steel Community (ECSC) declined from 39 per cent in June 1950 to 21 per cent in January 1952. A year later, in March 1953, only 19 per cent said it had "not been a mistake" for Germany to join in this arrangement, while 75 per cent were either undecided (15 per cent) or uninformed (60 per cent).[37] By April 1956, the

[32] *Jahrbuch I*, pp. 342–43.
[33] *Jahrbuch II*, p. 345.
[34] "Ideologies," p. 9.
[35] *Jahrbuch I*, pp. 339, 341; *Jahrbuch II*, pp. 342, 344.
[36] "Ideologies," p. 11.
[37] *Jahrbuch I*, pp. 343–45.

number of uninformed had risen to 74 per cent, 11 per cent were undecided, and only 10 per cent said that it had not been a mistake for Germany to join.[38]

The projected European Defense Community (EDC), which was to
include German troops under a common European command, was endorsed by 33 per cent in March 1950, and 37 per cent in September
1954, expressed regret for the failure of the project.[39] Throughout the
period, however, polls always recorded more opponents than supporters
of any German troop contribution to a Western European defense force,
but the levels of both support and opposition usually remained below
those for or against an independent German army.[40]

The German membership in the North Atlantic Treaty Organization
(NATO) seems to have had even less popular backing. In April 1954,
while 48 per cent of Germans polled knew at least approximately the
meaning of EDC, only 24 per cent could even approximately identify
NATO.[41] Another poll, in June 1954, showed only 20 per cent correct
identifications of NATO; 80 per cent were: vague (6 per cent), incorrect (11 per cent), or "Don't know" (63 per cent).[42] By December
1956, the number of those who could identify NATO correctly had risen
slightly, to 28 per cent.[43]

It is noteworthy that despite these low levels of popular support, the
Adenauer government succeeded in securing parliamentary ratification
of the NATO, ECSC, and EDC treaties, and that the EDC treaty failed
because of French opposition, not German.

The Issue of Rearmament

Among the popular images of major foreign policy goals, one is conspicuous by its absence. This missing goal is national rearmament: no
popular majority is pressing for it. At best it may be said that the existence
of an independent military establishment has been reluctantly accepted.
Between November 1950—when a new German army first became an
issue—and June 1956—by which time an independent army had been
established—opposition to it in twenty-one public opinion polls ranged
between 49 per cent and 33 per cent and support between 46 and 31 per
cent. In June 1956, opposition was almost as great as in November 1950
(47 per cent and 48 per cent, respectively), support even somewhat lower
(31 compared with 33 per cent).[44] Thereafter, approval—given for the

[38] *Jahrbuch II*, p. 349.
[39] *Jahrbuch I*, pp. 357, 362.
[40] See charts, *Jahrbuch I*, pp. 360–61, 372–73.
[41] "Ideologies," pp. 7–8.
[42] *Jahrbuch I*, p. 90.
[43] *Jahrbuch II*, p. 339.
[44] *Jahrbuch I*, pp. 372–73; *Jahrbuch II*, pp. 296–97.

greater part reluctantly—increased. By November 1956, after the Hungarian revolt, 46 per cent of respondents supported an independent army in principle, but 46 per cent remained opposed.[45] In another poll, in December 1956, respondents were offered a specific choice between a range of statements expressing varying degrees of acceptance for or opposition to a German army. Some degree of acceptance was expressed by a majority, 53 per cent (18 per cent unconditionally and 35 per cent with qualifications), while 33 per cent gave negative replies (18 per cent "unconditionally" and 15 per cent not "at this time").[46] Another question in October and December 1956 offered a choice between maintaining the army and abolishing it. Those who wanted to keep the army rose from 38 to 51 per cent, presumably under the impact of the intervening events in Hungary, but those who wanted to abolish the army declined only from 43 to 36 per cent.[47]

Much of the opposition has come from German women, and to a lesser extent from the young men, while men over sixty have been the martial group. Thus in a poll in May 1955, men split almost evenly for and against having an army, 46 to 44 per cent, while women were far more negative, divided 34 to 47 per cent respectively. Among age groups, the reluctance of Hamlet clashed with the vigor of Polonius. The age group of eighteen to twenty-nine rejected the army, 48 to 34 per cent, while those over sixty years old endorsed it, 45 to 37 per cent.[48] By October 1957 the share of men, regardless of age, who favored an army had increased to 56 per cent and opposition had shrunk to 39 per cent. Among two slightly different age groups of young men, that is, potential conscripts, support for an army also increased from 50 per cent in July 1956 to 56 per cent in October 1957, but opposition also rose, from 38 to 44 per cent.[49]

Assuming that there would be an army, a system of voluntary enlistment was preferred in May 1956 by 49 per cent, while 39 per cent favored conscription. In a poll in July 1956, almost two-thirds of the men under sixty-five replied that they would become soldiers "only very reluctantly or not at all"; and in August 1956 more than three-quarters of the men and 70 per cent of the women polled said that a man looked better in civilian clothes than in uniform.[50]

This lack of military enthusiasm was shared by the young. When asked in July 1956 whether they would volunteer for eighteen months

[45] "Ideologies," p. 5.

[46] *Jahrbuch II*, p. 305.

[47] *Ibid.*, p. 305.

[48] *Ibid.*, p. 295.

[49] *Ibid.*, pp. 152, 295; Lang letter, 1958. For the views of men over sixty and other details see polls in *Jahrbuch II*, pp. 297, 301–3, 307–8.

[50] "Ideologies," pp. 4–6. For similar replies in February 1956, see *Jahrbuch II*, p. 297.

rather than await conscription, 79 per cent of young men said unconditionally no; only 12 per cent said yes, and the rest attached conditions
or were undecided. In the same poll, 80 per cent said they were "not
interested" in becoming professional soldiers—now or later; only 10 per
cent said "yes."[51] Similar attitudes appeared in a number of other polls
of young men in 1955 and 1956.[52]

What the German government does in the way of rearmament is thus
a response to international considerations or conceivably to special interest groups; it is not being driven to rearmament by any domestic
popular pressure. There is, in fact, reason to think that the German
government has been mindful of public feeling on this point. The levels
of German armament envisaged by NATO in the early 1950's—500,000
men and eighteen months compulsory military service—were substantially reduced. By early 1958 no more than 125,000 men were in uniform, only 200,000 men were expected by March 1959,[53] and conscripts
had to serve only twelve months. The German military budget remained
at about 4 per cent of the national income, similar to levels prevailing
in Scandinavian countries, at a time when France and Great Britian
spent 7 and 8 per cent of their national incomes, respectively, and the
proportional burden on the United States was still higher.[54] These relatively low levels of military contribution to the Western alliance were
in no sense an indication of bad faith on the part of the Adenauer government, but they suggested how limited the burdens were which German political consensus would support.

Regardless of popular feelings on any matter of foreign policy, however, German foreign policy makers have a great deal of leeway so far
as domestic opinion is concerned. There is a long-standing German tradition of leaving such complicated matters to experts and persons of authority; and the German government may count on popular acquiescence
even to relatively unpopular foreign policy moves. Thus the Adenauer
government, without encountering serious domestic opposition, has been
far more friendly to France on the issue of the Saar territory, and to
Israel on the issue of German reparations, than public opinion would
have liked it to be, as indicated by many poll results.[55] After the return

[51] *Jahrbuch II*, pp. 153, 159.

[52] Rolf Fröhner, *Wie stark sind die Halbstarken?* pp. 125–27, 326–33; *Jahrbuch II*, pp.
152–59, 308–11.

[53] Statement by German Defense Minister Franz Josef Strauss, cited in Associated
Press, "Bonn Role in NATO Grows," *The Christian Science Monitor*, December 18, 1958,
p. 9:6–8.

[54] For 1955 data, see United Nations, *Economic Survey of Europe, 1955*, Table 4, p. 7.

[55] See polls in *Jahrbuch I*, pp. 130, 322–28, 331. By January 1957, about one-sixth of
Germans thought that there were obstacles on the German side to German-French friendship, while twice as many saw obstacles on the French side; one-third thought there were
no obstacles on either side; and more than one-third were undecided. "Ideologies," pp.
11–12.

of the Saar to Germany, however, a plurality in December 1956 credited
Adenauer with the achievement.[56] The extent of Adenauer's freedom of
action vis-à-vis domestic opinion was strikingly confirmed in the matter
of the reparations agreement with Israel. Although the proposed indemnity of more than $700 million to Israel in lieu of the property of Jews
killed or despoiled in the Hitler period was approved by only 11 per
cent in a poll in August 1952, with 44 per cent flatly opposing and 24
per cent favoring a lesser amount, an agreement was concluded to pay
this sum to Israel in goods over a ten-year period.[57]

How Stable Are Current German Political Images and Attitudes?

A general characteristic of German poll data between 1947 and 1957
is the relative stability of many of the attitudes revealed. Particularly
since 1950, shifts in opinion have rarely exceeded a few percentage
points. This is somewhat in contrast to the relative volatility of public
opinion in the United States on matters of foreign policy topics, which
such studies as Gabriel Almond's have documented.[58]

German politics today thus looks remarkably sober, even pedestrian;
no startling changes appear at all probable. Yet it is worth remembering that German political life presented a similar appearance during the
heyday of the Weimar Republic between 1925 and 1929, only a few
years before its collapse and the National Socialist seizure of power.[59]

[56] *Jahrbuch II*, p. 330.

[57] Cf. *Jahrbuch I*, p. 130. For a more detailed account, see below, pp. 168–76.

[58] *The American People and Foreign Policy*, pp. 69–115. For a theory of long-term
swings in American opinion, in addition to the short-term changes traced by Almond, see
also Frank L. Klingberg, "The Historical Alternation of Moods in American Foreign Policy," *World Politics*, 4:2 (January 1952), 239–73.

[59] For an example of the deceptive appearance of German political stability in 1928–29,
see Joseph A. Schumpeter, "Das soziale Antlitz des Deutschen Reiches," *Aufsätze zur
Soziologie*, pp. 214–25; and Karl W. Deutsch, "Joseph Schumpeter as an Analyst of Sociology and Economic History," *Journal of Economic History*, March 1956, pp. 41–56. For
another example of contemporary optimism, see J. W. Angell, *The Recovery of Germany*
(New Haven, Yale University Press, 1929), *passim*.

While economists and social scientists read stability in the boom statistics of the 1920's,
a poetic writer had a different vision:

"Something has happened. Something has happened which has not yet eventuated.
The old spell of the old world has broken, and the old, bristling, savage spirit has set in.
The war did not break the old peace-and-production hope of the world, though it gave it
a severe wrench. Yet the old peace-and-production hope still governs, at least the conscious-
ness. Even in Germany it has not quite gone.

"But it feels as if, virtually, it were gone. The last two years have done it. The hope
in peace-and-production is broken. The old flow, the old adherence is ruptured. And a still
older flow has set in. Back, back to the savage polarity of Tartary, and away from the
polarity of civilized Christian Europe. This, it seems to me, has already happened. And it
is a happening of far more profound import than any actual *event*. It is the father of the
next phase of events . . .

"And it all looks as if the years were wheeling swiftly backwards, no more onwards.

We find a similar contradiction between long-lasting stolid competence and occasional romantic daring in many popular images of the German national character. It is difficult and dangerous to say anything about the character of a people as a whole, but it would be no less misleading to pretend that all peoples are alike and that the same behavior patterns and personality types are distributed in the same manner among them. In assessing the factors limiting or influencing foreign policy decisions we must take some note, therefore, of the modern literature on national character, and on German character in particular.[60]

There is a good deal of agreement about some particular German behavior patterns in recent decades, and these are borne out by poll results. Asked to name the best qualities of the German people, 72 per cent of Germans polled in July 1952 said "diligence, efficiency, endeavor." In second place, 21 per cent named "orderliness, reliability, thoroughness, cleanliness"; 12 per cent said "benevolence, good will," 11 per cent said "loyalty," 9 per cent said "intelligence, ingenuity," 8 per cent said "persistence," and 3 per cent named "modesty." As one might well expect from human nature, there was less agreement on the worst German qualities; 18 per cent named "lack of unity," 13 per cent said "arrogance," 11 per cent said "lack of nationalism," and 10 per cent said "excessive trustfulness and gullibility."[61]

The image of one's own people as "hard-working" is more strongly held in Germny than in other countries. In a UNESCO poll in eight countries in 1948-49, such a self-image was endorsed in seven countries by majorities or pluralities ranging from 43 per cent in Norway to 68

Like the spring that is broken, and whirls swiftly back, so time seems to be whirling with mysterious swiftness to a sort of death. Whirling to the ghost of the Middle Ages of Germany, then to the Roman days, then to the days of the silent forest and the dangerous, lurking barbarians."

Written February 19, 1924, from D. H. Lawrence, "A Letter from Germany," *Selected Essays* (Harmondsworth, Middlesex, Penguin Books, 1950), pp. 177 and 178.

[60] For general discussions of national character, and of German national character in particular, cf. Almond, *The American People and Foreign Policy*; Henry V. Dicks, "Some Psychological Studies of the German Character," in T. H. Pear, *Psychological Factors of Peace and War*; Willy Hellpach, *Der Deutsche Charakter*; Alexander Inkeles and Daniel J. Levinson, "National Character: The Study of Modal Personality and Socio-Cultural Systems," in G. Lindzey, ed., *Handbook of Social Psychology* (Cambridge, Addison-Wesley, 1954), II, 977–1020; Paul Kecskemeti and Nathan Leites, *Some Psychological Hypotheses on Nazi Germany*; Robert H. Lowie, *Toward Understanding Germany* (Chicago, University of Chicago Press, 1954); Margaret Mead, "National Character," in A. L. Kroeber, ed., *Anthropology Today* (Chicago, University of Chicago Press, 1953), pp. 642–67; Thomas Mann, "Germany and the Germans," *Yale Review*, XXXV, No. 2 (December 1945), 223–41; Helen Peak, "Observations on the Characteristics and Distribution of German Nazis"; Bertram Schaffner, *Father Land: A Study of Authoritarianism in the German Family*; M. Waehler, *Der deutsche Volkscharakter* (Jena, Diederichs, 1937); Henry C. Wallich, *Mainsprings of the German Revival*, pp. 328–43.

[61] *Jahrbuch I*, p. 126. These were replies to open-ended questions, not choices from set questionnaires.

per cent in the United States; but in Germany a solid 90 per cent described their own nation as "hard-working." Only a minority would concede this property to any other nation, and the gap between the vote for this favorable self-estimate and the vote for the next highly esteemed nation in this respect, China, was nearly twice as high as it was in any other country polled.[62] Majorities of German respondents—60 per cent in 1955 and 56 per cent in 1956—reaffirmed the belief that their own people were "more efficient and gifted than the other peoples."[63]

The German national character, like that of other peoples, has changed several times in history. In the sixteenth century, Germans impressed foreign observers with their lack of discipline; in the late seventeenth century, they were reputed to be deficient in soldierly courage. In the course of the nineteenth century, the national character changed again when many South and Central Germans learned to model their behavior on that of Prussians, and the German reserve officer became a distinctive social type.

These changes, however, took time. The dramatic reversals of German politics within a single generation, say from 1928 to 1958, included the Weimar Republic, the Nazi dictatorship, occupation by foreign powers, and the Federal Republic. These events followed upon each other too rapidly to become embodied in stable patterns of personality and culture, and hence in a new kind of national character. Rather, the West Germans of the late 1950's seemed to have very much the same basic character as their fathers in the 1920's, along with a very different heritage of personal memories. Together, this character and these memories were bound to create contradictions—some manifest and some beneath the surface.

Both the "national character" studies and the poll results leave the impression of unresolved contradictions in the psychology and character of present-day Germans, corresponding to some extent to the legacy of unresolved contradictions from their country's past. "In Germany," writes an uncommonly well-informed observer, "a truly unresolved past . . . introduces upon the present."[64] At the same time, this past was rich in memories of periods of steadfast continuity, alternating with abrupt reversals of foreign and domestic policies, which were discussed earlier in this chapter. How stable would German foreign policy alignments prove to be this time, in the age of nuclear energy and intercontinental missiles? One indication of the chances for stability might be found in the social structure and ideological group alignments in the German Federal Republic.

[62] W. Buchanan and H. Cantril, *How Nations See Each Other*, pp. 46–47.
[63] *Jahrbuch II*, p. 139.
[64] Speier, *German Rearmament and Atomic War*, p. 30.

CHAPTER 3

Conditions of stability: Social classes and cleavages in ideology

The Germans of the Federal Republic are largely an urban and industrial people. By 1956, 33 per cent of Germans above eighteen years of age lived in large cities above 100,000 population; another 15 per cent lived in middle-sized cities of between 20,000 and 100,000 inhabitants. This left 28 per cent for small towns (2,000–20,000 population) and 24 per cent in smaller, mostly rural communities. In part as a result of war losses, 55 per cent were women as against only 45 per cent men. As many as 21 per cent of the total were sixty years old or older; 24 per cent were under thirty, and the rest were nearly evenly divided between those above and below forty-five.

Almost half (48 per cent) were workers, and another 4 per cent were rural laborers; 18 per cent were private white-collar employees and 5 per cent were public officials, bringing the total share of wage or salary earners up to three-quarters of the total. The remaining quarter were self-employed persons, 12 per cent peasants or farmers, 12 per cent businessmen and artisans, and 1 per cent professionanl men such as doctors, architects, or lawyers.

Educational levels are not high. Only 4 per cent of Germans over eighteen had the equivalent of a junior college education (*Abitur*). Another 12 per cent had the equivalent of ten years' schooling (*Mittlere Reife*), and the remaining 84 per cent had no more than the equivalent of eight years' schooling (*Volksschule*).[1]

No political group can win a majority in Germany without the support of at least part of these urban and industrial groups; but there are enough peasants, white-collar workers, and others of middle-class status or aspirations to permit a variety of political combinations, and to reward political appeals designed to unite at least some wage and salary earners with some self-employed groups. This situation limits the effectiveness of class appeals and favors politicians who can present their views as serving the interests of the nation.

From a survey of West German social strata in 1955, three striking facts emerged.

[1] All these data from *Jahrbuch II*, pp. xliv and 4. For other data, see tables in Appendix II.

First, the distribution of German social strata in 1955—their shares in the total population—was remarkably close to what it had been in 1939 in the days of Hitler's power.

Second, the incumbents of these social class positions had changed to a considerable extent: while the top, middle, and bottom drawers of the social system had remained much the same, there had been considerable mobility among the persons who filled them. Thus only about three-quarters of the upper-middle class had retained their positions from 1939 to 1955; 25 per cent of the upper-middle-class persons of 1955 had themselves risen from some lower social position held in 1939; and 21 per cent of those who had been in the upper-middle class in 1939 had dropped into lower-class positions in 1955. Not quite 51 per cent of the upper-middle-class fathers had upper-middle-class sons.

Third, the changes between the generations of fathers and sons, both as to class structure and incumbents of such class positions, had been much greater than the changes experienced by individual Germans in their own careers. Nearly one-half (49.4 per cent) of the children of upper-middle-class fathers had been reduced by 1955 to lower social positions; and those sons of upper-middle-class fathers, who had retained their social position, now formed a minority of less than one-third in the much larger upper-middle class of 1955. On the other hand, more than one-third of the children of skilled workers had risen in the social scale, while only about one-fifth of the children of this class had descended into the "lower-lower" class of unskilled and semiskilled labor. Less than one-third of the skilled workers of 1955 were second-generation members of their class, and only a bare majority were descended from fathers in any of the traditional "working classes," including unskilled workers and rural laborers.[2]

Generally, there had been so much mobility across class lines from one generation to the next that it suggested a decline in the potential

[2] Morris Janowitz, "Social Stratification and Mobility in West Germany," *American Journal of Sociology*, 64:1 (July 1958), 6–24; see also tables in Appendix II. The authors are indebted to Professor Janowitz for making available to them a prepublication draft of this article. Professor Janowitz's findings of the stability of the German occupational structure appear confirmed in other sources.

Despite the impact of World War II, changes in the proportion of self-employed persons in the occupied population of Western Germany have been smaller than those in neutral Sweden and Switzerland. Computations based on a United Nations survey give the following figures:

Per Cent Self-Employed in Total Occupied Population

	1936	1940	1941	1950	1953	1954	No. of Years	Total% Change	Change per Decade
Sweden	—	28.5	—	22.2	—	—	10	−6.3	−6.3
Switzerland	—	—	28.7	24.6	—	—	9	−4.1	−4.5
Western Germany	28.0	—	—	23.0	—	—	14	−5.0	−3.6
Denmark	—	26.0	—	25.6	25.3	—	13	−0.7	−0.5
France	29.1	—	—	—	—	28.6	18	−0.5	−0.3

(From data in United Nations, *Economic Survey in Europe in 1956* (Geneva 1957), Ch. VIII, p. 19, Table 9.)

appeal of symbols of class, while leaving unimpaired—or even enhanced—the potential appeal of symbols of the nation. Moving upward or downward in the social scale, or maintaining his father's social status, a man still remained German. Any political appeal expressed in terms of his nationality might count on an echo from personal and family memories unimpaired by any changes in his own position.

Other conditions reduce the effectiveness of sectional or denominational politics and encourage political appeals to images of national interest. Interregional mobility has been intense. Vast population movements took place during and after the last war. The great cities, largely destroyed and depopulated at the end of the war, have regained for the most part their prewar population levels, but one-third of their present inhabitants are newcomers.[3] Above all, regional mobility in postwar Germany is the result of the expulsion or flight of millions of Germans from areas now under Soviet control, including the German Democratic Republic. Almost one-fourth of the adult population of the Federal Republic consists of such expellees and refugees, who settled in large numbers in areas formerly distinguished by parochialism in national politics, such as in Bavaria. The newcomers are not likely to respond to appeals based on the interests of a single region or section.

Many of these expellees are of middle-class background, and whatever their present occupations may be, their memories and style of thinking are still at least partly middle-class. To the 47 per cent who are now in middle-class or white-collar occupations there must thus be added an appreciable group of wage earners with middle-class memories and an even larger group of wage earners with middle-class aspirations—all of which could lend themselves to expression in national terms.

The results of this great social and regional mobility have been hailed by one German student of nationalism as "the birth of a new people," and they have led a German sociologist to speak of a "standardization of social design," a "far advanced breakdown of social distinctions," and the emergence of "a relatively equal and uniform social class."[4] Such relative social uniformity may well offer serious obstacles to the success of class appeals, but not necessarily to the appeals of nationalism, moderate or even potentially extreme.

A similar consideration applies to the religious groupings. With the population above eighteen almost evenly divided between Protestants (52 per cent) and Roman Catholics (44 per cent, but somewhat better organized), Germans could only expect deadlock from religious quarrels.[5] Finally, the main ideological cleavages inherited from the

---

[3] Helmut Schelsky, "Elements of Social Stability," *German Social Science Digest* (Hamburg, Claassen Verlag, 1955), p. 115.

[4] *Ibid.*

[5] Data from *Jahrbuch II*, pp. xliv, 3.

days of the Empire, the First (Weimar) Republic, the Nazi dictatorship, and two world wars all cut largely across regional, religious, and class boundaries.

The Persistent Split in Ideology

The most important underlying cleavage in Germany is between friends and enemies of the Republic, supporters of democracy and adherents of dictatorship. In practical terms, this still means the inconspicuous but persistent difference between Nazis and anti-Nazis—between those who would like to see some equivalent of the Hitler dictatorship restored and those who wish to maintain democratic institutions.

The Unpopularity of Communism

As a domestic problem, Communism has survived at most as a negative symbol. The Communist party was outlawed, but even before this happened it had attracted practically no supporters. In the election of 1953, the party received less than 3 per cent of the votes and in a July 1956 poll only 1 per cent of respondents professed to prefer it to other parties.[6] However, many West Germans saw Communism as an internal threat, linked to the external threat from the East. In February 1956, 55 per cent of respondents to a poll agreed that there was "a fairly extensive and influential" Communist underground movement in Western Germany, and only 24 per cent denied this.[7]

The large majority of West German voters and politicians are against Communism as they are against sin. Nazi sympathizers are alternately vehement in denouncing Communism and ready to play with the thought of making alliances with Communists against the West, in line with the old Stalin-Hitler pact of 1939 and with some more recent "national-bolshevist" propaganda themes. But it is in their appeal to the traditions of nationalism and authoritarianism that the potential strength of the Nazis must be sought; it is here that the supporters of democratic institutions will have to resist them.

The Supporters of Democracy

The consistent supporters of democracy seem to number about one-fourth of the adult population. On some issues this figure has declined to one-fifth or less. In a December 1952 poll, 21 per cent approved in

[6] *Jahrbuch II*, p. 149. In earlier polls, the number of those professing a favorable view of Communism had dropped from 8 per cent in 1950 to 2 per cent in 1955. *Jahrbuch I*, p. 272; "Ideologies," p. 8.

[7] Affirmative replies were particularly prominent among men (64 per cent) and were fairly evenly distributed among supporters of all major parties. See *Jahrbuch II*, p. 276.

theory of resistance against Hitler in wartime, but in an April 1956 poll only 18 per cent would name a new school after one of the leaders of the abortive 1944 plot against Hitler.[8]

On the whole, this democratic group has held remarkably steady. Exactly the same proportion of respondents, 25 per cent, said both in November 1953 and in June 1956 that they would do all they could to keep a new Nazi party from coming to power.[9] Some 25–28 per cent affirmed in October 1948 that they had been "opposed to both the domestic and foreign policies" of the Hitler regime, and had rejected National Socialism as an idea. The same percentage in June 1952 expressed unqualified condemnation of Adolf Hitler; in May 1954 favored the black, red, and gold flag of the German Federal Republic against the black, white, and red of the Hohenzollern empire and the Nazis; in October 1954 asserted that men who had worked in Germany in the resistance movement against Hitler should be eligible for high governmental positions;[10] and in October 1956 endorsed democracy in terms implying an awareness of shared responsibility and duties as well as rights.[11]

With time, this hard core of the democratic vote may have grown. By June 1956, support for the black, red, and gold flag of the Republic had risen to 30–34 per cent, depending on the wording of the question.[12] Approval for the Constitution—the so-called "Basic Law"—remained substantially unchanged, however; it declined fractionally from 30 per cent in May 1955 to 29 per cent in June 1956.[13] However, 50 per cent of respondents in a poll in June 1956 indicated a clear awareness of a connection between dictatorship and "acts of violence . . . such as in those days in the concentration camps"; and 56 per cent preferred a system of government "in which several people have something to say in the state."[14]

Not all Germans who favor democracy speak up for it in public. A study of 1,800 Germans in extended group discussions in the winter of 1950–51 revealed only 10 per cent of the speakers as strongly in favor of democracy; but these persons were replying to a deliberately provocative item of Western criticism of the German people, and among the 68 per cent of speakers who appeared to favor democracy "conditionally" many endorsed it in principle. Clear-cut approval of democracy was stronger among young people under twenty; of these, 15 per cent

[8] *Jahrbuch I*, p. 138; *Jahrbuch II*, p. 145.
[9] *Ibid.*, p. 276; *Jahrbuch II*, p. 27.
[10] *Ibid.*, pp. 133–34, 136, 139, 159.
[11] "Ideologies," p. 2.
[12] *Jahrbuch II*, p. 173.
[13] *Ibid.*, p. 165.
[14] *Ibid.*, pp. 172–73.

gave it unconditional endorsement.[15] More recently, 39 per cent of a group of young people between fifteen and twenty-five interviewed in November 1955 strongly expressed their readiness to speak up for the political institutions of the Federal Republic against criticism, and 74 per cent expressed some degree of positive attitude toward their form of government.[16]

On many issues, the strong or all-weather democrats find broader support among their less clearly committed countrymen. Thus 36 per cent denied in May 1955 that "Hitler without the war would have been one of the greatest statesmen," and this rose to 38 per cent in a similar poll in June 1956. The proportion replying in the affirmative declined from 48 to 42 per cent. Still, it is sobering to know that this many respondents voted Hitler's greatness on these terms, with dictatorship, concentration camps, and all.[17] In several polls taken between 1951 and 1954, about 40 per cent generally approved the resistance movement against Hitler; in July 1952, 47 per cent had a bad opinion of Hitler, and 68 per cent were at least willing to agree that Hitler's "fatal deeds and qualities predominated by far" in his record. Of other prominent Nazi leaders the late propaganda minister Joseph Goebbels was flatly condemned by 61 per cent, and the late secret police chief Heinrich Himmler by 78 per cent—a near-record in unpopularity.[18] The number who blamed Nazi Germany for the outbreak of war in 1939 increased from 32 per cent, in a 1951 poll, to 47 per cent in 1956; over this same period, the proportion who blamed "other states" declined from 24 per cent to 12 per cent.[19]

Nazis, Extreme Nationalists, and Their Sympathizers

On the other side, there is a hard core of unreconstructed Nazis and a penumbra of their partial sympathizers. In Germany between 1950 and 1957, about one German in eight was for most political purposes such a Nazi. That is, in poll ofter poll between 7 per cent and 15 per cent said that they liked Hitler and Goebbels, professed race doctrines about Jews, and announced that they would welcome the return of a new National Socialist party to power.[20] Among young people between fifteen and twenty-five, polls in November 1953, 1954, and 1955 showed about 10 per cent professing favorable opinions of Hitler and of National Socialism.[21] In a June 1956 poll of both men and women 16 per cent of respondents in the eighteen to twenty-nine age group declared they

[15] Friedrich Pollock, ed., *Gruppenexperiment: Ein Studienbericht*, pp. 139–51.
[16] Fröhner, *Wie stark sind die Halbstarken?* pp. 314–15.
[17] *Jahrbuch I*, p. 277; *Jahrbuch II*, p. 278.
[18] *Ibid.*, pp. 135–36, 138–39.
[19] *Jahrbuch II*, p. 142.
[20] *Jahrbuch I*, pp. 126, 132, 136, 138, 174, 276; *Jahrbuch II*, pp. 141, 277–79.
[21] Fröhner, *Wie stark sind die Halbstarken?* pp. 119–21, 305–10.

would welcome the efforts of a new Nazi party to come to power; and in July 1956 an equal proportion in a separate poll of young men declared without qualifications that National Socialism had been "a good idea."[22]

With somewhat less fervor, about one German in four was an emotional supporter of the Nazis or extreme Nationalists in general, professing a "predominantly favorable" opinion of Hitler, his deputy Hess, and the Nazi Youth leader von Schirach. About the same proportion of Germans consistently expressed an unfriendly attitude toward democracy and toward the black, red, and gold flag of the Federal Republic. An equal number felt that Germany had lost the war mainly because of domestic sabotage and treason. Not surprisingly, almost as many (24 per cent) wished to bar from high government positions any man who took part in the wartime resistance against Hitler.[23]

The camp of Nazi sympathizers has its own version of anti-Communism: 22 per cent insisted "unconditionally" in June 1956 that Germany in 1933 had had no other choice except either National Socialism or Communism; another 15 per cent said "perhaps"; only 28 per cent denied the exclusiveness of these alternatives.[24]

On many specific issues, however, a much larger number of Germans have held views in line with Nazi traditions or policies. Thus about one-third of Germans polled in 1952 expressed anti-Semitic views, and about two-fifths opposed legal punishment for anti-Semitic propaganda. Nearly the same proportion, 37 per cent, said in December 1952 and in April 1956 that it was "better for Germany not to have any Jews within the country,"[25] and a German study reported in 1957 "unequivocally anti-Semitic responses" from 30 per cent of persons polled. Anti-Semitic or not, 88 per cent declared themselves "not interested" in the problem of anti-Semitism. Although it is generally estimated that about 6 million Jews lost their lives through Nazi persecution, nearly two-thirds of respondents rejected a lower estimate of Jewish dead—5 million—as "too high"; a familiar 37 per cent of the total called it "grossly exaggerated."[26] The persistence of anti-Semitic sentiments contrasts with the actual decline of the Jewish population from 560,000 in 1933 to about 30,000 in

[22] *Jahrbuch II*, pp. 149, 279.

[23] *Jahrbuch I*, pp. 135–37, 139; *Jahrbuch II*, pp. 170, 172–73.

[24] *Jahrbuch II*, p. 144.

[25] *Ibid.*, p. 126.

[26] Erich Lüth, "Deutsche und Juden heute," *Der Monat*, x, No. 110 (November 1957), 47, 49. According to the American Jewish Committee, as reported in a Paris dispatch to *The New York Times*, March 28, 1958, one-third to two-thirds of respondents in a poll expressed anti-Semitic sentiments. Such views were stronger in the age group over thirty-five and, among farmers, weakest among young men below thirty-five. Inquiries about this poll at the American Jewish Committee in New York City produced the statement that this poll was conducted for internal use of the German Federal government by a German polling organization and that the information reported "leaked" to a representative of the American Jewish Committee.

Western Germany in 1957, and with the prospective further decline of this over-aged group to an expected 20,000 by the late 1960's.[27]

A similar number, 39 per cent, opposed in 1954 the admission of former anti-Hitler refugees to high positions in the Federal Republic. Slightly more than one-half of a group of Germans polled in 1951 favored lifting the ban on the wearing of Nazi World War II decorations with the swastika symbol (almost every other German man had at least one such decoration); and they opposed the idea of reissuing these decorations with the swastika omitted. A majority rejected the notion of German war crimes. More than one-half (55 per cent) felt in 1953 that the German soldiers of World War II had nothing to reproach themselves for in their behavior in the countries they had occupied, while as many as 70 per cent of the Germans polled in 1949 had said that they could not consider, or ever have considered, marrying a person of Jewish descent.[28]

Finally, we may recall what we noted earlier about the image of history which Germans hold today. More than four German adults out of every five polled have favorable memories of one or the other of the two authoritarian systems of government in Germany during the twentieth century: the Hohenzollern monarchy before 1918 and Hitler's Third Reich between 1933 and 1945.[29]

The Limits of Consensus

Most of the large popular majorities on particular foreign policy issues thus seem to arise in instances in which many or all of the 25–30 per cent all-weather democrats and many or all of the 20–25 per cent antidemocratic Nazi sympathizers can agree. In such instances, a considerable part of the usually undecided or ambivalent persons are likely to join them. We have surveyed the main issues that tend to produce this kind of agreement between pro- and anti-Nazis, adherents of nationalistic dictatorship and adherents of democracy, friendly and hostile critics of the United States, France, and the United Kingdom. They are the familiar issues of opposition to Communism, preference for Western economic and political connections and living standards, and eagerness to increase Germany's national prosperity and international prestige and bargaining power.

The nature of this consensus implies its limits: most voters will not follow nationalist goals to the brink of war; most democrats will not

---

[27] *Ibid.*, p. 49.

[28] *Jahrbuch I*, p. 131. In 1957, Lüth reported, however, that 61 to 79 per cent of respondents agreed that it was possible for "two young people in love, one of them Jewish" to find happiness in marriage ("Deutsche und Juden heute," p. 49).

[29] For this and the preceding paragraphs, see polls in *Jahrbuch I*, pp. 125, 126, 128, 131, 137, 379. Cf. also F. Pollock, *Gruppenexperiment*, pp. 139, 151–52, 162, 220.

increase German international bargaining power to the point where extreme nationalists and militarists would actually ragain major power in domestic politics; most of the right-wing extremists do not wish to deepen their alliance with the West to the point where they would have to drop their anti-Semitism, their admiration for much of the Nazi system, and their contempt for democracy. Wherever those limits of consent are reached, democrats and Nazi sympathizers separate again; many of their countrymen withdraw into silence or indifference; and policy decisions, though sometimes delayed or compromised, are left in the hands of the government which has tended to follow the democratic sectors of opinion and what it judged to be the relevant international opinion.

Ideologies and Social Groups

A look at the distribution of ideologies among particular sectors of the population confirms this picture. Democratic opinions were expressed in 1950–51 to an extent significantly above the average by persons with higher education (*Abitur*) but lacking a university degree, by those under twenty or over fifty years of age, by women in general, by students, and by housewives. Still somewhat above average on the prodemocratic side were white-collar employees, persons with no past military service, and skilled workers. Close to average were persons with less than two years of military service, persons aged twenty to thirty-five, persons with tenth-grade education (*Mittlere Reife*), and unskilled workers. Somewhat below average—i.e., above average in nationalistic and antidemocratic opinions—were men in general, persons with only grade-school education, those with two to six years of military service, and those between thirty-five and fifty—perhaps an indication of the effects of Nazi indoctrination of young people in the 1930's.

Most inclined to rabidly nationalistic, anti-Western, and pro-Nazi views were peasants, men with more than six years of military service, and persons with university degrees, in that order, perhaps another legacy of Nazi selection and indoctrination of military and academic personnel. Nazi ideologies thus seem to have survived most strongly not only in the small villages of Bavaria and Lower Saxony, but also in important academic and military circles—a situation with which a democratic leadership must cope as best it can.[30]

Ideology and Military Service

The seriousness of this problem is underlined when one considers the one-tenth to one-quarter proportion of strong nationalists and Nazi sympathizers in relation to the near two-thirds proportion of men under

[30] Cf. Pollock, *Gruppenexperiment*, pp. 236–72.

sixty-five who had said in 1956 that they would serve in the armed forces "only very reluctantly or not at all." (See p. 30.) Among young men under twenty-five, it may be recalled that in repeated polls about 10 to 16 per cent expressed favorable opinions about Hitler and National Socialism, while only 10 to 12 per cent of this age group said that they would like to become soldiers. (See *Jahrbuch II*, pp. 153, 159, cited on p. 32.) The number of Nazi sympathizers, while small in proportion to the total population, seems large in relation to those likely to volunteer for military service, and it could well be as high as 40 or 50 per cent of this latter group.

A similar inference is suggested by another consideration. The proportion of 25 per cent all-weather democrats, indicated by many poll results discussed earlier in this chapter (see pp. 38–42), includes many Social Democrats, perhaps not less than one-half. These Social Democrats and their sympathizers, however, according to the stand taken repeatedly by their party and stressed in its electoral campaigns, are cool —to say the least—toward rearmament. It seems plausible that most of them were included among the two-thirds of Germans who expressed strong reluctance to render military service. Thus, the proportion of all-weather democrats willing to volunteer for the armed forces would seem to be at most one-eighth of all men under sixty-five, and less than one-half of the potential volunteers.

In October 1958, the Bundestag deputies of the Social Democratic party (SPD) explicitly approved of party members joining the armed forces, and decided on a country-wide effort to build up contacts with the military establishment and personnel, including "better contacts" between regional socialist organizations and troops stationed in their areas.[31] This shift in policy was met with some misgivings by the government, however, particularly since the SPD rejected at the same time the appeal of the federal government for a bipartisan military policy; and the whole episode did not seem likely to change substantially the continuing problem of recruiting a democratic army from not necessarily prodemocratic volunteers.

Two other factors aggravate the problem. While Nazi sympathizers by reason of their ideology are likely to favor the military life, all-weather democrats may not necessarily do so; hence an even larger proportion of the actual volunteers may come from the ranks of strong nationalists and Nazis than from among the supporters of democratic institutions. The second aggravating factor is the increasing reliance of the government on long-term volunteers, rather than on conscripts, to fill the ranks of the armed forces. Both of these factors operated in the days of the Weimar Republic and helped to produce a conspicuously nondemocratic, and potentially antidemocratic, army.

[31] Sydney Gruson, "Socialists Reject Bonn Unity Plea," *The New York Times*, October 19, 1958, p. 2:5–6.

To keep Bonn from repeating the experience of Weimar, the federal government relies on considerably more elaborate screening and supervisory procedures than were used by its luckless predecessor. These safeguards may indeed prove effective, if recruitment remains slow and limited in numbers, but they may well be overtaxed if large numbers of officers and men should have to be recruited in a hurry. Since an army, navy, and air force, once organized, are not easily made over, the reluctance of both government and opposition to speed the military build-up of the Federal Republic may well be based on serious long-term considerations of domestic policy.

The Climate of Prosperity

To the casual observer, however, and even to many Germans, these problems seemed remote. Despite their heritage of ideologies, the West Germans in the mid-1950's seemed a highly "nonideological" people. None of the old abstract slogans of monarchy, republic, socialism, or capitalism could move a majority of the population to firm commitment or active support. Homes, jobs, security, and opportunity for individuals and families appeared far more important.

Prosperity thus became a central political fact for many voters. The net national product rose from $340 per capita in 1949 to $510 for the average of 1952–54, and wages and other incomes rose less steeply but perceptibly.[32]

By mid-1955, almost one-fifteenth of all German households had automobiles; a slightly higher fraction had pianos or phonograph consoles or both. About one-tenth had electric refrigerators, electric washing machines, hot water heaters, motorcycles or motor scooters, electric shavers. Almost one-sixth had electric stoves, and a similar fraction had typewriters. Almost one-third had gas stoves; more than one-third had cameras; almost two-fifths had vacuum cleaners; nearly three-fifths had sewing machines, bicycles, wrist watches; over four-fifths had radios; and nearly nine-tenths had electric irons.[33]

To be sure, this prosperity was not perceived equally by all. Compared to the period before World War II, 41 per cent claimed to be worse off, and only 24 per cent said "better." Of the age group between thirty and fifty-nine years, 40 to 57 per cent considered themselves in May 1955 worse off, and only between 15 and 26 per cent reported improvement. A plurality of persons under twenty-nine—who had been children before the war—believed that their lot had improved; 36 per

---

[32] United Nations Statistical Office, *Per Capita National Product of Fifty-Five Countries 1952–54* (Statistical Papers, Series E, No. 4; New York, 1957), p. 7; and *National and Per Capita Incomes of 70 Countries in 1949* (Statistical Papers, Series E, No. 1; New York, 1950).

[33] *Jahrbuch I*, pp. 27–28. See also Schelsky, "Elements of Social Stability," p. 116.

cent said so, and only 21 per cent felt that they were faring worse. Old folk over sixty overwhelmingly reported themselves poorer.[34] In contrast to the Soviet world, however, and to conditions in Eastern Germany, there was no doubt whatever in the minds of West Germans that their own levels of prosperity and consumer goods were far higher, and this was a matter of very great importance.

The German people did not have to vote about the Western way of life in terms of ideology alone. They had already voted about it in terms of their posessions.

Wanted: A Foreign Policy of Caution

Above all, German public opinion in the mid-1950's wanted to avoid unpalatable choices. The cumulative evidence of many opinion polls, interviews, and electoral results indicated that most Germans favored a foreign policy of firm symbolic attachment to the West, coupled with caution and a preference for limiting the extent of actual commitment. There was a clearly accepted general goal, to raise the prosperity and prestige of the German people to the level of the leading Western nations; and there were at least four agreed-upon major goals: (1) to keep Western Germany free of major Communist influence; (2) to preserve peace; (3) to retain United States friendship and support for German aspirations; and (4) to reunify Eastern and Western Germany, substantially on West German terms. Two less salient goals—the recovery of former German territories east of the Oder and Neisse rivers, and Western European integration—were endorsed by majorities but were perceived as less urgent for the time being, and perhaps also as less important in the long run.

Clearly, German opinion rejected anti-Communism at the price of war, as well as peace at the price of Communist rule. It rejected national reunification at the price of either Communist penetration or the loss of Western friendship. It favored neutrality, provided this could be coupled with continuing close and friendly association with the West, but it would not favor any overt displays of neutralism that might alienate Germany's Western allies.

These preferences corresponded fairly well to the very limited range of opportunities offered to German foreign policy by the international situation of the time. The two great power blocs, led by the United States and the USSR, respectively, appeared in a position of near-stalemate. Neither side could count on a clear and certain shift of power in its favor in the immediate years ahead. At the same time, all major countries in Europe were committed to one of the two blocs. There

[34] *Jahrbuch II*, p. 35.

was no effective bloc of neutral countries: Sweden, Finland, Austria, and Switzerland counted for little in military terms, leaving only Yugoslavia with a respectable army that was not firmly committed to either side. These countries could not form any effective combination offering positive attractions or opportunities to Germany.

Under these conditions, some of the determinants of German foreign policy were likely to be negative: to avoid or delay any decisions that might make matters worse. So long as really attractive positive opportunities either were lacking or, like Western European integration, seemed at best very slow in coming, German public opinion was most likely to favor a policy of cautious advance, designed to limit German risks and to increase quietly and steadily the extent of German bargaining power. Yet, if German foreign policy should succeed in bringing about a substantial increase in German power, there was little or no consensus as to how this power was to be used; and if German prosperity should fail to continue, or German power and prestige should shrink, even the existing limited consensus might become threatened. German political stability seemed likely to be endangered by any major change: the impact of an economic recession, a major political crisis, or a heavy drive toward nuclear armaments might prove equally unsettling.

Pending such potentially unsettling developments, the popular image of the tasks of German foreign policy in the 1950's was thus quite limited. What was the image of its makers? They should be experts, competent to make all necessary changes within the broad limits of the goals outlined. They should be cautious, but determined on essentials; they should be persevering, persistent, resourceful; they should try every promising approach, but not make any major concessions or compromises at the expense of long-run goals. They did not have to be open or explicit; they should not bother the voters with the burden of decisions; above all, they should be united. If they could also be "crafty" or "foxy," so much the better; "prudence," "diplomacy," "shrewdness," and "foxiness" were all considered major traits of Chancellor Adenauer in January 1955, a time when his popularity was rising.[35]

There was less public concern about the constitutional, legal, and administrative details of the way in which foreign policy was supposed to be made. Nevertheless, these arrangements are important, and it is to them that we must now direct our attention.

---

[35] *Jahrbuch I*, p. 163.

II
INSTITUTIONS AND ELITES

CHAPTER 4

Who is supposed to act: The role
of formal governmental institutions

Under the Constitution of the German Federal Republic foreign policy is the responsibility of the federal government. The ten constituent states of the Republic and their governments are bound by federal actions in the realm of foreign policy; if required, they are expected to pass enabling legislation to incorporate into state law commitments undertaken by the federal government toward foreign governments. This principle was weakened, however, by a recent decision of the federal constitutional court in a special case. This decision involved the old Concordat of 1933, between Nazi Germany and the Vatican, which the federal government of Chancellor Adenauer sought to uphold. The court ruled that the treaty was binding on the Federal Republic as the legal successor of the Third Reich, but that the new constitution did not oblige the individual states to fulfill the treaty.[1]

To a limited extent, the states participate in the formation of foreign policy through the upper house of the federal legislature (*Bundesrat*); this house is composed of representatives of the ten state governments, and each state has from three to five votes according to the size of its population. This chamber has an absolute veto over all constitutional changes, but only a suspensive veto over ordinary legislation. Prior to the conclusion of treaties affecting the particular interest of one or more states, the state governments have the right to make their views known, but these opinions are not binding on the federal government and may formally be ignored by it, though political considerations may induce the federal government to take them into account in deciding a course of action. As under the constitution of the Soviet Union, and unlike the United States system, the states have the right to conclude treaties of their own with foreign nations—subject to the approval of the federal chancellor—when these deal with matters not specifically reserved for federal jurisdiction or with subjects of concurrent jurisdiction not yet preempted by the federal government. These, however, are minor matters; in the main, foreign policy is federal in theory and practice.[2]

---

[1] Cf. Speier and Davison, *West German Leadership and Foreign Policy*, p. 42, Editors' note.

[2] The informal influence of state governments on federal foreign policy has also re-

The Key Role of the Chancellor

Within the federal government, the federal chancellor (*Bundeskanzler*) is constitutionally the principal decision maker in the realm of foreign policy. His cabinet, the federal president, the two chambers of the federal legislature, and the federal constitutional court may under certain circumstances share in the decision-making process, but constitutionally the final source of authority is the chancellor, who alone has the power and responsibility for determining public policy (*"bestimmt die Richtlinien der Politik"*).

The framers of the "Basic Law" of 1948—the Constitution of the Federal Republic—deliberately endowed the chancellor with considerable power in the hope of avoiding the sort of governmental instability which is common in many countries where an all-powerful legislature is divided into many bitterly antagonistic factions. At the same time, they wanted to prevent a recurrence of the sort of irresponsible executive absolutism which had prevailed in Germany before 1918 and in the early 1930's. Designed for the traditional German multiparty system, the Basic Law strives for executive responsibility by providing for a chief of government elected by and responsible to a majority of the popularly elected lower house of the federal legislature. It strives for governmental stability by providing that a chancellor remain in office until (1) a majority, or at least a plurality, of the lower house agree on a replacement or (2) a new lower house is elected, or (3) the incumbent chancellor dies or resigns. The chancellor cannot be impeached. Thus, it was hoped by the fathers of the constitution, neither the disintegration of a coalition nor the opposition of a parliamentary majority unable to agree on a replacement should force the fall of a government. "Chancellor Government" (*"Kanzlerregierung"*) is intended to make the head of the government less dependent upon the legislature than under a pure parliamentary system, yet more so than under our own presidential form of executive leadership.

In accordance with these principles, the chancellor alone—and not the entire government—is supposed to determine government policy, see to its execution, and account for it to the legislature. There is no collective responsibility of the entire government. Accordingly, the chancellor in effect appoints and dismisses the members of his cabinet; his recommendations are binding on the federal president who has the formal power of appointment and dismissal. In turn, the ministers of the chancellor's government are solely responsible to him as his advisers and subordinate administrators; their tenure ends automatically with his.

---

mained unimportant. For examples of cases, see Samuel L. Wahrhaftig, "The Development of German Foreign Policy Institutions," in Speier and Davison, *West German Leadership and Foreign Policy*, pp. 39–40, 47–49.

Constitutionally, neither the president nor the legislature can compel the chancellor either to include anyone in his government or to dismiss any minister. Chancellor Adenauer successfully maintained this point in 1955, when one of the parties in his coalition broke with him and sought to withdraw its representatives from the government. The ministers, Adenauer insisted, were his agents once they joined the government, and not those of their party. Subsequently, he dropped some cabinet members on his own because their presence in the government apparently no longer seemed politically advisable to him. Adenauer's actions underlined the fact that a strong chancellor who commands a majority in the lower house of the legislature can afford to defy suggestions concerning the composition and size of his government. On the other hand, a weak chancellor—that is, one who did not command such a majority or even a plurality—presumably would have to be far more considerate toward the leaders of parties whose support he sought in connection with the make-up of his cabinet. In order to gain such support he may be forced to accommodate them, to give ministerial portfolios to representatives of parties whose support he wants, create new portfolios, or appoint minsters without portfolios. He may have to offer important ministries to powerful political leaders who are not necessarily qualified for these posts but will bring him the parliamentary support he needs.

Other Offices and Officials

Individually, the members of the chancellor's government are supposed to administer the affairs of their ministries in accordance with the general policy determined by their chief. As in the case of the chancellor himself, the personality, experience, and qualifiications of the incumbent play an important part in determining the actual role he plays in the decision-making process and the extent to which he relies upon subordinate officials.

Chief among the ministries concerned with foreign policy is, of course, the Foreign Office (Auswärtiges Amt). It is officially charged with "attending to foreign affairs," and unless the chancellor makes special exceptions (as in the case of the Minister for Economic Cooperation in the second Adenauer government), other ministries may deal with foreign governments and international organizations only with its approval. Jurisdictional conflicts are resolved either by the entire cabinet or by the chancellor alone.

Other ministries directly or indirectly concerned with foreign policy decisions are those of Defense (Bundesministerium für Verteidigung), Finance (Bundesministerium für Finanzen), Economics (Bundesministerium für Wirtschaft), the Ministry for Expellees, Refugees, and Victims of War (Bundesministerium für Vertriebene, Flüchtlinge, und

Kriegsbeschädigte)—which was especially created to attend to the interests of some twelve million citizens who fled or were expelled from German and East European territories now dominated by the Soviet Union; and the Ministry for All-German Affairs (Bundesministerium für gesamtdeutsche Fragen)—whose special responsibilities are matters pertaining to the reunification of divided Germany. The second Adenauer government (1953–57), as previously mentioned, also included a Minister for Economic Cooperation (Bundesminister für wirtschaftliche Zusammenarbeit) who dealt with questions pertaining to European economic cooperation. Of these ministries, the Ministries of Economics and Finance exercise significant influence on international negotiations on trade and other economic matters, since the Foreign Office, which is nominally in charge, has to lean heavily on their trained personnel.[3]

Collectively, the ministers form the chancellor's cabinet and, as such, are supposed to advise him on matters of general policy decisions and to decide upon government proposals to be submitted to the legislature. The actual role of the cabinet and its individual members in decision making would also appear to depend very largely upon the personalities and relative political power of the chancellor and of his minister. A strong chancellor, such as Adenauer, can largely dictate policy; a weaker chancellor would be more dependent upon the approval and support of at least the most powerful of his ministers.

A relatively recent creation is the Federal Defense Council (Bundesverteidigungsrat), a sort of inner cabinet, somewhat similar to the American National Security Council. Its members are selected by the chancellor. In 1956 it included, in addition to the chancellor, the vice-chancellor and the ministers for Atomic Questions (Atomfragen), Defense, Foreign Affairs, Interior (Bundesministerium des Inneren), Finance, and Economics. Other ministers and important officials may be invited to attend meetings at the chancellor's discretion.

Two other agencies of the executive branch of the federal government have in recent years played a considerable role in the making of German foreign policy, largely owing to the intimate relationships existing between their respective chiefs and Chancellor Adenauer. The first of these, the Chancellor's Office (Bundeskanzleramt) is formally charged with assisting the chancellor in his relations with other branches of the government and important nongovernmental agencies, with keeping him informed on political developments at home and abroad, and with preparing for the decisions which the chancellor may decide to take on the basis of this information. The second, the Press and Information Office of the Federal Government (Presse und Informationsamt der Bundesregierung), is supposed to assure close relations between the executive branch and the mass

[3] *Ibid.*, p. 31.

media—both foreign and domestic—to gather and evaluate data on public opinion, and, generally, to interpret the policies, decisions, and actions of the government to the public at home and abroad. In terms of actual as well as potential influence over foreign policy-making process, the leading officials in both these offices have been important members of the decision-making elite within the executive branch, although the extent of their influence varied with the prevailing relationship between their incumbents and the chancellor.

Reserved for Special Cases: The Powers of the President

As in many other countries, the office of the president enables its incumbent to direct public attention to any foreign policies or issues he chooses. The president's role as an opinion leader usually remains secondary to that of the chancellor, but the ceremonial duties of the president provide him with special opportunities to turn a routine statement into a message of national and international significance. The 1958 New Year's message of President Theodor Heuss illustrates these possibilities. The President, commenting on East-West relations, called upon statesmen to "disentangle" themselves "from the web of slogans and ideologies," which were treated by some as "a missionary substitute for religious or scientific dogma," and he reminded his listeners of "the temporary character of social beliefs and economic principles." He found it "painful" that Soviet technical advances were "judged . . . merely from a military point of view," and insisted that "politically controlled war can no longer happen," and that, therefore, "war must appear today as political bankruptcy." He further praised "old-fashioned" secret diplomacy and the "confidential reconciliation between Washington and Moscow" which had preceded the lifting of the Berlin blockade in 1948. A reference to "the cautious and brilliant George Kennan" attracted particular attention since this prominent former United States diplomat had just called for East-West negotiations on a highly controversial subject: the neutralization of Germany and the withdrawal of Soviet forces to the Soviet Union and American forces at least to countries west of Germany. Referring to current German-Soviet trade negotiations, the President expressed his "hope for a successful continuation of the talks in Moscow—that they may not be suffocated by petty legal terms." The speech was interpreted by some observers as "a thinly veiled attack" on the policies and methods of United States Secretary of State John Foster Dulles, as well as of West German Foreign Minister Dr. Heinrich von Brentano and his closest advisers.[4] Despite the

---

[4] M. S. Handler, "Heuss Advocates More Diplomacy, Less Propaganda," *The New York Times*, January 1, 1958, pp. 1–2. Cf. also "Kennan on Germany: A Symposium" and M. S. Handler, "West Germans Split on Unification Issue: Kennan Plan Attracting Support in Wake of NATO Meeting," both in *The New York Times*, December 29, 1957, p. E5. For details on Mr. Kennan's views, see his *Russia, the Atom and the West* (New York, Harper, 1958).

wide attention it attracted, the President's statement was not followed by any significant changes in German foreign policy.

Generally, the impact of such presidential pronouncements on the actual conduct of German foreign policy is apt to depend on the amount of political power at his command. This power may vary greatly with political conditions.

The formal role of the federal president in the foreign policy-making process is normally extremely limited. While he has the right to nominate a candidate for the chancellorship to the lower house of the legislature, he must appoint the choice of the majority of the deputies, whether he approves or not. The incumbent chancellor is supposed to keep the president informed and to consult with him on the policies of his government, but the president, for his part, is considered constitutionally bound to cooperate loyally with a man who has the support of a majority of the deputies. He must sign such treaties, bills, and decrees as are submitted to him by the chancellor or his ministers, appoint or dismiss officials on the chancellor's advice, and, in general, exercise his formal powers at the discretion of the chief of government, who bears ultimate responsibility for the actions of the executive branch. Some constitutional commentators would concede the president limited influence over diplomatic negotiations, but even here a strong chancellor would appear to have the final word as principal decision maker.

The president's role becomes crucial only if parliament is so deeply divided that it will neither support the chancellor nor agree on a successor. In this situation—which would resemble the last crisis years of the Weimar Republic before Hitler's rise to power—the Basic Law provides for several contingencies. Thus, should a chancellor fail to receive the vote of confidence which it is his right to demand at any time in the lower house, he has fourteen days within which to exercise his privilege to get the president to dissolve the hostile chamber and order new elections—unless a majority of the deputies can agree on a successor. However, should the incumbent chancellor lose his majority in the lower house, yet prefer not to ask for a vote of confidence or let it come to an electoral contest, his dependence upon the president would increase considerably. Unless or until the lower house agreed on a successor, the president could either grant the chancellor limited powers to govern for a short time without the lower house, or he could compel his resignation. Provided the upper house consents, the president may proclaim a state of legislative emergency (*Gesetz-notstand*) under which all but budgetary items may become law without the consent of the lower house. On the other hand, should the president— or the upper house—refuse the support of such a step and, in effect, compel the chancellor to resign, he may then recommend a successor of his choice to the lower house and appoint him if his candidate should get at least a plurality in the chamber. He then might support his man in the above manner until the latter found a working majority or the chamber replaced him. Finally, should the president's nominee for the chancellorship fail even to get the support of a plurality of the deputies, the president has the right to dissolve the lower house at his own discretion and order new elections which may produce a legislature more favorable to the man of his choice. Whenever parliament and the chancellor should become deadlocked, the role of the federal president in the political process and his influence over foreign policy might thus increase a great deal.

The Powers of Parliament: The Bundestag

Of the two chambers of the federal legislature, the lower house (Bundestag) has by far the greater power in most matters, including foreign policy. Although it cannot initiate foreign policy, its consent for many measures is essential. Treaties which regulate the political relations of the Federation or relate to matters of federal legislation can become the law of the land only with the approval of the Bundestag. Similarly, the transfer of sovereign rights of the state to international institutions, such as the European Coal and Steel Community, require legislative action. Finally, all treaties and other legislation which conflict with the Basic Law require constitutional amendments, which must be approved by two-thirds of the membership of the lower house.

Apart from its legislative functions, the lower house is granted certain other powers which are designed to give the members a voice in the foreign policy-making process. A majority elects a chancellor and can dismiss him by choosing a successor. The deputies of the lower house provide half the votes in the Federal Assembly (Bundesversammlung), which every five years chooses a federal president, and can initiate impeachment proceedings against him before the federal constitutional court.

In the lower house, the deputies have the right to investigate and criticize the actions of the executive in plenary sessions or in committees. They may summon and question members of the government when they choose; the latter, for their part, have the right to demand to be heard by the deputies at any time, thus providing the chancellor and his ministers with potential opportunities to influence important deliberations of the house at decisive moments.

Most of the important contacts between the executive branch and the deputies occur in the sessions of the standing and select committees of the lower house, rather than in plenary sessions. It is here that experts from the various parties examine the actions and requests of the government and question its members thoroughly. The vote in the committee is usually decisive, and committee recommendations are usually approved in subsequent plenary sessions. With respect to foreign policy issues, the key committees are Foreign Affairs (Auswärtige Angelegenheiten), Defense (Verteidigung), Budget (Haushalt), Expellees (Heimatvertriebene), All-German Affairs (gesamtdeutsche Fragen), Border Questions (Grenzlandfragen), European Security (europäische Sicherheit), and Foreign Trade (Aussenhandel).

The role which the deputies of the lower house may play in the realm of German foreign policy appears to depend primarily on the authority which the chancellor exercises in the chamber. If he commands a stable majority, or, better, two-thirds of the votes, his powers are fairly absolute and his position firm. However, if he lacks such strength, his freedom of action would seem to be more limited; he may be forced to rely on the cooperation of uncertain and demanding allies in order to see his program through the legislature and prevent the election of a successor.

In the case of constitutional disputes arising out of foreign policy issues the federal constitutional court might enter the picture. It may be called upon to adjudicate jurisdictional disputes between the federal government and the states—as in the case of the validity of the 1933 Concordat[5]—or between the executive and the legislative branches of the national government. The court may also be asked to render advisory opinions on the constitutionality of certain pending actions, either upon the joint request of executive and legislative, or upon that of the federal president alone. The latter has the right to refuse to place his signature on treaties, acts of the legislature, or government decrees pending an advisory opinion from the court. Thus, in 1952, President Theodor Heuss tried to withhold his signature from the treaty providing for the arming of the Federal Republic until the constitutional court had advised him that it did not conflict with the Basic Law, but finally signed the treaty on Chancellor Adenauer's advice.

To summarize what has been said about the formal role of various governmental institutions in making of foreign policy: foreign affairs are a federal matter and, within the federal government, the principal decision maker is the chancellor, while lesser roles are assigned to the ministers, president, legislature, and constitutional court of the Republic. How this formal arrangement actually functions depends primarily on the prevailing relationship between a chancellor and the lower house of the legislature. A strong chancellor who commands a comfortable majority in the lower house will have a great deal of freedom in the conduct of foreign affairs; a chancellor who lacks such support is likely to be far more dependent on either the cooperation of the legislature or that of the president or both.

Experience during the first seven years of the Republic's existence indicates that the chancellor's position vis-à-vis both cabinet and legislature rests largely on his relationship to his party and on that party's

---

[5] Discussed above, p. 51.

strength and cohesion. A future chancellor might not necessarily be a party man at all—not even a member of the legislature—nonetheless, his power of making decisions would still depend primarily on his ability to gain the support of the majority party or coalition of parties in the legislature. The formal organization of the foreign policy-making process thus assumes a functioning party system; it provides the chancellor only with limited means of governing temporarily without parliamentary support, should the parties fail to produce a stable majority behind him.

CHAPTER 5

Key groups for decisions:
Political parties and their leaders

The formal arrangements for making and executing foreign policy decision in the Federal Republic—as in other states—provide only a partial and somewhat superficial picture of the way the system actually functions. Much of foreign policy is determined by various elites, while the general public is only indirectly involved. Such elites are, generally speaking, those groups in the population who are better informed about policy matters and who have a greater influence upon policy decisions than the rest of their countrymen. They constitute, in the words of Gabriel Almond, "the articulate policy-bearing stratum of the population which gives structure to the public, and which provides the effective means of access" to the various interests and groupings which make up the general public. Decisions and actions affecting the Republic's relations with other nations thus result largely from interaction between German and foreign elite groups, from interaction between members of various elite groups within the Federal Republic, and from interaction between these German elite groups and their "constituents" among the general public, in whose name the elite members claim an influence in the making of foreign policy.

Using Almond's fourfold classification of foreign policy elites in the United States,[1] we may divide the German elites into political elites, administrative or bureaucratic elites, interest group elites, and communication elites. (See Tables 9.1–9.7, pp. 133–40.) The role which elite members may play in the foreign policy-making process is determined principally by (1) their formal membership in important governmental and nongovernmental agencies and organizations and (2) a network of informal personal relationships among elite members. Bonds of the latter kind, such as political, economic, social, and religious ties, tend to be at least as significant in the political process as formal links within and between governmental and nongovernmental institutions. Similarities or differences in age, background, and experience can be as important as formal institutional affiliations in determining common or divergent views toward specific foreign policy issues among members of the elite. Thus, in Germany today, informal cliques and camaraderies, based on common ex-

[1] Gabriel A. Almond, *The American People and Foreign Policy*, pp. 139–43.

periences under the Third Reich and in World War II, play a significant role. Contacts and friendships were made in industry or local government, in the army or in the resistance movement, in government offices or in prison, in the universities, in the officially controlled press and film organizations, in student groups, in concentration camps, in exile or as prisoners of war—and all these human ties continue to have political effects in regard to elite membership and sometimes even to elite behavior.

It would be highly desirable, therefore, to be able to analyze elite groups in terms of income, social origin, and social status. No published data of this kind, however, were readily available for the German foreign policy elites, except for aristocratic titles and the more indirect evidence of university degrees. Standard reference works permitted, however, the tabulation of certain other data of potential significance for elite behavior in regard to foreign policy. Information about previous occupation and educational level attained indicates at least something about the skills of individuals, as well as about their past and present social status, and about the homogeneity of elite groups in these respects. Moreover, changes in occupation from the Weimar Republic to the Nazi period, and again after the fall of the Hitler regime, may be quite suggestive of a man's political past.

The decade of birth tells us something about generations of elite members with different past experiences and memories, about their representation in different groups, and about the possibility of informal links across elites among members of the same generation. Records of military service in World War I or II, or in both, indicate an even more intense kind of potentially unifying experience, as well as possible common attitudes toward past and current questions of war and peace, allies and enemies, armament and disarmament.

Data about geographic origins identify potentially important groups: Central and East Germans who usually have a greater personal interest in the reincorporation of their Soviet-dominated native regions, either by force or negotiation; West Germans with greater potential concern for industrial interests; both South and West Germans with closer links to Western and Southern Europe; and North Germans with potential interests in overseas trade and shipping. Finally, the significance of data on professed religion, or political affiliation before and after the Nazi era, and on any major anti-Nazi record (i.e., as to imprisonment or exile) appears obvious.

In the sections that follow, the kinds of available data just discussed will be used as aids in characterizing particular elites. They should indicate the extent of homogeneity or difference among them, and perhaps their potential interest in specific policies and their possible response to particular appeals.

The Political Elite

For the purpose of this analysis of foreign policy making in the Federal Republic, the German political elite may be divided into two major groups. First, there is the constitutional formal political leadership, consisting of (1) the chief policy makers in the executive branch of the federal government—the chancellor and his ministers—and (2) the leadership of the second chamber of the federal parliament—its leading officers, the chairmen of committees directly or indirectly concerned with foreign policy, and the leaders of major party groups. Second, there is the nongovernmental para-constitutional component of the political elite, consisting of the leaderships of the major political parties. Because of their dominant position in the present political system, the role of the latter in the making of foreign policy will be considered first.[2]

The Role of the Political Parties and Their Leaders

The Basic Law of the Federal Republic is unique in its specific recognition of the decisive role of political parties in the formulation of national policy. Through their representatives in the executive and legislative branches of the national government the parties are expected to act as the responsible agents of the electorate in the conduct of government. The existing electoral law compels all aspirants for seats in the popularly elected lower house to belong to a party and thus to identify themselves with and bear responsibility for its policies and actions. Referenda, plebiscites, and other devices for "direct democracy," bypassing parties and legislature, have been deliberately omitted from the constitution; its framers were all too aware of the antidemocratic uses to which such devices had been put in the past by demagogues who appealed to the "popular will" against the "selfish" interests of parties.

Anyone may organize a political party in the Republic, as long as its objectives and organization accord with the democratic principles of the constitution and do not aim at the overthrow of the present state. In fact, however, the electoral laws have made it almost impossible for any party receiving less than 5 per cent of the electoral votes to gain representation in the national legislature.

The constitution permits the suppression of parties, regardless of size, if the constitutional court, acting upon petition by the federal government, declares them to be unconstitutional, i.e., hostile to "the free democratic basic order" (Art. 18 of the constitution). Two minor parties have been suppressed in this fashion, the neo-Nazi Socialist Reich party (SRP) in

---

[2] For an outstanding treatment of German political parties, see Sigmund Neumann, "Germany: Changing Patterns and Lasting Problems," in S. Neumann, ed., *Modern Political Parties*, pp. 354–92.

1953 and the Communist party in 1956. The suppression of both was accepted by the public without major repercussions.[3]

Contrary to the apparent expectations of the framers of the constitution, recent years have seen the gradual elimination of the traditional German multiparty system and the emergence of two major parties as the principal representatives of the electorate. These are the Christian Democratic Union and the Social Democratic party. Between them, these parties received 60 per cent of the votes and 67 per cent of the seats in the election for the first Bundestag in 1949; 74 per cent of the votes and 83 per cent of the seats in the election of the second Bundestag in 1953; and 82 per cent of the votes and 88 per cent of the seats in the 1957 election of the third Bundestag.[4]

Among the political elites, the national leaderships of the two major parties are at the present time undoubtedly the most important groups. To a large extent, they owe their prominent role to the fact that they had a head start over most other elite groups in the process of social realignment which followed the collapse of the old order in 1945. They were able to consolidate their position in the immediate postwar period with the permission—often indeed the blessings—of the foreign occupying powers, and without having to contend with the rivalry of other elite groups. Political leaders relatively uncompromised by past Nazi associations were sought out and encouraged by the military governments to fill the vacuum left by the elimination of the former political elites. With the exception of the church hierarchies, practically all the elite groups of the Nazi period were at least temporarily barred from playing a role in public life; and

[3] Sentiment for these prohibitions increased with time. Of the two parties, the Communists were by far the more unpopular, particularly among women.

	1950 April	1952 Jan.	1952 Nov.	1954 June
For banning:				
SRP (neo-Nazis)				
Total	—	23	37	—
Women only	—	19	31	—
Communists				
Total	46	43	—	55
Women only	50	48	—	62
Against banning:				
SRP				
Total	—	32	22	—
Women only	—	22	14	—
Communists				
Total	34	35	—	30
Women only	23	25	—	18

From polls in *Jahrbuch I*, pp. 272–74.

[4] These electoral results confirmed the trends disclosed by polls. A series of 45 polls from early 1950 to September 1957 showed that the share of the two major parties rose from 58 per cent to 82 per cent of those who indicated any party preference, but that on the average more than a third of those polled gave no such preference. *Jahrbuch II*, Chart, pp. 252–53, and *Jahrbuch II*, Chart, pp. 262–63.

by the time some of them began to reassert themselves, the party leaders had firmly established their dominant role.

The Christian Democratic Union

The Christian Democratic Union (Christlich-Demokratische Union), CDU—operating in Bavaria as the Christian Social Union (Christlich-Soziale Union), CSU—represents a departure from the traditional German parties. Instead of following the traditional pattern of parties in Germany and becoming closely identified with some particular ideology, religious group, or economic interest, the CDU/CSU has managed to attract the support of rather heterogeneous elements among the voters in the name of its "Christian principles." Moderately conservative in its domestic economic and social program, the CDU has professed a wide range of foreign policy aims. Prominent among these have been the reunification of Germany "in peace and freedom," the peaceful recovery of the German lands presently "administered" by Poland and the Soviet Union, permanent and intimate collaboration with the Western powers, and the economic, military, and—ultimately—political integration of the states of Western Europe.

The CDU was founded after the war by prominent lay leaders of the Roman Catholic and Protestant churches, along with conservative businessmen and trade union officials, with the intent of establishing something entirely new in German politics—an interconfessional "Christian" party identified with no single class or social stratum. In election after election, the CDU has received the votes of a broad cross-section of the German population. The party has consistently drawn above-average support from regular churchgoers; from civil servants, farmers, and members of the professions; from Roman Catholics; from those over sixty years old; from rural laborers; and from women. Independent artisans and businessmen who had shown only average support in a 1952 poll strongly endorsed the CDU by fall 1956. This increasing support on the part of businessmen may have added significance quite out of proportion to their voting strength in terms of greater tangible financial aid for the CDU from this group. Such aid may have been significant in successful CDU efforts to attract at election time in 1957 a majority of the 40 per cent of adult Germans who claimed to be ambivalent or indifferent about the party between national elections.

The most prominent symbol of the CDU in the minds of its supporters is "Christian attitude." In practice, its general spirit and policies are middle-class and conservative. Substantial majorities of its adherents describe themselves as "right of center" in politics (59 per cent; only 3 per cent said "left of center") and endorse candidates who are "thoroughly *bürgerlich*" (71 per cent)—a word connoting at one and the same time "bourgeois," "civic," and "civilian." A large minority (42 per cent) of the CDU supporters endorse the symbol "conservative," but one-half are uninformed (30 per cent) or undecided about this highbrow word. Nearly one-half of CDU adherents (49 per cent) said that they "would not like to live in a country without rich or poor, where all would have equally much, as nearly as possible"; but another 42 per cent said that they would like just such equality.[5]

The ideology of the CDU is thus specific enough to be identifiable, but broad enough to be inclusive. It has been a party not only of integration but of action. It has been able to get things done. In this respect it has been more similar to the major political parties in the United States. Like these, it has united diverse groups for the realization of specific policies and for the mutual advancement of specific interests, rather than for the pleasures of ideological and emotional self-expression. The CDU represents the day-to-day interests and compromises of its members rather than their hopes and dreams. The latter might be too diverse in a single party, and some of them might be less careful, sober, and moderate than CDU policies have been in practice. Some day, if daily realities should seem more disappointing, dreams and ideologies might again seem more attractive, particularly to the young. Throughout most of the 1950's, however, the practical successes of the CDU have served to consolidate the loyalties of its members and to make the party popular in its own right.

The CDU has substantial strength, independent of its leader. Chancellor Adenauer was shown by polls to be running behind his party in popularity in 1950 and 1951, ahead of his party—by a large but gradually diminishing margin—between 1953 and spring 1957, and again behind his party from April 1957 to the time of the September 1957 election. (See Table 5.1.)

TABLE 5.1*

TRENDS IN POPULARITY: ADENAUER VS. CDU

	1950	1951	1952	1953	1954	1955	1956	1957	Jan.–Apr. 1957	May–Sept. 1957
Per cent approving foreign policy:										
Of Adenauer	—	46	53	32	—	—	—	—	—	—
Of CDU or German govt.	—	—	—	—	32	35	22	—	—	—
Per cent approving:										
CDU	31	26	32	40	42	43	41	44	42	46
Adenauer	27	24	34	49	50	52	44	44	44	44

* Averaged from poll data in *Jahrbuch I* and *II* as follows: Row 1: *Jahrbuch I*, pp. 170, 181, 259, 260; *Jahrbuch II*, p. 170; Rows 2–3: *Jahrbuch I*, pp. 172–73, 252–53, 258; Rows 3–4: *Jahrbuch II*, Charts pp. 182–83, 262–63.

[5] Polls of March 1955, February, March, July, and August, 1956, *Jahrbuch II*, pp. 48, 118–24, 265.

This table suggests some intriguing speculations. In 1950–52, winning concessions from the West was highly popular; the CDU was far less so, and Adenauer still less. As Germany became accepted as a Western ally, Adenauer may have transferred his popularity from the foreign policy successes of 1951–52 to his domestic leadership in 1953–55, and perhaps consolidated it with the further successes in foreign policy in the latter years. Since the fall of 1955, however, there were no conspicuous new foreign policy successes comparable to the earlier ones. Adenauer's popularity declined moderately, but that of the CDU continued to rise, overtaking Adenauer's own by the second half of 1957. Already by July 1956 a plurality of respondents (45 per cent), including a majority of men (57 per cent), expressed their belief that Adenauer was "no longer in firm control" of his government and party; only 30 per cent thought that he still was.[6] Increasingly the CDU thus has had to rely on its own popularity; and its popularity as a party has come from domestic as much as, or more than, from foreign affairs.

The attempt to form a multi-interest "party of integration" thus has proved, on the whole, remarkably successful. Most of the traditional elite groups—the hierarchies of the churches, business leaders, higher civil servants, farm leaders, and the military men—directly or indirectly seek to exercise influence upon public policy through the CDU. The composition of its national executive (Bundesvorstand) reflects both the heterogeneity of the party's supporters and its strong local roots, particularly in Southern and Western Germany. Formal power in the executive is carefully divided between leaders of regional organizations (*Landesverbände*) and the party's leading representatives in the national government and legislature, between Protestants and Catholics, between conservative businessmen and trade unionists.

Within the CDU, the focus of actual decision-making power on foreign policy issues has shifted in recent years more and more away from the large and rather unwieldy national executive into the hands of the party's ministerial and parliamentary leaders at the capital. In part, this development has been the result of the party's control of the national government and the powerful influence of its chairman, Chancellor Konrad Adenauer. However, it is also due to the growing influence on the federal level of nation-wide organizations affiliated with the CDU, but not under the control of its local leaders, and the increasing dependence of a party with a relatively small dues-paying membership upon financial support from national business organizations.[7]

As a result, an increasing number of the party's leaders and deputies, directly or indirectly, have come to identify themselves with national rather

6 *Jahrbuch II*, p. 185.
7 Cf. A. J. Heidenheimer, "Germany Party Finance: The CDU," pp. 369–85.

than regional interests—particularly on foreign policy issues. While formerly state and regional politics tended to dominate Christian Democratic activities at the federal level, in more recent years political considerations of the party's leaders in the federal government, based on national issues, have frequently determined CDU strategy in the various states. Thus, Adenauer's desire to control a two-thirds majority of the votes in the upper chamber of the legislature—composed of representatives of the state governments—induced CDU leaders in various states to form coalition governments with otherwise uncongenial partners. On the other hand, the intervention of the leaders in Bonn on some occasions also caused the dissolution of such coalitions.

In recent years, an inner party elite thus seems to have determined Christian Democratic policies on foreign affairs. This group was led by Chancellor Adenauer, the party chairman, and included the four vice-chairmen of the CDU, its cabinet ministers, and its parliamentary leaders.[8] In December 1956 this group numbered 23 men, many of whom simultaneously occupied prominent government and party positions. It was a far more homogeneous group than the formal supreme decision-making organ of the party, the executive. Most of its members hailed either from Western or Southern Germany (87 per cent) and professed the Roman Catholic faith (65 per cent). A majority had grown up in prewar Imperial Germany (52 per cent). It was a well-educated group: more than two-thirds of its members had gone to university and almost half of these had received the doctorate. Roughly 61 per cent had seen military service— 39 per cent in the First World War and 22 per cent in the Second—but none had served in both wars. A large minority (39 per cent) had, before the establishment of the Nazi dictatorship, been prominent members of the Catholic Center party or its offshoot, the Bavarian People's party. While none had gone into exile during the Nazi era, 35 per cent had been imprisoned for anti-Nazi activities, 39 per cent had an anti-Nazi record, and only 4 per cent had served the Hitler government in any official capacity.[9]

The composition of this elite resembled in many ways the composition of the CDU delegation of 250 members who sat in the Bundestag from 1953 to 1957. A comparison of the CDU top elite and the Bundestag

---

[8] The parliamentary leaders in this group consisted of the chairman of the CDU delegation in the Bundestag and his two deputies; the chairman of the CSU delegation (who happened also to be a cabinet minister) and his deputy; and the chairmen of five major Bundestag committees concerned with foreign affairs (one of these latter men was also a vice-president of the Bundestag). For a complete list of the group, see Appendix III.

[9] Another analysis of the CDU inner elite, based on its composition about five months earlier, August 1956, revealed only minor deviations from the December group, except that at the earlier date a still higher proportion, 74 per cent, had listed themselves as Roman Catholic. For details, see Tables 9.1–9.7, Group B, Political elites.

delegation is given in Table 5.2. The two groups are closely similar in regard to religious composition, average age, and social origins, but the

TABLE 5.2

A COMPARISON OF PARTY LEADERSHIP GROUPS, 1956

(*Data in percentages*)

Characteristic and classification	CDU Party Elite 1956	CDU B'tag Deleg. '53–57	SPD Party Elite 1956	SPD B'tag Deleg. '53–57	Bundestag[a] Leg. Elite 1956	Bundestag[a] Total Deputies '53–57
Total number analyzed..................	23	250	29	162	44	507
Age structure:[b]						
–1890	17	14	3	11	14	13
1891–1900	35	35	28	28	39	33
1901–1910	26	33	52	36	34	34
1911–1920	22	15	17	20	11	17
1921–1930	0	3	0	5	2	3
1931–1940	0	0	0	0	0	0
1941–	0	0	0	0	0	0
NI	0	0	0	0	0	0
Total	100	100	100	100	100	100
Religion:						
Protestants	35	38	35	32	43	43
Roman Catholics	65	62	0	14	34	37
Others and none...................	0	0	9	34	5	12
NA and NI........................	0	0	55	20	18	8
Total	100	100	100	100	100	100
Education:[c]						
Primary	17	30	28	56	11	34
Secondary	9	14	31	16	18	22
University	70	52	35	28	66	42
NA and NI........................	4	3	7	0	5	2
Total	100	100	100	100	100	100
Anti-Nazi record (political persecution):						
Arrest, prison	35	13	26	32	14	18
Exile	0	0	33	16	5	5
NI or NA.........................	65	87	41	52	82	77
Total	100	100	100	100	100	100
Early training, or social origin:[d]						
Aristocracy	4	n.a.	3	n.a.	0	n.a.
Middle class	74	78	28	55	68	74
Labor	22	21	48	44	30	25
NI (or none)......................	0	1	21	1	2	1
Total	100	100	100	100	100	100

[a] All computations for Bundestag delegations taken from Martin Virchow, with the collaboration of Rudolf Holzgräber, "Die Zusammensetzung der Bundestagsfraktionen," in Wolfgang Hirsch-Weber and Klaus Schuetz, *Wähler und Gewählte*, pp. 353–92.

[b] Age structure for Bundestag delegations was computed from ages given in ten-year periods, e.g., 50–59 as of December 31, 1953. Even distribution was assumed over the decade so represented, and to make the figures comparable with the figures in this table, the numbers were prorated as in the following example: 30 per cent of those who were 50 to 59 years old as of December 31, 1953, plus 70 per cent of those 40 to 49 equals the number of delegates born between 1901 and 1910.

[c] No information concerning doctorates was discovered for the delegates. Otherwise, figures are comparable with elites.

[d] For Bundestag delegates, information concerns "Early training." There is therefore no data applicable for "Aristocracy."

Bundestag delegation was less well educated—30 per cent had not gone beyond primary education. Far fewer of them had a clear-cut anti-Nazi record: only 13 per cent of the deputies had been arrested or imprisoned by the Nazis as against 35 per cent of the top elite, and none of the CDU deputies nor of the CDU leaders reported having been in exile. Since it seems plausible that the top elite of the party will be replenished in time from the middle-level leaders who were still in the Bundestag in the mid-1950's, the percentage of top CDU leaders with clear-cut anti-Nazi records seems likely to decline.[10]

In his dual role of party chairman and federal chancellor, Konrad Adenauer dominated this CDU elite since the inception of the Republic in 1949. Notwithstanding some occasional mutterings against his personalized leadership of the party, mainly from the ranks of local leaders and from members of the CDU youth organization (Junge Union), Adenauer's astute intraparty political activities, his unrivaled prestige, and his political power assured him the loyal support of the Christian Democratic elite for his foreign policy decisions as chancellor. Despite the heterogeneous character of the party and its supporters, the CDU has usually supported Adenauer's policy of close military and political collaboration with the Western powers, his efforts to overcome age-old Franco-German differences, his leadership in the integration of Western and Southern Europe, and his reluctance to yield to Soviet overtures for closer collaboration between Russia and Germany.

On at least one important issue, however—the Bundestag vote on the reparations agreement with Israel—the Chancellor was deserted by a sizable portion of his party. On two other issues—his proposals for 18 months' conscript service and for the goal of a 500,000-man army by 1960—CDU support notably faltered.[11]

Despite his power, the Chancellor has known when to be flexible. Popular criticism of some of his moves, translated into pressure from the CDU and other elite groups, occasionally caused him to modify his position—as in reducing or slowing down certain aspects of the armament program sought by the United States, and in the establishment of diplomatic relations with the Soviet Union.

Like most democratic statesmen, Chancellor Adenauer was more concerned with maintaining his power than with insisting on every detail of his policies. Where necessary, he modified his policies to maintain power by preserving the necessary minimum of popularity and elite support in his party. The main policies that emerged from this process were those acceptable to the CDU elite, and they seemed likely to survive him.

[10] Data from Martin Virchow, "Die Christlich-Demokratische Fraktion," in Wolfgang Hirsch-Weber and Klaus Schütz, *Wähler und Gewählte*, pp. 356–65.
[11] See below, pp. 201–2, 205; Table 16.1, cols. 7–8.

The Social Democratic Party

The Social Democratic party (Sozialdemokratische Partei Deutsch-lands), SPD, is more strongly rooted in the past than the CDU/CSU—in terms of both its objectives and its supporters. It is also far more a party of interest representation than interest integration.[12] Basically, it has remained what it had been for decades before Hitler outlawed it in 1933, the party of German workers, despite the efforts of some of its leaders to transform it into a broader party of integration. It draws most of its support from organized labor—though the trade unions are no longer formally affiliated with the party—and it is a nonconfessional rather than an interconfessional party like the CDU. Far more homogeneous in both membership and electorate than the CDU/CSU, the SPD reflects in its domestic program the desire of the workers for social and economic betterment through economic planning, "codetermination" in basic industries, and moderate nationalization of key enterprises.

In its foreign policy the SPD has strongly opposed the CDU/CSU. While definitely a pro-Western party, it has maintained that too close collaboration with the Western powers would prevent both reunification and the recovery of the eastern territories. It has advocated the permanent neutralization of a united Germany in the hope that such an arrangement would induce the Soviet Union to agree to reunification.

With by far the largest membership of all the German parties and the highest ratio of members to voters, the SPD derives most of its financial support from membership dues rather than, like the CDU, from the contributions from powerful economic interest group elites. Particularly in the early years after the war most of its some 600,000 members were themselves either members of the SPD before the Nazi period or the children of old party members.[13] However, recent poll data indicate that this is not the case for over four-fifths of its present supporters.[14] The old-time party members are closely tied to the leaders by a strong sense of solidarity, loyalty to the party and its traditions, and a common distrust toward "outsiders"—even within the party—who do not share this in-group identification. The strong roots linking postwar party members to the pre-Nazi party enabled the SPD leadership to reestablish quickly a tightly knit, loyal and efficient national organization throughout the territory of the present Federal Republic, staffed largely by long-time

---

[12] For a discussion of the distinction between the party of representation and the party of integration, cf. Sigmund Neumann, "Toward a Comparative Study of Political Parties," in his *Modern Political Parties*, pp. 404–5. On the SPD in particular see also pp. 378–80 in the same volume.

[13] Of the 162 SPD deputies elected to the Bundestag in 1953, over 70 per cent were members of the party before 1933 and had belonged to it for decades. See Virchow, "Die sozialdemokratische Fraktion" in Hirsch-Weber and Schütz, *Wähler und Gewählte*, p. 373.

[14] *Jahrbuch I*, p. 261; *Jahrbuch II*, p. 270. Polls of October 1952 and March 1955.

party functionaries. However, the preeminence of old party members in the organization and their distrust toward newcomers undoubtedly have handicapped the efforts of some of the top leaders to transform the SPD into a popular reform party by attracting the support of members of the middle-class and the independent professions.

Apart from many trade union leaders, few of the members of other elite groups support the SPD. Among the voters, the party has been singularly unsuccessful in gaining the support of farmers, professional men, civil servants, white-collar employees, women, businessmen, and unorganized workers, while it has been consistently supported by a majority of organized industrial workers.[15] In the public mind the SPD has been identified as a "left wing" party; however, as indicated by a poll in February 1956, twice as many West Germans think of themselves as "right" rather than "left" in their political preference. In July 1956 only 36 per cent of those asked in a poll whether they thought of the SPD as a middle-class party believed that it was one, while 35 per cent did not. By contrast 58 per cent considered the CDU a middle-class party and only 16 per cent did not. The SPD appealed to 61 per cent of those indicating a preference for it because it "represented the interest of the workers"; far fewer liked it because of its "courageous opposition" (9 per cent), its "rejection of rearmament" (7 per cent), or its "representation of the national interests" (6 per cent).[16]

Though a workers' party, the SPD is not seen as a revolutionary party. Indeed, a near-majority of its own supporters in a poll in July 1956 considered it middle-class or bourgeois—"bürgerlich"—in character.[17] As its appeal to class interest softened, the SPD's efforts to appeal to national sentiment increased. In polls from 1952 to 1956 twice as many Germans chose consistently the SPD, rather than the CDU, as the prime champion of national reunification, but a plurality saw no difference between the two parties on this score; and all this did not broaden substantially the SPD's popularity at election time. In the national elections of 1949, 1953, and 1957, the share of the SPD remained nearly constant at about 30 per cent of the votes cast, even though its popularity had been usually somewhat higher—often around 35 to 40 per cent—in off-year polls.[18]

The focus of decision-making power in the Social Democratic party, perhaps even more than in the past, is the party executive committee (Parteivorstand), whose authority rests solidly on the loyal support of the disciplined party membership. Regional and local leaders have less

---

[15] *Jahrbuch I*, p. 264; *Jahrbuch II*, p. 264.
[16] *Jahrbuch II*, pp. 47–48, 267–68.
[17] *Ibid.*, p. 267.
[18] *Jahrbuch I*, pp. 252–53; *Jahrbuch II*, pp. 262–63.

—far less—influence over the decisions of the national leadership than in the CDU. SPD deputies in the federal legislature have consistently voted according to the instructions of the executive committee; as a group they have held a record of disciplined solidarity unrivaled by the deputies of any other party. Differences between parliamentary delegation and executive committee have never become manifest; the latter group can always impose its will on the deputies, not only because many of them are employed by the party, but also because the most prominent members of the parliamentary leadership of the SPD are members of the executive committee of the party as well. In 1956, eleven of the twenty members of the parliamentary leadership (Fraktionsvorstand)— whose decisions are binding on the entire parliamentary delegation— were also members of the executive committee. They formed thus a majority of the parliamentary leaders, but only a minority of the executive committee of the party.

The Social Democratic executive committee is a highly homogeneous group dominated by no one personality or group—in contrast to the inner elite of the CDU. A strong sense of identification with the party and its traditions, common persecution by the Nazi regime, and—in many cases—long service within the party organization unite its members and have created an intense in-group sentiment among them. Particularly since the death in 1952 of Kurt Schumacher, the dynamic postwar chairman of the party, collegial leadership has been the rule. While one or another of the leaders may occasionally sway the vote of his associates on certain issues, once a decision has been reached in secret conference, all the members will support it with at least an outward show of unanimity.

The SPD executive committee elected in August 1956 consisted of thirty members. Fifteen of these were also federal deputies—including the chairman and vice-chairman—and three others were salaried employees of the party in charge of its headquarters. An analysis of the background of twenty-nine members for whom adequate biographical data were available may help to explain their attitudes and decisions on foreign policy issues—particularly when compared with that of the CDU elite. The SPD leaders formed a relatively homogeneous group: 72 per cent had been active in the party before 1933, 20 per cent in leading positions; 70 per cent had anti-Nazi records, at least 33 per cent had been in exile, and 24 per cent had been in prison or concentration camps during the Nazi regime. A majority of the former exiles had worked together against Hitler abroad. In strong contrast to the inner elite of the CDU, none of the members of the SPD elite professed the Roman Catholic faith; 35 per cent declared themselves Protestants, while the rest acknowledged no religious affiliations. Forty-one per cent hailed from German lands now under Communist control; another 14 per cent came from Northern Germany, and only 38 per cent from Southern and Western Germany. The Social Democratic elite was on the whole a younger and formally less educated group than that of the CDU: only 31 per cent had spent their youth in Imperial Germany, while 69 per cent grew up either during or immediately after the First World War; 59 per cent indicated no university studies and only 14 per cent held doctoral degrees. Ten per cent had seen service in the First World War, 14 per cent in the Second, and 3 per cent in both wars; better than 72 per cent gave no indication of any military service. No record was found of any member of the Social Democratic executive committee having served the Nazi regime in any official capacity.

The top elite of the SPD can again be compared with the 162 deputies of the party in the 1953–57 Bundestag who may be considered as part of the middle-level leadership of the Social Democratic movement. The parliamentary delegation was somewhat older than the top elite; it was less well educated; a majority—56 per cent—had not gone beyond primary school as against only 28 per cent whose formal education had stopped at the level among the top leaders. A majority of the Social Democratic deputies—55 per cent—admitted middle-class origins; among the top leaders only 28 per cent admitted as much, but 21 per cent gave no data. Strikingly, however, the record of arrest or imprisonment of the Social Democratic parliamentarians was even stronger than that of the top leaders; 32 per cent of the Bundestag delegation, as against 26 per cent of the top leaders, had been arrested or imprisoned during Hitler's rule. The percentage of the deputies who had been exiles under the Nazi regime, however, was less than half of what it was among the top leaders, 16 per cent as against 33 per cent. If most of the Social Democratic deputies should move up to replenish the top-level leadership, it would seem unlikely that the strong anti-Nazi record of the party would be diminished.[19]

Among all the major foreign policy elites in the Federal Republic, the SPD leadership has alone consistently opposed the course of Adenauer's government and party. Primarily, this opposition has been based on differences with the ruling group over ways and means to bring about the reunification of Germany and the recovery of German territory presently "administered" by Poland and the Soviet Union. A large proportion of the Social Democratic elite have strong personal ties to these regions and feel themselves in a sense as aliens in the present Federal Republic. Moreover, of the two large parties the SPD has suffered the greater political disadvantages from the division of Germany. The chief support for the party before Hitler had come from the urban areas of Central and Eastern Germany; and, before the SPD was outlawed in

---

[19] See data in Table 5.2, based on Martin Virchow, "Die sozialdemokratische Fraktion," in Hirsch-Weber and Schütz, *Wähler und Gewählte*, pp. 366–77.

the Soviet zone in 1946, there were strong indications that its postwar strength would also come primarily from these areas. The SPD elite feels that it has a far greater political stake in their recovery than does CDU, which draws its principal support from the Catholic regions of Southern and Western Germany. However, the failure of the Western powers and the Soviet Union to reach an agreement on the reunification question—not to speak of the recovery of the lands east of the Oder-Neisse line—has made it increasingly difficult for the Social Democratic elite to develop a realistic alternative to the CDU's position on reunification and general foreign policy. While it has declared itself willing to buy Soviet agreement to reunification through a "neutralization" of Germany and the severance of military ties with the West, the SPD elite has been as insistent as the leaders of the CDU and the Western powers in demanding free elections in the Communist areas prior to reunification, which the Soviet Union has consistently refused.

Soviet policy has made it increasingly difficult for the SPD elite to appeal to the voters with a program based on hypothetical assumptions concerning Soviet good intentions and on persistent antagonism to membership in NATO as an obstacle to reunification. In order to achieve a more positive position and to gain some influence over foreign policy making, the party leaders have been compelled to modify their earlier categorical opposition to the Adenauer course. As a result, their differences with the CDU policies have in fact diminished, protestations of both major party elites to the contrary. As a leading periodical in the Federal Republic observed at the outset of the 1957 parliamentary campaign: "Our foreign policy is more bipartisan than either of the two [major] parties will admit."[20] While some of the leading members of the CDU elite in recent years have granted that it might be desirable for German foreign policy to be less closely tied to that of the Western powers and more flexible toward the Soviet Union, the SPD leadership has at least implicity admitted by some of its actions that it is prepared to accept many of the political and economic features of Christian Democratic foreign policy. In fact, the chief differences in foreign affairs between the two groups has been reduced to the desirability of Germany's membership in NATO and the military commitments which this implies.

Within these limits, however, the indirect influence of the SPD on foreign policy has been far from negligible. By exercising pressure on the government, the party has contributed to modifications of unpopular measures. By placing controversial policies before the public, such as the question of diplomatic relations with the Soviet Union, the SPD sometimes paved the way for their later adoption by the government.

Even unwittingly, the SPD has served as a foil for the government.

[20] "Wo findet der Wahlkampf statt?" *Die Gegenwart*, March 1957, p. 1 f.

In the absence of a significant West German Communist movement, the party has supplied the Chancellor with the appearance of a neutralist electoral threat to which he could point in order to win greater concessions from the Western powers.[21]

The Minor Parties

None of the minor parties represented by the remaining 12 per cent of the deputies in the present Bundestag have played a very significant role in matters of foreign policy. The largest of them, the Free Democratic party (Freie Demokratische Partei), FDP, has vainly aspired to a balance of power position between the two major parties and has oscillated between opposing and supporting the CDU/CSU. Extremist parties have been conspicuous by their absence; the small neo-Nazi Socialist Reich party was banned in 1953 by the constitutional court; the insignificant Communist party had had no representation in the national legislature even before it was outlawed in 1956; other extremist parties have been singularly unsuccessful in gaining support among the electorate.

The leaders of the minor parties have had relatively little influence on foreign policy. However, many of their followers are middle-class persons of anticlerical or Protestant orientation, with relatively stronger ties to Northern and Eastern Germany, and a more acute interest in reunification. In economic matters, they have been likely to agree with the CDU, but in contrast to the predominantly Catholic and West German leadership of the CDU, these minor parties and splinter groups sometimes like to make common cause with the SPD in pressing for a somewhat greater willingness to explore Russian offers of negotiation.

[21] Samuel L. Wahrhaftig, "The Development of German Foreign Policy Institutions," in Speier and Davison, *West German Leadership and Foreign Policy*, p. 54.

CHAPTER 6

Official actors:˙ Formal
legislative and executive elites

The Formal Political Elite

The formal, constitutional political elite in the Federal Republic consists of the members of the cabinet and the legislative leaders of the lower house of parliament. Mostly prominent functionaries of their respective parties, the members of this formal political elite influence and are influenced in a process of constant interaction with fellow party leaders not belonging to it. In the case of the governing Christian Democratic Union the weight of decision-making power in foreign policy matters has tended to rest in the hands of the party leaders who are also members of the formal political elite: the chancellor, cabinet ministers, and parliamentary leaders of the party. On the other hand, in the case of the opposition, the Social Democratic party, and some of the smaller parties, members of the party leadership not belonging to the formal political elite have played an important, if not decisive, role in determining policy.

The dominant position of Chancellor Konrad Adenauer in the formal political elite of Germany has tended to obscure the potential role of other members of this elite in the making of foreign policy. In Adenauer's case the already great constitutional power of the chancellor has been strongly reinforced by his political power as absolute leader of the majority party in both the government and the legislature. A less powerful chancellor might find himself far more dependent upon other members of the formal political elite in his government and in parliament, particularly if he should not command the support of a majority party. Even Adenauer has on occasions been forced to modify his position on certain issues in the face of determined opposition from powerful ministers or parliamentary criticism. Particularly the role of the parliamentary elite has tended to become more important in recent years when leaders of government and opposition parties joined in criticizing actions of the executive branch.

The formal political elite in the executive branch of the government consists of the chancellor and his ministers who, as a group, make up the cabinet. Individually and collectively the cabinet members are supposed to give political guidance to the actions of the entire government under the direction of the chancellor.

In August 1956 the Adenauer coalition cabinet included twenty men, most of them prominent functionaries of the CDU/CSU, the others representing the minor parties in the coalition.[1] Because of the dominant position of the CDU/CSU leadership in the coalition government, the cabinet had many of the same collective characteristics as the inner elite of the governing party and the legislative leadership in the second chamber of the parliament.

However, this cabinet differed in marked degree from the average German cabinet in the past. It contained more avowed Roman Catholics, more members of the middle class, more highly educated men, and far more representatives of industrial Western Germany than the average cabinet between 1890 and 1945. (See Table 9.8, p. 141.) The average age of its members, fifty-eight years, was somewhat below that of the CDU/CSU elite, but above the average of former cabinets. Roughly 55 per cent had grown up in Imperial Germany, 35 per cent during or immediately after the First World War, and 10 per cent during the First (Weimar) Republic, before the establishment of the Nazi dictatorship. Thirty-five per cent of the cabinet members had been politically active before the Nazi era, 10 per cent in parties of the moderate right and 25 per cent in the Catholic Center party. Of all the political elites, the cabinet had the poorest anti-Nazi record. Twenty per cent of its members had belonged to the Nazi party or one of its major affiliates, such as the SS, while only 15 per cent had been imprisoned for anti-Nazi activities, and no cabinet member had been in exile during the Hitler regime.[2]

Individually and collectively, the members of the Adenauer cabinets have probably not exercised as much influence on foreign policy as potentially they might under another chancellor. In gathering information, conducting negotiations, seeking advice, and making decisions, Adenauer has tended to rely heavily upon an ill-defined and changing "Kitchen Cabinet" of personal advisers. Among them have been the permanent undersecretaries (*Staatsekretäre*) of the Chancellor's Office and the Foreign Office, the German ambassador to the headquarters of NATO, the

[1] One minister, a technical expert not officially affiliated with any party, was the only member of the cabinet not a member of the Bundestag. These data, and those for the rest of this chapter, unless otherwise indicated, correspond to those in Tables 9.1–9.7, Group A.

[2] A minor cabinet change in October 1956 reduced the number of members to seventeen, but did not alter the basic picture. The age groups changed slightly to 47, 35, and 18 per cent, respectively, for the older, middle, and younger political generations. The percentage of persons who had held high positions during the Nazi era was 18 per cent, but this was a somewhat broader category than the test of organizational Nazi membership applied to the mid-1956 group. On the other hand, the share of those arrested or imprisoned by the Nazis had risen to 24 per cent. The regional overrepresentation of Western Germany continued. Data on this group correspond to those in Tables 9.1–9.7, Groub B, Cabinet.

chief of the Press and Information Office, and a prominent banker. It has seldom been entirely plain which of Adenauer's personal advisers happened to be most influential at any one time, since the Chancellor has tended to rely at various times on different men. Nevertheless, even careful observers of the decision-making process in the federal government have found it difficult to tell at times which of the two groups, the official or the unofficial cabinet, exercised greater influence in the making of German foreign policy.

In foreign affairs, as in other matters, Adenauer's leadership has been highly personalized and independent from his formal foreign policy advisers. In his relationship to the president, to his ministers, and to his lieutenants in the legislature he has occupied an even more dominant position than is granted to the chancellor by the constitution. In the conduct of foreign affairs he has taken very literally the chancellor's right to determine policy. Even after he finally surrendered the formal role of foreign minister to Heinrich von Brentano, the new incumbent was permitted to devote himself only to secondary international problems. Adenauer himself continued to deal with all important issues, such as the question of German reunification, relations with the United States and the Soviet Union, and all other matters relating to the East-West conflict. For advice and assistance he has largely relied on his lieutenants, rather than on his formal foreign policy advisers, the foreign minister and his staff. When, early in 1957, Adenauer sought to discover American intentions toward the German question and to acquaint U.S. policy makers with his own views, he bypassed the foreign office and sent in quick succession his press chief, the head of the Chancellor's Office, and two parliamentary leaders of his party to Washington.

The legislative component of the formal political elite concerned with foreign policy issues includes the president of the lower house, the parliamentary leaders and deputy leaders of the major parties, and the chairmen of the eight committees that deal with foreign affairs. (See pp. 57–58.) In July 1954 this group consisted of twenty-one deputies, including eleven members of the majority party, the CDU/CSU, and five members of the SPD, the leading opposition party; the rest belonged to splinter groups.

This legislative elite was a somewhat younger group than the CDU and the cabinet elite: 48 per cent had grown up in Imperial Germany, 38 per cent during and immediately after the First World War, and 14 per cent during the Weimar Republic. As far as geographic origins were concerned, industrial Western Germany, with 43 per cent of the legislative elite but only 35 per cent of the population, was overrepresented, though less strongly than in either the CDU or the cabinet elite. Twenty-nine per cent of the legislative elite came from Eastern and Central Germany, regions presently under Communist control, and 29 per cent from

Southern Germany—compared with 26 and 24 per cent respectively of the population; 10 per cent had been born abroad, but not one member of the legislative elite came from Northern Germany, though roughly 15 per cent of the population lived there.

As in the case of the CDU and the cabinet elite, a large proportion of the legislative elite, 43 per cent, declared itself Roman Catholic, with only 19 per cent professing the Protestant religion; 38 per cent did not list any religious affiliation. It was a comparatively well educated group; 62 per cent had attended a university, including 33 per cent who held doctoral degrees; however 19 per cent had only a primary and 14 per cent a secondary education. (There were no data for the remaining 5 per cent.) The legislative elite included comparatively few veterans in comparison with the cabinet and CDU elite: 5 per cent had seen service in the First World War, 38 per cent in the Second, another 5 per cent had been in both wars, while 52 per cent indicated no military service at all. Its anti-Nazi record was poorer than that of either of the two major party elites: roughly 14 per cent had been imprisoned by the Nazis and another 14 per cent had gone into exile, while over 71 per cent showed no anti-Nazi record. A majority were relative newcomers to politics: only 38 per cent had been in politics before the Nazi period, either in the Catholic Center or the Social Demorcatic party.

A broader group of 44 legislative leaders, in 1956, including the chairmen of all parliamentary committees, showed similar characteristics. The members of this general legislative elite were somewhat older, with more veterans from World War I, and more of them came from Western Germany. This group had practically the same share of persons arrested by the Nazis, but only one-third of the proportion of former exiles as had the legislative foreign policy elite of 1954.[3]

The potential influence of legislative leaders was considerable. As in other European parliaments which are elected entirely or at least partly by means of a system of proportional representation in which the elector votes for a party rather than for an individual, the lower chamber of the German legislature is generally dominated by the party leaders. Among the deputies, those of the Social Democratic party have followed the instructions of their leaders most persistently, while those of the CDU/CSU showed least inclination to observe directions from their leadership. However, on most foreign policy votes the deputies of all parties tend to toe the line once their leaders have settled the issue in caucus meetings of the respective party groups. Votes on the floor of the chamber are thus usually predetermined, but interparty deliberations in the committees, which precede party caucuses, provide somewhat greater opportunity for prominent deputies to exercise an influence over foreign policy, inde-

---

[3] For details, see Tables 9.1–9.7, Group B, Legislature.

pendent of the party elites. While committee members consider themselves representative of their various parties and usually coordinate their actions with the party leaders, occasionally committee chairmen have managed to induce the cabinet or the party elites to amend their previous position in accordance with the wishes of, a committee. Particularly in the CDU/CSU—almost never in the SPD—prominent party leaders acting in their capacity as spokesmen for parliamentary committees have at various times in recent years compelled their party chairman and chancellor to agree to changes in government bills.

In the long run the potential influence of this parliamentary elite, like that of the cabinet, may be far greater in the field of foreign policy than has been apparent during the Adenauer regime. The extent of such influence depends primarily on three factors: (1) the power of the chancellor in the chamber, (2) the influence of nonparliamentary party leaders over the deputies, and (3) the relationship between the parliamentary leaders of the different parties. A strong chancellor has little to fear from the legislature and its leaders, especially if—like Adenauer —he controls the majority party. Strict control of the parliamentary delegations of the various parties by their respective party elites also leaves the parliamentary leadership little or no freedom of action; the deputies of the Social Democratic party, for instance, are in effect simply party functionaries subject to the orders of a nonparliamentary body, the executive committee. It has been demonstrated, however, that cooperation between the legislative leaders of the various parties—in opposition to, or by sufferance of, their party elites—might considerably strengthen the potential role of the parliamentary elite in foreign affairs. Constructive criticism on the part of Social Democratic legislative leaders has on occasion met with a sympathetic response from the legislative leaders of the Christian Democratic Union and the smaller parties, with the result that the federal executive was compelled to yield to the combined pressure of the members of the parliamentary elite.

Such instances, however, have been relatively rare. Under present conditions, the legislative elite as such is unlikely to gain sufficient independence from the party elites to play a more active role in the making of foreign policy vis-à-vis the political and executive elites than heretofore. The nature of the German party system and the constitutional limitations imposed upon the legislature combine to deny its leaders the important role which the legislative elite enjoys in the making of foreign policy in the United States.

The Administrative Elite

In general, the administrative or bureaucratic elite of the German Federal Republic may be said to consist of those professional, "nonpolitical" employees of the executive branch who exercise special power and influence over the making of policy by virtue of their positions, their technical skills, and their experience. They are the top civilian and military administrators of the professional civil and armed services whose duties, formally or informally, involve the formulation of policies and their execution on behalf of the formal political elite in the government.

In Germany, this civilian and military administrative elite has traditionally enjoyed considerable power and prestige; the extent of its influence over policy making has varied more or less inversely with the power of the political elite. In the Empire, when practically all the positions in the executive branch were occupied by civilian or military members of the administrative elite, its influence was enormous—particularly between 1890 and 1918. After the resignation of the "Iron Chancellor," Otto von Bismarck, the unstable Emperor William II fell increasingly under the influence of his official and unofficial advisers in the administrative elite—the real, if politically irresponsible, rulers of Germany. The traditional administrative elite survived the fall of the Empire in 1918. It regained influence during the First Republic when weak political leadership, resulting from governmental instability and parliamentary anarchy, left many vital policy decisions in effect in the hands of the military civil "servants" of the state. Under the strong political leadership of Hitler the influence of the professional administrative elite was practically eliminated as a factor in policy making.

Traditionally, German administrators and professional military men have considered themselves the faithful servants, not of the public, but of the State—an abstraction which has always played a great role in German political theory. By tradition and training, they were imbued with the image of the civil and military services as the politically neutral guardians of the "national interest," the defenders of the State against the "selfish" interests of political factions and pressure groups. In fact, however, the administrative and military services sought at every possible opportunity to influence foreign policy along traditionalist and nationalist lines and to inhibit democratic and internationalist trends. The administrative elite in both the civil and military services jealously defended their claim to recruit and train members of the services, and they bitterly resisted the rather weak efforts of the democratic political leaders of the First Republic to reform the services. Hitler ruthlessly subjugated the civil and military services to his political leadership, but he left the old professional corps more or less intact. For their part, the civil and military administrative elites loyally served the Nazi state. Only a few prominent civil servants and military leaders joined the anti-Nazi opposition; most of the members of the administrative elite clung to the belief that it was their duty to obey the chief of the Nazi state to the bitter end.

The Senior Civil Service

After the war it appeared for a while as if the old German administrative elite had gone down with the Nazi state. The victorious occupying powers declared that foreign military governments would rule a
demilitarized Germany for a long time to come. Before long, however,
administrative problems and political developments paved the way for
the return of the old professionals. The division of Germany and the
establishment of a sovereign German state in the western half brought
with them the restoration of a professional administrative elite to provide expert advice and assistance to the relatively inexperienced political
elite. Time and men were lacking to create an entirely new civil and military elite, and the political leaders of the new state were compelled to
call back into service many of the professional administrators of the
Nazi state. With the establishment of the Federal Republic in 1949 there
began a great migration of former civil servants to the new capital at
Bonn. Former associates in the government service recruited each other,
and entire staffs of former ministries and military organizations were reunited in the offices of the executive branch of the federal government,
sharing common traditions and experiences which went back to the Nazi
era and beyond.

In the realm of foreign affairs, three groups among the administrative elite stand out for their potential influence on policy making: the
undersecretaries (*Staatssekretäre*) of those government ministries and
agencies particularly concerned with foreign policy matters, the leading
diplomats, and the military leaders. In general, all three groups consist
of former servants of the Nazi state.

The permanent undersecretaries in the German executive branch
occupy greater positions of responsibility and power than their counterparts in most other major Western nations. The formal political leaders
cannot bring into office with them political associates to serve as their
deputies—as in Britain and France—but must rely on these senior civil
servants for prosessional advice and for carrying out their orders at the
lower levels of administration. In contrast to the changing political
leadership of the state, these leading civil servants thus represent continuity in the administration of the affairs of state. The permanent undersecretary not only acts as a chief of staff, but may take the place of his
political superior in the latter's absence and represent him in parliament
and in sessions of the cabinet. The more inexperienced a minister is in
the affairs of his office, the more he tends to be dependent upon his permanent undersecretary, who stands between him and other officials in the
ministry. Similarly, the less confidence a chancellor may have in a minister, the more likely he is to circumvent him and to rely directly on the

permanent undersecretary. The potential influence of these top civil servants on policy making and execution is thus considerable.

In 1956, six of the eight undersecretaries of the executive agencies particularly concerned with foreign policy matters (Chancellor's Office, Foreign Office, and the Ministries of Finance, Interior [2], Defense, Expellees and Refugees, and All-German Affairs) had been members of the civil service in Nazi Germany; five had been in the national civil service already before Hitler. None had a major anti-Nazi record, and none claimed to have been politically active either before or during the Nazi era. A majority had grown up under the Empire, and none was born later than 1910. It was a highly educated group: all but one had attended university and four of the eight held doctoral degrees. Five of the eight came from industrial Western Germany and one from Northern Germany; two failed to indicate their geographic origins.[4]

For purposes of comparison, an analysis was made of a much larger group of sixty-seven high-level civil servants, consisting of all undersecretaries and division chiefs on whom data were available in all ministries. This group thus was not restricted to the field of foreign policy. It was slightly older, and more evenly recruited from all regions, except that South Germans were still underrepresented. A larger proportion—over three-fifths—held doctoral degrees, but far fewer—less than one-fourth—indicated any military service. The proportion of those with anti-Nazi records was very small—3 per cent—but higher than among either the foreign policy bureaucracy or the total population.[5]

The Diplomats

Before Hitler, the leading diplomats of the German Foreign Office had exercised considerable influence on the conduct of foreign affairs. Weak efforts to reform the foreign service after the Revolution of 1918 and to recruit persons more in sympathy with the new democratic order were quite unsuccessful. The career officials of the old Imperial foreign service retained firm control and frequently made German foreign policy, in the absence of firm political leadership and parliamentary control. The Hitler regime did not destroy the career service, but simply transformed it into a pliable tool of Nazi foreign policy.

Following the drastic decline of its influence during the Nazi regime, the diplomatic elite temporarily disappeared from the scene while foreign conquerors ruled Germany. With the recovery of sovereign powers by a German government came the reorganization of the old foreign office.

---

[4] Tabulations by the authors.

[5] For details, see Tables 9.1–9.7, Group B, Civil Service.

The old career official who took charge of the Auswärtiges Amt insisted that the services of the old professionals could not be dispensed with, even if many of them had been members of the Nazi party. In the beginning, many of the more sensitive diplomatic assignments in Western capitals went to nonprofessionals—often, it has been claimed, in payment of political debts, or to rid Chancellor Adenauer of opponents in the ruling coalition.[6] Gradually, however, these men were replaced by trained diplomats. Still, in 1954, 36 per cent of the forty-four leading diplomats for whom biographical data were available were noncareer officials; the rest had been members of the foreign service before 1945. While the nonprofessionals were usually assigned to conspicuous posts in major Western capitals, the old professionals were sent at first to smaller nations. There, however, they had greater opportunities to influence German policy toward their countries of assignment than their noncareer colleagues in Washington, London, and Paris. The latter were given far less independent responsibility. Chancellor Adenauer was said to supervise them closely, and he often bypassed them through the use of personal emissaries.[7]

Of the forty-four top administrators and chiefs of missions of the foreign office, 59 per cent had been in the diplomatic service under Hitler, and 52 per cent had served both the Nazi regime and the preceding democratic republic; only 2 per cent of the leading diplomats had been imprisoned, and 5 per cent exiled, because of their opposition to the Nazi regime. For most of the forty-four, the important formative period of their youth had coincided with the phenomenal ascent of the prewar German Empire to the position of a world power; 77 per cent had been born before 1901, and none later than 1908. Thirty-six per cent of the diplomatic elite of 1954 hailed from German lands presently under Communist rule, and only 27 per cent professed the Roman Catholic faith—in contrast to the 4 per cent and 74 per cent, respectively, in the case of the elite of the governing party, the Christian Democratic Union.[8]

This rather aged diplomatic elite will gradually be replaced by younger men, as trained new foreign service officers become available. Already by 1956, one-half of the leading German diplomats had been born in this century.[9] How the successors are recruited and trained will play an important role in determing the future character and influence of the professional career service. The old professional diplomats are naturally inclined to select men who give promise of conforming to their image

[6] Samuel L. Wahrhaftig, "The Development of German Foreign Policy Institutions," in Speier and Davison, West German Leadership and Foreign Policy, p. 33.

[7] Ibid.

[8] See Tables 9.1–9.7, Group A, Diplomats.

[9] For the 1954–56 shift in age composition and other details, see Tables 9.1–9.7, Group B, Diplomats.

of the service and its functions, and to train new recruits accordingly. The dominant political elite of the Adenauer government, for its part, has ostensibly been endeavoring "to train a new generation of diplomats who would be anti-militarists, democrats, and good Europeans," and thus loyal administrators of the present foreign policy. In contrast to the 59 per cent preponderance of former Nazi diplomats among the diplomatic elite of 1954, only 28 per cent of the entire foreign service were taken over from the Nazi government and only 34 per cent had been members of the Nazi party.[10]

Two years later, the share of diplomats with major anti-Nazi records of arrest or exile had risen from 7 per cent in 1954 to 12 per cent in 1956. More broadly defined anti-Nazi records appeared in the biographies of 21 per cent of the 1956 group. This was a proportion well in line with that for all elites, and far above that for the total population.[11]

The Military Men

Even more than the top diplomats, the military elite played an important role in the making of German foreign policy before Hitler. As in the case of the foreign service elite, this influence was greatly weakened during the Nazi era. With the collapse and occupation of Germany in 1945 it was entirely eliminated until the Federal Republic became a sovereign power after 1949 and began organizing a military establishment. At that time the political elite professed a strong desire to prevent the restoration of military influence. The leaders of the major parties joined in drafting laws and regulations governing the new military establishment and the selection of its leaders, which were intended to make certain that the new military elite would stay out of politics and follow loyally the directions of the political leaders of the state. However, strong pressure from American leaders and NATO officers for rapid German rearmament compelled the Adenauer government to entrust Hitler's soldiers with the task of organizing the new military establishment; they were the only competent professional men available.

A semiofficial list of fifty-four members of the new military elite, published in *Das Wehrarchiv*, in 1957, indicates that the military leadership consists of experienced career officers who, like the diplomats, differ considerably in their background from the governing political elite. Better than 83 per cent of these fifty-four officers had been born after 1900 and had largely grown up during the turbulent years during and following the First World War; most of them had received their training in the

---

[10] See "34% of Bonn's Diplomatic Corps Recruited from Ex-Nazi Ranks," *The New York Times*, March 25, 1954.

[11] See Tables 9.1–9.7, Group B, Diplomats.

small professional army of the First Republic and had later served as command and staff officers in the Nazi forces. The Junker element seemed weakened: less than 20 per cent bore aristocratic names.

Interestingly enough, almost 41 per cent of the new military elite had been born in Central and Eastern Germany—in contrast to 29 per cent of the Adenauer cabinet of late 1956 and 4 per cent of the leadership of the governing Christian Democratic party, the CDU. Over 83 per cent of the military leaders professed to be Protestants—compared to 41 per cent of the cabinet, 35 per cent of the CDU elite, and 43 per cent of the general legislative elite of 1956. Not one of the fifty-four officers listed claimed to have been politically active at any time in his life; two had been arrested by the Nazis, but none had been in exile during the Third Reich. As in the case of the top administrators and leading diplomats, this record of service under the Nazi regime contrasts sharply with the anti-Nazi record of the political elite, a large number of whose members had either been imprisoned or exiled in the Hitler era.[12]

The contrast between postwar military leaders and civilian elite appears mitigated on closer examination. Military leaders who actively took part in resistance activities against Hitler, such as in July 1944, were likely to be shot rather than arrested or permitted to escape into exile; those who survived were at most questioned by the Gestapo, and were punished, usually not by arrest but rather by demotion, sudden retirement, or transfer to the front. None of these latter measures—which do indicate some kind of anti-Nazi record within the framework of the military establishment of that time—are emphasized in the current *Wehrarchiv* biographies. Autobiographies and other data, however, indicate this sort of past conflict with the Nazi regime in the careers of such older generals as Hans Speidel, Adolf Heusinger, Hans Roettiger, and Joseph Kammhuber, all of whom are currently holding high office in the Federal Republic. The picture is less clear, however, for the younger men on the levels below the top. On balance, and allowing for all special circumstances, the difference in background between the present military and political elites is worth remembering.

The Bureaucrats and Foreign Policy

It seems apparent that considerable contrasts in background and experience divide the political and the administrative components of the German foreign policy elites: different formative experiences and training, different geographic origins, different relationships to the fallen Nazi dictatorship. Thus, while much of the dominant formal and informal political leadership at the present time is Roman Catholic and

---

[12] Hans-Henning Podzun, *Das Wehrarchiv: Handbuch des Wehrwesens der Gegenwart*, *passim*.

West German, the military elite is primarily Protestant, and a good part of its members come from Communist-controlled Central and Eastern Germany. The members of the political elite on the whole had no part of the Nazi regime and, in many cases, actively opposed it; most of the members of the present administrative elite are united by the common experience of government service under the dictatorship and by a sense of grievance against the postwar denazification and demilitarization policies of the Western occupation powers, which sought to bar the return of the civil and military servants of the fallen regime. To what extent these factors are likely to affect the future course of German foreign policy remains to be seen.

Little is known at the present time concerning the attitude of the administrative elite toward the foreign policy of the Adenauer government. A study by John H. Herz on the political views of the German civil service in 1953 indicated that government servants in general were inclined to accept American guidance for German foreign policy, but expected the Federal Republic to take the leadership among the lesser Western powers; Britain was considered barely an equal, France was despised as an inferior power, and other Western nations were considered unimportant. Russia was despised and feared.[13] However, this study did not include the administrative foreign policy elite groups considered here and, therefore, is not a reliable guide to their views. Some recent reports have claimed that there is sentiment among officials for more "flexibility" than heretofore in dealing with the Communist nations of Eastern Europe, particularly Poland.[14]

Another elite study in 1956, based on sample interviews, revealed a striking difference between the foreign policy views of the military and political elites. It suggested a far higher measure of agreement, however, between the political elite and the higher civil servants. In particular, it showed the civil servants at one with the politicians in favoring overwhelmingly a policy of Western alliance and economic collaboration. The military, on the other hand, endorsed a Western alliance, but were far from enthusiastic about any scheme of European integration, military or civilian, such as ECSC or EDC.[15]

Formally, the role of the administrative elite in the decision-making process is carefully circumscribed and limited to advising and assisting the responsible political leadership of the state. Potentially, however,

---

[13] Published as "Political Views of the West German Civil Service," in Speier and Davison, *West German Leadership and Foreign Policy*, pp. 96–135.

[14] See, for example, M. S. Handler, "Bonn Pondering East Europe Ties," *The New York Times*, October 14, 1957, p. 7:1.

[15] This study—to be published shortly—was carried out by the Institute for Social Research at the University of Cologne, under the sponsorship of the Center for International Studies at the Massachusetts Institute of Technology. The authors are indebted to Daniel Lerner and Suzanne Keller for making available to them a draft version of their findings.

even these formal functions can be of considerable importance. Even as strong and self-willed a political leader as Chancellor Adenauer—who was said to control the personnel policies of the various ministries —apparently relied a good deal on certain members of the administrative elite in the conduct of foreign policy. A chancellor less certain of his course, and of his role as principal decision maker, a political leadership more closely linked to the administrative elite than the present one, may come to depend far more on the permanent civil and military services for advice and guidance. The extent of the future influence of the administrative elite in foreign policy matters thus depends primarily on political developments. Apparent failure of the present foreign policy to "pay off" in terms of the conceived national interests of the foreign policy elites may give the administrative elite a greater voice, but basically its future role would seem to depend upon its relationship to the political leaders of the state. Unstable and weak governments are likely to become more dependent upon guidance from the permanent officialdom than would be the case with strong political leaders, able and willing to formulate and put into effect their own views on foreign policy issues.

CHAPTER 7

Parties behind the parties:
Interest groups and interest elites

For the purpose of this analysis, the interest group elites in the German Federal Republic may be said to consist of the leaders of powerful nongovernmental associations—other than political parties—which seek to influence the formulation and conduct of foreign policy in accordance with the conceived interests of their constituents. Specifically, the leaders of interest groups seek to influence the decision-making process in the government by (1) assuring themselves access to one or more key points of decision through the *recruitment and placement of decision-making personnel* sympathetic to their interests in government and parties;[1] (2) providing for the *allocation of decision-making power* in government and parties to individuals accessible to their influence and sympathetic to their interests; and (3) pressing for the *adoption of their own values and goals* by key decision makers in government and parties. The members of the interest group elite seek to accomplish these "facilitating intermediary objectives"[2] directly, through personal contacts with key decision makers—in which case common background and experiences are particularly important—and indirectly, by bringing pressure to bear upon the key decision makers to support their interests, through the organization of public opinion in support of or in opposition to decisions and decision makers in governments and parties.

The Role of Interest Groups in German Politics

The constitution grants all Germans the right to form organizations to represent their particular political, economic, or religious interests, as long as such groups are not directed against "the principle of international understanding." As in the United States, there exist in the Federal Republic numerous associations which in one way or another seek to influence the conduct of foreign affairs in accordance with their perceived interests. However, German interest groups are more inclusive, more tightly organized, and occupy a more privileged position in public life than do their American counterparts.

The methods pursued by interest groups in German public life have

---

[1] On the importance of access see David B. Truman, *The Governmental Process*, p. 264.
[2] *Ibid.*

varied considerably according to the political context in which they had to operate at different times. In the days of the Empire, interest group influence over government policy was most effectively exercised through intimate contacts with prominent members of the administrative elite. After the First World War the interest group leaders shifted their attention to a considerable extent from the administrative to the political elite, since the leaderships of the various parties played an important role in the turbulent political affairs of the Weimar Republic. Under the totalitarian rule of Hitler, such interest groups as were permitted to survive sought to achieve their aims largely through the elite groups of the Nazi state. The destruction of the totalitarian state, and the establishment of a new democratic order, confronted interest group elites with a new situation. New interests were to be represented, and the new methods needed to exercise influence in national affairs were quite different from those of the preceding period of Nazi rule. In general, the influence of interest groups in the conduct of foreign affairs has increased in direct proportion to the gradual restoration of German sovereignty and the recovery of independence of action by the government of the Federal Republic. Most of them have endeavored to exercise their influence over national policy through the political parties and, particularly, through party leaders in the executive and legislative branches of the federal government.

The specific methods which contemporary interest groups employ to influence foreign policy decisions are generally shielded from public view. It seems that, in recognition of the present pivotal role of party elites, most of the powerful interest groups tend to concentrate their efforts in the major parties, rather than in the government. Aided by the trend toward the concentration of political power in the hands of relatively small party elites, interest group leaders seek to influence party leaders who—directly or indirectly—play a role in the making of government policy. For the moment, attempts to exert a direct influence on the formal political and administrative decision makers in the government itself appear to be of only secondary importance; however, this pattern might change should the party elites lose their present positions of preeminence.

Methods employed vary, of course, with different interest groups and different situations. A financially powerful or numerically strong group may find it advantageous to trade money or votes for a voice in the nomination and election of friendly politicians, and possibly in the distribution of key positions in the executive branch and in parliament. Direct access to and close personal ties with key government and party officials, on the other hand, may give a smaller and poorer group disproportionate influence over the making and execution of government policies. In practice, efforts of various German interest groups to influence the decisions of the political elite take primarily the form of (1) direct representation within the leadership of the parties, (2) formal and informal contacts between members of interest group and party elites, and (3) financial support and publicity on the part of interest groups for political leaders and parties which give promise of supporting their objectives.

Direct Interest Representation in the Bundestag

A large number of leading functionaries and federal deputies of all the major parties are closely identified with different interest groups. A study of 461 deputies of the German Bundestag in the years 1949 through 1952 gave some indication of the heavy representation of interest groups in the various party delegations. Broadly speaking, 59 per cent of these deputies were identified at least informally with one or more economic interest groups. In some cases, they were identified by current associations, in others, by past associations. The inference from past occupation to present interest may not hold in every individual case, but it should be useful in indicating trends of interest representation among larger numbers, particularly in the absence of any specific indication of a sharp break with previous connections or interests. Thus 14 per cent were identified with organizations of employers, 21 per cent with trade unions and cooperatives, 10 per cent with farm interests, 10 per cent with the free professions, and 4 per cent with the interests of independent artisans and craftsmen. A considerably smaller number— 24 per cent—were openly affiliated with economic interest associations, mostly as prominent functionaries. Leading in this latter group were representatives of trade unions and cooperatives (9 per cent), employers' associations (7 per cent), and farm organizations (5 per cent). Only slightly more than 3 per cent of these 461 deputies identified themselves as leaders of associations of refugees and expellees from German lands now under Communist control. These spokesmen, however, might expect to find sympathetic listeners among the much larger number (19 per cent) of deputies who had lived part of their adult life in these territories, and whose past residence no doubt influenced indirectly their attitude toward questions affecting German reunification and the "liberation" of the areas east of the Oder-Neisse line now held by the Soviet Union and Poland.

A more recent analysis of the Bundestag elected in 1957 found that of 467 deputies at least 13 per cent openly represented business interest groups, another 13 per cent represented farmers and their associations, while 10 per cent were officials of trade unions and social welfare organizations (*Sozialverwaltung*).[3]

---

[3] "Die interessante Zahl," *Junge Wirtschaft*, V (December 1957), 522 (using data from a survey of the German Industry Institute [*Deutsches Industrie Institut*]); Heinz Hartmann, "Authority and Organization in German Management," typescript, Princeton University, 1958, pp. 281–82.

Interest group representation has been particularly pronounced in the committees of the lower house of parliament, with different interest groups sending their spokesmen into committees likely to deal with bills of particular concern to them. Thus, of twenty-one members of the Committee for Foreign Trade in the 1949–52 legislature, almost 50 per cent either were leaders of employers' associations or occupied leading positions in private business. In the Committee for Refugee Affairs, 70 per cent of the twenty-seven deputies were refugees from Communist-controlled German lands.[4] In the second Bundestag, from 1953 to 1957, representatives of business interests held more than one-third of the seats on four committees, those for Economic Policy, Nationalization, Foreign Trade, and Patents; they held slightly less than one-third of the seats in the Committee on Money and Credit and slightly less than one-fourth in the Committee on Transport. Furthermore, these representatives held four chairmanships and five vice-chairmanships in the twelve permanent committees of the legislature.[5]

In the opinion of one American observer, this plethora of interest group representatives in the German Bundestag contributes significantly to the previously noted ineffectiveness of the legislative elite relative to other elites in the Federal Republic. "In national politics, as within the political parties and the pressure groups," he writes, "one has the impression of a pattern of political discussion in which a few giants speak from the heights of government ministries, the central party organs, and the *Spitzenverbände* . . ."[6]

Influence Groups and Parties

Less apparent and more covert than the direct representation of interest groups in parliament is the influence which their leaders exercise in the political parties through personal contact with party functionaries, through financial contributions, and through free publicity in interest group publications. Numerous coordinating committees and affiliated organizations of the political parties link party and interest group elites—particularly in the case of the center and right-wing parties. Thus, the ruling Christian Democratic Union maintains a Committee of Christian Employers, a Committee of Christian Trade Unionists, a Committee for Refugee Problems, and a highly important Committee for Economic Policy (Auss-

---

[4] Cf. Rupert Breitling, *Die Verbände in der Bundesrepublik*, pp. 102–17, 130–33, and *passim*.

[5] Kurt Pritzkoleit, *Die neuen Herren* (München, Desch, 1955), p. 254; quoted by Hartmann, "Authority and Organization in German Management," p. 286.

[6] Gabriel A. Almond, "The Politics of German Business" (multigraphed; The RAND Corporation, Santa Monica, California, 20 June 1955), p. 27. See also Speier and Davison, *West German Leadership and Foreign Policy*, pp. 195–241.

chuss für Wirtschaftspolitik) to serve as liaison agencies between the party leaders and leaders of economic, religious, and social interest groups. In addition, every major interest group supports a liaison staff in the capital, to maintain continuous contact with important party and government leaders and to exert pressure upon them in support of interest group objectives.

Politics, like war, requires money. Article 21 of the Basic Law calls for the parties to give "an open accounting" of the sources of their income, but it remains a dead letter: the necessary implementing legislation has never been passed. The Social Democratic party alone gives a public accounting of its income, most of which is derived from dues paid by its large membership which comprises about 10 per cent of its electorate. However, in recent years unidentified "miscellaneous" contributions from other sources have become increasingly important items in the party's published income figures. The Christian Democratic Union and the smaller parties derive relatively little income from membership dues. They are almost entirely dependent on outside contributions, most of which come from the business community.[7] Trade associations and *ad hoc* committees of special industrial groups, such as the large industrial concerns of the Rhine-Ruhr area, have generously contributed to the coffers of the CDU and, to a lesser extent, to the smaller right-wing parties. All parties solicit contributions from well-heeled interest groups, sometimes quite openly in special fund appeals, more often covertly through personal contacts between party and interest group elites. Thus prominent bankers and industrialists have served as intermediaries between business and the CDU leaders, while trade union functionaries have served as contact men between the trade union leaders and the SPD elite.

Finally, various interest groups provide free publicity for political leaders sympathetic to their interests by providing free space in their official and unofficial publications and urging their members to support selected candidates and parties. On the other hand, interest groups often purchase advertising space in party publications, which has the added advantage of listing such financial contributions as "promotional" or business expenditures for tax purposes.[8]

Among the German political parties, the Christian Democratic Union is unique because of its association with a large number of diverse interest groups. The other parties are largely supported by one major interest group, or at most by a few. In the case of the Social Democratic party, there are two such interest groups, with overlapping memberships:

[7] Cf. A. J. Heidenheimer, "German Party Finance: The CDU," *passim*. For the Weimar period, cf. James K. Pollock, *Money and Politics Abroad*, pp. 227–45.

[8] For an excellent discussion of the employment of all these means by German interest association in the 1953 election campaign, see Wolfgang Hirsch-Weber and Klaus Schütz, *Wähler und Gewählte*, pp. 54–75.

the trade unions and the consumers' cooperatives. Twenty per cent of 151 Social Democratic Bundestag deputies, studied in the previously cited survey, were leading officials in trade unions and cooperatives, accounting for thirty-one of the thirty-three Social Democratic deputies who indicated any direct affiliation with an interest group. In contrast, only 4 per cent of the CDU/CSU deputies and 9 per cent of the entire group of 461 deputies indicated such trade union affiliation. Thirty-eight per cent of all Social Democratic deputies were members or former members of trade unions and cooperatives, compared with about 16 per cent of the CDU/CSU deputies and 21 per cent of the 461 deputies studied from all parties. Among the deputies of the third largest party, the Free Democratic party, 31 per cent were identified with employers' interests and 20 per cent admitted direct affiliation with such interests, compared with 14 per cent and less than 7 per cent respectively of the entire group of 461 deputies.[9] Almost all the deputies of the small refugee party—the Bloc of Expellees and Dispossessed (BHE)— occupied prominent positions in major associations of Germans expelled from Communist countries of Eastern and Southeastern Europe.

The Christian Democratic Union owes its dominant position largely to the fact that it has managed to receive the support of numerous and diverse interest groups without apparently becoming too closely identified with any one of them. Financially largely dependent upon big business, it has received the electoral support of most farmers, artisans, Roman Catholics, as well as of a large proportion of the labor and Protestant vote. The diversity of interest group representation within the party was indicated in the above-mentioned survey of 461 deputies of the first Bundestag (1949–53). Close to 16 per cent of 158 CDU/CSU deputies were identified with employers' interests, close to 6 per cent with the interests of artisans, and almost 18 per cent with those of farmers, compared with 14, 4, and 10 per cent respectively among all deputies. In general, the study indicated that the Christian Democratic Union counted among its deputies more representatives of farm associations, professional organizations, and craft associations than any other party, more trade unionists than any other party but the SPD, and almost as many employers' representatives as the Free Democratic party—supposedly the party of big business. While only 7 per cent of the 461 deputies occupied leading positions in the major religious organizations, 17 per cent of the Christian Democrats were prominent in either the Roman Catholic Church (11 per cent) or the Protestant Church (6 per cent), accounting for most deputies with those affiliations.[10]

The success which the Christian Democratic Union has had in becom-

---

[9] Cf. Breitling, *Die Verbände in der Bundesrepublik*, pp. 102–9.
[10] *Ibid.*

ing an aggregated, multi-interest party has apparently freed rather than tied the hands of its leaders with regard to various interest pressures. As the CDU is supported by the votes of businessmen, farmers, artisans, employees, and professional men, and has taken care to acknowledge the interests of religious associations and various socioeconomic interest groups—such as war veterans and German refugees from Communist dominated areas—its leaders presumably have greater opportunity to resist individual interest group pressure than do those of parties more subject to the influence of one particular interest group. Although multi-interest representation among the CDU/CSU deputies has somewhat weakened the relative cohesiveness of its parliamentary delegation, the Christian Democratic leadership has apparently considerable freedom of maneuver among the diverse interest groups; it can point out that its position as a governing party depends upon the CDU/CSU not becoming too closely identified with any one interest at the expense of others supporting it. Astute leaders, such as Chancellor Adenauer, seem to have managed to hold in check different interest pressures by stressing the need for restraint and balance of interests if the party is to retain its heterogeneous mass base in the electorate.[11]

Access to Government Officials

Blocked at the front door, interest groups may come to make greater efforts to gain access to key governmental officials through the back door. Should the present trend toward the evolution of a few, multi-interest parties prove to be a permanent development, the German interest group elite may be induced to try to circumvent uncooperative party leaders by shifting their efforts to influence government policies more to the administrative elite. In matters of foreign policy, such a development would increase the significance of formal and informal contacts between key diplomatic and military personnel in the government and members of private interest groups.

Common background, shared experiences, and long-standing associations appear to link many key officials in the present German civil and military services to prominent members of certain economic and social interest groups, such as employers' and veterans' associations. The new state is of too recent origin to have established as yet a government service relatively free of outside influences. Old friendships, professional contacts, and group affiliations, often dating back to the Nazi regime, appear to play a more-than-usual role in providing certain interest group representatives with access to, and influence over, government personnel participating in the formulation and execution of foreign policy. The

[11] On this point, cf. Almond, "The Politics of German Business," p. 36; and Sigmund Neumann, "Germany: Changing Patterns and Lasting Problems," *Political Parties*, pp. 380-82.

greater the differences in background, professional skills, and experiences between the political and administrative elites in the government, the greater would seem the opportunity for interest group spokesmen to bypass the "politicians" in seeking access to like-minded military men and civil servants in the government. In particular, professional "experts" on military, economic, and diplomatic matters inside and outside the government may find it easier to communicate with each other than with "political" outsiders who appear to them to lack the necessary skill and understanding to handle complex "technical" problems

A well-informed observer has described some of the implications of this situation:

> The Foreign Office readily admits that there is a limited number of qualified persons available for duties involving negotiations. Those in government service are frequently augmented by experts from industry and banking. Thus economic interests are able to make their influence felt on foreign policy, at least during negotiations for trade and commerce agreements.
>
> Their influence extends to the Ministry for Foreign Affairs through yet another avenue, for many professional civil servants in the Foreign Office have had previous experience in industry. Industries with extensive interests abroad frequently used to employ former Foreign Office officials, and at times the Foreign Office gave diplomatic appointments to executives from certain industries. Some members of the Foreign Office who went over to private industry before 1945 and represented leading German firms abroad—usually chemical, machinery, or electrical firms—have now found their way back into the Foreign Office and hold leading diplomatic positions.[12]

Various advisory councils of nongovernmental experts, which presently are attached to different ministries, also offer interest groups ready access to government officials. Particularly in matters affecting foreign policy decisions and personnel, links between members of administrative and interest elite groups appear to have assumed a certain significance. Thus, it has been claimed that the major association of former professional soldiers, the German Soldiers' League, "exercised powerful behind-the-scenes influences on the selection of officers for commissions in the new armed forces"—contrary to the announced selection policy of the governing political elite.[13]

A recent study by a member of the British Royal Institute for International Affairs maintained that leaders of the association of Germans expelled from Czechoslovakia were collaborating with diplomats of the Foreign Office in opposition to Chancellor Adenauer's foreign policy.[14] If substantiated, such developments might eventually threaten the present dominance of the political elite in the formulation and execution of foreign policy.

[12] Samuel L. Wahrhaftig, "The Development of German Foreign Policy Institutions," in Speier and Davison, *West German Leadership and Foreign Policy*, p. 32.

[13] See *The New York Times*, April 13, 1957.

[14] Elisabeth Wiskemann, *Germany's Eastern Neighbors*, p. 207 f.

Specific Interest Groups

Economic and sociopolitical interests are organized into large national organizations (*Spitzenverbände*), all of which are ostensibly nonpartisan, but by no means nonpolitical. Religious interests are primarily represented by the two major churches, the Roman Catholic and the Protestant, and their affiliated lay organizations. Economic interest groups in the Federal Republic fall roughly into two major categories: (1) employers' organizations and (2) organizations representing employees, independent farmers, independent craftsmen, and the professions. The former groups have the greater financial resources, the latter the greater voting strength to offer to political leaders and parties. While reliable figures on financial support are lacking, some of the potential voting power of different economic interests may be apparent from the 1955 percentage figures of gainfully occupied persons and their dependents, given earlier in Chapter 3.[15] According to the 1950 census, 38.7 per cent of the population of the Republic was engaged in industry or the crafts, 14.9 per cent in agriculture and forestry, 14.4 per cent in trade and transport, 13.7 per cent provided various service (including government and domestic services), and of the remaining 18.3 per cent indicating no occupation, a large proportion were undoubtedly dependent upon one or another of the other groups.

While this occupational distribution permits broad maneuvering by political parties, all the important interest groups—employers' associations, farm and labor organizations, and the major churches—are functionally specific. They pursue the specific interests of particular economic or religious elements in the population, rather than the diverse interests of a number of different groups. Our general survey permits neither a definitive identification of the effective leaders of these groups nor a true measure of their influence over foreign policy making; these matters await more detailed investigations than are presently available. However, a brief analysis of the formal leadership of some of the most prominent of these interest groups may provide some clues to the character of the various components of the interest group elite, their links to other foreign policy elites, and the extent to which the attitude and behavior of such elite members may be the product of background, training, and past experience.

Employers' Organizations and the Business Elite

German employers are organized both regionally and by economic sectors (*Fachverbände*). Most employers belong to one of the eighty regional Chambers of Industry and Commerce—membership is compul-

[15] See pp. 35–37.

sory in some parts of the country—which are represented nationally by the Diet of German Chambers of Industry and Commerce (Deutscher Industrie und Handelstag). The DIHT is perhaps the most powerful of the employer groups. Next in importance—some would place it first— is the Federation of German Industry (Bundesverband der deutschen Industrie), which represents the interests of the thirty-nine affiliated national federations of various branches of German industry. Better than three-fourths of all industrial enterprises belong to the BDI. The Co-ordinating Committee of German Trade and Industry (Gemeinschaftsaus-schuss der deutschen gewerblichen Wirtschaft) includes all major em-ployer groups and acts as a coordinating agency among the component interest groups. Other important employer interest groups concerned with foreign affairs are the Federal Association of Private Banking (Bundesverband des privaten Bankgewerbes), the Association of German Wholesalers and Exporters (Gesamtverband des deutschen Gross- und Aussenhandels), the Central Organization of German Retailers (Haupt-gemeinschaft des deutschen Einzelhandels), the German Shipowners As-sociation (Verband der deutschen Reeder), the German Section of the International Chamber of Commerce (Deutsche Gruppe der interna-tionalen Handelskammer), and the Committee for Foreign Trade of German Business (Arbeitsgemeinschaft Aussenhandel der deutschen Wirt-schaft). In addition to these permanent national organizations various business groups frequently will form temporary alliances for special ends, such as export drives or tariff reform.[16]

Big business, tightly organized into national interest associations and dominated by relatively few men, has long been the most powerful effective private interest group in Germany. James Pollock and others have vividly described the powerful influence of large business elites in the political life of pre-Nazi Germany.[17] The rapid and intensive indus-trialization of the German Empire brought with it the rising influence of large employers' associations, which effectively commanded tariff pro-tection and other forms of government support for their interests. Be-tween 1918 and 1933, during the First Republic, the influence of the business elite in the national government increased even more. German banks, corporations, and business associations generously subsidized po-litical parties and leaders who appeared willing and able to further their interests in the executive and legislative branches of the government. By and large, the business elite supported conservative and right-wing nationalist politicians who opposed the liberal democratic system of

---

[16] For a more detailed discussion on contemporary German employers' organizations, cf. Almond, "The Politics of German Business," pp. 211–17, and Hartmann, "Authority and Organization in German Management," pp. 258–301.

[17] J. K. Pollock, *Money and Politics Abroad*, pp. 246–61; Franz Neumann, *Behemoth: The Structure and Practice of National Socialism* (New York, Oxford University Press, 1942), pp. 235–40.

Weimar; the role which leading industrialists and bankers played in helping Hitler to power is well known.

Under the Nazi regime the business elite failed to get the rewards which many of its members had expected in return for their support; particularly, Hitler denied the business leaders any effective influence over foreign policy making, but his regime took many measures to help German businessmen to expand their economic power abroad. With the approach of war, Nazi control over economic life became more intense, and foreign trade and investment opportunities rapidly diminished. Many business leaders who had heretofore supported the Nazi system became disillusioned. However, to the very end of the Nazi dictatorship the business leaders retained perhaps more power than any other elite group besides the Nazi bosses; as Franz Neumann and others have shown, they played a prominent role in mobilizing the German economy in support of the war effort.[18]

Despite allied efforts during the period of occupation to diminish the concentration of German business organizations and the power of their leaders, the German business elite today exercises an influence in national affairs which rivals that of any period in the past. The phenomenal economic recovery of Germany since 1948 benefited the big business community more than any other group, and it immensely increased the political power of its leaders. Today, as in the Weimar Republic, the leaders of the major interest associations of German business are determined to assert to the fullest their actual and potential influence over public opinion, parties, legislatures, and governments.[19] Vast financial contributions for, and extensive representation in the governing political elite, as well as intimate personal ties to key government leaders, have given leading members of the business elite very considerable influence within the inner councils of the Adenauer government.

Eight national associations of German employers were mentioned earlier as interested participants in the making of foreign policy.[20] In 1956, ten men stood at the head of these associations, all of them powerful business leaders in their own right. None had been born later than 1910 and the majority had grown to adulthood during the era of the Empire. Four of the ten came from areas now under Communist control, five from Western Germany and one from Southern Germany.

---

[18] Cf. United States Strategic Bombing Survey, *The Effects of Strategic Bombing on the German War Economy*, Washington, 1945; F. Neumann, *Behemoth*, pp. 240–361.

[19] Hartmann, "Authority and Organization in German Management," p. 280. For some evidence of this influence in the lower house of the legislature, see pp. 91–92, above.

[20] The Diet of German Chambers of Industry and Commerce, the Federation of German Industry, the Federal Association of Private Banking, the Association of German Wholesalers and Exporters, the Central Organization of German Retailers, the German Shipowners Association, the German Section of the International Chamber of Commerce, and the Committee for Foreign Trade of German Business.

Half of the members of the group professed to be Protestants, while the rest did not indicate any religious affiliations in their biographies for the German *Who's Who*. All had been prominent businessmen before the accession of Hitler, and all but two indicated that they had remained the same in the Nazi area. Not one admitted to having been in political life either before or during the Third Reich, and only one of the ten claimed to have been imprisoned as an opponent of the Nazi regime. Judging by the formal leadership of these major employers' associations, the contemporary German business elite appears to be closer in background and experience to the foreign service and military elites discussed earlier than to the political elite which presently rules Western Germany.

A separate analysis of the collective characteristics of a much larger group of leading German businessmen in 1956 tends to confirm many of the findings for this smaller foreign policy business elite. Two-thirds of forty-seven directors and board chairmen of the major German employers' associations had been born before 1900 and had grown up under the Empire. By far the largest number, over 38 per cent, came from the western parts of the country; professed Protestants outnumbered Roman Catholics two to one, and 44 per cent of the total group laid claim to a university education. Only two of the forty-seven claimed an anti-Nazi record, three listed themselves as prominent business leaders in the Third Reich, while most remained silent about their activities before 1945.[21]

In general, the German business elite has on the whole supported the Adenauer government and its strongly pro-Western foreign policy. However, it has been divided on the economic integration of the non-Communist nations of continental Europe and the elimination of trade barriers between them. Some of the most prominent members of the business elite played leading roles in the creation of the European Coal and Steel Community and in the negotiations leading to the conclusion of treaties providing for a common market and an atomic energy pool among the nations of Southern and Western continental Europe. On the other hand, the Federation of German Industry fought proposals to expand the Coal and Steel Community in the mid-1950's.[22] The business elite has favored reciprocal trade and investments between the Federal Republic and its Western allies—particularly the United States—which have created stronger economic ties to Western nations than perhaps at any previous period.

Political developments since the end of the war practically severed the extensive bonds which once tied German business to markets in nations now under Communist rule, including China. However, German business leaders have lately sought to renew some of these bonds—even in the face of objections from Chancellor Adenauer, if newspaper accounts are to be

---

[21] For further details and comparisons, see Tables 9.1–9.7, Employers (pp. 133–40).
[22] Hartmann, "Authority and Organization in German Management," p. 259.

trusted. In 1955 German businessmen had still stood aside while government officials went to Moscow to negotiate a trade agreement with Russia. However, in the summer of 1958 two groups of leading industrialists visited the USSR. When the visit of one group turned out to coincide with demonstrations before the German Embassy in Moscow, it was reported that Chancellor Adenauer asked the group to return at once, and that, while three years earlier German industrial leaders had acknowledged "the primacy of the national and governmental interests" in dealing with the Soviet Union, in 1958 those in Moscow refused to accede to the Chancellor's wishes.[23]

Such support as the business elite has given the Adenauer government and its foreign policies appears to be based largely on purely economic interests, rather than on political or even ideological considerations. On the basis of a study of the political attitudes of leading German businessmen in 1954, Gabriel Almond concluded that they supported the Adenauer government "because it has followed a sound economic policy from their point of view, and because it has been successful in rehabilitating Germany on the international scene." The "basic pattern of political irresponsibility" which characterized the business elite in the past, Almond found "fundamentally unchanged." He discovered no evidence pointing either to the survival of widespread nationalist, militarist, or authoritarian points of view, or to the emergence of firm democratic beliefs. Rather, the business elite appeared generally indifferent to political issues which did not directly seem to affect its interests, so that its members seemed only somewhat uncertain supporters of close collaboration between the Federal Republic and other Western nations, while "an economic recession and a decline in foreign trade" might render the business community seriously vulnerable to Soviet pressure.[24]

Other Economic Interest Groups: Trade Unions, Farmers' and Artisans' Associations

Roughly one-fourth of all gainfully employed adult citizens of the Federal Republic belong to one or another of the large associations of workers, salaried employees, civil servants, independent artisans, and farmers.

Among employee groups, by far the largest and most important is the German Confederation of Trade Unions (Deutscher Gewerkschaftsbund). With 6.1 million members (1955) it not only includes all wage earners' unions but is also the largest organization of salaried employees

---

[23] *Ibid.*, p. 296*a*, with references to "Tadel aus Bonn," *Der Spiegel*, 12:27 (July 2, 1958), 17; and *Der Stadt-Anzeiger* (Köln), June 26, 1958, p. 1.

[24] Almond, "The Politics of German Business," pp. iii–v, 8, 19, 30, 35, and *passim*; and in Speier and Davison, *West German Leadership and Foreign Policy*, pp. 218–41.

and civil servants. About 35 per cent of all wage earners, 12 per cent of all salaried employees, and 41 per cent of all civil servants in the Federal Republic belong to the Confederation. Eighty-three per cent of its members are wage earners (11 per cent salaried employees, 6 per cent civil servants) and the large industrial enterprises are the most thoroughly organized and represented with the Confederation. The largest single industrial union, IG Metall, contributes 25 per cent of the total membership of the entire Confederation. The German Employees' Union (Deutsche Angestelltengewerkschaft), with some 420,000 members (1955), includes about 8 per cent of all salaried employees, and the German Federation of Civil Servants (Deutscher Beamtenbund), with some 517,000 members (1955), about 43 per cent of all civil servants. Between them, these three groups thus include about 35 per cent of the wage earners, 20 per cent of the salaried employees, and 84 per cent of the civil servants in the Republic. Individually or collectively, these organizations endeavor to influence the foreign policy-making process whenever they consider their special interests involved.[25]

In 1956, three-fourths of sixteen leaders of the major German trade unions had been born between 1890 and 1910, with the remainder evenly divided between those born before and in the decade following. Half of these trade union leaders were natives of the western regions of the Federal Republic, not quite a fifth came from Communist-controlled German lands, and another fifth from Southern Germany. Most failed to indicate their religious preference, but Protestants and Catholics were evenly divided among those who did. Almost two-thirds had only a primary education. Of these sixteen top trade union leaders, eight had been trade union functionaries before the Hitler era, four had been members of the SPD before 1933, and four had been imprisoned by the Nazi regime. Thirty-one per cent had an anti-Nazi record and none indicated any close association with the Hitler regime.[26]

In general, the top trade union leadership in the Federal Republic is thus primarily of West and South German origins, like the governing political elites and the employers' elite. The anti-Nazi record of the trade union leaders is considerably above the average for all elites, but not as strong as that of the CDU elite, and there are among them less than half as many former active anti-Nazis than among the leaders of the SPD. In terms of domestic politics, the trade leadership thus stands squarely

[25] Figures from the *Statistisches Jahrbuch für die Bundesrepublik Deutschland 1956*, pp. 111, 128; and from *Jahrbuch I*, pp. 3–4.

[26] Fourteen of these trade unionists were top leaders of the German Confederation of Trade Unions, the other two were the national leaders of the German Employees' Union and the German Federation of Civil Servants. For further details and for comparison of this group with a smaller group of top trade union and farm organization leaders, see Tables 9.1–9.7, Groups A and B, Employees.

in the camp of the anti-Nazi democratic forces. With regard to foreign policy issues, the trade union leaders have relatively weaker ties than most elites to the Communist-controlled areas of the former German Reich—though their ties are still stronger than those of the dominant CDU elite. The trade union leaders may thus be somewhat less interested in the reincorporation of these regions than the SPD leaders, whose foreign policy position they have thus far generally tended to support—despite their claims to be nonpartisan.

Only a minority of workers and salaried employees belong to trade unions—a fact that weakens the claim of the trade union leaders to represent all employee interests. Even among their constituents, the trade union leaders command far less authority than in the past, particularly in matters not directly related to economic interests. After some abortive attempts to influence the direction of German foreign policy directly, the trade union leadership appears to have decided to restrict its activities in this realm mainly to bread-and-butter issues of concern to union members, such as international wage agreements and the importation of foreign labor into Germany. Under present conditions of full employment this may suffice; however, as in the case of the business elite, a serious recession and decline in foreign trade might render the trade union leadership vulnerable to strong Communist pressure in favor of a more neutralist or even potentially pro-Soviet course in foreign policy.

Among organizations representing the interests of farmers and artisans, two are by far the strongest and most important. The League of German Farmers (Deutscher Bauernverband) with 1.3 million members (1952) represents 77 per cent of all independent farmers. Perhaps its most important objective has been the protection of the high-cost, small German farm units against cheaper agricultural imports, not only from overseas but also from Germany's European neighbors, such as the Netherlands. The League of German Artisans (Zentralverband des deutschen Handwerks) with 864,000 members includes practically all the independent craftsmen in the nation. Its interest in foreign affairs appears to be limited primarily to the protection of its members against cheaper imports and the promotion of the export of their products.

The numerical strength of all these organizations is no measure of the influence of their leaders in the making of foreign policy. These may claim to speak for millions of voters, but, at least on matters of foreign policy, they have failed to translate their membership figures into effective political power. In the realm of foreign policy the interests of the League of German Farmers and the League of German Artisans are restricted to such matters as tariff protection—and developments in the late 1950's toward lowering German tariffs seemed to indicate that even here the influence of their spokesmen was quite limited.

Some Special Interest Organizations:
Refugees, Expellees, and Veterans

Organizations concerned with such matters as migration, trade, investment, tourism, and banking are obviously interested in asserting influence in the foreign policy-making process, but other groups, too, may take a strong interest when their particular economic sector is thought to be affected, as in the case of tariffs, international marketing arrangements, and wage price agreements. Special issues may lead to temporary alliances between groups which on other issues may disagree. Farm and industry groups may jointly seek tariff protection, employer and employee organizations in particular industries may temporarily unite to fight for or against proposed international agreements that affect them, or export industries may ally themselves to gain government support for trade expansion.

Only a few of the special sociopolitical interest groups play any significant role in the Federal Republic. The most important of these are the organizations of expellees, German citizens and/or ethnic Germans who were expelled from or fled German lands east of the Oder-Neisse line presently "administered" under the Potsdam Agreement of 1945 by Poland and the Soviet Union and from other parts of Eastern and Southeastern Europe. There are about 8.6 million of these expellees living in the Federal Republic today, constituting about 17 per cent of the total population; about half of them are former residents of Silesia and the Sudetenland.

Only a fraction of the expellees are organized into the various groups that claim to defend their common interests. The most important of these are the League of Expelled Germans (Zentralverband Vertriebener Deutscher) and the League of Regional Groups (Verband der Landsmannschaften), with its major affiliates of Silesians (Landsmannschaft Schlesien) and Sudeten Germans (Sudetendeutsche Landsmannschaft). There are also about 2.6 million refugees from the Soviet zone of Germany in the Federal Republic (5.2 per cent of the population), but while there are numerous organizations which would like to represent their interests, few of the refugees belong to them. Together, expellees and refugees number about 11 million persons or 22 per cent of the population, but most of them appear to have found adequate representation of their interests in the major political parties.

A refugee party, the BHE, suffered a crushing defeat in the 1957 election and failed to gain the 5 per cent of the votes necessary to send at least one representative into the parliament. The younger age groups among the refugees and expellees, in particular, appear to shun the organizations claiming to represent their interests.

While the mass organizations claiming to represent the interests of refugees and expellees may be losing such influence over the making of foreign policy as they may have had—if any—this does not mean that such interests are likely to be ignored by the dominant elites. Too many among both the elites and the general public retain strong emotional ties to their former homeland to permit the issues of reunification and the recovery of the Oder-Neisse territory to be forgotten in the formulation of German foreign policy. The absorption of the refugees and expellees into the two major parties has actually given greater weight to their spokesmen in the councils of these parties. The refugee and expellee interest thus continues to be represented through the mechanism of the major parties rather than directly as in the early 1950's.

Another potentially powerful interest group has thus far not used its potential. Sixty-nine per cent of all German men are war veterans, 48 per cent of the Second World War, 15 per cent of the first, and 6 per cent of both wars.[27] There are close to 1200 veterans' organizations in the Federal Republic, but few, if any, of them appear at this time to exercise any major influence in German politics. The largest and, potentially, most influential is the League of German Soldiers (Verband deutscher Soldaten), primarily an organization of present and former professional soldiers. Among its stated objectives are "loyalty to an undivided fatherland," the rehabilitation of all "defamed" former soldiers, and the liberation of still imprisoned soldiers convicted of war crimes. The pre-Hitler, right-wing veterans' organization "Steel Helmet" (Stahlhelm) is a much smaller association with apparently little influence. The same appears true for the Air Force Circle (Luftwaffenring), composed of former members of the German air force.

The Major Churches and Their Spokesmen

According to the 1950 census, 51.2 per cent of the population of the Federal Republic professed the Protestant and 45.2 per cent the Roman Catholic religion, compared with 60.6 per cent and 33.3 per cent respectively in prewar Germany. In terms of relative strength the potential influence of the Roman Catholic Church in national affairs has thus increased considerably. However, no more than 11 million West Germans—about half of these professing the Roman Catholic faith—are thought to be active members of their church; in the case of the Protestants the proportion is about one-eighth.[28] Of the two major churches the Roman Catholic is probably politically the more active and influential; many of its leaders have vigorously supported the Christian Democratic party in every national election. Both major churches, however, are

[27] Calculated from data in a 1956 poll, reported in *Jahrbuch II*, p. 4.
[28] *Jahrbuch I*, pp. 10–11.

thought to wield considerable influence within the dominant political and economic elites.[29]

The supreme organ of the Roman Catholic Church, the annual meeting of the hierarchy at the town of Fulda (Fuldaer Bischofskonferenz), also claims jurisdiction in the Soviet-controlled German Democratic Republic. Nonetheless, the influence of the Church is largely restricted to the Federal Republic, for not only are less than 20 per cent of the Germans living in the Soviet zone Roman Catholics, but the Communist government has greatly restricted contacts between the West German hierarchy and Roman Catholics living in the Democratic Republic. In the Federal Republic the Church maintains a liaison office at the capital to represent its interests. With the encouragement of the hierarchy, the members of numerous lay groups affiliated with the Church endeavor to translate Catholic interests into Catholic action by playing an active role in public life. Among the members of the two faiths, Roman Catholics have tended to favor the CDU, Protestants the SPD. In a 1956 poll, 55 per cent of the Catholics but only 30 per cent of the Protestants supported the CDU, while only 30 per cent of the Catholics but 47 per cent of the Protestants supported the SPD.[30] In the 1957 national election, at least one member of the Roman Catholic hierarchy openly urged the faithful to vote for the CDU.

The Roman Catholic leadership of the Federal Republic has strong ties to Southern and Western Germany but far weaker links to the Communist-dominated German territories to the east. At the end of 1956, 80 per cent of twenty leading members of the Roman Catholic Church came from either Western (40 per cent) or Southern Germany (40 per cent); only 5 per cent came from the areas now under Soviet domination.[31] In terms of religious background and training, and experience,

[29] Henry J. Kellermann, "Party Leaders and Foreign Policy," in Speier and Davison, *West German Leadership and Foreign Policy*, p. 61. On the role played by church leaders, particularly by those of the Roman Catholic Church, in the national election campaign of 1953 see Hirsch-Weber and Schütz, *Wähler und Gewählte*, pp. 68–73.

[30] *Jahrbuch II*, p. 264. An earlier poll, in 1952, indicated that among regular churchgoers from both denominations, 45 per cent preferred the CDU, and only 22 per cent the SPD. About three-fourths of regular churchgoers are Roman Catholics, which indicates the relatively greater influence of the Roman Catholic hierarchy over public opinion compared with that of the leaders of the numerically larger Protestant Church. In Germany, most people belong nominally to one or the other of the two churches for purposes of taxation and population statistics, but in twenty-three polls through 1955 and 1956 only about 30 per cent reported going to church "regularly." Another 27 per cent or so claimed to go "irregularly"; another 27 per cent said "rarely," and perhaps 16 per cent said "never." See chart in *Jahrbuch II*, p. 29. These figures suggested a slight rise in churchgoing habits as against the 1952–54 period. Cf. *Jahrbuch I*, p. 10; also pp. 3, 11, 12, 258, 264.

[31] These twenty Roman Catholic leaders included all the bishops and archbishops of the church. A slightly different survey, at a somewhat earlier date, yielded very similar results, although it included the leaders of four major lay affiliates: the Central Committee of German Catholics, the League of Catholic Employers, the Association of Catholic Employees, and the Association of German Catholic Publicists. See Tables 9.1–9.7, Group A, Roman Catholics.

these members of the Roman Catholic hierarchy are linked to their opposite numbers in the Catholic countries of Western and Southern Europe,
such as France, Italy, Belgium, and perhaps even Spain, by bonds which
are in many respects not less strong than those to the relatively few
German Roman Catholics—about 13 per cent—living under Communist
rule. While ties between the hierarchy and church members in the Soviet-
controlled areas of Germany have been greatly weakened in recent years
owing to the division of the country, those between the Roman Catholic
leaders of the Federal Republic and of the nations of Western and Southern
continental Europe have been strengthened since the fall of the Nazi
regime. There is every indication that these latter ties have been of considerable importance in the postwar movement for closer association
between the countries of Catholic Europe, a movement led largely by
prominent Roman Catholic politicians, including Konrad Adenauer,
Robert Schuman and the late Alcide de Gasperi.

The position, attitude, and behavior of the present Roman Catholic
hierarchy in German public life undoubtedly are strongly influenced by
the fact that it is practically the only elite which moved from the Nazi
state into the postwar political system without serious change in its status
and personnel. Unlike the political elite, it did not have to make a new
start after twelve years of Nazi oppression; unlike the administrative and
big business elites it was not temporarily eclipsed in the immediate postwar period; unlike the Protestant leadership it was not weakened by loss
of influence over a large proportion of the members of the Church living
under Communist rule. Its position of eminence relatively unaffected by
various drastic changes in the political order over the last four or five
decades, the hierarchy currently may be more influential than ever before,
since the proportion of Roman Catholics among the population has never
been as great since the creation of a German state in 1870.

This permanence and continuity of the Roman Catholic hierarchy is
reflected in its present composition. Sixty-five per cent of its twenty
leaders mentioned above were born before 1901 and entered the service
of the Church during the Empire; all who had been old enough at the time
indicated in their official biographies that they had served the Church
before 1933, and all had done so during the Nazi regime. Not one of the
Roman Catholic leaders reported having been in prison or exile during
the Third Reich, but one dignitary indicated an active anti-Nazi record.

The German Evangelical Church (Evangelische Kirche in Deutschland), EKD, is a union of German Protestant churches in both the Federal
Republic and the Communist Democratic Republic. As over 80 per cent
of Germans living under Communist rule are Protestants and their Church
still exercises considerable influence over them, the EKD and its member
churches have considerably stronger ties to and interest in the population
of the Democratic Republic than the Roman Catholic Church. The Synod,

Council, and Conference of the Evangelical Church are the recognized representatives of the Protestants in both parts of the divided country, the annual rally (*Kirchentag*) of the German Evangelical Church is held alternately in the Federal Republic and in the Democratic Republic, and the EKD maintains a liaison office at the seat of each government. Through its Church Office for Foreign Affairs (Kirchliches Aussenamt) the Church maintains relations with other churches in both Communist and non-Communist countries.

The orthodox Lutherans among German Protestants have traditionally shunned political action on behalf of their church. Today, too, they exert only indirect influence in political affairs through their tacit support of the dominant liberal leadership of the Evangelical Church. The leaders of this liberal wing, while numerically in the minority, occupy most of the positions in the EKD and in this capacity endeavor to exercise some influence in both the Federal Republic and the Democratic Republic. In the Democratic Republic this has involved the Church in many bitter clashes with the Communist rulers; in the Federal Republic its participation in public life is neither as extensive nor as intensive as that of the Roman Catholic Church. While individual Church leaders occasionally speak out on public issues, organized Protestant groups play a comparatively small role in the political process.

"Nonetheless," says a well-informed observer, ". . . both Catholics and Protestants play an influential role in the CDU. The Catholic Church seems to have achieved predominance within the party, but Protestant leaders are also found in important positions, particularly in Southwest and Northwest Germany. Of particular importance is the work of the 'Evangelical Academies' which, under the leadership of Protestant lay and clerical leaders, are bringing together representatives from all areas of public life in meetings devoted to a serious diagnosis of political and social developments. The academies have played a major part in introducing ethical considerations into political discussions."[32]

The present leadership of the German Protestant Church in the Federal Republic to a large extent represents the anti-Nazi wing which bitterly fought the totalitarian ambitions of the Hitler regime. At the end of 1956, some 33 per cent of 18 leading Protestant churchmen indicated in their biographies that they had been imprisoned by Hitler, and 44 per cent had an anti-Nazi record.[33] With some 14 million German Protestants

[32] Kellermann, "Party Leaders and Foreign Policy," p. 61.

[33] These 18 were all the leaders of the German Evangelical Church listed in a standard reference work, for whom any data were available. A somewhat earlier survey of fourteen leaders of the Church, including also the head of the Committee of the Christian Churches (Arbeitsgemeinschaft Christlicher Kirchen), the Annual Rally of the Evangelical Church of the Union, and the League of Evangelical and Reformed Churches, gave similar results, except that the proportion of those arrested by the Nazis was as high as 64 per cent. For details, see Tables 9.1–9.7, Group A, Protestants.

living today under Communist rule in the Soviet zone—about 37 per cent of all German Protestants—the leaders of that Church are also more directly involved in the battle against the claims of the East German regime than are their Roman Catholic counterparts. Moreover, the Protestant leadership has far stronger personal ties to the German lands east of the Elbe River than the Roman Catholic: in sharp contrast to the Roman Catholic hierarchy 22 per cent of the 18 leading Protestant churchmen of the Federal Republic come from these regions. Another 33 per cent come from Northern Germany, a region strikingly underrepresented in the cabinet and the CDU elite, while about 39 per cent hail from Western and Southern Germany, the regions from which such a large portion of the members of the political elites of the Federal Republic is recruited.[34]

With the Protestant Church in the Soviet zone engaged in a struggle for survival against the totalitarian claims of the Communist regime, the leaders of the Church in the Federal Republic are naturally far more concerned about the problem of German reunification than are other foreign policy elites less closely tied to the Soviet zone by personal and organizational bonds. Reunification would free the oppressed Protestants of the Soviet zone and reestablish the Protestant Church in its former position of preeminence among the German churches: the proportion of Protestants would rise from a bare majority of 51 per cent in the present Federal Republic to at least 61 per cent in a unified German state. At the same time, German Protestant leaders have viewed with some apprehension moves toward the inclusion of the Federal Republic in a continental European federation whose population would be overwhelmingly Roman Catholic. There have been indications that at least some German Protestant leaders fear that a federated Europe which did not include the Scandinavian states and Britain would fall under the religious dominance of the Roman Catholic Church.

Protestant efforts to maintain some influence in the Soviet zone, and the traditional reluctance of the leaders of the Protestant churches to become involved in political problems, have largely restrained Protestant leaders in the Federal Republic from openly trying to influence foreign policy. Covertly, however, some leaders appear to have sought to have a voice in governmental foreign policy decisions which they felt directly affected their interests. However, they have lacked allies. Although common geographic roots and political interests would seem to suggest cooperation between the Protestant leadership and the opposition Social Democrats, efforts for closer collaboration between the two groups have been singularly unsuccessful. While far more Protestants than Roman Catholics support the Social Democratic party, the Protestants' leadership has

---

[34] In the earlier survey, the geographic contrast to the other elites was much larger: 36 per cent of the Protestants in the earlier group came from East and Central Germany and only 21 per cent from the South and West.

either supported the governing Christian Democrats or maintained a neutral position between the two major parties. Not only do traditional differences between the Protestant Church and the Social Democratic party stand in the way of closer cooperation between the two groups, but both as a governing party and as a pronounced interdenominational "Christian" party, the Christian Democratic Union has continued to attract as much, if not more, Protestant support than the avowedly non-religious SPD. Whether popular interest in the issue of German reunification could ever become strong enough to bring Protestant leaders and Social Democrats into some sort of political alliance or alignment remains to be seen.

CHAPTER 8

Gatekeepers of opinion: Influential editors and publishers

The Influence of the Press

The effective leaders of the German press—the most influential of the news media—control vital channels of communication between various foreign policy elites and the general public. Publicly owned radio and television networks and privately owned newsreel companies provide only limited factual reports of news items of general interest; the average German, insofar as he is concerned about foreign policy issues at all, depends primarily on newspapers and periodicals to explain to him what is going on in the world. Not only do these mass media provide him generally with a more extensive record of international developments than radio, television, and newsreels, but the periodicals in particular furnish him with cues for interpreting these events. This role of the press—traditionally important in a highly literate country—appears to be as highly significant as ever.

In Germany, perhaps even more than in the United States, the "attentive public,"—insofar as it lacks the private sources of information available to members of elite groups—relies largely on newspapers and periodicals for its "images of reality." These images, furnished by the press, contribute to the public's general perception of other nations and their leaders, as well as of the attitudes and actions of the leaders of their own country, and of the changing conditions which affect Germany's position in the world. The leaders of the press are thus in the position of "gatekeepers" who determine what the public will read and who at least influence what it may remember. They have the power to emphasize certain news items or to play them down; they can conceal or expose, support or attack particular courses of action in German foreign policy; they can supply their readers with "interpretive cues" by suggesting that particular events or policies should be viewed as friendly or hostile, serious or trifling, deserving respect or contempt. In all these ways, editors and publishers of important newspapers and periodicals influence foreign policy decisions by acting as mediators between the interested sectors of broad public opinion and the various foreign policy elites; they present and interpret elite views and actions to their readers and, at the same time, exert influence over members of the elites in the name of the public which they claim to represent.[1]

The present and potential influence of the contemporary German press has not been clearly tested. There have been few, if any, cases of major conflict between the press and the federal government, nor has the press usually acted as a whole. It has remained divided by regions and interest groups and much of its influence has remained indirect. Yet its long-run, cumulative effects, as well as its short-run potential, should not be underrated.[2]

The Readership of the Press

Ninety-one per cent of all adults in the Federal Republic read a newspaper at least once a week; at least 55 per cent read one daily. Men outnumber women among the regular newspaper readers by a ratio of about two to one.[3] More than half of the men and more than one-quarter of the women read first of all the first pages which contain more political and international items; but one-third of the women and one-sixth of the men start with the last pages which carry mostly news features, local news, and sports.[4]

The "attentive public"[5] in international affairs comprises less than two-fifths of the adult population. Almost three out of four Germans polled in March 1955 said that they almost always read local news; but only 46 per cent followed the news about domestic politics, and only 39 per cent said they followed political news from abroad. However, attention to political and international news was far higher among men: 64 per cent of the men read international news regularly and 70 per cent followed domestic politics, while only 18 per cent of the women followed international news and 26 per cent regularly read domestic political items.[6] In May 1953, only 5 per cent of readers felt that the newspaper which they usually read was unfriendly to the Bonn government; 38 per cent thought their paper was friendly to the regime, and 19 per cent believed it was neutral.[7]

Taken together, these figures suggest something about the limits of

[1] An excellent analysis along these lines has been given for the role of the American press in foreign policy making in the United States in Richard C. Snyder and Edgar S. Furniss, Jr., *American Foreign Policy*, pp. 532–38.

[2] For a divergent opinion by a well-qualified observer cf. W. Phillips Davison, "The Mass Media in West German Political Life," in Speier and Davison, *West German Leadership and Foreign Policy*, pp. 242–81, especially 242–54.

[3] *Jahrbuch II*, p. 51.

[4] *Jahrbuch I*, pp. 53–55.

[5] For a discussion of this concept, see Almond, *The American People and Foreign Policy*, pp. 138–39, 228.

[6] *Jahrbuch I*, p. 56.

[7] *Ibid.*, p. 53.

direct newspaper influence. A predominantly pro-government press dis-
seminates news which presumably is on the whole favorable to democracy
and to the West; but this news is mainly read by men whose attitudes,
as many tests have shown, are often quite cool toward democracy, the
Western powers, and the Bonn regime; and the same news is largely
ignored by the women who are far more friendly to the West and whose
votes have done much to keep the present government in power.

Among political news competing for the attention of readers, reports
from Bonn were picked as first choice by 37 per cent of persons polled
in September 1953; they were followed by items from Moscow which
were the first choice of 23 per cent; New York was picked by 8 per cent;
Paris 5 per cent; and Rome 3 per cent.[8] The total of choices for first and
sececond place in order of attention gave the same rank order: Bonn 55
per cent, Moscow 37 per cent, New York 31 per cent, Paris 14 per cent,
and Rome 8 per cent. Striking was the interest in news from Moscow;
the high interest in second place for news from the United States (New
York, 23 per cent); and the low interest in news from Paris and Rome,
the capitals of Germany's main partners in the European Coal and Steel
Community.[9]

Particularly salient for German readers is that international news
which combines some human interest with a strong domestic news appeal.
In such a category is news about German returnees from the East (e.g.,
emigrants or repatriated prisoners of war), and news about Soviet proposals regarding German reunification. In a poll in March 1955, the
returnee item topped all others in reader appeal, including all German
domestic news; it was ranked first by 49 per cent of all respondents, and
by 52 per cent of the women. The item "New Russian Proposal on
Reunification" ranked second among readers in general (46 per cent)
but was the first choice for 56 per cent of the men. These two were followed by domestic items; "Modern Weapons for German Army" ranked
ninth with 23 per cent for all readers, and fifth for men; finally, items
from France and Britain ranked at the bottom of reader interest.[10] Another
poll in April 1956 contained no returnee or reunification item, but showed
otherwise a similar picture. Domestic items ranked highest in reader
interest. An item on proposed labor legislation was put first by 43 per
cent, and outdrew by a margin of two to one the highest ranking foreign
news item, "Russians Make New Disarmament Proposal," which appealed to 21 per cent, including 29 per cent of men. Among men, four of the
top-ranking five items were domestic, dealing with taxes, strikes, and the
minister of finance. Yet the Russian disarmament proposal outdrew "New
Weapons for the German Army," which held top interest only for 16 per

[8] The rest of the answers were indifferent or scattered. *Ibid.*, p. 54.
[9] *Ibid.*
[10] *Ibid.*, p. 56.

cent of all readers, including 27 per cent of men. At the bottom of the list was the only political item touching upon Western Europe: "New Plans at the European Coal and Steel Community"; only 7 per cent would have cared to read it first.[11]

In 1956 there appeared 1,432 dailies in the Federal Republic, with a combined circulation of 15.9 million, or 318 copies for every thousand inhabitants (U.S.: 346/1,000). Better than half of these dailies were merely local editions (*Nebenausgaben*) of large regional newspapers (*Stammausgaben*) which provided them with their national and international news and most of their editorial material. Thus, the twelve largest dailies accounted for about one-third of the total circulation of the daily press, ranging from the illustrated *Bild-Zeitung* of Hamburg with a reported circulation of 2.5 million to the influential *Frankfurter Allgemeine*, which claimed a circulation of 166,000.[12]

Almost all dailies feature editorial articles—usually on the front page —and in 1954, 77 per cent of these dealt with political issues.[13] However, only 23.9 per cent of the newspapers (with 18.4 per cent of the total circulation) admitted a definite political orientation; the rest claimed to be "independent" or withheld information concerning their editorial orientation. Slightly less than half of those papers overtly identified with a political orientation were publications of the two major political parties, the CDU and the SPD; most of the rest called themselves "Christian" dailies.[14]

Only a few of the most prominent dailies employ their own foreign correspondents; most of them rely for news from abroad on free-lance correspondents and on the German Press Service (Deutsche Presseagentur), which has correspondents in most major capitals of the world and also uses the services of such international news agencies as the Associated Press, United Press International, and Reuters. In addition, various governmental and nongovernmental agencies, political parties, the Press and Information Office of the Federal Government, foreign embassies, and the major churches provide the daily press with news from abroad.[15]

With one or two outstanding exceptions, the periodical press has far fewer readers than the daily press. Nonetheless, by mid-1955, about 70 per cent of Germans were reading at least one periodical each month.[16] The influence of periodicals in public affairs is often considerable. One

[11] *Jahrbuch II*, p. 60.

[12] *Die Deutsche Presse, 1956*; and *Political Handbook of the World, 1957*.

[13] Max Dovifat, in *Die Deutsche Presse, 1956*, p. 35.

[14] *Die Deutsche Presse, 1956*, p. 124 f.

[15] Hans Joachim von Merkatz and Wolfgang Metzger, *Deutschland-Taschenbuch: Tatsachen und Zahlen*, p. 207.

[16] *Jahrbuch I*, p. 58, chart of 11 polls, 1950–55; *Jahrbuch II*, p. 52.

of the most popular and outspoken is the illustrated weekly *Der Spiegel*, which is modeled after *Time* magazine and attracts the same people who are the regular newspaper readers. Specializing in political exposés, *Der Spiegel* has been highly critical of the Adenauer government and most of its foreign policy, but it has not spared the opposition either. Not nearly as popular, but nonetheless influential, are some of the less sensational journals concerned with political issues, such as *Aussenpolitik*, *Gegenwart*, *Die Zeit*, *Frankfurter Hefte*, *Rheinischer Merkur*, and *Christ und Welt*, which are read by opinion leaders and policy makers both inside and outside the government. While these journals receive their news items more or less from the same sources as the dailies, they interpret, rather than report the news. Although ostensibly nonpartisan on major issues of German foreign policy, most journals are usually on the side of one or the other of the major parties; more rarely they wish a plague on both houses.

Public opinion polls are postwar innovations in Germany and have as yet not gained the public attention and influence they enjoy in the United States. The main opinion-polling organizations are the Institut für Demoskopie at Allensbach-am-Bodensee; the EMNID Institute at Bielefeld; and the somewhat smaller DIVO Institute at Frankfurt/Main. In addition, university Institutes of Social Research, such as those of the Universities of Frankfurt and of Cologne, are also carrying on survey work.

While the influence of opinion polls and surveys appears to be increasing, there are as yet no studies of its extent. There is reason to believe that German diplomats and civil servants have displayed very little interest in public opinion polls, and little appreciation of any potential importance of their results.

Politicians, on the other hand, seem to have been distinctly more interested in such polls, and on occasion they seem to have been more responsive to their findings. Thus, at least some of the propaganda methods and electoral slogans of the CDU seem to have been pretested systematically in opinion polls. German polling experts have claimed that the major political parties, as well as the federal government and Chancellor Adenauer himself, are all making systematic use of public opinion polls, not only by following their published results but by arranging for specific studies to be made for their own use by professional polling organizations. The responsiveness shown particularly by the CDU and by Chancellor Adenauer on some occasions to trends of public opinion would well accord with such claims. It seems, therefore, that the federal government is making its decisions about each foreign policy issue with a fairly accurate knowledge as to whether it has the support of mass opinion or whether it has to override it at least temporarily in some particular case.

Other Media of Mass Communication

Other mass media are less influential, but still significant. Radio and television are controlled by public corporations which are enjoined by law from adopting partisan positions. These media provide important forums for the presentation of political commentaries and speeches by representatives of various partisan groups—important parliamentary debates are both broadcast and televised and the leaders of the government and parties frequently employ the media—but they serve merely as media in the endeavors of others to influence public opinion; they are not themselves original opinion-forming agents. By the mid-1950's, more than 90 per cent of Germans were listening to the radio; about 80 per cent were doing so for at least one hour each day; and about 55 per cent had bought radio sets after 1948.[17] Sixty-four per cent listen to a newscast at least once a day and about 79 per cent of radio listeners like to listen to news; 46 per cent enjoy listening to political commentaries, but only 33 per cent care to listen to reports of events abroad. The number of regular listeners to the "Voice of America" dropped from 22 per cent of radio listeners in March 1950 to 14 per cent in March 1955.[18]

Motion pictures are also an important medium. By November 1956, polls indicated that more than one-half of the adult population were attending motion pictures at least once a month; more than three-quarters attended at least sometimes, but 18 per cent said they had not been to the pictures in years. Two-thirds of the filmgoers or more than half of the adult population were "very much interested" in newsreels. However, while 33 per cent of respondents in a 1956 poll believed that political events dominated in the newsreels, only 19 per cent expressed a particular interest in this subject. More than 20 per cent of the population and 30 per cent of those who had recently been to the movies felt sure in March 1953 that the newsreels were politically neutral; only 7 per cent of recent filmgoers or 4 per cent of the total denied this; the rest did not know or did not care.[19]

Television by early 1957 had not yet reached in Germany the status of a medium of such political importance and effectiveness as it had in the United States. In a September 1955 poll, 28 per cent of those questioned had never seen television, 14 per cent saw it often, and four per owned a television set.[20] Recent reports indicate that West Germans are rapidly acquiring sets or watching television in public places, as more and larger stations are blanketing the country. As television comes to make its political impact more fully, it may enhance the influence of the gov-

[17] *Jahrbuch I*, pp. 62–65. *Jahrbuch II*, p. 63.

[18] This is only a drop from 17 per cent to 13 per cent of the adult population, since the proportion of radio listeners in general rose from 76 per cent in December 1948 to 92 per cent in February 1955. *Jahrbuch I*, pp. 62, 73–74; *Jahrbuch II*, p. 79.

[19] *Jahrbuch I*, pp. 59–60; *Jahrbuch II*, pp. 60, 62–63.

[20] *Jahrbuch II*, pp. 81–82.

ernment and of those groups who will have not only more or less equal
access to a share of television time, but also the money and the skill to
make the most of its potentialities. As yet, however, no distinct elite of
television experts has appeared in German politics.

The Communications Elite

The control of the mass media lies in the hands of a somewhat amor-
phous group, which includes members of most of the elites we have discussed. Radio and television networks are government-owned, but their
control is shared between government officials and representatives of
party and interest group elites who sit on the boards of these public
corporations. Newspapers and periodicals frequently represent the views
of some other elite, even when they call themselves "independent." Sometimes control is quite overt, more often it is hidden. While this situation
permits only the most tentative analysis of the actual communications
elite, the information which is available enables us to say something about
the publishers and editors who, at least overtly, control the leading newspapers and periodicals in the Federal Republic.

By the mid-1950's, leading editors and publishers played a more independent and influential role in public life than in any other period of
German history. Until 1918, freedom of the press was seriously limited
by the autocratic leaders of the Empire, who used both police powers
and secret funds to protect themselves from journalistic criticism. During
the Weimar Republic the German press enjoyed unprecedented freedom
from government interference, but was largely controlled by powerful
political parties and interest groups. Thus, Alfred Hugenberg, the leader
of the Nationalist party of conservative industrialists and Prussian aristocrats, exercised control over a huge empire of newspapers, news and advertising agencies, and newsreels, which he used eventually to assist
Hitler's rise to power. As soon as the Nazis assumed control of the state
in 1933, they placed all German news media under the Ministry of Propaganda, which exercised complete control over the domestic and foreign
press in Germany from 1933 to 1945. Journalists and editors were still
paid by the publisher but were primarily responsible to the government
and could not be hired or dismissed without its approval.[21]

After the unconditional surrender of Germany in 1945, the Western
occupation powers—and particularly the United States—set out to create
a new and free press as an integral part of the problem of restoring or
creating democratic institutions. The occupation authorities licensed a
limited number of German papers and periodicals between 1945 and 1949,
which were headed by carefully selected editors and publishers and super-
vised by the occupation authorities. These efforts were directed toward

[21] See Henry P. Pilgert, *Press, Radio and Film in West Germany 1945–1953*, pp. 11–12.

ensuring the permanent eradication of Nazi influence and the creation of a democratic and independent communications elite. Editors and publishers were selected primarily on the basis of their record of opposition to, or noninvolvement with, Nazism; and only secondary consideration was given to their professional qualifications.

The result was that many of the licensed publishers and editors were survivors of the anti-Nazi parties of the Weimar period (including some Communists who were eventually weeded out). Most of these men had received their journalistic training before 1933 and could prove that they had not supported the Nazi regime. Some were of advanced age, their stamina weakened by long periods of imprisonment in concentration camps; some lacked the vigor which their new tasks demanded of them. The older men were handicapped, too, by twelve years of enforced journalistic inactivity during the Nazi regime, while the younger were inexperienced. Both age groups included persons of working-class origin with little formal schooling. Thus, of 113 editors and publishers given newspaper publishing licenses by American military government between 1945 and 1949, about 40 per cent had been imprisoned by the Nazis; 25 per cent had no previous journalistic experience; about 62 per cent had no university training, and 19 per cent had not gone beyond primary school.[22] The American military goverment, and the British and French, too, sought through ordinances and financial assistance to establish these licensed editors and publishers as a new German communications elite. Printing plants owned by former Nazis were forced to conclude long-term contracts with the licensed newspapers and periodicals, most of which lacked funds to purchase their own plants; paper, newsprint, and other essential items in short supply were made available by the occupying powers. By mid-1949, there were in the American zone fifty-nine licensed newspapers with a total circulation of over four million copies.[23]

When licensing of approved editors and publishers ceased in 1949, many American officials in Germany feared that the editors and publishers sponsored by the Western occupation powers would not be able to hold their own against the competition of former Nazi journalists now free to return to the publishing field. Indeed, several hundred new publications appeared to challenge the former licensed press, most of them produced by persons who had not been able to qualify for a military government license because of a Nazi record. A long and bitter circulation war ensued, but the former licensed press managed on the whole to maintain its dominant postion. Casualties among the newcomers were far more numerous, although they had in many cases generous financial assistance and—unlike the former licensed press—owned their own printing plants. In 1952, two years after the suspension of licensing, the circulation of the

22 *Ibid.*, pp. 20–21.
23 *Ibid.*, p. 47.

former licensed press stood at 3.3 million—compared with 4 million in 1949—while the post-license papers had a circulation of 1.3 million. By 1953, the former licensed press had a circulation about three times that of newspapers which sprang up after licensing ended. According to a report of the U.S. High Commissioner for Germany, most editors who had assumed their positions between 1945 and 1949 with the blessings of military government not only had retained their posts, but had inspired many of the new editors to follow their leadership in defending the press against governmental interference.[24]

Undoubtedly, many of the former licensed editors and publishers owed their survival to a large extent to continued support from the United States authorities. In 1950–51, to protect the ex-licensees against the termination of forced leases with printing plant owners concluded earlier under military government pressure, all decisions over such leases were kept out of the jurisdiction of German courts, and concentrated under a Newspaper Leases Control Board controlled by the Allied authorities. This arrangement prevailed in the early 1950's. Another effective Allied instrument to influence the recruitment and attitudes of the owners and editors of the German press was a Press Fund, supported largely out of funds provided by the American government, which provided loans and grants to editors and publishers "meeting certain policies and criteria" determined by American authorities and by German ex-licensed journalists selected by United States officials. By early 1952, this Fund had spent almost three million dollars and it had enabled most of the former licensed journalists to acquire their own printing plants or to make satisfactory leasing arrangements. It also had provided valuable support for new publications found worthy of financial assistance by the directors of the Fund. Finally, the American authorities sent hundreds of selected German journalists to the United States for varying periods of study, observation, and training.[25]

What has been the effect of better than ten years of direct and indirect American efforts to create an "independent and democratic" German press and a communications elite sympathetic to United States interests and values? To find out, two groups were analyzed. The first and more highly selected Group A consisted of twenty-one people and included the publishers or editors in 1956 of all newspapers with a circulation of over 600,000 and of a number of leading journals dealing with foreign policy matters.[26]

[24] *Ibid.*, p. 101; cf. also pp. 20, 21, 47, 50, 119.
[25] *Ibid.*, pp. 21, 43, 50, 51–52, 64, 101.
[26] Included were the editors and/or publishers of the following newspapers and periodicals: *Frankfurter Allgemeine Zeitung, Schwäbische Landeszeitung, Süddeutsche Zeitung, Westdeutsche Allgemeine Zeitung, Hamburger Abendblatt, Bild-Zeitung, Welt am Sonntag, Aussenpolitik, Deutsche Rundschau, Die Welt, Deutsche Kommentare, Deutsche Zeitung und Wirtschaftszeitung, Münchner Merkur, Christ und Welt, Rheinischer Merkur, Das Andere Deutschland, Der Spiegel, Die Gegenwart, Frankfurter Hefte, Zeitschrift für Geopolitik, Die Kultur.*

The second and broader group analyzed, Group B, consisted of 41 people, including publishers or editors in 1956 of all newspapers with a circulation of over 100,000 and of leading periodicals, as well as a few directors of radio networks.[27] Data for both groups are given in Tables 9.1–9.7. in the text, we will discuss only the characteristics of the larger Group B of 41 persons, unless otherwise indicated.

On the whole, former opponents of the Nazi regime appear to have maintained considerable control over the news media, while overt Nazis seem to have had little success in establishing themselves in the major news media. Forty-two per cent of the communications group had anti-Nazi records, while only 2 per cent had held influential positions in the Third Reich; 32 per cent had been imprisoned by the Nazis. This is 8 per cent less than the group of former U.S. Military Government licensees analyzed by Pilgert in 1953,[28] but another 5 per cent of our 1956 group had been exiled by the Nazis. On the whole, United States efforts to establish a democratic, anti-Nazi communications elite in Germany appear to have been quite successful.

In other respects, however, the 1956 group was quite different from the ex-licensees of 1953. They were much better educated: where 19 per cent of the 1953 group had had no more than a primary school education, only 2 per cent of the latter group indicated less than secondary school training; 42 per cent held doctoral degrees, compared with 12 per cent of the ex-licensees. A slightly higher proportion (80 per cent) of the 1956 group indicated journalistic experience than the ex-licensees analyzed in 1953 (75 per cent). However, while presumably none of the ex-licensees had been active in journalism during the Nazi period (with

---

[27] A comparison of the characteristics of the two groups will be found in Tables 9.1–9.7, Groups A and B, Press. The second group included the editors or publishers of the following newspapers and periodicals (December 1955 circulation in parentheses): *Schwäbische Landeszeitung* (161,916), *Braunschweiger Zeitung* (120,857), *Ruhr-Nachrichten* (150,000), *Westfälische Rundschau* (248,963), *Rheinische Post* (219,033), *Neue Ruhr-Neue Rhein Zeitung* (259,000), *Westdeutsche Allgemeine* (358,538), *Frankfurter Allgemeine* (166,000), *Frankfurter Neue Presse* (119,025), *Frankfurter Nachtausgabe* (115,280), *Frankfurter Rundschau* (120,000), *Westfalenpost* (122,221), *Bild-Zeitung* (2,436,000), *Hamburger Abendblatt* (304,908), *Hamburger Abendblatt Sonntagsausgabe* (287,472), *Die Welt* (198,358), *Welt am Sonntag* (404,248), *Hannoversche Allgemeine* (115,038), *Hannoversche Presse* (167,127), *Kölnische Rundschau* (156,046), *Mannheimer Morgen* (116,431), *Münchner Merkur* (164,154), *Süddeutsche Zeitung* (205,415), *Nürnberger Nachrichten* (155,194), *Passauer Neue Presse* (100,684), *Stuttgarter Zeitung* (132,201), *Christ und Welt* (72,750), *Deutsche Zeitung und Wirtschaftszeitung* (48,000), *Rheinischer Merkur* (69,000), *Der Spiegel* (230,000) *Aussenpolitik* (2,200), *Das Andere Deutschland* (25,000), *Deutsche Rundschau* (8,500), *Frankfurter Hefte* (15,000), *Die Gegenwart* (14,000).

Directors of the following broadcasting networks were also included in the group: Südwestfunk, Hessischer Rundfunk, Süddeutscher Rundfunk, Radio Bremen, Norddeutscher Rundfunk, Nord- und Westdeutscher Rundfunk und Fernsehverband, Bayrischer Rundfunk.

[28] Pilgert, *Press, Radio and Film in West Germany 1945–1953*, pp. 20–21.

the possible exception of a few former exiles), almost one-third or 29 per cent of the 1956 group indicated journalistic activity during the Nazi period, 33 per cent claimed other activities (including schooling), and 38 per cent simply gave no indication of professional activities during the Third Reich. (The data in the preceding two sentences are based on the smaller Group A.) Only five of the forty-one men in the 1956 group said they had been politically active before 1933. Three had been Social Democrats and two members of the Center party.

The present communications elite includes more young men, born after 1910 than many other foreign policy elites. Almost 10 per cent grew up under the Weimar Republic and 5 per cent spent their impressionable years of adolescence under the Nazi regime. However, only 22 per cent claimed military service, 10 per cent in the First and 12 per cent in the Second World War. Among the most highly selected leaders of the national German press in 1956 as listed in Group A, at least one-third hailed from Communist-controlled German lands, and 5 per cent had been born abroad. The larger group, including more of the editors of regional papers, had a pattern of geographic recruitment very similar to that of the general population. Members of both groups were reticent about religion: 24 per cent of the larger professed to be Protestants, and 20 per cent claimed Roman Catholicism as their denomination, while the rest gave no indication of religious affiliations.

While American efforts during the licensing era had aimed at preventing the reestablishment of large press empires controlled by a few press lords or political leaders, financial difficulties in the post-licensing era led many smaller papers to merge with larger ones. Newspaper chains (*Zeitungsringe*) developed and many of the smaller newspapers became merely local editions of larger papers which provided them with most of their news items and editorials. In 1956, 28 per cent of all German newspapers belonged to newspaper chains, and 54 per cent of the total circulation of all newspapers was taken up by local editions of the major papers (compared with 30 per cent in 1954). However, in the opinion of a leading German authority, this trend toward concentration does not threaten, for the present at least, either the independence or the political pluralism of the German press.[29]

On the whole, German publishers and editors have vigorously asserted their independence against all efforts to impose government controls; in contrast to former times, only a small proportion of newspapers are openly affiliated with political parties or private interest groups. The Adenauer government has both overtly and covertly sought to influence press opinion, particularly through the Press and Information Office of the federal government, but the evidence presently available does not indicate that these

---

[29] Dovifat, in *Die Deutsche Presse*, 1956, pp. 27–36.

efforts have had much success. In general, elite and public opinion appears to be opposed to government efforts to reinstitute anything even remotely resembling the totalitarian control over the press exercised by the Nazi regime.[30] Unfortunately, reliable information and studies concerning more indirect control over German newspapers by political parties and powerful interest groups are lacking. That it exists is indicated by the tendentiousness of many supposedly "independent" papers, and by occasional incidents discussed in periodicals.

The German periodical press itself is far more extensively and openly associated with various interest groups than the newspapers. In 1956, two-thirds of 5,630 periodicals appearing in the Federal Republic were directly affiliated with some political, economic, social, or religious interest group, indicating, in the opinion of a German expert, "the fundamentally political nature of the periodical press."[31]

Openly and covertly, most of the German periodicals are the instruments of interest group elites seeking to mold opinion and influence political developments. The German Chamber of Industry and Commerce in 1956 published 79 periodicals, with a combined circulation of over 400,000; other employers' associations published an additional 97 periodicals, with a combined circulation of over half a million. The League of German Farmers published 38 periodicals, with a combined circulation of almost 1.5 million, while the Confederation of German Trade Unions published 69 periodicals (circulation 7.5 million), the German Employees' Union 23 periodicals (circulation 538,323), and the German Association of Civil Servants 22 periodicals (circulation 892,495). Among religious interest associations, the Protestant Church published 310 periodicals, 267 of which had a combined circulation of 4.7 million, the Roman Catholic Church 221 periodicals, which had a combined circulation of over 10 million. Veterans' Associations published 29 periodicals, with a circulation of 237,750, and Refugee and Expellee Associations published 340 periodicals with a combined circulation of 1.6 million. In comparison with these figures, the overt publications of the major political parties were comparatively few. In 1956 the Christian Democratic Union published 10 periodicals, seven of which had a combined circulation of about 450,000, while the Social Democratic party published 14 periodicals, 12 of which had a combined circulation of almost 400,000.[32]

Far fewer in number and circulation than the overt publications of the interest groups, a number of ostensibly independent journals dealing

[30] In this connection, see M. S. Handler, "Germans Alerted on Press Control," *The New York Times*, June 15, 1954, and "Wenig Beifall für Propaganda-Ausschuss," *Frankfurter Rundschau*, June 13, 1954.

[31] F. Medebach, "Die deutsche Zeitschrift," *Die Deutsche Presse, 1956*, p. 56 f.

[32] Data from *Die Deutsche Presse, 1956*, pp. 38–83.

with political matters appear to have nonetheless considerable influence among the "attentive public" and particularly among important members of elite groups. The influence of Rudolf Augstein, publisher of *Der Spiegel* (circulation 230,000), Rudolf Pechel, publisher of *Die Deutsche Rundschau* (circulation unknown), Benno Reifenberg, publisher of *Die Gegenwart* (circulation 14,000), Herbert von Borch, editor of *Aussen-politik* (circulation 2,200), and a few other editors and publishers of independent political journals appears to be considerable among German opinion leaders and decision makers—far greater than the circulation figures of their periodicals might indicate. On the whole, most of these journals are committed to a pro-Western course in German foreign policy, though in many cases with strong reservations. In particular, many of their editors and publishers often have been highly critical of the close identification of the Adenauer government with American military and foreign policy, and have urged upon the government greater independence and flexibility in the conduct of foreign affairs.

Another Kind of Communications Elite:
the Heads of the Universities

While newspapers, periodicals, and radio serve as media of rapid and direct communication to large numbers, educational institutions communicate more indirectly and slowly to most members of the community outside their own student bodies. Nonetheless, their influence is often pervasive in the long run. Among German educational institutions, the universities play a key role in educating future elite members, and in setting patterns of aspiration and prestige for the whole community. Since the rectors of German universities are chosen by their college and usually serve short terms without reelection, they may serve as an acceptable sample of the most respected and influential faculty members. Accordingly, the rectors of the 38 institutions of higher education (universities, institutes of technology, medical schools), for whom data were available, were analyzed for purposes of comparison with other elite groups.

The rectors are surprisingly young, in comparison with the cabinet, the civil service, the diplomats, and with the average of all elites; and they are strikingly homogeneous in age. A majority were born within a single decade: 58 per cent were born after 1900, but only 5 per cent after 1909. Their geographic origins resemble roughly those of the total population. All are university-educated, but only 79 per cent report doctorates. They are one of the most highly Protestant groups in the country, second only to the military: 50 per cent of the university elite are listed as Protestants, but only 13 per cent as Catholics. Only 6 per cent list any military service, 3 per cent for each World War, respectively. Not a single person in the university elite lists any anti-Nazi records.

CHAPTER 9

Chances for cooperation: Elite
characteristics and possible alignments

The preceding discussion indicates that German foreign policy elites differ in a number of ways from their counterparts in the United States. In the first place, the leaders of civic organizations, such as the foreign policy associations and women's organizations, play a relatively insignificant role in the making and execution of German foreign policy. In the second place, control by the "constituents" of various elites, such as ordinary party and interest group members, over elite members appears to be comparatively weak. To be sure, the rank and file may occasionally compel the leadership to adopt a certain position on issues appearing crucial to its interests, but the size and complexity or organizations headed by important foreign policy elites prevent continuous control and, ordinarily, permit the leaders to operate more or less independently. Last, there appears to be far less competition in the "opinion market" among various foreign policy elites than in the United States owing to the more rigidly stratified, less pluralist character of German society. The almost total compartmentalization of the society into functionally specific organizations designed to look after political, economic, religious, and social interests of various groups in the population leads to formal and informal logrolling arrangements between such groups, designed to achieve the harmonious accomodation of various interests. This traditional German pattern leaves few organizations uncommitted to specific interests; at the same time it allows various elites to command more all-embracing loyalty from their "constituents" to the organizations' interests—as interpreted by them—than is the case among foreign policy elites in the United States.[1]

In our discussion of the German foreign policy elites the point was made earlier that informal bonds between members of different elites tend to be at least as significant in the political process as formal links. Similarities or differences in age, background, and experience, it was stressed, can be as important as formal institutional affiliations in determing common or divergent views toward specific foreign policy issues among members of the elites. Specific links between individuals, such as old friendships and particular experiences shared in common, are difficult to trace,

[1]For some contrasting conditions in the United States, see Almond, *The American People and Foreign Policy*, p. 142.

but informal bonds between different elite groups of a more general kind may be deduced from some of the data about elite members taken from standard German biographies. In particular, it is possible to indicate relevant similarities and differences in background and experiences, which may affect the attitude of different foreign policy elites toward each other and toward foreign policy issues.

The background condition most frequently cited in studies of this sort is social origin. Is the elite aristocratic or middle-class in character? Are there many, few, or any workers among them? One does not have to overstress the significance of class in politics in order to find such information interesting. The political significance of class has been formulated rather happily by one of the most imaginative critics of Karl Marx, the late Joseph Schumpeter, when he wrote:

. . . it is an essential property . . . of the phenomenon of class that the members of one class behave toward one another in a characteristically different manner than they do toward members of other classes; that they maintain closer connections among each other, understand each other better, cooperate more easily, join together among themselves and close ranks against outsiders; that they are looking with similarly predisposed eyes from similar points of view in the same direction into the same segment of the world. . . . Social intercourse within the boundaries of class is fostered by the influence of the identity of manners, of habits, of things valued positively or negatively and considered interesting. In communication across class boundaries, on the contrary, there are differences in all these respects, which repel and inhibit sympathy, so that there is always a larger or smaller territory of delicate topics which must be avoided, and of matters which appear strange or even ridiculous, and which must be labored or paraded and become unnatural and forced. The difference between communication among members of the same class and communication with outsiders is that between swimming with the current and swimming against it.[2]

In the German Federal Republic, these barriers of class have become greatly simplified, compared to the past, and in many cases weaker. In terms of social origins, all elites are now predominantly middle-class, with the exception only of the SPD and trade union leaders. The aristocracy has largely disappeared, and labor has not made a substantial contribution to any elite other than the trade union leaders and the Socialists. For the average of all twelve elites,[3] 70 per cent are of middle-class background, while only 8 per cent bear aristocratic names and 10 per cent indicate some working-class background; for the remaining 12 per cent, no indication as to social origin was found.[4] This contrasts with a middle-

[2] Joseph Schumpeter, "Die sozialen Klassen im ethnisch homogenen Milieu," in *Aufsätze zur Soziologie*, p. 152.

[3] As listed in Tables 9.1–9.7, Group B (excluding State cabinet and Educators) and comprising a total of 418 incumbents of foreign policy elite positions.

[4] The picture holds for domestic matters. An enlarged elite inventory of 529 incumbents—broadened by the addition of members of state cabinets and all heads of German institutions of higher learning, and thus not limited to direct relevance for foreign policy—showed very nearly the same distribution. See Tables 9.1–9.7, Group B, Total elites.

class share of at most 48 per cent in the total adult population of the Federal Republic, and with a small majority, 52 per cent, of workers and rural laborers; far less than one-half of one per cent are aristocrats.[5]

The only elites within which a significant remnant of aristocrats has persisted are the military (19 per cent), the diplomats (17 per cent), and, at some distance, the federal cabinet (12 per cent) and the higher civil service (9 per cent). The press elite is just average, with 7 per cent bearing noble names. The remainder of aristocratic elite members is fairly evenly diffused. Almost every other elite includes at least one nobleman. This is true even of the Social Democrats and the trade union leaders; only the legislative leaders and the Roman Catholic bishops lack this distinction.

Workers have been at best a source of minority recruitment, mainly for the SPD (48 per cent), the trade union leaders (38 per cent), and the CDU elite (22 per cent). The legislative leaders, of whom 30 per cent indicate working-class origin, reflect, of course, the elite composition of the major parties. The state cabinets with a working class share of 14 per cent and the federal cabinet with 12 per cent of working-class background lag conspicuously behind the composition of the leading bodies of the major parties. Among the other elites, only the Roman Catholic bishops report two men—10 per cent—of labor background.

The rest of the German foreign policy elites seem to have remained as impermeable to persons of working-class origin as they have ever been. The press elite and the university leaders each include just one man of labor background. There is not a trace of working-class background about any member of the remaining elites: the diplomats, the military, the civil servants, the employers, and the Protestant church leaders. While opportunities and recruitment patterns may have broadened in other respects, the old social segmentation of German leadership has persisted, and not least so in the executive branch of the Bonn government and in most of the foreign policy elites.

Other background characteristics are more widely distributed, and may have a bearing on attitudes to foreign policy issues, now or in the future. Thus, geographic origins may well be an important element in determining the attitude and behavior of various foreign policy elites toward such vital issues as German reunification, the recovery of German lands presently under Soviet and Polish administration, European integration, and cooperation with the Western powers. Perhaps most significant in terms of the geographic origins of elite members is the under-representation of Southern and Northern Germany among all elites, the preponderance of natives of industrial Western Germany among some

[5] *Jahrbuch II*, p. xliv. However, in 1954, 17 per cent of the members of the Bundestag Committee on Foreign Affairs bore aristocratic names. The next highest parliamentary committee in this respect was that on All-German Affairs, with 10 per cent. From lists in Fritz Sanger, *Handbuch des deutschen Bundestages* (Stuttgart, Cotta, 1954), pp. 174–97.

elites, and the large number of natives of Communist-controlled Central and East Germany among others. These differences are not large, though they are discernible, for the average of all elites.[6]

In 1956, the preponderance of West Germans—35 per cent of the total population—was conspicuous among the legislative elite (50 per cent), the trade union leaders (50 per cent), the CDU elite (48 per cent), the federal cabinet (47 per cent), and the Roman Catholic hierarchy (40 per cent). By contrast, natives of Central and Eastern Germany— 23 per cent of the adult population and 26 per cent of the total population—were strongly represented in the Social Democratic leadership (41 per cent) and among the military elite (41 per cent). Other factors being equal, common geographical roots might be significant in determining a common attitude toward important foreign policy issues among members of elites in which West or Central and East Germans are particularly numerous and might serve to divide them from other elite members.

Two other types of experiences appear to be of particular significance insofar as personal memories may influence the attitude and behavior of elite members toward foreign policy issues and toward each other. The first of these is the formative impact of the sociopolitical environment during the important years of adolescence, which is generally recognized as having an important influence upon political attitudes in adulthood. The second experience which may significantly affect behavior and attitudes pertains to the past behavior of elite members toward the Nazi regime.

In terms of all her foreign policy elites, Germany is not governed by old men. Only 11 per cent of all elite members were born before 1890, which is somewhat below the 14 per cent average for the entire adult population. These older men—now well past their middle sixties—spent their adolescence in the era of the rise of the autocratic German Empire to the position of a world power. Members of this generation are rapidly disappearing from most elites, largely because of death or retirement.

The old men are more strongly entrenched, however, in particular elites. In 1956 they were particularly well represented among leading businessmen (24 per cent), the Roman Catholic hierarchy (20 per cent), and the federal cabinet (18 per cent)—all groups not affected by mandatory retirement rules. On the other hand, only 5 per cent of the leading diplomats, 3 per cent of the SPD leadership, and not one of the military elite belonged to this generation.

Leadership is predominantly exercised by men in late middle age, somewhere between 45 and 65. In 1956 nearly three-fourths of all elite members belonged to the generations born between 1890 and 1909. Thirty-six per cent were born between 1890 and 1899 and another 36

6 See Tables 9.1–9.7, pp. 133–40.

per cent in the decade following—compared with 14 and 19 per cent, respectively, for the entire adult population of the country.

As these figures show, the generation born between 1890 and 1899 is most strongly overrepresented. It is the generation that was decimated by the First World War and embittered by its aftermath. The memories of their adolescent years are rooted in the period of the decade immediately preceding the First World War—characterized by an aggressive though vacillating foreign policy on the part of the autocratic leaders of the Wilhelmian Empire—and the early years of that war, when Germany seemed to be winning. By 1918–19, when Germany lost, the adolescence of this group was largely over; their personalities had to a large extent been formed, and they had to live a postwar world of the 1920's to which their personalities had often not been fully adjusted. Some of them responded by concentrating their efforts on some special world of professional interest, others joined Nazi or Communist protest movements in the 1920's and early 1930's and, with the defeat or decline of these movements, lost their chance for an elite career in the new Bonn Republic. This generation was most strongly represented among the leaders of the Protestant Church (56 per cent), the diplomatic elite (45 per cent), and the employers (40 per cent). It was weakest among the military (17 per cent) and the SPD (28 per cent).

The adolescent years of the generation born between 1900 and 1909 coincided roughly with the turbulent era which witnessed the military defeat and collapse of Imperial Germany, revolution, civil strife, foreign occupation of portions of Germany, and the desperate efforts of the founders of the Weimar Republic to establish a lasting democratic order in Germany. A large portion of the members of this generation had been indifferent toward the Republic, or even hostile, particularly when inflation or depression shocked them into political activity. Many were willing to believe that Germany had lost the war because it had been "stabbed in the back" by traitors at home and humiliated by the victors' peace terms, many had joined the rabidly nationalistic Nazi movement, which received from them initial mass support. Another part of the same generation defended the Weimar Republic at the risk of sacrifice; but whether as cynics or as defenders, few or none could take the Republic simply and pleasantly for granted. Among the foreign policy elites, this generation is most strongly represented within the military elite (57 per cent) and the Social Democratic leadership (52 per cent). In contrast with the SPD leaders, few, if any, of the military may be presumed to have been strong supporters of the Weimar Republic. This generation is also well represented among the top diplomats (50 per cent) and the trade union leaders (44 per cent). It was relatively weak among the CDU leaders (26 per cent), the Protestant churchmen (28 per cent), and the business elite (32 per cent).

Only 11 per cent of the members of the 1956 foreign policy elites belonged to the important generation born between 1910 and 1919—as against 16 per cent of the adult population. Merely one per cent were born after 1919 and none later than 1929—compared with approximately 27 per cent of the adult population. This is the generation whose members were largely adolescents when the democratic Weimar Republic succumbed to the onslaught of its domestic enemies. Its younger members were youths when Hitler came to power; in the Nazi youth organization and, subsequently, in the compulsory labor and military service, they were more thoroughly exposed to intensive Nazi indoctrination than the members of any other generation represented in the contemporary German foreign policy elites. These had been the youths who witnessed the dictator's unhindered progress toward world conquest. Later, past their adolescence, they marched to war at his command in 1939—first to conquer and then to be defeated in a bitter and savage struggle. Almost one-fourth of the military elite and over one-fifth of the CDU elite belonged to this generation in 1956. Its members were also relatively numerous within the cabinet (18 per cent) and the Social Democratic leadership (17 per cent), in comparison with the average for all elites and the adult population. On the other hand, none of the diplomats and none of the Protestant leaders, and only 4 per cent of the business elite had been born later than 1909.

The post-1919 generation was represented in only three elites, the press elite (5 per cent), the legislative leadership (2 per cent), and the military elite (2 per cent).

All the members of the present foreign policy elites share memories and experiences of the Nazi era and witnessed as adults, first, the success of Nazi foreign policy, and, subsequently, its catastrophic consequences. With but few exceptions, elite members experienced totalitarian rule and war at first hand—at the front or in the allied bombing raids that devastated most German cities—and memories of these experiences undoubtedly influence their present attitude and behavior in matters of foreign and military policy. These memories have not made them think all alike about specific policies, such as EDC or German national rearmament, but they have given most of them a deep aversion to slogans, romantic gestures, and any policies of reckless adventure.

Many elite members served the National Socialist regime in an official capacity, particularly members of the diplomatic, military, and civil service elites. On the other hand, certain elites include a significant number of members with a major anti-Nazi record, men who were imprisoned or lived in exile in the Nazi era. While at most 2 per cent of the present population are believed to have a major record of opposition to the Hitler dictatorship, 23 per cent of the foreign policy elites have such a record; 13 per cent were arrested and imprisoned by the regime and 4 per cent were in exile, and 6 per cent reported other forms of persecution during the Third Reich. The Social Democratic leaders have by far the strongest record of opposition (70 per cent), followed by the Protestant leaders (44 per cent) and the CDU elite (39 per cent). The CDU elite had the largest number of individuals arrested by the Nazis (35 per cent), followed by the Protestant leaders (33 per cent), the press elite (32 per cent), and the SPD leaders (26 per cent). On the other hand, the Social Democratic leadership included more exiles by far than any other group (33 per cent). No former exiles belonged to the CDU and to most other elites—even though a good number of Germans of elite caliber had been in exile.

There was no elite group among those analyzed for 1956 which did not include at least one former opponent of the Hitler regime. However, certain elites—such as the press elite and the business elite—included no more than one or two men who included in their official biographies data on anti-Nazi activities. None of the Roman Catholic bishops and archbishops, none of the senior civil servants, and only two of the military leaders claimed to have been arrested by the Nazis. On the other hand, close to one-fifth of the senior civil servants, and almost as large a proportion of the cabinet members, had held prominent positions in the Third Reich.

Similarities or differences in education and religious affiliation may also play a role in determining the relations of different elite members toward each other and toward foreign policy issues. Seventy per cent of all elite members indicated in their official biographies that they had attended a university—compared with only 4 per cent of the adult population of the Federal Republic. Thirty-three per cent of all elite members held doctoral degrees. In contrast to the 84 per cent of the adult population who had only a primary school education, merely 8 per cent of the elite members had not gone beyond *Volksschule*.

The proportion of university-trained elite members and holders of doctorates varied considerably. Not surprisingly, the religious elites were among the most highly educated. The Roman Catholic hierarchy was entirely university-educated in 1956, and 85 per cent of its members held doctorates. The Protestant leaders were also entirely university-trained, and one-third of their number held doctorates. As the Federal Republic has adhered to the traditionally high educational standards required of diplomats and high civil servants, it was also not surprising that 97 per cent of the diplomats proved to be university-educated, and 81 per cent the holders of doctorates. Of the top civil servants, 93 per cent were university-trained and 63 per cent possessed doctorates. Other highly educated elites included the Adenauer cabinet (83 per cent of its members had attended university and 35 per cent held doctorates) and the press elite (76 per cent university and 42 per cent with doctorates).

Among the elites with the least amount of formal education were the top trade union officials and the Social Democratic leaders. Almost two-thirds of the former and better than one-fourth of the latter group had only had a primary school education; another one-third of the Social Democratic leaders had no more than a secondary school education.

Between these polarities of highly educated and relatively poorly educated elites stood the military elite (69 per cent of whose members had had a secondary school education and 31 per cent had attended university [including 9 per cent with doctor's degrees]), and the legislative and business elites (each with 66 per cent university-trained members). The CDU elite showed once again the integrative, cross-class character of the party: 70 per cent were university-educated, but as many as 17 per cent had had only a primary education.

Summed up somewhat differently, the elites with the largest share of self-made men who had risen from a mere grade school education were all more or less political in character. These were the trade union leaders, and the SPD, CDU, and legislative elites. The highest proportions of secondary school graduates were among the military and the SPD. All other elites were dominated by university men. Politics and the military life still seem to offer the best chance for elite status to those Germans who lack the relatively rare good fortune of a university education.

More difficult to determine is the religious affiliation of elite members. Roughly, 37 per cent of those investigated failed to indicate any religious preference in their official biographies. Thirty-eight per cent listed themselves as Protestants and 23 per cent said they were Roman Catholics. Among other than religious elites, professed Protestants predominated heavily over Roman Catholics among the military (83 per cent as against 13 per cent Catholics), the legislative elite (43 per cent Protestants, 34 per cent Roman Catholics), and the Social Democrats (35 per cent Protestants, with no indication for the rest). Professed Protestants also outnumbered Roman Catholics among the diplomats (27 against 12 per cent, respectively), the business elite (24 against 13 per cent), and the press leaders (24 against 20 per cent, respectively). On the other hand, Roman Catholics strongly predominated within the CDU elite (65 per cent as against 35 per cent Protestants) and in the Adenauer cabinet (53 per cent, as against 41 per cent Protestants), despite official claims of the completely interdenominational character of the governing party. The trade union leaders and the civil service elite were in 1956 roughly evenly divided between professed members of the two major churches.

Indications of military service in either the First or Second World War, or both, might also provide some interesting clues to attitudes and relationships among the foreign policy elites, but here official information is rather scanty. Sixty-nine per cent of all adult men in the Federal Republic are veterans, 15 per cent of the First World War, 48 per cent of the Second, and 6 per cent of both. By way of contrast, over 62 per cent of all elite members investigated failed to indicate any military service in the biographical data they provided for standard references (see list of sources, Table 9.1). All the military leaders, of course, claimed such service—all in the Second World War and 19 per cent in both wars. Government leaders stressed their war experience; 71 per cent of the members of the 1956 Adenauer cabinet claimed military service (47 per cent in the First and 24 per cent in the Second World War), as did 61 per cent of the CDU elite (39 per cent in the First, 22 per cent in the Second World War). On the other hand, only 11 per cent of the employers' elite, 19 per cent of the top diplomats, 22 per cent of the press leaders, and 28 per cent of the Social Democratic leaders claimed military service in either war.

In late 1958, all major interests groups and elites, except the trade unions and the Social Democrats, were lined up in support of the strongly pro-Western policies of the Adenauer government. This alignment seems likely to persist. It appears more stable, and more acceptable to the elites concerned than any alternative that can now be seen as practical.

Yet even that which is stable is not necessarily eternal. Pressures for a revision of foreign policy and a realignment of elites have been ineffective but persistent. Changes in political or economic conditions in Germany or in the world at large could give them added strength, and some elites are less solidly anchored than others, in terms of their own structure and composition, to an all-out pro-Western course in foreign affairs. Among persons from Northern and Central Germany, among diplomats and soldiers, and among Protestants and Social Democrats there are signficant groups who are more concerned about German reunification, and somewhat less concerned about close formal ties to a Western military alliance, than the Adenauer government has been. If greater risks and sacrifices should be demanded of Germany by her Western allies, if more attractive offers should be made by the Soviet Union, or if Western prosperity and economic cooperation should falter, some of these elites might well urge some reconsiderations and readjustments of the course of German foreign policy.

The chances for such readjustments in the near future are hard to judge. They are small, but not small enough to be ignored.

A tabulation of the interest group data that might be relevant for assessing the background conditions for any such interest group alignments are given in Tables 9.1–9.7; and a comparison of German cabinets, indicating some of the changes of elite alignments that have occurred in the past, is presented in Table 9.8.

TABLE 9.1*

SOME GERMAN FOREIGN POLICY ELITES—AGE STRUCTURE

(Comparative Data in Rounded Percentages)

	Total No. Analyzed	Before 1890	1891–1900	1901–10	1911–20	1921–30	1931–40	1941–	NI	Total
Population:										
Total, 1954	49.8	11	11	15	12	13	16	22	0	100
Over 14 yrs., 1954 ...	38.9	14	14	19	16	17	20	0	0	100
18 yrs. and over, 1955	36.8	14	15	20	17	20	15	0	0	100
GROUP A										
Total elites	250	17	36	36	10	1	0	0	0	100
Admin. elites:										
Diplomats, 1954	44	27	50	23	0	0	0	0	0	100
Civil serv., 1956	8	0	63	38	0	0	0	0	0	100
Military, 1956	31	0	19	48	32	0	0	0	0	100
Political elites:										
CDU, 1956	23	26	30	26	17	0	0	0	0	100
SPD, 1956	27	4	30	56	11	0	0	0	0	100
Cabinet, 1956	20	20	35	35	10	0	0	0	0	100
State cabinet, 1956..	—	—	—	—	—	—	—	—	—	—
Legislature, 1954 ...	21	10	38	38	14	0	0	0	0	100
Interest group elites:										
Economic, 1956										
Employers	8	20	50	30	0	0	0	0	0	100
Employees	9	45	11	44	0	0	0	0	0	100
Religious, 1956										
Protestants	14	14	57	29	0	0	0	0	0	100
Roman Catholics..	22	27	27	41	5	0	0	0	0	100
Communications elites:										
Press, 1956	21	19	33	29	10	10	0	0	0	100
Educators, 1956	—	—	—	—	—	—	—	—	—	—
GROUP B[a]										
Total elites	529	10	35	42	11	1	0	0	1	100
Minus state cabinet										
and educators	418	11	37	41	11	1	0	0	1	100
Admin. elites:										
Diplomats, 1956	42	5	45	50	0	0	0	0	0	100
Civil serv., 1956	67	6	42	40	9	0	0	0	3	100
Military, 1957	54	0	17	57	24	2	0	0	0	100
Political elites:										
CDU, 1956	23	17	35	26	22	0	0	0	0	100
SPD, 1956	29	3	28	52	17	0	0	0	0	100
Cabinet, 1956	17	18	29	35	18	0	0	0	0	100
State cabinet, 1956..	73	10	32	40	15	0	0	0	4	100
Legislature, 1956 ...	44	14	39	34	11	2	0	0	0	100
Interest group elites:										
Economic, 1956										
Employers	47	24	40	32	44	0	0	0	0	100
Employees	16	13	31	44	13	0	0	0	0	100
Religious, 1956										
Protestants	18	15	56	28	0	0	0	0	0	100
Roman Catholics..	20	20	35	40	5	0	0	0	0	100
Communications elites:										
Press, 1956	41	15	34	37	10	5	0	0	0	100
Educators	38	5	37	53	5	0	0	0	0	100

* Sources, Tables 9.1–9.7: *Taschenbuch des öffentlichen Lebens* (1956, 1957); *Statistisches Jahrbuch für die Bundes-republik Deutschland* (1956); *Who's Who in Germany* (1956); *Wer Ist's* (1955); *Amtliches Handbuch des deutschen Bundestages* (1953); *Das Wehrarchiv* (1956–57); A. Köhler, *Die Bundesrepublik* (1954/55, 1956/57), *Handbuch für die Bundesrepublik Deutschland* (1953, 1954); *Taschenbuch für Wehrfragen* (1956); *Die Deutsche Presse* (1956); H. Tross-man, *Der Zweite Deutsche Bundestag* (1954); *Jahrbuch I and Jahrbuch II*; *International Who's Who* (1957); British Ministry of Economic Warfare, *Who's Who in Nazi Germany* (1944).

a In Elite Sample B age structure was calculated in terms of the following age groups: 1880–1889, 1890–1899, 1900–1909, 1910–1919, 1920–1929, and 1930 and over. This may have distorted the comparison slightly and more seriously in the oldest age groups, where fixed retirement age may be relevant.

TABLE 9.2

SOME GERMAN FOREIGN POLICY ELITES—GEOGRAPHIC ORIGIN
(Comparative Data in Rounded Percentages)

	Total No. Analyzed	Western Germany[a]	Northern Germany[b]	Southern Germany[c]	Cent. & East Germany[d]	Abroad[e]	Not Available	Total
Population:								
Total, 1954............	49.8	35	15	24	26	0	0	100
Over 14, 1954..........	38.9	—	—	—	—	—	—	—
18 and over, 1955......	36.8	——————77——————			23	0	0	100
GROUP A								
Total elites..............	36.8	——————77——————			23	0	0	100
Admin. elites:								
Diplomats, 1954........	44	41	14	8	36	0	0	100
Civil serv., 1956........	8	63	13	0	0	0	25	100
Military, 1956.........	31	26	10	23	42	0	0	100
Political elites:								
CDU, 1956............	23	48	0	44	4	4	0	100
SPD, 1956.............	27	33	11	11	41	4	0	100
Cabinet, 1956..........	20	50	0	20	30	0	0	100
State cabinet, 1956.....	—	—	—	—	—	—	—	—
Legislature, 1954.......	21	43	0	29	19	10	0	100
Interest group elites:								
Economic, 1956								
Employers	8	50	0	10	40	0	0	100
Employees	9	56	11	33	0	0	0	100
Religious, 1956								
Protestants	14	14	36	7	36	0	7	100
Roman Catholics.....	22	50	5	41	5	0	0	100
Communications elites:								
Press, 1956............	21	19	19	19	33	5	5	100
Educators, 1956........	—	—	—	—	—	—	—	—
GROUP B								
Total elites..............	529	34	14	20	22	5	5	100
Minus state cabinet and educators.......	418	35	12	20	24	6	4	100
Admin. elites:								
Diplomats, 1956........	42	31	12	12	29	2	14	100
Civil serv., 1956........	67	36	15	15	25	3	6	100
Military, 1957.........	54	22	6	20	41	7	4	100
Political elites:								
CDU, 1956............	23	48	0	39	4	9	0	100
SPD, 1956.............	29	28	14	10	41	7	0	100
Cabinet, 1956..........	17	47	0	24	29	0	0	100
State cabinet, 1956.....	73	26	27	22	10	4	11	100
Legislature, 1956.......	44	50	9	27	9	5	0	100
Interest group elites:								
Economic, 1956								
Employers	47	38	9	19	21	11	2	100
Employees	16	50	19	13	19	0	0	100
Religious, 1956								
Protestants	18	22	33	17	22	7	0	100
Roman Catholics.....	20	40	10	40	5	0	5	100
Communications elites:								
Press, 1956............	41	27	17	20	20	10	5	100
Educators, 1956........	38	29	18	21	24	5	3	100

[a] Including Rhineland, Westphalia, Lippe, Hesse, Saar.
[b] Including Schleswig-Holstein, Hamburg, Oldenburg, Bremen, Hanover, Brunswik.
[c] Including Bavaria, Baden-Württemberg.
[d] Including Berlin, Brandenburg, Pomerania, Silesia, East Prussia, Mecklenburg, Saxony, and Thuringia, as well as "Volksdeutsche" from Eastern and Southeastern Europe (but not Austria).
[e] Including Austria.

TABLE 9.3

SOME GERMAN FOREIGN POLICY ELITES—RELIGION

(Comparative Data in Rounded Percentages)

	Total No. Analyzed	Protestant	Roman Catholic	Other and None[a]	NA and NI	Total
Population:						
Total, 1954	49.8	51	45	4	0	100
Over 14, 1954	38.9	—	—	—	—	—
18 and over, 1955	36.8	52	44	4	0	100
	GROUP A					
Total elites	250	39	34	0	28	100
Admin. elites:						
Diplomats, 1954	44	41	27	0	32	100
Civil serv., 1956	8	13	13	0	75	100
Military, 1956	31	77	16	0	7	100
Political elites:						
CDU, 1956	23	26	74	0	0	100
SPD, 1956	27	33	0	0	67	100
Cabinet, 1956	20	40	50	0	10	100
State cabinet, 1956	—	—	—	—	—	—
Legislature, 1954	21	19	43	0	38	100
Interest group elites:						
Economic, 1956						
Employers	10	50	0	0	50	100
Employees	9	0	44	0	56	100
Religious, 1956						
Protestants	14	100	0	0	0	100
Roman Catholics	22	0	100	0	0	100
Communications elites:						
Press, 1956	21	38	19	0	43	100
Educators, 1956	0	0	0			
	GROUP B					
Total elites	529	37	21	1	40	100
Minus state cabinet and educators	418	38	23	1	37	100
Admin. elites:						
Diplomats, 1956	42	27	12	0	60	100
Civil serv., 1956	67	22	18	2	58	100
Military, 1957	54	83	13	0	4	100
Political elites:						
CDU, 1956	23	35	65	0	0	100
SPD, 1956	29	35	0	9	55	100
Cabinet, 1956	17	41	53	0	6	100
State cabinet, 1956	73	27	11	1	60	100
Legislature, 1956	44	43	34	5	18	100
Interest group elites:						
Economic, 1956						
Employers	47	24	13	0	64	100
Employees	16	12	12	12	63	100
Religious, 1956						
Protestants	18	100	0	0	0	100
Roman Catholics	20	0	100	0	0	100
Communications elites:						
Press, 1956	41	24	20	0	56	100
Educators, 1956	38	50	13	0	37	100

[a] Including Jews and "no affiliation."

135

TABLE 9.4

SOME GERMAN FOREIGN POLICY ELITES—EDUCATION[a]

(Comparative Data in Rounded Percentages)

	Total No. Analyzed	Primary	Secondary	University	Doctorate	NA and NI	Total
Population:							
Total, 1954..............	49.8	—	—	—	—	—	—
Over 14, 1954...........	38.9	—	—	—	—	—	—
18 and over, 1955.......	36.8	84	12	4	na	na	100
GROUP A							
Total elites...............	250	9	20	26	42	3	100
Admin. elites:							
Diplomats, 1954.........	44	0	2	18	80	0	100
Civil serv., 1956........	8	0	0	38	50	13	100
Military, 1956..........	31	0	81	10	10	0	100
Political elites:							
CDU, 1956.............	23	17	9	35	35	4	100
SPD, 1956..............	27	22	37	18	18	4	100
Cabinet, 1956..........	20	10	10	35	45	0	100
State cabinet, 1956......	—	—	—	—	—	—	—
Legislature, 1954........	21	19	14	29	33	5	100
Interest group elites:							
Economic, 1956							
Employers	8	10	10	40	40	0	100
Employees	9	44	22	11	11	11	100
Religious, 1956							
Protestants	14	0	0	64	36	0	100
Roman Catholics......	22	15	0	18	73	5	100
Communications elites:							
Press, 1956.............	21	0	14	38	38	10	100
GROUP B							
Total elites...............	529	8	15	27	43	7	100
Minus state cabinet and educators........	418	8	17	36	33	6	100
Admin. elites:							
Diplomats, 1956.........	42	2	0	17	81	0	100
Civil serv., 1956.........	67	0	3	30	63	5	100
Military, 1957..........	54	0	69	22	9	0	100
Political elites:							
CDU, 1956.............	23	17	9	39	30	4	100
SPD, 1956..............	29	28	31	21	14	7	100
Cabinet, 1956...........	17	12	6	47	35	0	100
State cabinet, 1956......	73	14	15	25	33	14	100
Legislature, 1956........	44	11	18	32	34	5	100
Interest group elites:							
Economic, 1956							
Employers	47	2	11	23	44	21	100
Employees	16	63	0	13	0	25	100
Religious, 1956							
Protestants	18	0	0	67	33	0	100
Roman Catholics......	20	0	0	15	85	0	100
Communications elites:							
Press, 1956.............	41	2	15	34	42	7	100
Educators, 1956.........	38	0	0	21	79	0	100

[a] "Primary" education in Germany ends at 14 years, somewhat equivalent to junior high school in the United States. "Secondary" education has two levels: *Mittlere Reife*, which corresponds to the eleventh grade in high school, and *Abitur*, which corresponds to graduating from junior college.

For the population at large, the only readily available data came from polls of the population above 18 years in the Federal Republic, including West Berlin, between 1947 and 1956. (*Jahrbuch II*, p. 4.) These poll data have been used to put under "secondary" (*Mittlere Reife*) persons with the equivalent of 11 years of schooling, and under "university" persons with the quivalent of junior college (*Abitur*), which made them eligible for university study, whether they eventually did attend a university or not. These data are not quite comparable with the biographical data for elite members, which may count persons with the mere *Abitur* as having had only a "secondary education," and which count under "university" only those persons who after their *Abitur* actually became university students.

TABLE 9.5

Some German Foreign Policy Elites—Military Service
(Comparative Data in Rounded Percentages)

	Total No. Analyzed	World War I	World War II	Both I and II	NI	Total
Population:						
Total, 1954...................	49.8	—	—	—	—	—
Over 14, 1954...............	38.9	—	—	—	—	—
18 and over, 1955[a]..........	36.8	15	48	6	31	100
GROUP A						
Total elites....................	250	14	24	4	58	100
Admin. elites:						
Diplomats, 1954..............	44	23	2	5	70	100
Civil serv., 1956..............	8	38	25	0	38	100
Military, 1956...............	31	0	81	19	0	100
Political elites:						
CDU, 1956...................	23	35	26	0	39	100
SPD, 1956...................	27	7	22	0	70	100
Cabinet, 1956................	20	45	25	0	30	100
State cabinet, 1956..........	—	—	—	—	—	—
Legislature, 1954.............	21	5	38	5	52	100
Interest group elites:						
Economic, 1956						
Employers	8	10	0	0	90	100
Employees	9	0	11	0	89	100
Religious, 1956						
Protestants	14	7	7	0	86	100
Roman Catholics...........	22	0	9	0	91	100
Communications elites:						
Press, 1956..................	21	0	14	0	86	100
GROUP B						
Total elites....................	529	12	21	2	65	100
Minus state cabinet						
and educators.............	418	13	24	2	62	100
Admin. elites:						
Diplomats, 1956..............	42	12	2	5	81	100
Civil serv., 1956..............	67	10	13	0	76	100
Military, 1957...............	54	0	100	0	0	100
Political elites:						
CDU, 1956...................	23	39	22	0	39	100
SPD, 1956...................	29	10	14	3	72	100
Cabinet, 1956................	17	47	24	0	29	100
State cabinet, 1956..........	73	11	22	3	64	100
Legislature, 1956............	44	21	23	9	48	100
Interest group elites:						
Economic, 1956						
Employers	47	6	4	0	89	100
Employees	16	6	19	6	69	100
Religious, 1956						
Protestants	18	18	5	0	78	100
Roman Catholics...........	20	0	5	0	95	100
Communications elites:						
Press, 1956..................	41	10	12	0	78	100
Educators, 1956..............	38	3	3	0	95	100

[a] Estimated for male population over 18 in 1956 from data in *Jahrbuch II*, pp. 4–5.

TABLE 9.6
SOME GERMAN FOREIGN POLICY ELITES—ANTI-NAZI RECORD
(*Comparative Data in Rounded Percentages*)

	Total No. Analyzed	Political Activity				Political Persecution			
		Nazi Era Elites[a]	Anti-Nazi[b]	NI	Total	Arrest, Prison	Exile	NI	Total
Population:									
Total, 1954	49.8								
Over 14, 1954	38.9								
18 and over, 1955	36.8					2[c]	0.1[d]	97.9[d]	100
GROUP A									
Total elites	250	—	—	—	—	16	6	77	100
Admin. elites:									
Diplomats, 1954	44					2	5	93	100
Civil serv., 1956	8					0	0	100	100
Military, 1956	31					3	0	97	100
Political elites:									
CDU, 1956	23					35	0	65	100
SPD, 1956	27					26	33	41	100
Cabinet, 1956	20					15	0	85	100
State cabinet, 1956	—	—	—	—	—	—	—	—	—
Legislature, 1954	21					14	14	71	100
Interest group elites:									
Economic, 1956									
Employers	8					10	0	90	100
Employees	9					33	0	67	100
Religious, 1956									
Protestants	14					64	0	36	100
Roman Catholics	22	0				0	0	100	100
Communications elites:									
Press, 1956	21					14	5	81	100
GROUP B									
Total elites	529	5	20	75	100	12	4	85	100
Minus state cabinet and educators	418	6	23	72	100	13	4	83	100
Admin. elites:									
Diplomats, 1956	42	10	21	69	100	10	2	88	100
Civil serv., 1956	67	19	12	69	100	1	1	98	100
Military, 1957	54		6	94	100	4	0	96	100
Political elites:									
CDU, 1956	23	4	39	57	100	35	0	65	100
SPD, 1956	29	0	69	31	100	26	33	41	100
Cabinet, 1956	17	18	18	65	100	24	0	77	100
State cabinet, 1956	73	3	18	80	100	10	2	87	100
Legislature, 1956	44	0	23	77	100	14	5	82	100
Interest group elites:									
Economic, 1956									
Employers	47	6	2	92	100	4	0	96	100
Employees	16		31	69	100	25	0	75	100
Religious, 1956									
Protestants	18		44	56	100	33	0	67	100
Roman Catholics	20	0	5	95	100	0	0	100	100
Communications elites:									
Press, 1956	41	2	42	56	100	32	5	63	100
Educators, 1956	38		0	100	100	0	0	100	100

[a] Members of Nazi political elite (Nazi party and affiliated organizations) and of Nazi nonpolitical elite (bureaucratic, communications, economic, and educational elite positions, as defined in this study). Data from British Ministry of Economic Warfare, *Who's Who in Germany and Austria* (1945), and from other biographical reference works listed under Sources, Tables 9.1–9.7, page 239.

[b] Members of anti-Nazi organizations and others with anti-Nazi resistance records.

[c] Estimated from data in G. Weisenborn, *Der lautlose Aufstand* (Hamburg, 1953), pp. 38–40, 255.

[d] About 300,000 Germans are estimated to have sought refuge abroad from Nazi persecution, but no more than 30,000 of these may be presumed to have returned. Cf. Lewis J. Edinger, *German Exile Politics* (Berkeley and Los Angeles, 1956), pp. 205–7.

TABLE 9.7

SOME GERMAN FOREIGN POLICY ELITES—SOCIAL ORIGIN
(Comparative Data in Rounded Percentages)

	Total No. Analyzed	Aristocracy	Middle Class	Labor	NI	Total
Population:						
Total, 1954....................	49.8					
Over 14, 1954.................	38.9					
18 and over, 1955.............	36.8	—	48	52		100
GROUP A						
Total elites......................	250	—	—	—	—
Admin. elites:						
Diplomats, 1954...............	44					
Civil serv., 1956...............	8					
Military, 1956.................	31					
Political elites:						
CDU, 1956....................	23					
SPD, 1956....................	27					
Cabinet, 1956.................	20					
State cabinet, 1956............	—					
Legislature, 1954..............	21					
Interest group elites:						
Economic, 1956						
Employers	8					
Employees	9					
Religious, 1956						
Protestants	14					
Roman Catholics.............	22					
Communications elites:						
Press, 1956....................	21					
GROUP B						
Total elites......................	529	7	68	10	15	100
Minus state cabinet and educators...............	418	8	70	10	12	100
Admin. elites:						
Diplomats, 1956...............	42	17	83	0	0	100
Civil serv., 1956...............	67	9	79	0	12	100
Military, 1957.................	54	19	81	0	0	100
Political elites:						
CDU, 1956....................	23	4	74	22		100
SPD, 1956....................	29	3	28	48	21	100
Cabinet, 1956.................	17	12	71	12	5	100
State cabinet, 1956............	73	3	60	14	23	100
Legislature, 1956..............	44	0	68	30	2	100
Interest group elites:						
Economic, 1956						
Employers	47	2	79	0	19	100
Employees	16	6	25	38	31	100
Religious, 1956						
Protestants	18	6	67	0	28	100
Roman Catholics.............	20	0	55	10	35	100
Communications elites:						
Press, 1956....................	41	7	68	2	22	100
Educators, 1956...............	38	8	66	2	24	100

ᵃ From *Jahrbuch II*, p. xliv. The proportions given are based on extrapolated German census data. Workers (48.2 per cent) and rural laborers (3.6 per cent) were lumped together as "labor." All other occupations— farmers, white-collar employees, public officials, self-employed, "in trade and commerce," and "free professions" —were lumped together under middle class. If white-collar employees had been counted as labor—which most of them would find distasteful—the proportion of "labor" would amount to 69 per cent.

TABLES 9.1–9.7

CATEGORIES

	Group A		Group B	
	Criteria	Number	Criteria	Number
Administrative elite:				
Diplomats (where data available)	Chiefs of mission and top administrators, 7/1954	44	Chiefs of mission, 12/31/1956	42
Civil service (where data available)	"Staatssekretäre" of ministries concerned with foreign affairs, 7/1956	8	"Staatssekretäre" and division chiefs of all ministries, 12/1956	67
Military	Officers on active duty, rank of major and above, listed in *Wehrarchiv*, 12/1956	31	Officers on active duty, rank of major and above, listed in *Wehrarchiv*, 7/1957	54
Political elite: CDU/CSU	CDU/CSU members of cabinet and parliamentary leaders of CDU/CSU, 7/1956	23	Same 12/31/1956	23
SPD	SPD Executive Committee, 9/1956	27	Same	29
Cabinet	8/1956	20	12/1956	17
State cabinet	———	—	Members of all state cabinets for which biographical data available	73
Legislature	Officers of BT, leaders of 3 major parties, and 8 chairmen of committees concerned with FP	21	Officers of BT, leaders of 2 major parties, chairmen of all committees	44
Interest group elites: Employers	Directors and board chairmen, 8 leading trade associations, 1956	8	Directors or board chairmen, 47 major employers' associations, 1956	47
Employees	6 TU leaders, 2 farm leaders, 1 artisan leader, 1956	9	Leaders of DGB and smaller TU's, 1956	16
Protestants	Principal lay (2) and religious leaders (12) of EKD, 1956	14	Principal religious leaders of EKD, 1956	18
Roman Catholics	Archbishops, bishops, and principal lay leaders (4), 1956	22	Archbishops and bishops only, 12/1956	20
Communications elite: Press (when data available)	Publishers and/or editors, newspaper circulation 600,-000 and over, and leading periodicals, 1956	21	Publishers and/or editors, newspaper circulation 100,-000 and over, of leading periodicals, and directors of radio network	41
Educators	———	—	Rectors of all major universities and THS, 12/1956	38
Total		250		529

TABLE 9.8

A COMPARISON OF GERMAN CABINETS, 1890–1956*

(Percentages)

	Population		Empire (1890–1918)	First Republic (1918–1933)	Third Reich (1933–1945)	Second Republic (Dec. 1956)
	1871 (by birth)	1955 (by residence)				
Geographic distribution of birthplace:						
Northern Germany	10.5	15	3.9	12.3	9.1	0
Southern Germany	20.1	24	14.4	23.9	33.4	24
Western Germany	22.6	35	14.5	26.2	18.2	47
Central & Eastern Germany (now under Communist control)	46.8	26[a]	63.2	34.6	24.2	29
Abroad	—	—	2.6	3.0	12.1	—
Not indicated	—	—	—	—	3.0	—
Total	100.0	100.0	99.9	100.0	100.0	100.0
Religious affiliation:						
Protestants	66	51.2	13.2	27.9	45.5	41
Roman Catholics	32.6	45.2	13.2	25.4	9.1	53
Other (Jews, etc.)	1.3	3.5	1.3	15.7	—	—
None indicated	—	—	72.3	31.1	45.5	6
Total	99.9	99.9	100.0	100.1	100.1	100.0
Social origin:						
Aristocracy		64.5	11.5	27.3	12	
Middle class		35.5	77.8	69.7	76	
Labor		—	10.7	3.0	12	
Total		100.0	100.0	100.0	100.0	
Education:						
Primary (to 14 yrs.)		84.0	1.3	12.3	3.0	12
Secondary (to 18 yrs.)	12.0	12.0	21.1	12.4	21.2	6
University		4.0[b]	59.2	70.4	75.8	82
Not indicated		—	18.4	4.9	—	—
Total		100.0	100.0	100.0	100.0	100.0
Military experience:						
Indicated		34.2	27.1	72.8	71	
Not indicated		65.8	72.9	27.2	29	
Total		100.0	100.0	100.0	100.0	

* Source for 1890–1945 data: Maxwell E. Knight, *The German Executive, 1890–1933*, Stanford, 1952 (some data corrected with author's assistance).

[a] Residents of West Berlin, and refugees and expellees now residing in the Federal Republic.

[b] Eligible for university study through the *Abitur* (see Table 9.4, footnote).

III
THE SYSTEM IN OPERATION

CHAPTER 10

Money is not everything: American dollar inputs and the influence of the United States

The actual operation of German foreign policy making is heavily influenced by three factors: the aims of German policy makers, the pressure of various domestic interest groups, and the massive involvement of the German economy with the United States, through various forms of United States aid and through private business relations. The intra-German factors will be discussed below, but the German stake in United States–German political and economic relations is so substantial that we must try to say something about its magnitude at the outset.

To indicate even the order of magnitude of the American dollar flow into the Federal Republic and West Berlin is not an easy task. If politicians have been described sometimes as practitioners of "strategic obfuscation," governmental agencies engaged in administering economic aid have not been eager to publicize the full magnitude of the entire program either to American taxpayers or to the German electorate. The aid has been given in a large variety of ways, under a bewildering succession of alphabetical agencies, GARIOA, ECA, MSA, FOA, etc. While these accounted publicly for their operations, data for other channels of dollar inputs into the German economy have not been so readily available. In the case of Germany, as in that of some other countries, many of these extraordinary dollar receipts, as a report of the U.N. Economic Commission for Europe points out, ". . . belong to the twilight zone of quasi-strategic information: at best, only general orders of magnitude are known . . ."[1]

The Scale of Dollar Aid

What is this general order of magnitude? The German Federal Ministry for Economic Cooperation acknowledged in 1956 that Germany has received almost $10 billion up to June 30, 1956, presumably for a period since early 1948.[2] Of the exact total of $9,935 million, $6,355 million

---

[1] United Nations, Department of Economic Affairs (Economic Commission for Europe), *Economic Survey of Europe in 1953*, pp. 19–20.

[2] Germany, Federal Republic, Bundesministerium für wirtschaftliche Zusammenarbeit. *Der Europäische Wirtschaftsrat—OEEC: Handbuch, 1956*, p. 70.

are listed as aid to the Federal Republic in general, and $3,580 million as aid to West Berlin.[3] Even if one assumes that this total includes all dollar aid since 1946, one would arrive at an average of $1 billion per year; or approximately $20 per year for every German man, woman, and child. If the sums should be limited to the years 1948–56 (since the OEEC program discussed in this publication began in 1948), this figure of annual per capita aid becomes about $25. This amount of $20–$25 per year per German accords well with the estimates of dollar aid as having amounted to not more than 5–6 per cent of German national income, as given by several writers.[4]

Of this amount, only parts can be readily located in official statistics. More than $1.6 billion were spent between 1946 and March 1950, chiefly for relief purposes, under the auspices of GARIOA (Government and Relief in Occupied Areas).[5] Another $1.5 billion are reported as spent between 1948 and 1956 by the United States agencies ECA (Economic Cooperation Administration), MSA (Mutual Security Agency), and FOA (Foreign Operations Administration).[6] Together with funds from smaller United States aid programs, these amounts totaled about $3.6 billion, for 1946–53, or about $0.5 billion per year.[7] Another official United States government tabulation puts the total United States nonmilitary "net grants and credits" to Germany for the years 1945–55 at almost $3.9 billion.[8]

The remainder of about $6 billion may have flowed into Germany in a variety of ways. American economic aid to Germany in the form of commodity surpluses, the expenditures of American troops in Germany,

[3] *Ibid. Time* Magazine offers a more recent figure: ". . . the U.S. and West German governments have poured almost $4 billion in direct aid since 1950 [into West Berlin]—the equivalent of about $1,800 apiece for every West Berliner." *Time*, May 25, 1959, p. 20.

[4] Cf. Henry C. Wallich, *Mainsprings of the German Revival*, p. 356 (for 1948–49); Michael L. Hoffman, "Germany's Recovery—A Problem for Allies," *The New York Times*, January 3, 1954 (for 1948–53). Germany, Federal Republic, The Press and Information Office of the German Federal Government, *Germany Reports, 1953*, p. 238, n. 2 ($28.30 per capita for 1950); Germany, Federal Republic, Bundesministerium für den Marshallplan, *Fünfter und sechster Bericht der Deutschen Bundesregierung über die Durchführung des Marshallplanes, Oktober 1950–März 1951*, pp. 34–35; etc.

[5] Germany, Federal Republic, Bundesminister für wirtschaftliche Zusammenarbeit, *Siebenter und achter Bericht der Deutschen Bundesregierung über die Fortführung der Amerikanschen Wirtschaftshilfe (FOA)*. 1. Januar 1954 bis 30. Juni 1954, p. 11, and footnote; see also annual figures, *ibid.*, p. 71.

[6] International Cooperation Administration, Washington, D.C., *Operations Report*, Data as of March 31, 1956, p. 43.

[7] Wallich, *Mainsprings of the German Revival*, p. 355 (amount to June 1954); Horst Mendershausen, *Two Postwar Recoveries of the German Economy*, Contributions to Economic Analysis, VIII, 105 ("The total of the Post-War-II aid, from 1946–1953 on a net basis, came to $3,634 million . . ."), (with reference to U.S. Department of Commerce, *Foreign Aid by the United States Government*, 1940–51, Washington, D.C., 1952, p. 82, and supplement, September 1953).

[8] U.S. Department of Commerce, Office of Business Economics, *Foreign Grants and Credits by the United States Government*, December 1955 quarter, Table 2, p. S-10; cf. also p. S-27.

American offshore procurement of military supplies from German firms are some channels that come most readily to mind, but the full story of American aid to West Berlin and of economic cooperation between Germany and the United States in the "twilight zone of strategic information" remains to be written.

Other forms of dollar aid to the German economy presumably are not even included in the total of $9.9 billion given by the German Ministry. There are loans from international agencies, such as the World Bank, in which the United States wields considerable influence; there are loans and investments from American private industry; and there are other forms in which American economic resources and connections have contributed to the "German economic miracle."

The effectiveness of these dollar inputs into the German economy was greatly increased by the manner in which they were employed, and through the efficient response of German management and labor. Through counterpart funds and other devices, a considerable part of these funds was used to increase capital investment and thus the technological equipment of German industry, without any of the sacrifices which German consumers otherwise would have had to make for an investment program of this magnitude. The result was an increase in both capital equipment and consumer goods. "To use a medical term," says a German government publication, "it was 'dollar therapy' and the tonic effect of an American blood transfusion. . . . Every Marshall Plan dollar spent in Germany has resulted in $10 to $20 worth of goods produced and services rendered."[9]

Those dollar aid programs which were openly accounted for have tended to succeed one another in time with only partial overlap, so that a new program provided new inputs of dollars into Germany as the flow under an earlier program tapered off. United States economic aid to Germany has thus always appeared to be drawing to a close without actually ever quite ending. The same relation holds still more strongly for the overt aid programs as a whole as against the military, or "semi-strategic" dollar inputs under programs not accounted for in detail in any readily accessible public data.

A figure for United States data on military aid for Western Europe as a whole has been given in the amount of $9,690 million for the years 1945–55,[10] but it is not clear whether it includes all programs: what other channels of dollar inputs into Germany are excluded, and what Germany's share in this Western European figure has been in various years. Generally, it seems safe to assume that this German share has increased as German rearmament got under way. Dollar flows to Germany under military and related programs have thus increased presumably

---

[9] Germany, Federal Republic, *Germany Reports*, 1953, pp. 239–43.

[10] U.S. Department of Commerce, Office of Business Economics, *Foreign Grants and Credits by the U.S. Government*, December 1955 quarter, Table 2, pp. 5–8.

after 1953 or 1954, just as the earlier and publicized nonmilitary German aid programs had dwindled to a low level. The total figure of nearly $10 billion aid up to June 1956 to the Federal Republic and West Berlin, given by the Federal Ministry of Economic Cooperation and cited earlier in this section, suggests an annual per capita average of $20–$25 for the entire period 1946–56, as against a per capita average of about $28 for the year 1950, a peak year of aid under the Marshall Plan. To keep a ten-year average 1946–56 anywhere near this figure would require a substantial increase in defense-oriented dollar flows to Germany in the last years before 1956. This, in fact, appears to have occurred, and as the German contribution to the Western military establishment under NATO increases, substantial flows of United States defense aid, as well as of dollar inputs under other headings, may well continue in the future.

The Changing Forms of Assistance: Some Side Effects of American Military Spending and Military Aid

Another approach to the maze of German and American civilian, military, and partly military aid statistics for the 1950's is through the analysis of German balance of payments data, as released by German authorities and by the International Monetary Fund.[11] These statistics show that outright American dollar aid declined to very low levels by the end of 1952, and became a mere trickle thereafter. During the same years, however, another item rose strikingly. This was the German credit balance for receipts for "services," including "foreign payments for sales to armed forces"—which were largely payments from "dollar countries," that is, from the United States.

In 1950, this balance had amounted to about $210 million, and thus to somewhat less than one-half of the $480 million direct foreign aid to Germany in that year. It increased tenfold, however, between 1950 and 1957. In the latter year alone, it amounted to $2,228 million, over one-fifth more than the entire German export balance, and more than four times the annual direct foreign aid to the Marshall Plan years.

The service balance includes relatively nonpolitical items, such as foreign earnings of German shipping and airlines, but it also includes items which are imbued with political interest. The specific item of greatest political interest is government receipts from services to foreign military agencies. These also rose sharply during the years for which we have data, from $199 million in 1952 to $540 million in 1957. In each of these years military receipts were greater than foreign aid, and by 1957 the yearly income from sales to military agencies was greater

---

[11] The authors are indebted to Professor Robert Triffin for expert advice, without wishing to impute to him any responsibility for their views.

than annual foreign aid receipts in any of the preceding years. The rise of this item, and its rapid overshadowing of the declining amounts of direct foreign aid, can be seen in Table 10.1.

TABLE 10.1

GERMAN BALANCE OF TRADE IN GOODS, RECEIPTS FROM SERVICES, INCLUDING FOREIGN MILITARY PAYMENTS, AND FOREIGN AID, 1950–1957*

(*Millions of U.S. Dollars*)

	(1) Net Balance of Exports of Goods	(2) Total Receipts from Services	(3) Receipts for Services to Foreign Military Agencies	(4) Foreign Aid	(3) + (4) Foreign Aid Plus Military Receipts
1950	—561	210	—	430	480
1951	+365	389	—	428	428
1952	535	704	199	115	314
1953	875	895	263	63	326
1954	952	1,124	233	69	302
1955	812	1,415	273	31	304
1956	1,398	1,765	381	31	412
1957	1,849	2,228	540	17	557

* Sources: International Monetary Fund, *Balance of Payments Yearbook, 1956–1957* Vol. 10, Washington, D.C., 1958, Germany, Federal Republic, p. 1. *Ibid.*, *1955–56*, Vol. 9, 1957, Germany, Federal Republic, p. 1. *Ibid.*, *1950–54*, Vol. 8, 1957, p. 87.

Data on receipts from services to foreign military receipts from *Monthly Report* of the Deutsche Bundesbank (Frankfurt am-Main), September 1958, p. 36.

For further tabulations see Appendix III.

Figures for 1953–57 were converted from DM figures at the rate $.233 = 1 DM.

Information covers Federal Republic and West Berlin's transactions with rest of world, except Soviet zone of Germany, and excludes military imports under grants.

But how can service receipts and foreign aid ever be added together? Is it permissible to look in any sense whatever upon service receipts as an equivalent of direct foreign aid? After all, foreign aid is a gift, but service receipts have to be earned by goods and services. If the German economy had been underemployed, there would be little doubt that the input of dollar purchasing power through American military purchases would have been beneficial. In the German full-employment economy of the 1950's, however, did not all German goods and services, sold to the American military establishments, have to be diverted from their probable export to other countries, or else from the needs of German consumers, so that American purchases would have mainly tended to enhance the pressures for inflation?

Yet it is a fact that American purchases increased, and that prices in Germany rose far less than they did in other countries. From June 1950 to June 1957, German prices rose by less than 16 per cent, while rising 18 per cent in the United States, 31 per cent in Italy, 33 per cent in the Netherlands, 36 per cent in Denmark, 39 per cent in France, 44 per cent in Britain, and 56 per cent in Australia.[12]

[12] Press- und Informationsamt der Bundesregierung, *Leistung und Erfolg, 1957: Die Bundesregierung berichtet* (1958), p. 22.

Part of the answer may rest in a fundamental peculiarity of the West German economy. Even when fully employed, it is not closed. It can always count on more labor in the form of refugees entering from Eastern Germany —labor that for most practical purposes is indistinguishable from its West German counterpart. The annual inflow of such refugees in fact has been around 260,000 persons in the later 1950's, most of them adults, with a relative concentration of the young and the skilled. Yet there has been no unemployment. (If there had been, fewer refugees might have cared to come.) Nor has there been inflation. What happened, it seems, was that the steady and large built-in demand from American purchases played its share in underwriting the productive employment of these refugees, and that the additional goods and services resulting from their employment in turn contributed to the successful containment of the forces of inflation.

Prescription for an "Economic Miracle"

The updraft in the German economy in the mid-1950's was aided by the coincidence of six sets of conditions:

1. the general boom in Europe and the continuation of a high level of prosperity in the United States;

2. the steady supply of relatively cheap skilled labor from East Germany, and also of cheap labor from Italy, and, to a much lesser degree, from elsewhere in Western Europe;

3. the willingness of German trade unions, and of the Social Democrats, to accept technical changes making for higher productivity, and not to press too vigorously for shorter hours or higher wages, thus permitting a normal 50-hour work week to continue through the mid-1950's;

4. the full recovery of confidence in the German economy by both German and foreign businessmen, facilitating both capital imports and high rates of reinvestment;

5. the steady and substantial flow of dollar-earning orders to Germany for goods and services, stemming in considerable part from American defense-connected spending; and

6. the absence of excessive tax burdens on German employers, workers, or consumers for the expensive military hardware for their army, which was supplied to Germany free of charge in the form of end items of American military aid, or in the form of American dollar credits for the purchase of defense items for the German army from other countries.

The second and third of these six sets of conditions favoring the German economic boom were closely connected with the leadership displayed by the West German government and by its loyal Social Democratic opposition, and with the skills and work habits of the German people. The last three of the six conditions, however, were obviously and substantially related to policies of the United States[13] There is ample evidence that German government leaders clearly anticipated the large scale and the beneficial economic effects of American military aid, and that they staked to some extent their political fortunes on it.[14]

Over a longer period, the Bonn government's commitment to full employment policies, and its need for some form of American aid, were no less serious. For political reasons, the flow of East German refugees could not have been reversed, even if there had been a depression. It would have been unthinkable for West German leaders, as well as for public opinion, to send large numbers of individual Germans back into a Communist-ruled territory, once they had taken the risk of leaving it. American orders thus underwrote and overbalanced what otherwise might have been a significant source of anxiety for German policy makers.

Some writers have considered these American purchases as unstable, on the grounds that they drop sharply in the event of a major change in American policy, following upon some change in American domestic conditions, political or economic. The German government, on the contrary, has insisted on considering these expenditures as stable—just as stable as the American military commitment to defend the Federal Republic, and to keep troops on its territory. The present Bonn government has worked, and can be expected to work, for keeping these American commitments stable, for they correspond in their minds to stable German needs, economic, political, and psychological.

With the over-all growth of the German economy in the later 1950's, the economic component in the German need for American aid has been declining, but in the late 1940's and early 1950's, it was substantial, and the spectacular effects of American dollar aid in those years have left a deep mark in the minds of many of the men who were still guiding the Bonn government nearly a decade later.

The Decreasing Importance of American Dollar Inputs in the Future

By the mid-1950's, the German economy had grown so much that even dollar flows for military purchases on the scale of the grants of the Marshall Plan years loomed much less large in the German economic picture.[15]

---

[13] For details on many of these points, as they were discussed in the contemporary German press, see Lewis J. Edinger, *West German Armament*, pp. 67–82, with many references. Cf. also Bruce M. Russett, *Economic Impact of German Rearmament* (Williamstown, Mass., Williams College, 1957).

[14] Edinger, *West German Armament*, pp. 76–81.

[15] Finance Minister Ludwig Erhard reported that the German gross national product had risen by 70 per cent from 1950 through 1957. (Press- und Informationsamt der Bundesregierung, *Leistung und Erfolg, 1957: Die Bundesregierung berichtet*, n.p., n.d. (1958), p. 9.) An input of about $0.5 billion of direct American dollars, which amounted to roughly 2.5 per cent of the *c.* $16 billion German national income in 1950, would thus amount only

Certainly by the late 1950's the American instruments for economic pressure on Germany, even if anybody in the United States government had wanted to use them, had become relatively much smaller. In terms of simple economic power, the United States leverage vis-à-vis Germany has declined, and it seems likely to decline still further.

Since 1953 or 1954, Germany is as much or more dependent on the European community in economic matters as it is on the United States. If backed by most of Western Europe, a neutralist Germany could afford to risk even the intense displeasure of the United States, just as, if backed by the United States, Germany could risk the displeasure of her West European neighbors. In fact, of course, the German government has been anxious not to displease either America or Western Europe, and rather to improve relations with both in every possible way. But what was once a policy dictated by inescapable and palpable necessity is now becoming ever more a policy pursued by choice.

In economic terms, Germany today is perhaps no more dependent upon the United States than is any other large West European country. If an open American endorsement of his policies still helps a German politician where it would embarrass a Frenchman, the reason is perhaps not so much any remaining difference between the economic positions of France and Germany as in the historical and psychological setting of their politics.

Germany needed to establish her credit—moral, political, and economic —not only in the eyes of her neighbors but also in the eyes of her own investors, her own citizens, and perhaps, deep down, even in the minds of some of the members of her own political elites. In France, American backing and the need for it reminded Frenchmen of their diminished fortunes. In Germany, the national fortune had hit bottom in 1945; the need for foreign aid had been self-evident; and the presence of American backing had been a major symbol of the improvement in Germany's fate and of the restoration of the self-respect of her people.

In one form or another, a substantial part of the dollar inflow from the United States thus has been continuing in 1956 and thereafter. At the same time, an appreciable amount of German private investment has begun to flow to the United States, and a growing number of German and

---

to about 1.7 per cent of *c.* $31 billion German national income in 1957, using current prices in both years. If the actual 1957 inputs of American dollars into the German economy— mainly in the form of defense purchases on the services account—should have been in fact closer to $1 billion, they would still have amounted only to about 3 per cent of the German national income in that year. Moreover, the last 3 per cent of income in the prosperous Germany of 1957 was obviously less critical than the same 3 per cent would have been relative to the smaller German national income in the lean years before 1950. Viewed in purely economic terms, the economic relations with the United States are becoming ever less critically important to Germany. (German gross national product from data in DM, given in United Nations, Statistical Papers, Series H, *Statistics of National Income and Expenditure*, No. 8, September 1955, p. 81; No. 10, January 1957, p. 97.)

American corporations have entered into close association. Few if any German voters or even policy makers know the exact figures that are involved in all these relationships, but they do know beyond doubt that their economic stake in cooperation with the United States is large and continues to be so. Their foreign policy decisions are made in full awareness of this fact.

Perhaps even more important, the economic influence of the United States is heavily reinforced by psychological, social, and military considerations which make American friendship appear as the most important basis of what security the members of the West German foreign policy elites can hope for in this uncertain world. The results of this relationship have been conspicuous. In every major German foreign policy decision the government of the United States thus has been an invisible—and sometimes not so invisible—partner.

Nevertheless, there has been a growing autonomous component in German foreign policy making. The interplay of German aims and United States influence, and of the various domestic German interests, can be seen best by glancing briefly at a few actual cases of such policy decisions. The questions of German membership in the European Coal and Steel Community; of German rearmament, of German reparations to Israel, and of negotiations with the Soviet Union about German reunification—these are the cases in which we shall try to watch German foreign policy making in operation.

CHAPTER 11

Toward the recovery of German influence: The European Coal and Steel Community treaty (ECSC)[1]

A primary objective of German foreign policy since the creation of the Federal Republic in 1949 has been the recovery of German influence in international affairs. There have been differences between various elite groups and among the public at large over the means to be employed, but solid unanimity concerning the general objective. The man primarily responsible for the conduct of German foreign policy from 1949 to 1957, Chancellor Konrad Adenauer, was singularly successful in his efforts to regain for Germany independence of action in the conduct of foreign policy without losing the political, military, and economic support of the Western allies—particularly the United States.

Adenauer's policy was to establish Germany as the leading power and the senior partner of the United States on the European continent by means of adroit and subtle moves which gained for the Federal Republic full sovereignty and a leading position within the Western alliance system in the course of a few years. In the face of frequently bitter opposition from some foreign policy elites, especially the Social Democratic leadership, and often without the specific support of public opinion, he gained his ends through close collaboration with the Western powers, particularly the United States. Adenauer gambled successfully that temporary concessions would eventually yield major gains for German foreign policy and that the voters would sustain him at election time.

Adenauer owed his success to a combination of factors, including his unrivaled position as the leader of the governing political elite, his remarkable prestige inside and outside Germany, his ability to enlist the support of crucial German elites for specific foreign policy moves in spite of public opposition or indifference, his influence among leading policy makers in Western countries, and last, but not least, the exigencies of the international situation. In general, he has exploited to the fullest his great formal and informal powers as chancellor and leader of the largest

---

[1] The authors are indebted to Ernst B. Haas for permitting them to use for this analysis material from the draft manuscript of his perceptive and thoroughgoing study *The Uniting of Europe: Political, Social, and Economic Forces, 1950–1957* (Stanford, Stanford University Press, 1958). See also Henry L. Mason, *The European Coal and Steel Community: Experiment in Supranationalism*, pp. 1–34.

German party—if necessary in the face of widespread public opposition at home and abroad—in order to gain his ends in foreign affairs.

The first step toward the recovery of German sovereignty and liberation from allied controls after the creation of the Federal Republic was taken with the creation of the European Coal and Steel Community (ECSC), popularly known as the Schuman Plan.

Under the Occupation Statute of 1949, the new German state had gained only limited independence from control over its affairs by the three Western occupation powers, the United States, Great Britain, and France. A tripartite Allied High Commission was established, endowed with broad powers designed to assure that the Federal Republic would conform to Western plans for a democratic and demilitarized Germany and would honor the political and economic obligations it had undertaken in return for allied agreement to the establishment of the new state. The Allied High Commission controlled the organization and operation of German business, endeavoring to prevent its reconcentration in cartels and trusts and diverting a considerable share of the production of the Ruhr coal to foreign countries that had been victims of German aggression; it regulated political and economic relations between the new state and foreign countries and, for all practical purposes, represented the interests of the Federal Republic and its citizens abroad.

The new German government, a coalition led by Adenauer, immediately sought ways and means to gain freedom from allied supervision. These efforts were helped immeasurably by the rapid economic recovery of the new German state—aided largely by generous financial assistance from the United States government—and by the intensification of the conflict between the Western allies and the Soviet Union. Failure to achieve agreement with the Soviet Union on the reunification of Germany and the belief that Russia might attack Western Europe through the territory of the Federal Republic led the Western occupation powers to yield to Adenauer's demands for complete sovereignty.

This change in the political climate began early, and Adenauer made the most of it. Well before the outbreak of the Korean conflict in July 1950, Western policy had begun to shift from treating the Federal Republic as a defeated enemy to seeking its inclusion in the Western alliance system as a major bulwark against Soviet aggression. These developments played directly into the hands of the leaders of the Federal Republic, who offered intimate collaboration to the Western powers in return for independence and complete German equality in the councils of the Western alliance. Their first opportunity to move toward their objective came almost as soon as the new state had come into being, in May 1950, when French Minister Robert Schuman called for the pooling of Franco-German coal and steel production in an economic union which he invited other interested European states to join.

The French foreign minister made his proposal for a variety of political, economic, and military reasons, including the desire to prevent the restoration of an independent German power on the Continent that might once more become a threat to French security. Conscious of the rapid recovery of German power, Schuman sought to make a virtue of apparent necessity by proposing a close organic bond between the Federal Republic, France, and other states of Western and Eastern Europe which, he hoped, would permit resurgent German power to benefit, rather than threaten, the anti-Communist nations of Europe. Schuman advertised his proposal as the first step toward the economic and political unification of Europe which, he claimed, would put an end to past Franco-German conflicts and prove advantageous to all participating states.

Chancellor Adenauer immediately hailed Schuman's proposal as "epoch-making" and called for its speedy implementation in the form of a treaty. However, the spokesman of the Federal Republic let it be known that their country would join the proposed community only if all existing restrictions on its sovereignty, imposed by the occupation powers, were removed. While this appeared to be "sheer blackmail" to some Frenchmen,[2] in effect most of this price was paid in return for additional German undertakings, particularly to participate in the common defense of Europe in a supranational European Defense Community. The Occupation Statute of 1949 was gradually revised in the course of the negotiations leading to the signing of the European Coal and Steel Community treaty in April 1951. The Federal Republic was given partial control over its foreign relations and some of the most severe allied controls over its domestic affairs were gradually dropped. In January 1952, the Bundestag approved the ECSC treaty by a vote of 232 to 143.

Bundestag approval of the ECSC treaty was not due to overwhelming public support. The "attentive public" in favor of the proposed coal and steel community declined steadily during negotiations, while opposition increased. The largest number of Germans, however, appear to have become increasingly indifferent toward the issue, leaving it to the foreign policy elites to make the final decision. As Table 11.1 shows, very nearly one-half of the attentive public has at all times favored the treaty, and less than one-sixth of the attentive group has remained in opposition. Among the population at large, however, the Coal and Steel Community seems to have stirred up a tidal wave of apathy.

Adenauer and State Secretaries Hallstein and Blankenhorn—two senior civil servants—managed to negotiate treaty terms which met the various aspirations of leading German foreign policy elites and, at the same time, satisfied corresponding elites in France, Italy, Belgium, and the Netherlands who spearheaded the integration movement in these countries. In

---

[2] Susan Strange, "The Schuman Plan," *The Year Book of World Affairs*, p. 127.

TABLE 11.1

PUBLIC OPINION AND THE ECSC TREATY, 1950–1956

(*Percentages*)*

Event and Date of Poll:	Treaty Proposed June 1950	Treaty Initialed June 1951	Bundestag Debate Sept. 1951	Treaty Ratified Jan. 1952	ECSC in Operation March 1952	ECSC After Four Years Apr. 1956
Attentive public:						
Approved	39	25	18	21	19	10
Opposed	13	20	20	24	6	5
Undecided	25	15	27	12	15	4
Total	77	60	65	57	40	19
No opinion or uninformed	23	40	35	43	60	81
Total	100	100	100	100	100	100

* Source: *Jahrbuch I*, pp. 343–44; *Jahrbuch II*, p. 349.

leading the movement, Adenauer was joined by the two other outstanding Roman Catholic statesmen of Europe. French Foreign Minister Robert Schuman, a leader of the M.R.P., like Adenauer a Rhinelander by birth, had served in the German army in the First World War and spoke fluent German; in confidential conversations with Adenauer and other CDU leaders he had gained their encouragement and support for his proposal before he made it public. Alcide de Gasperi, the Italian Prime Minister and leader of the Christian Democrats, had been born and educated in a section of Italy which was Austrian in his youth, and also spoke fluent German. Most of the members of the CDU elite were natives of Southern and Western Germany, regions which had far stronger historical, religious, and cultural ties to the predominantly Roman Catholic nations of Latin Europe than other areas of Germany. Finally, many members of the Christian Democratic elite were strongly dedicated to the sincere belief that antinationalism, Franco-German collaboration, and European union based on Christian values offered Germans redemption for the sins committed by the Nazis in their name.

While ideological motivations were extremely important, political and economic considerations also influenced the CDU elite. ECSC appeared to promise the liberation of the German Federal Republic from the "fetters" imposed by the victorious allies and its elevation to at least equal status with one of the "Big Three" Western powers—France. To the representatives of German industry within the CDU elite, the ECSC treaty held out the promise of the abolition of restrictions imposed by the allies on business concentrations and cartels and greater control over the production and sale of Ruhr coal than was the case under the International Ruhr Authority. On the other hand, economic liberals within the CDU elite hoped that the Coal and Steel Community would curb cartels, protect private enterprise against government control, and encourage free competition within the common market.

The leaders of the three smaller parties belonging to the Adenauer coalition government were somewhat less enthusiastic than the CDU elite about the ECSC treaty, but Adenauer managed to enlist their support to carry the treaty through parliament. The small refugee party (BHE) demanded total abolition of all allied controls over the German economy and definite assurances that France would return the Saar to German control before it would approve the treaty, but last-minute assurances from allied quarters that all controls would be lifted as soon as the treaty was ratified led the refugee party leaders to support it. The nationalist German Party (DP) endorsed ECSC because it hoped that it would further Western unity against Communism and spur efforts to liberate Central and Eastern Germany from Soviet control. At least some of the leaders of the conservative Free Democratic party, representing particularly big business and the Protestant middle class, at first feared that the European Coal and Steel Community would prove disadvantageous to the interests of German industry and strengthen Roman Catholic influence in the Federal Republic. However, they were persuaded that ECSC would in fact further German political and economic aspirations, and in the end the fifty-one votes of the Free Democratic party helped to carry the Treaty in the Bundestag.

Among the economic interest group elites, the leaders of German industry were lukewarm in their support of ECSC. Many feared that French industrialists would use the proposed common market arrangement to dump their own surplus production in other member countries, while German industry would be at a disadvantage in a freely competitive common European market for coal and steel. The German coal industry feared for the survival of its marginal producers, protected in the past by national marketing arrangements. However, in the end most German coal and steel producers—though by no means the entire big business elite—were persuaded by the CDU leaders that promised advantages outweighed possible drawbacks in the ECSC scheme. The Ruhr was expected to be the greatest beneficiary as it appeared to enjoy natural cost advantage over other producers in the proposed market, particularly since Adenauer had successfully resisted French efforts to raise German production costs by providing for the equalization of wages and taxes within the community. Moreover, German industrialists expected ECSC to permit reconcentration of the coal and steel industry to at least as high a level as existed in other countries of the proposed market and to provide German producers with greater influence over their own production and marketing than under the International Ruhr Authority—hopes which proved to be fully justified after the scheme went into operation.

The attitude of the trade union elite toward ECSC presented an interesting illustration of *ad hoc* coalitions between employer and employee elites when their common interests were affected. Despite close ties to the Social Democrats—who bitterly opposed the treaty—the trade union leaders on the whole supported the scheme. They were led by the powerful leaders of the coal and steel workers unions, which had just gained a voice and an interest in the management of their industries under a "codetermination" arrangement. Identifying the interest of their own constituents with those of the industrialists, these union leaders also hoped that ECSC would permit at least partial reconcentration of the coal and steel industries and lead to the removal of allied controls; they argued that trade union support might lead to the extension of "codetermination" to the international level through the representation of the unions in the controlling organs of the proposed coal and steel community. While some union leaders joined employers opposed to the scheme, those in the coal and steel industries fought alongside management to participate in the common market on the best possible terms for German producers.

Alone among the leading foreign policy elites, the Social Democrats opposed the proposed common market to the bitter end, to be easily outvoted in the Bundestag by the coalition supporting Adenauer. Under the leadership of their dynamic chairman, the late Kurt Schumacher, they claimed that ECSC would delay, if not prevent, the reunification of Germany. They charged that the scheme would lead to a supercartel of international big business and to the subjugation of the Federal Republic to the control of a "Black International" of conservative, Roman Catholic parties. While they professed to favor European union, they asked that it should follow, not precede, the reunification of Germany, and that it should include the predominantly Protestant countries of Scandinavia and Britain, in which socialist parties were strong. Deliberately or inadvertently, the German Socialist leadership served as a foil for Adenauer and his allies, who used its opposition to ECSC to gain concessions from the Western allies and support from anti-Socialist German elites, which might otherwise have rejected the community plan. The Social Democrats categorically demanded the immediate abolition of all allied controls, leading the Western allies to meet the more moderate demands of Adenauer; they charged that ECSC would handicap, if not prevent, their plans for the socialization of basic industries, thus helping to enlist the support of large and small businessmen.

In 1956, four years after ratification of the Treaty, a large majority or all of the elites had remained attentive to the Coal and Steel Community, and a smaller, but still large majority had come to endorse it. This was brought out strikingly in a study of 600 Germans who occupied leading positions in business, in politics, in the mass media, and in the government in 1956.

Acceptance of ECSC was highest among politicians, civil servants, journalists, and white-collar workers. This was a confirmation of the acceptance of EDC among Social Democrats and their sympathizers who contribute a significant share of three of these four groups. Among the

TABLE 11.2*

ENDORSEMENT OF THE EUROPEAN COAL AND STEEL COMMUNITY IN 1956

(Percentages)

	For	Against	No Opinion	Total
Politicians	81	13	6	100
High civil servants	79	21	—	100
Journalists	74	13	13	100
White-collar workers	71	13	14	100
Medium business	70	20	9	100
Big business	68	22	10	100
Professions	62	16	21	100
Small business	59	23	18	100
Military	50	44	6	100
All elites	70	19	11	100

* From data in Suzanne Keller, "Attitudes Toward European Integration of the German Elite," M.I.T. Center of International Studies, October 1957, multigraphed, pp. 2 and 26. The authors are indebted to Dr. Keller and to Professor Daniel Lerner for making materials from this study available to them.

business community, a minority of nearly one-fourth has remained opposed. The military had remained intensely attentive but plainly skeptical as a group. Barely one-half endorsed the Community, but nearly one-half remained in open opposition.

Whatever anyone's opinions were about the ECSC as an institution, there was no doubt about the popularity of the gains in Germany's international position that came with the ratification of the Treaty. Another issue, however, was to pit the popular desire for further improvements in Germany's international position against the no-less-popular desire to avoid all excessive risks or burdens. This was the issue of German armament.

CHAPTER 12

Bargaining about armaments:
EDC, NATO, and the Paris Agreements[1]

On the morning of May 9, 1955, the black, red, and gold flag of the German Federal Republic rose at the Supreme Headquarters, Allied Powers Europe (SHAPE), while the band played the old German national anthem, "Deutschland, Deutschland, über alles, über alles in der Welt." It signified the admission of a free and sovereign German state to the North Atlantic Treaty Organization (NATO)—almost ten years to the day that its new allies had dictated armistice terms to a vanquished Germany. After almost six years of determined efforts to throw off Western allied controls over German affairs, Chancellor Adenauer and his associates appeared at last to have obtained their goal.

Their gains were impressive. In exchange for the promise of a German military contribution to the defense of Western Europe they had gained, for the Federal Republic, "the full authority of a sovereign state over its internal and external affairs," a national military establishment, a major voice in the councils of the Western powers, assurances of Western military and political support against Soviet Russia, and, finally, Western recognition of the Bonn government as "the only German Government . . . entitled to speak . . . as the representative of the [entire] German people in international affairs.[2]

As in the case of ECSC, the negotiations leading to the abolition of Western controls and the recognition of the Federal Republic as a sovereign and equal member of the NATO alliance demonstrated the far-reaching and generally uncontested independence of German foreign policy decision makers from the influence of domestic public opinion. The price which the Adenauer government agreed to pay for sovereignty and NATO membership was the establishment of a national military establishment, a decision consistently opposed throughout the period of negotiations by more Germans than supported it.[3]

[1] Portions of the following discussions are based on material in Lewis J. Edinger, *West German Armament, passim.*

[2] See U.S. Congress, Senate, *Protocol on the Termination of the Occupation Regime in the Federal Republic of Germany and Protocol to the North Atlantic Treaty on the Accession of the Federal Republic of Germany.*

[3] See Chapter 2, pp. 29–31.

For five years official Western policy in Germany conformed to the principle proclaimed by the "Big Three" at Potsdam in 1945: "the complete disarmament and demilitarization of Germany and the elimination of all German industry that could be used for military production." Although four-power cooperation in the occupation of Germany soon broke down and the Soviet Union withdrew from the Allied Control Council in 1948, the three Western occupation powers sought to maintain existing agreements and regulations concerning German disarmament and demilitarization.

Western allied approval of the creation of the Federal Republic in 1949 was conditioned on German assurances that allied provisions for "the liberation of the German people from militarism" were to remain in force. The new German government of Konrad Adenauer declared "its earnest determination to maintain the demilitarization of the Federal territory and to endeavor by all means in its power to prevent the re-creation of armed forces of any kind."[4] However, Chancellor Adenauer appears to have had strong mental reservations in making this declaration and almost immediately proceeded to suggest to the Western allies a German military contribution for the defense of Western Europe against Soviet attack, in exchange for partial or complete lifting of allied controls over German affairs imposed by the Occupation Statute of 1949.

Adenauer and his closest associates sought to achieve their objective—as in the case of the European Coal and Steel Community—in the name of European integration. In December 1949, Adenauer launched a trial balloon by suggesting that Germany should contribute to the defense of Europe in a European Army.[5] Apparently anticipating early Western demands for a German defense contribution, on the basis of formal and informal current suggestions along these lines from Western political and military leaders, he maintained his position in the following months despite violent opposition both in the Federal Republic and abroad. Adenauer sought to impress upon Western leaders the value of the Federal Republic as an ally and the crucial role which it might play in a future conflict between the Soviet Union and the NATO powers. He claimed that the industrial and demographic resources of the Federal Republic might prove decisive in a future war, he stressed the danger of large-scale Soviet troop concentrations in Central Germany and the growing power of the so-called "People's Police" of the Communist-dominated German Democratic Republic, and suggested that short of a military contribution from the Federal Republic the Western powers lacked the forces to repel an attack from the East. For political as well as military reasons, Adenauer maintained, the Western powers needed the loyal support of the people of the German Federal Republic; he offered it in exchange for an end to allied controls and

[4] C. G. D. Onslow, "West German Armament," *World Politics*, 3:4 (July 1951), p. 451.
[5] *Ibid.*, p. 453 ff.

the termination of existing limitations on the sovereignty of the Federal Republic.

To gain his objective, Adenauer was willing to risk Soviet threats against the Federal Republic and the possibility that the reunification of Germany might be deferred indefinitely; as in the case of ECSC, he was prepared to sacrifice *potential* sovereign rights in return for the surrender of actual sovereign powers by other nations participating in the creation of a European defense community. The same ideological motives which influenced the CDU elite, under Adenauer's leadership, to support the Schuman Plan of May 1950 also led it to support concurrent proposals for the creation of a European army.[6] However, political considerations were every bit as important. Membership in a European integration scheme for a German state both wealthier and more populous than any other Continental state held out the prospect not only of equality for the Federal Republic in such a union, but potential leadership of the democratic nations of continental Europe. Instead of remaining merely a rump German state, facing the prospect of indefinite occupation and control by foreign powers, the Federal Republic might at least become "first among equals," playing a leading role in international affairs as the leader of the Continental nations, particularly toward the United States and the Soviet Union, the two superpowers of the world. Finally, such a role for Germany in a European military union promised to make it less dependent on foreign powers and to give its leaders a greater voice in matters affecting the defense of the Federal Republic against attack from the East. To gain these ends, Adenauer was prepared to defy popular opposition to German rearmament. Sovereignty and equality for the Federal Republic through European integration was to him worth the price of a German military contribution, as Adenauer's official biographer was to note.[7]

Adenauer's arguments for a German military contribution to the defense of Western Europe against Communist attack seemed substantiated by the North Korean attack on South Korea in July 1950. Particularly in the United States government, military and political leaders—some of whom had favored a German military contribution, at least since 1949[8]—reportedly interpreted the unexpected invasion as a clear warning that either the Soviet Union herself, or her East German satellite, might invade the Federal Republic too. Western allied forces in Germany, never very

---

[6] See Chapter 11, pp. 156–57.

[7] See Paul Weymar, *Konrad Adenauer: Die autorisierte Biographie*, pp. 500, 557. See also Fritz Rene Allemann, *Bonn ist nicht Weimar*, pp. 187–212.

[8] See Edinger, *West German Armament*, pp. 5–7. The desire for a German military contribution was spurred by the explosion of a Soviet nuclear device, revealed by President Truman in September 1949. *Ibid.*, p. 51. Cf. also Walter Millis, *Arms and the State* (New York, Twentieth Century Fund, 1958), pp. 336–38; and L. W. Martin, "The American Decision to Rearm Germany" (typescript, Princeton University, 1959, publication forthcoming).

strong and further weakened by the diversion of military resources to Korea, appeared inadequate to meet the threat. Simultaneously, the French government informed the United States that it was not interested in an allied strategy that depended primarily on U.S. air-atomic power, but wanted Western Europe to be defended by ground forces as far east as possible.

While United States leaders sought desperately to stem the North Korean sweep down the Peninsula, Chancellor Adenauer pointed with increasing emphasis to the exposed situation of his country, and Western Europe in general. In August 1950 he suggested to the Western allies the formation of a "special force of German volunteers" of the same size and strength as the "People's Police" in the Soviet zone of Germany—estimated to consist of from 50,000 to 80,000 trained soldiers. He coupled this appeal with the renewed suggestion that the Federal Republic might make a sizable contribution to a European army in return for an end to allied controls and complete equality within such a defense arrangement. Simultaneously, Adenauer appointed a former general to head a new office in the federal government which was to lay plans for such a German military contri- bution. The United States government, upon the urgings of its military leaders, replied to Adenauer's proposals by calling openly for the use of German productive resources and military manpower for the defense of Western Europe. Secretary of State Dean Acheson asked British and French government leaders to agree to the inclusion of about ten German divisions in the NATO forces in Europe. But, in the face of French oppo- sition to the creation of an independent German army, the three Western governments agreed that the German military contribution demanded "by democratic leaders in Germany" rather should become part of an inte- grated European army.

Urged on by United States leaders, the governments of the Federal Republic of Germany, of France, Italy, Belgium, the Netherlands, and Luxembourg for over two years hammered out a scheme for a European Defense Community (EDC) which would more or less parallel the pattern agreed upon for the Coal and Steel Community. While French negotiators, led by Adenauer's friend, Foreign Minister Robert Schuman, sought to limit German influence in the proposed military arrangement, the repre- sentatives of the Federal Republic demanded complete equality and the termination of allied controls over German affairs. The German spokes- men were aided not only by strong United States support—even on the level of personal relations, the U.S. High Commissioner for Germany, John McCloy, happened to be related by marriage to Konrad Adenauer— but, paradoxically, by popular opposition to any rearmament in Germany itself. Pointing to gains for the opposition Social Democrats—strongly opposed to the scheme—in various local elections, Adenauer extracted major allied political concessions for the more "cooperative" German leaders.

When the EDC treaty was finally signed in May 1952, it provided for the creation of twelve German divisions, an air force, and a small navy, which were to become major components of a European military establishment. True, the German Federal Republic was not yet admitted to NATO, but Chancellor Adenauer had no doubts that membership would follow as soon as the German defense contribution had begun to take concrete form. Simultaneously with the signing of the EDC treaty, the Federal Republic concluded a Contractual Agreement with the three Western occupation powers which was to replace the Occupation Statute of 1949. In effect, this agreement terminated the occupation and put an end to practically all allied controls. However, Western forces remaining in Germany as "allies" retained the right to intervene in case the democratic order in the Federal Republic should be threatened either from within or without.

In May 1953, the Bundestag approved the two agreements by a majority of fifty-nine votes, a considerably smaller margin of victory for Adenauer's policies than in the case of the ECSC vote only a few months earlier. The treaties became the major issues of the campaign for the election of a new parliament, which followed ratification. The Christian Democratic elite, supported only diffidently by leaders of the smaller parties in the Adenauer coalition, claimed a major political victory for Germany. Opposition came largely from a peculiar alignment of militarists, pacifists, nationalist opponents of European integration, and neutralists who feared that military alignment with the West would prevent any Soviet agreement to the reunification of Germany. The Social Democratic and trade union elites, this time united, claimed that rearmament would restore the anti-democratic and bellicose German military leadership of the past and perpetuate the division of Germany. The Protestant elite was divided. Important members—like the Social Democratic leaders particularly sensitive to the needs of their silent "constituents" living under Soviet control in Central and Eastern Germany—claimed that membership in EDC would constitute a "betrayal" of their "oppressed brethren." The old military elite was also divided into proponents and opponents of EDC. Some supported Adenauer's claim that the political and military gains for Germany outweighed whatever disadvantages the agreements might include. Others maintained that the limitations imposed upon a new German military establishment were unacceptable and asked that rearmament be deferred until political conditions and popular opinion had become more favorable.[9] Strenuous Communist efforts, directed from the Soviet zone, to draw the various opposition groups into a united "patriotic" front, proved unsuccessful.

Despite widespread popular opposition to rearmament, the promised restoration of German sovereignty and the gains in Germany's international position impressed many voters in the electoral campaign that

---

[9] See, for example, excerpts from a memorandum by former Fleet Admiral Heinrich Gerlach, reprinted in *Der Spiegel*, April 3, 1957, p. 16.

followed in the summer. Even the Social Democrats played down the issues of EDC and German rearmament, on which they had opposed the government so vehemently earlier in the year.[10]

Adenauer won a resounding personal victory in the election of 1953. His prestige and deputation as an effiective representative of German interests gave the Christian Democrats for the first time an absolute majority in the Bundestag; the ruling coalition now commanded the two-thirds majority required for constitutional changes which armament might require. Adenauer's policy of German political recovery in international affairs through European integration was dealt a setback in August 1954, when the French National Assembly rejected the EDC treaty and thus defeated the scheme. However, only 37 per cent of the respondents in a German poll following this defeat expressed regret for the failure of the project.[11]

Adenauer immediately demanded complete sovereignty for the Federal Republic maintaining that it had fulfilled its part of the bargain and was not to blame for the failure of the armament scheme. However, the British and American governments insisted that a German military contribution agreed to by the French remained the *sine qua non* for political sovereignty. On British initiative, representatives of the United States, Britain, Canada, and the six Continental countries which had signed the EDC treaty formulated a hasty substitute. It provided for the creation of a national German military establishment and the admission of the Federal Republic to the North Atlantic Treaty Organization as a sovereign and equal partner, subject only to certain limitations on its future military power and the retention of a few formal rights on the part of the former occupation powers pertaining to West Berlin and German reunification. By May 1955 all the governments concerned had ratified these "Paris Agreements." Though not exactly in the manner intended by the Chancellor, a major goal of his foreign policy since 1949 had been achieved.

Public and elite opinion seemed well satisfied with the result. Clearly, the immediate political gains for the Federal Republic were even greater than under the proposed EDC arrangement. To be sure, many of the personally involved proponents of European integration among the German foreign elites paid the price only reluctantly. To them, the immediate gains of sovereignty, NATO membership, and a national military establishment did not appear worth the sacrifice of the European army scheme and its apparent promise of German leadership of a European political union. Among the bulk of the elites, as well as among the public the Paris Agreements, which gave sovereignty to Germany, were more popular than EDC.

A survey taken two years later showed, however, that the Western European Union Treaty, which formed a part of the Paris Agreements,

[10] Hirsch-Weber and Schütz, *Wähler und Gewählte*, p. 20.
[11] See Chapter 2, p. 29.

was markedly more popular than were the entire Agreements under their own name. (See Table 12.1.) The Agreements retained the allied rights to maintain their armies of occupation in Germany under the title of "Allied forces," and to take "immediate action appropriate for their protection" if these forces should be "imminently menaced," including presumably the possibility of hostile action by German nationals.[12]

The Western European Union Treaty itself, on the other hand, was more innocuous. The Council of Union, consisting of the representatives of the six ECSC countries and the United Kingdom, had only the right to set ceilings on the national armed forces permitted to each of the members, and to supervise national defense build-ups accordingly, and in the absence of a two-thirds vote of the Council, Germany was not to manufacture guided missiles, submarines, warships larger than 3,000 tons, and so-called A.B.C. weapons for atomic, biological, and chemical warfare. In the mood of the mid-1950's, these restrictions seemed innocuous enough. Altogether, the WEU Treaty carried for some Germans the glamor of the name of "Western European Union," and the added prestige of an association with Great Britain, but unlike EDC it did not impose such restrictions on German sovereignty as would have repelled major sections of opinion.

TABLE 12.1

OPPOSITION AND SUPPORT TO EDC, PARIS AGREEMENTS, AND WEU

	WEU		Paris Agreements		EDC	
	Against	For	Against	For	Against	For
All elites	7	91	17	74	28	64
Public opinion	7	69	27	40	35	40
Men only	8	75	34	44	41	43
Particular elites:						
Medium business	6	92	13	82	23	69
Small business	3	95	14	65	24	67
Big business	5	90	7	80	25	63
Politicians	5	94	18	77	26	69
Professions	8	89	13	70	26	57
High civil servants..............	4	96	20	80	29	63
White-collar workers	10	86	26	64	33	56
Journalists	13	85	28	62	36	64
Military	19	81	20	70	38	56

The picture seems consistent. The business elites were most favorable to European integration, the intellectuals less so, and the military least. All elite groups agreed in preferring more German sovereignty to less: they preferred WEU to the Paris Agreements, and the Paris Agreements to EDC. But while both public and elites preferred a looser form of European collaboration to a tighter one, they remained interested in the national unity of Germany—and this meant eventual reunification with the Soviet zone.

[12] Suzanne Keller, "Attitudes Toward European Integration of the German Elite," M.I.T., Center for International Studies, multigraphed, October 1957, p. 26.

CHAPTER 13

Details of a test case:
The reparations agreement with Israel

The conclusion of a reparations agreement between the Federal Republic and Israel in 1952 is a good example of the latitude which the German government enjoys in adjusting to international situations, even in the face of relatively unfavorable opinion at home.

The facts of the case can be summarized briefly. Almost all German Jews and many Jews in other countries, as well as many persons of Jewish descent, had been killed or expelled by the Nazis, mainly in the course of World War II. Altogether perhaps as many as six million men, women, and children had thus lost their lives, and an even larger number had lost their homes and property. After the war, the new state of Israel received a substantial number of Jewish survivors from Germany and Central Europe, who there found new homes. Their claims for compensation for injuries, loss of family members and property were directed against the Federal Republic—which had become the legal successor to other financial obligations of the Nazi regime in such matters as public debt, pensions, and the like—and these claims were championed by the government of Israel. The latter government also asked compensation for the lives and properties of those Jewish families which had been exterminated by the Nazis, so that no individual heirs had survived.

These claims had been announced in substance against defeated Germany in September 1945 by Dr. Chaim Weizmann on behalf of the Jewish Agency for Palestine.[1] The new state of Israel, which proclaimed its independence on May 15, 1948, made these claims its own. After the German Federal Republic had been established in 1949 and had gained a measure of sovereignty in 1950, the Israeli government pressed this claim formally in two notes, of January 16, and March 12, 1951. The notes were addressed not to the Federal Republic but to the four occupying powers. They referred to the notable economic recovery of Germany and demanded acceptance of financial liability by the Federal Republic for indemnification laws (jointly and separately with the German states), the speeding up of actual payments, the facilitation of transfer of German

---

[1] Letters to the governments of the United Kingdom, United States, USSR, and France, September 20, 1945, cited in Kurt R. Grossmann, *Germany's Moral Debt: The German-Israel Agreement*, pp. 6–7.

payments in Deutsche Mark into dollars, and the acceptance by the Federal Republic of an obligation to contribute to the cost of rehabilitation of Jewish survivors in their new homeland, Israel.

The official reaction of the Western powers to the Israeli notes came in July 1951. In effect, they advised Israel to seek direct negotiations with the Federal Republic: The United States government "regrets," so the Israelis were told, "that it cannot impose on the government of the German Federal Republic to pay reparations to Israel."[2] Unofficially, the German government presumably was advised by the United States that it would be wise to seek some negotiated settlement with Israel. Solution of the German-Jewish problem widely considered abroad, as the then U.S. High Commissioner John J. McCloy once put it, as "a test for Germany's democracy."[3]

Many members of the German elite had long had a strong sense of ethical obligation in this matter. Moreover, considerations of morality were reinforced by "a decent respect for the opinions of mankind." At a time when neither Germany's legal sovereignty nor her moral and political credit was fully restored, and where so much depended on the good will of Western—and particularly American—public opinion, the international advantages of concluding a speedy and relatively amicable settlement with Israel were obvious to those who were well informed about foreign policy matters.

The well-informed and the strongly conscience-motivated, however, did not necessarily form a majority of all German political elites, and they did not have the support of a majority of the electorate. More than two-thirds (68 per cent) of the respondents to a poll conducted in late 1951 by a German opinion research institute for the High Commissioner in Germany agreed that Jews should get some economic help for their sufferings under the Third Reich, but 21 per cent were opposed outright, and 11 per cent said they did not know whether Jews should get any help or not. Moreover, out of the two-thirds majority who favored some help to Jews at some future time, 17 per cent specified that Jews should have the least right of all claimants to be helped, and therefore should come in last place, that is, after all Germans claiming damage from bombing, after refugees and expellees, etc. For practical purposes, 49 per cent or almost one-half of the respondents—and presumably of the electorate—thus could not be expected to support any restitution and indemnification measures in favor of Jews, regardless of their actual amount.[4] Later, in a poll in August 1952, when the approximate sum of the repara-

[2] *Ibid.*, p. 9; United States answer, July 5, 1951, to Israel note of March 12, 1951. Replying to a new Israeli note of November 20, 1951, the United States explicitly suggested direct negotiations between Israel and the Federal Republic. *Ibid.*

[3] *Ibid.*, p. 15.

[4] *Ibid.*, pp. 18–19.

tions to Israel under the proposed agreement had become known—three billion Deutsche Mark ($714 million), to be paid in goods over twelve years, were mentioned in the question—44 per cent flatly opposed any such payment as "superfluous"; another 24 per cent opposed the sum as "too high"; still another 21 per cent were undecided, and only 11 per cent—corresponding to one-ninth of the electorate—favored the agreement.[5] By that time, 84 per cent of all men said they were aware of the negotiations about the reparations agreement, and 75 per cent opposed the reparations sum as either superfluous or too costly. Of the women, only 54 per cent said they had heard of the negotiations, but 62 per cent opposed the agreement anyway, on one or the other of these grounds.[6]

Public opinion was thus not particularly favorable to any agreement embodying substantial payments to Israel, and at least some of the major interest groups, notably banking, industrial, and shipping circles, also were at least unenthusiastic about any such prospect.[7] In such a situation, much depended on the timing of the actions of various decision makers.

Both Adenauer and the leaders of the Social Democratic opposition in the Bundestag were quick to act. After the first Israeli note of January 16, 1951, to the occupying powers, the Bundestag debated in February the problem of restitution and indemnification. Speaking for the Social Democrats, Professor Carlo Schmid suggested that Germany propose to the allies the recognition of Israel as the successor to heirless property and indemnification claims, but the Social Democratic move on the matter of restitution legislation was referred to the legal committee of the Bundestag, where it remained for several months. "The few prominent Germans who took an active interest in this problem remained outside the limelight of publicity."[8]

However, after the second Israeli note to the Four Powers of March 12, 1951, Adenauer himself ordered a high German official, Ministerialdirektor Dr. Herbert Blankenhorn, who was then in London, to take up unofficial contacts with Jewish circles there. In these discussions, representatives of the World Jewish Congress put forward three demands: an official declaration by the German Chancellor before the Bundestag, accepting on behalf of the Federal Republic responsibility for the persecution of the Jews at the hands of the Nazi regime; a promise to make good the material damage; and an official invitation to representatives of Jewish people and of the State of Israel to enter into negotiations to that end.[9]

In April 1951, Adenauer on a visit to Paris received Israeli repre-

[5] *Jahrbuch I*, p. 130.
[6] *Ibid.*
[7] Grossmann, *Germany's Moral Debt*, pp. 21, 29, 32.
[8] *Ibid.*, p. 11.
[9] Paul Weymar, *Konrad Adenauer: Die autorisierte Biographie*, p. 626.

sentatives unofficially in the Hotel Crillon, but the interview ended without result. On September 27, 1951, however, Adenauer delivered before the Bundestag a declaration on behalf of the government which proclaimed restitution of Jewish material losses as a moral duty of the German people, and declared the willingness of the government to negotiate for this purpose with representatives of the Jewish people and with the state of Israel. Spokesman for all parties, with the exception of the Communists (who were still a legal party in the Federal Republic) and the extreme right, endorsed this declaration.[10] The extent of popular and interest group opposition to substantial reparations was not yet fully apparent; no appropriations had been asked for; and those legislators who disagreed with the Chancellor in this issue held their peace. Adenauer's declaration thus seemed to have safe legislative backing.

At first, however, this important gesture—which found a favorable echo in the British and American press—was not followed by any tangible action. Israeli disappointment was expressed in another note to the occupying powers of November 30, 1951.

According to his authorized biography, it was again Adenauer himself who at once took the initiative to arrange on the occasion of his forthcoming visit to London a meeting with Dr. Nahum Goldman, the chief negotiator on behalf of Israel and of the conference on Jewish Material Claims Against Germany, representing major Jewish organizations from many countries. The meeting took place on December 6, 1951, at the Hotel Claridge in London. The Chancellor at once told Dr. Goldman that it was "a matter of heartfelt need" for him to make good the wrong done to the Jews, and to open the way for a new relationship between Germans and Jews." Goldman in reply suggested the need for Germany to treat the matter as a moral problem and to respond to it with a "great gesture," so as to allay the acute bitterness among Jews in Israel and elsewhere, many of whom had felt it wrong to negotiate with Germany at all. Prolonged haggling about amounts of compensation would make matters only worse; hence Adenauer should accept then and there in principle the Israeli demand for one billion dollars compensation.

Adenauer did just that—without having any specific authorization from parliament or from the rest of the government—and wrote Goldman on the same day an official confirmatory letter, accepting explicitly on behalf of the German government Israel's "claims formulated in its note of March 12, 1951"—i.e., one billion dollars—"as the basis for . . . negotiations."[11]

In the Federal Republic, businessmen, bankers, and industrialists were quick to protest: Israel's claims were morally based on her having accepted

[10] *Ibid.*, pp. 627–31.

[11] Adenauer's letter to Dr. Nahum Goldman, December 6, 1951, and Dr. Goldman's account, *ibid.*, pp. 632–37. Cf. Grossmann, *Germany's Moral Debt*, pp. 17–18.

over half a million displaced Jews from Germany and from countries overrun by the Nazi armies, but in terms of accepted international law, her claims were at least open to dispute. On strictly legal grounds, therefore, the German government could have resisted them for a long time, perhaps indefinitely, and saved Germany from what looked like a major economic burden. At the same time, the Arab states protested on the grounds that such German payments would strengthen Israeli power; they threatened a boycott of German goods if a German-Israeli reparations agreement should come into force; and some German businessmen, fearful of losing Arab markets, joined the opposition to Adenauer's reparations policy.

The attitude of the press reflected the division among the different sections of the press elite, each of which represented a different set of interest groups. According to one study, the German press, insofar as it took up any attitude toward the agreement with Israel up to its signing in September 1952, appeared divided into three main groups:

The first group of thirteen newspapers, with a combined circulation of 1,300,000, favored unreservedly the Jewish claims and the principle of reconciliation with the Jews. This group included several newspapers of liberal attitudes in the former United States zone of occupation, such as the *Telegraf* of Berlin (circulation 227,000), the United States–owned *Neue Zeitung* (circulation 215,000),[12] the *Süddeutsche Zeitung* of Munich (circulation 208,000), and the *Frankfurter Rundschau* (circulation 150,000). Papers close to the Social Democrats, insofar as they commented on the issue, were also in this group.

The second group was by far the largest; it included sixty publications with a total circulation of nearly three million. In general, many of these papers were friendly to the CDU and to the other government parties. This group favored reconciliation with the Jews but with major reservations: it "placed Jewish claims after Germany's obligations to her own refugees, her trade interests, and her ability to make payments in hard currency." These reservations were expressed more frequently as Arab protests mounted. Papers in this group included the *Hamburger Abendblatt* (circulation 280,000), speaking for shipping and banking interests, the *Frankfurter Allgemeine Zeitung* (circulation 87,000), spokesman for powerful industrial interests; and the weekly *Rheinischer Merkur*, close to Adenauer on most other matters.

The third group consisted of seven papers, with a total circulation of almost one million, which explicitly opposed the Israel agreement. These included the illustrated weekly *Der Stern* (circulation 600,000), *Der Spiegel*, of Hamburg, "which sometimes vacillated in its attitude," and the *Aachener Nachrichten*.

---

[12] This paper ceased publication in September 1953.

The remaining papers took no stand on the question but merely reported on the progress of German-Jewish negotiations.[13]

Government and parliament likewise were divided; and another source of covert opposition may have arisen among a part of the high bureaucracy. German financial experts like Adenauer's adviser, the banker Hermann Abs, strongly backed by Finance Minister Fritz Schaeffer—and, presumably, some officials in his Ministry—sought to treat the German obligation to Israel on a basis similar to the old German foreign commercial debts from the Hitler era. Accordingly, they tried to keep open the possibility of reducing the obligation to Israel in proportion to the expected scaling down of these commercial debts, and sought to delay any firm agreements with Israel on actual amounts and conditions of payment.

These tactics produced a crisis in the German-Israeli negotiations at The Hague, which were suspended in early April 1952. On May 19, 1952, Abs, with the concurrence of Finance Minister Schaeffer, offered the Israelis less than one-half of the sum which Adenauer had accepted as basis for negotiations. On the same day, the two main German negotiators, Professor Franz Boehm and Dr. Otto Kuester, who were personally in favor of reaching an early agreement with Israel, resigned in protest against the delaying tactics of Abs and Schaeffer. Also on the same day, however, Nahum Goldman wrote to Chancellor Adenauer expressing his keen disappointment at the lack of any acceptable concrete German offer and a copy of his letter was forwarded to U.S. High Commissioner John J. McCloy.[14]

Once again Adenauer's intervention broke the deadlock. He met on May 28 with Dr. Goldman in Paris; and on June 9, on Adenauer's urgent invitation, Goldman and other Jewish and Israeli negotiators flew to Bonn, where they met with Secretary of State Walter Hallstein, Assistant Secretary Herbert Blankenhorn, Hermann Abs, and other German representatives. By the next afternoon, June 10, in a session in the presence of Adenauer himself, a basic agreement was reached—not without Adenauer's insistence that it should at once be formally recorded.[15] Detailed negotiations at The Hague from June to early September 1952 then produced the final agreement. On September 10 it was signed at Luxembourg by Chancellor Adenauer and Israeli Foreign Minister Moshe Sharett.

Ratification of the agreement by the Bundestag—which obligated Germany to pay 3,450 million Deutsche Mark (about $822 million) to Israel in goods over a period of twelve years—was the last hurdle. It

[13] Grossmann, *Germany's Moral Debt,* pp. 29–30.

[14] *Ibid.,* p. 23; text of letter, pp. 61–63.

[15] Weymar, *Konrad Adenauer,* pp. 637–41; Grossmann, *Germany's Moral Debt,* pp. 23–25.

was delayed for over six months while unsuccessful attempts were made by the government to negotiate a trade treaty with the Arab states. Franz Josef Strauss, a leader of the CSU (the Bavarian wing of Adenauer's party) and later Minister of Defense in Adenauer's cabinet, publicly demanded in January 1953 greater accommodation of Arab interests.[16]

When ratification finally came to a vote, it found Adenauer's coalition seriously divided. Less than one-half of the coalition deputies voted for ratification. It was the votes of the main opposition party, the Social Democrats, that were decisive in saving Adenauer's policy of agreement from defeat. The Social Democrats voted for the agreement as a matter of principle, having endorsed its general outlines explicitly and consistently on earlier occasions; their roll call vote was solidly in favor, without any abstentions. (See Table 13.1.)

Under the ratified agreement, Germany was to pay Israel in goods the equivalent of $48 million annually in 1953 and 1954; about $74 million per year for the nine years following; and about $26 million in the twelfth and final year. In every year thus far these sums have been much smaller than the total of the direct and indirect United States dollar inputs into the German economy which were discussed above. Economic and military aid—mainly indirect—has been flowing from the United States to Germany, while German direct reparations have been flowing on to Israel. Adenauer's policy thus contributed to the consolidation of

TABLE 13.1

ROLL CALL VOTE IN THE BUNDESTAG ON RATIFICATION OF THE LUXEMBOURG AGREEMENT
WITH ISRAEL, MARCH 18, 1953*

Party	Yes	No	Abstentions	Absent	Total	Per Cent in Favor
CDU/CSU	84	5	39	17	145	58
FDP	17	5	19	8	49	35
DP	5	5	10	—	20	25
Total coalition	106	15	68	25	214	49.5
SPD	125	—	—	5	130	96
FU (Federal Union)	3	—	13	3	19	16
KPD (Communists)	—	13	—	1	14	0
Independents (BHE, etc.)	5	7	5	6	23	22
Total opposition	133	20	18	15	186	71.5
Grand total	239	35	86	40	400	59.8

* Source: Kurt R. Grossmann, *Germany's Moral Debt: The German-Israel Agreement* (Washington, D.C., Public Affairs Press, 1954), p. 33.

[16] Grossmann, *Germany's Moral Debt*, pp. 27–28. The Arab states concerned in the trade negotiations were also acting through the Political Committee of the Arab League, which met in November 1952. Cf. Germany, Federal Republic, *Deutschland im Wiederaufbau, 1952*, p. 21.

the German moral and political position in the world, and it precluded the possibility that a quarrel over the smaller flow of German reparations to Israel might interfere in any way with the larger flow of direct and indirect benefits from the United States.

The Chancellor's policy may prove even more farsighted in the future. Any generous German treatment of Israeli claims was apt to improve the attitude of the Western powers to Germany's own debts, as well as the international reception of Germany's own claims for the return of the large properties of German corporations, which had been confiscated during World War II in the United States and other countries. At the end of 1952, the German Foreign Ministry reported that it was "currently following the developments of the situation of the seized German properties in the European and extra-European states."[17]

In 1953 the London Agreement about German Foreign Debts was concluded and ratified, cutting in half the sum of German prewar and postwar debts and interest arrears with the consent of the Western powers: the total was cut from about $7 billion to about $3.4 billion, with payments spread over a long period.[18] In the same year, 53 ships for inland navigation and 381 naval vessels were returned to Germany by the United States.[19] German foreign properties, seized during the war, were restored by Chile, Greece, and Iran, and the Foreign Ministry reported that in the matter of the far more substantial German properties in the United States, "as a result of the visit of the Chancellor [Adenauer] the way has been opened for a change in the former attitude, which has found expression in draft bills by Senators Dirksen and Chavez."[20] In the following years, the interest of the German government, and the personal interest of Chancellor Adenauer, in the restoration of the German properties in the United States continued, and was again expressed on the occasion of Adenauer's 1954 visit to the United States.[21] German government sources have put the recoverable value of these properties at about $350 million.[22]

[17] Germany, Federal Republic, *Deutschland im Wiederaufbau: Tätigkeitsbericht der Bundesregierung für das Jahr 1952*, p. 17. Other issues of this annual will be cited by brief title and year.

[18] *Deutschland im Wiederaufbau, 1953*, p. 27.

[19] *Ibid.*

[20] *Ibid.*, p. 34.

[21] *Deutschland im Wiederaufbau, 1955*, p. 60; cf. also *Deutschland im Wiederaufbau, 1954*, p. 40.

[22] Estimate communicated to the authors by the German Consulate, Boston, Spring 1958.

Some American press accounts have differed. By the Spring of 1957, it was estimated that by the restitution of these German properties in the United States to their German owners the United States Treasury would stand to lose between $400 and $500 million; and their current value, including accrued income, was put at $650 million. At that time a renewed drive by Senators Everett M. Dirksen and Olin D. Johnson for full restitution of these properties was attracting public attention, and the Board of Directors of the vast Ger-

However, none of these properties had been returned to Germany by late 1958, even though their eventual return did not seem too unlikely.

By 1958 Germany had paid substantial sums to Israel under the Agreement. It could be argued that, even if there had been no agreement, Germany's other debts would still have been scaled down to the same extent, the same restorations of German property would have occurred, the same further restorations of such properties might be expected in the years to come, and the same flow of indirect and direct American dollar benefits would have entered the German economy in 1954–58 and could be expected to continue to some extent and in some forms in the future. These arguments are necessarily speculative on both sides, while the payments to Israel under the agreements were certain and had to begin quickly.

On balance, Chancellor Adenauer's policy appears to have been enlightened and in the best national interests of Germany, as well as fully justified on moral grounds. It is worth noting, however, that these enlightened considerations apparently were not shared by a large part of public opinion, nor by some of the major interest groups, nor by a majority of coalition deputies in the Bundestag, nor by about two-fifths of the deputies of Adenauer's own party. Together with a dimly felt but real sense of moral obligation, which mitigated resistance to the Agreement, it was apparently Chancellor Adenauer's leadership and the ideological commitment of the Social Democrats which combined to produce the final decision. It seems that in the case of the settlement with Israel the Chancellor had perceived the possibility of acting in relative independence of any one interest group, as well as of the opinion of the general public, and that he had used it to secure action in the national interest as he saw it.

---

man corporation I. G. Farben expressed itself as "directly interested" in its success. (E. W. Kenworthy, "Bills Ask Return of Enemy Assets: Johnson and Dirksen Lead Drive in Senate to Hand Back Seized Property," *The New York Times*, April 1, 1957; and "I. G. Farben Backs Alien Property Bill," *The New York Times*, May 23, 1957).

CHAPTER 14

An unresolved issue: German reunification and relations with the Soviet Union

It has been suggested repeatedly in the preceding analysis that foreign policy makers in the Federal Republic have tended to show a great deal of independence from the pressure of public opinion. To this, there has been one conspicuous exception.

On the issue of German reunification no important leader has dared suggest that the Federal Republic is more than a provisional arrangement pending the "liberation" of the Soviet zone. During the years that German policy makers concentrated on gaining sovereignty and freedom of action for the "rump" German state, reunification as a policy objective took second place to these more immediate foreign policy goals, leading many non-German observers to underestimate its potential importance once sovereignty had been achieved. Since 1955, however, it has become increasingly apparent that peaceful reunification through some sort of arrangement with the Soviet Union has become one of the most crucial foreign policy issues confronting decision makers in the Federal Republic, one which is likely to affect significantly the future relationship between the Republic and its Western allies.

The Growing Popular Appeal of Reunification

Professions of support for European integration from official government spokesmen have tended to obscure the far stronger sentiment for reunification which has steadily gained strength in the Federal Republic.[1]

As mentioned earlier, three-quarters of the respondents in a public opinion poll in September 1956 considered the unification of the "Eastern and Western zones of Germany" more urgent than "European unification."[2] As long as economic and political recovery had appeared the most

[1] Experts on German affairs are divided on this point. Thus, Wallich (*Mainsprings of the German Revival*, p. 326) makes light of the reunification sentiment in the Federal Republic, while Allemann (*Bonn ist nicht Weimar*, p. 439) conceives the attainment of unity as the primary objective of the German people. The first view may fit the attitudes of the cabinet and the CDU elite, the second seems borne out by the bureaucracy, Protestant Church, and SPD elites, and by the poll data given in the text.

[2] See Chapter 2, pp. 29–31. The official report of the German Foreign Ministry for 1951 put European integration ahead of German reunification, but in all subsequent years reunification was put first. Cf. *Deutschland im Wiederaufbau*, volumes 1951 through 1955.

pressing immediate issues confronting the Federal Republic, public sentiment for government action on the reunification issue had been relatively
quiescent. Once these demands had been satisfied, the reunification issue
came immediately to the fore. (See Table 14.1.) Another poll in September 1956 showed that 53 per cent of respondents considered the division of Germany "unbearable"; 65 per cent explicitly refused to "let
time take care of" the reunification problem and held that West Germans
should "demand again and again" that Germany be reunified.[3]

TABLE 14.1

"The Most Urgent Task Facing the Federal Government, 1950–57"

(*Percentages*)

	Reunification	Housing	Employment	Integration of Expellees
January 1950	1	14	25	14
January 1951	12	10	11	12
January 1952	16	10	7	8
January 1953	12	9	8	6
January 1954	14	13	7	3
January 1955	21	9	3	2
January 1956	25	6	1	1
January 1957	27	5	1	0

* Source: EMNID Poll, *Der Spiegel*, April 17, 1957, p. 12. Another series of polls on a similar question
showed the reunification question rising in importance from third to first place between October 1951 and January
1955, while the number putting it first grew from 18 per cent to 34 per cent. See *Jahrbuch I*, p. 392. In
November 1955, reunification was put first as their personal choice among political slogans by 45 per cent of
respondents, ahead of "improvement of living conditions and lowering of prices," etc., *Jahrbuch II*, p. 293. A
U.S. HICOG poll of November 1954 showed reunification put first by 70 per cent of the respondents (as against
11 per cent who named rearmament); and a March 1955 poll of 15- to 25-year-olds showed 50 per cent putting
reunification first, ahead of peace (25 per cent) or European unity (10 per cent). See Research Staff, Office of
Public Affairs, Office of the U.S. High Commissioner for Germany, *Current German Opinion*, Report No. 206,
Series 2, December 6, 1954, and Alfred Rapp, "Die Jugend ruft nach Wiedervereinigung," *Frankfurter Allgemeine Zeitung*, April 1, 1955.

Not only do deep-rooted loyalties to the idea of a united German
nation appear at the present time far stronger than support for the supranational ideal of European unification, but intimate personal bonds link
a large number of citizens of the Federal Republic to German lands and
peoples presently under Communist domination. Twenty-four per cent
of the foreign policy elites and 26 per cent of the population are natives
of Soviet-ruled Central and Eastern Germany.[4] In February 1953, 44
per cent of the respondents in a public opinion poll claimed either relatives or friends living in the Soviet zone of Germany; when one adds to
these the number of West Germans with personal acquaintances, the share

    [3] *Jahrbuch II*, p. 316. This popular position conflicts with the counsels of patience from
leading American commentators on contemporary German politics. Thus, see for example
the observations by the last U.S. High Commissioner and first ambassador in the Federal
Republic, James B. Conant, in *Germany and Freedom* (Cambridge, Harvard University
Press, 1958), particularly p. 106.

    [4] See Tables 9.1–9.7, pp. 133–40.

of West Germans with such personal contacts should be well above one-half of the population of the Federal Republic.[5]

Many of these human contacts have remained active; in February 1953, almost two West Germans out of every five said they were sometimes writing letters to the East zone, and almost one in three had sent Christmas packages there.[6] According to the German federal government 24 million such packages were sent in 1956 and 30 million in 1957.[7] The 1956 figure of 24 million packages actually sent would more than confirm the one-third of persons who had claimed in the February 1953 poll just cited that they—that it, presumably, their families—had sent a package to East Germany.[8] The 1957 figure of 30 million packages might then suggest a not insignificant increase.

Travel between East and West Germany has also been increasing. Despite rigid travel restrictions imposed by the rulers of the Soviet zone, 2.4 million of its inhabitants visited the Federal Republic in 1956 and about 3 million in 1957.[9]

New contacts are added by migration. Every month several thousand refugees from the Soviet zone enter the Federal Republic, serving as a constant reminder that 18 million Germans remain outside the present "rump" German state. Between 1947 and 1954 an average of 165,000 so-called "resettlers" from Berlin and the Soviet zone entered the Federal Republic; in 1955 this migration increased to 230,000 and in 1956 to 291,000. In 1957 about 264,000 "resettlers" were reported by the federal government to have come to West Germany.[10] These people bring with them precious memories of relatives left behind, memories of cities, towns, and villages in which they grew up and to which they might return should Germany some day be reunified. They also are likely to bring with them an image of a reunited Germany quite different from the Federal Republic. Particularly the young people in their late teens and early twenties—who have made up an increasing proportion of these refugees—grew up in a Communist Germany, went to its schools and were exposed to its propaganda for a reunified Germany on a "socialist basis." Presumably few, if any, of these refugees are convinced Communists; many—though not necessarily a majority—were active opponents of the Communist regime. Neither, however, are they likely to feel strong sentiments for the "rump"

---

[5] *Jahrbuch I*, p. 24.

[6] *Ibid.*

[7] Presse- und Informationsamt der Bundesregierung, *Leistung und Erfolg 1957: Die Bundesregierung berichtet*, n.p., n.d. (1958), pp. 127–29.

[8] See note 6 above. It is interesting to note here that the record of actual behavior—i.e., packages sent—confirms the attitudes disclosed by polling.

[9] Presse- und Informationsamt der Bundesregierung, *Leistung und Erfolg 1957: Die Bundesregierung berichtet*, n.p., n.d. (1958), pp. 127–29.

[10] Press and Information Office of the Federal German Government, *Facts About Germany*, n.p., 1957, p. 23.

state in Western Germany. Rather, their loyalties are to a united Germany —as it existed before 1945—or to a new German state unlike either the Nazi Reich or its successor regimes in the Federal Republic or the Soviet zone.

In addition to national and personal sentiments, visions of potential political and economic gains motivate the demand for reunification. With a population of about seventy million and the largest area by far of all West and Central European states, a united Germany would once more rank among the leading powers of the world—second only to the United States and the Soviet Union. While present trade between the Federal Republic and Communist countries is negligible—even trade with the Soviet zone of Germany amounted in 1955 to only about 2 per cent of its total foreign trade—reunification might open up vast new markets. The Federal Republic, according to one of its leading "elite papers," would bring into a unified German state its great postwar genius for trade with non-Communist nations, while the present Soviet zone would contribute its intensive economic ties with the Communist nations of Europe and Asia. Trade in both directions might be greatly expanded once the resources of both parts of Germany were pooled.[11]

The magnitude and intensity of popular pressure for German reunification are evidenced by the attitudes of the elites. Opinion leaders in the Federal Republic have sought to outdo each other in denouncing the division of Germany as intolerable and in labeling reunification the most important national duty confronting the government. General agreement exists that reunification must be achieved peacefully and by means of free elections of a national assembly throughout Germany, and not through negotiations with the "puppet" regime of the Soviet zone. Elite views diverge, however, on the strategy which should be employed by the government of the Federal Republic in achieving reunification.

The Government's Policy and Its Critics

Most German leaders acknowledge—however reluctantly—that the government is not a free agent in the matter of reunification. German unity, they admit, depends in the last analysis upon agreement between the United States and the Soviet Union. Chancellor Adenauer and his supporters have taken the position that the best means of obtaining such an agreement consists in inducing the Western leaders—and United States leaders in particular—to adopt this German national objective as their own, and to treat it as more important than any other United States interest that might conceivably be served by an American-Soviet settle-

---

[11] See Hans Roeper, "Neue Chancen im Russlandgeschäft?" *Frankfurter Allgemeine Zeitung*, May 14, 1955. For 1954 and 1955 data on trade with East Germany, see Helmut Arntz, *Tatsachen über Deutschland*, p. 125, and its English language edition, *Facts About Germany* (same publishers and year), pp. 111, 115.

ment on other issues. Any general settlement of outstanding East-West differences, it is argued, would then have to include the unification of Germany on terms satisfactory to the government of the Federal Republic. To gain such support, however, the Republic and its leaders must convince Western leaders of their devotion and loyalty to the Western alliance, above all, they must convince them that a reunified Germany would be no threat to the peace of the world. According to Adenauer, the most affective way to earn such confidence and support is for the Federal Republic to take the leadership in the movement for European union. Therefore, the Chancellor has claimed, without the unification of Europe there can be no unification of Germany.

The Adenauer course for reunification has been opposed by a conglomeration of neutralist, pacifist, and nationalist elements that have otherwise little in common. It includes leaders of the Protestant Church, right-wing conservatives and nationalists, former officers, Social Democratic and trade union leaders, and businessmen. In general, they hold that the cause of German unity would be better served by loosening the ties which Adenauer has forged between the Federal Republic and the Western powers. Particularly the severance of present military bonds, they hold, would diminish Soviet opposition to German reunification by eliminating the fears of Russian leaders of resurgent German military power allied with the West. These elements dispute Adenauer's claim that German and Western interests regarding reunification are more or less identical, and, both overtly and covertly, they seek to influence the decision makers to adopt a more "independent" course in pursuit of what they conceive to be exclusively German national interest. The task of a dynamic German foreign policy, as they see it, is to create and exploit opportunities which would permit the government of the Federal Republic to avoid binding commitments to either of the two major power blocs, while using its bargaining power to mediate an agreement on German unification between them. Otherwise, it is claimed, the status quo will be perpetuated by a tacit understanding between the leaders of the Great Powers to shelve the issue of German unification indefinitely for the sake of some compromise on other issues, such as an agreement on disarmament.

From the inception of the Federal Republic in 1949 to its entry into NATO as a sovereign state in 1955, Chancellor Adenauer and his associates defended the policy of intimate collaboration with the Western powers and of European integration as aimed ultimately at the reunification of Germany. However, by 1958 Germany seemed no closer to this professed objective than in 1949. At best the foreign policy of the Adenauer government appeared to be preserving the status quo; at worst it seemed to be aggravating the division of the nation.

Adenauer's failure to register any concrete gains for a supposedly dynamic drive for reunification seemed all the greater in contrast with the apparent ease with which the Chancellor had previously managed to obtain concessions from the Western allies in establishing the Federal Republic as the leading power on the European continent. The opposition charged that Adenauer and his associates merely have paid lip service to the cause of reunification while they were, actually, anything but enthusiastic about joining the socialized economy and the Protestant population of the Soviet zone with the Federal Republic. The predominantly Roman Catholic, West and South German, and conservative elites supporting Adenauer and influencing his foreign policy decisions were said to fear the political and economic effect which reunification might have upon their present positions of power. Whether there is truth in these charges or not, the real reason for the paralysis of German foreign policy makers with regard to reunification appeared to lie beyond their control.

The International Deadlock

German foreign policy makers were faced with a deadlock between Soviet and Western leaders on a formula for German unity. Both sides conceived the potential status of a United Germany as a matter so vital to their respective interests that they have found it impossible to make the concessions which a compromise solution would require. Western leaders saw the terms for reunification proposed by the Soviet leaders as designed to give control over this strategic area to the USSR, while the latter insisted that a Germany united according to Western plans would constitute a menace to the Soviet Union and its allies in Eastern Europe. The resulting deadlock aroused widespread suspicions in the Federal Republic that neither Western nor Soviet leaders were genuinely interested in resolving the issue—protestations by both sides to the contrary—while the German government seemed unable to do anything about it.

"The German people . . . [are merely] the subjects of negotiations between foreign powers which pursue only their own interests," observed th leading foreign affairs journal in the Federal Republic after ten years of inconclusive four-power negotiations on German unification.[12] This sense of exasperation and frustration has repeadedly led to demands that the leaders of the Federal Republic take matters into their own hands and negotiate directly with the Soviet government. However, attempts in this direction have been singularly unsuccessful. This was illustrated by Adenauer's visit to Moscow in September 1955.

The Opening of Diplomatic Relations with the Soviet Union

The termination of the occupation regime in May 1955 was taken by many influential leaders of the Federal Republic as the signal for the start of direct negotiations with the Soviet Union on reunification. Such

[12] See "Glossen," *Aussenpolitik*, 4 (1955), 477.

sentiments were strengthened by the failure of the Geneva four-power talks on German unification the following July. Therefore, when Soviet leaders invited Adenauer to come to Moscow in September 1955, the Chancellor accepted, evidently sharing the widespread German view that his bargaining position was strong enough to extract favorable terms from the Soviet government.[13] It turned out, however, that he had overestimated his own position and underestimated that of the Russian leaders. The latter refused to discuss reunification, but suggested that he negotiate directly with the leaders of the German Democratic Republic—the satellite regime of the Soviet zone—which no political leader in the Federal Republic was then, and is now, willing to do. Adenauer refused, but agreed to the establishment of diplomatic relations between the Federal Republic and the Soviet Union in return for the release of several thousand German prisoners of war still in Soviet captivity.

To many opinion leaders in Germany it seemed that Adenauer had walked into a Soviet trap. By agreeing to the establishment of diplomatic relations he seemed to have accepted the Soviet claim that there were two German states, both represented in Moscow, and that unification could only come about by negotiations between their respective governments.

Adenauer quickly sought to dispel the impression that he had abandoned the claim of the federal government to be the only German government and that he was moving toward recognition of the Soviet zone regime. In fact, Adenauer had obtained the release of several thousand German prisoners of war which his Western allies had failed to procure. The presence of a Russian ambassador in Bonn and of a West German ambassador in Moscow represented a relative increase in German independence and bargaining power vis-à-vis the West; and Adenauer had gained these points without injuring in any way his reputation for rock-solid reliability as an ally of the Western powers.

Certainly—regardless of elite criticism—the West German public considered the trip a definite success. According to a poll taken after Adenauer's return, 48 per cent of respondents thought it an unqualified success, 31 per cent considered it a partial success, but only 9 per cent thought it no success at all. Sixty-eight per cent approved of the way the Chancellor had negotiated with the Soviet leaders and only 8 per cent thought he should have handled himself differently. As to positive accomplishments only 18 per cent actually thought Adenauer had bested the Russians, while 17 per cent thought it had been the other way around and 41 per cent called it a draw. However, 59 per cent thought that Adenauer's trip had improved the chances for an "understanding" between

[13] Apparently Adenauer believed that the Soviet regime had been greatly weakened since the death of Stalin in 1953, while, as he had told a British correspondent, the entry into force of the treaties giving the Federal Republic sovereignty and membership in NATO had increased his own bargaining position. See Alistair Horne, *Return to Power*, p. 405.

the Federal Republic and Russia—only one per cent thought such chances had gotten worse, while 27 per cent considered them unchanged.[14]

However, it was evident that the Federal Republic could ill afford to go much farther in the way of independent negotiations with the Soviet Union, and that it still depended upon the Western powers—and particularly the United States—to achieve the professed major foreign policy objective of its leaders: German unity.

Eastern and Western Fears of a Reunited Germany

Between 1949 and 1956 Germany foreign policy makers were highly successful in obtaining their objectives in negotiations with the Western occupation powers—primarily because the latter were willing and able to pay the price demanded. To obtain the political, military, and economic participation of the Federal Republic in the Western alliance against the Soviet Union, they agreed to Adenauer's demands for sovereignty and equality. Reunification is another matter. Tied by solemn commitments and functional integration—particularly in the economic and military fields—to the Western allies, the Federal Republic "is not free in her decisions," as Chancellor Adenauer himself pointed out in connection with the disarmament discussions of 1957.[15]

The leaders of the Federal Republic, no matter what their political affiliation might be, depend upon American, British, and French leaders to come to an agreement with the Soviet leaders on reunification, and it is not at all clear whether either Western or Soviet decision makers are willing to pay the price. No matter on what terms Germany might be unified, the laboriously established arrangement for the integration of Western Germany into an economic union with Western Europe and into the North Atlantic Treaty Organization would be shattered—a price which the Western leaders are not likely to be willing to pay in the near future. None of the Federal Republic's European allies are particularly eager to have an independent and united Germany dominate the Continent once more. The Soviet leaders, on the other hand, insist that a united German state must be "neutralized." Present ties between the Federal Republic and its allies accordingly would have to be permanently severed. Western leaders have adamantly refused to consider such terms, believing true "neutrality" out of the question for as powerful and strategic a country as a united Germany.

So long as international tensions remain acute, a united Germany may seem too dangerous to either side in the East-West context. Small or

[14] *Jahrbuch II*, pp. 187–88.

[15] This was in reply to questions submitted to him by *The New York Times* during a visit to the United States. See Dana Adams Schmidt, "Adenauer Gets Warm Farewell," *The New York Times*, May 30, 1957.

unarmed countries can be neutral in the sense that neither side is forced to count them as enemies or allies, but a large, armed country—armed perhaps with nuclear weapons—would be not so much neutral as just uncommitted; it might keep everyone in fear as to what it might decide to do at any time with its concentrated power. In the case of Germany, now still divided, neither Eastern nor Western leaders seem overly eager to hasten the day when such fears might become real.

Both sides have certain positive stakes in keeping Germany divided. For the Russian leaders the arming of Western Germany is of some value in maintaining their control over the satellite states, particularly Poland; even anti-Communist Poles greatly fear German rearmament and may reluctantly accept Soviet protection against an armed and reunited Germany. In the German Democratic Republic—the Soviet zone of Germany—the Russians have a buffer, a military staging area, an economic partner of growing importance, and a means of keeping Poland in a military and political vise.

The Western powers, on the other hand—and the United States in particuar—desire to retain West German military, political, and economic power in the competitive struggle with the Communist powers. Radar installations and missile bases, q 'te apart from military manpower, make the country too valuable a military asset to surrender readily.

The Problem of the Next Steps: Toward Reunification or Toward Other East-West Compromises?

While German reunification often has been described—particularly by German leaders—as a major means to lessen tensions between East and West, it seems possible that a reduction of international tensions through compromises on some other issues might make German reunification more acceptable to the other powers.

Thus, the great threat con ,onting the German objective of a reunited nation is the possibility of a tacit agreement between the great power leaders to leave the issue indefinitely in abeyance—as in the case of divided Korea and Indochina. This possibility has become particularly acute with recent attempts to halt the nuclear armament race between the Soviet Union and the United States. Prodded by Chancellor Adenauer, Western leaders formerly insisted that agreement on German reunification must precede agreement on disarmament, but indications have been abundant that their position need not remain rigid.[16] German unification,

---

[16] According to a Washington dispatch to *The New York Times* on June 7, 1958, a United States State Department announcement at the end of a meeting between Secretary Dulles and the German Foreign Minister, Heinrich von Brentano, "was carefully phrased to avoid the impression given by statements made after Chancellor Adenauer's visit . . . two years ago that West Germany sought to make reunification a prerequisite to significant disarmament."

unlike disarmament, has little appeal among either foreign policy elites or publics outside Germany. As one of the participants at a recent international conference on NATO put it: "For years now we have been saying that Germany must some day be reunited. But the fact is, and I say it with a heavy heart, maybe it is better for us if she is not."[17]

German decision makers could render the achievement of such East-West compromises on other issues more difficult. If they chose, they could exercise their influence to hamper or even block agreement on disarmament; they probably could intensify and dramatize the daily East-West frictions in divided Germany. But it is difficult to see how any such action would bring reunification any closer. At most they could use their insistence on the priority of reunification as a bargaining technique, in order to exact concessions from both East and West to German interests on other and more manageable matters.

[17] Gardner Paterson and Edgar S. Furniss, eds., *NATO: A Critical Appraisal* (Princeton, Princeton University Conference on NATO, 1957), p. 93.

IV
PROSPECTS AND PERSPECTIVES

CHAPTER 15

Landscape with crossroads: The unique
conditions of German foreign policy

It is time to sum up. What can we say, now that we have come near the end of our study?

German foreign policy is being made in the Federal Republic under highly unusual conditions. The process of its making is subject to unusual patterns of influence. These patterns of influence have changed considerably against the first half of the 1950's, and they promise to change further in the future.

The German Power Potential

German foreign policy deals with the international relations of a country that is potentially one of the three most powerful in the world. While the Federal Republic cannot expect to rival for the next decade either the United States or the Soviet Union in their respective combinations of population, area, and industrial strength, Western Germany ranks clearly ahead of Italy, Japan, China, and India in gross national product, and she is approaching the levels of the gross national product of France and Great Britain. It remains to be seen whether the Federal Republic, together with the now regained Saar territory, will eventually come to surpass France or even Britain, so as to gain third place in the world.[1]

It is illuminating to consider what would happen if the annual growth rates of the gross national products of each of the three countries were to continue in the future at the average levels of the years 1953–57. Annual economic growth averaged during these years 7.7 per cent for Western Germany, as against only 5.6 per cent for France and 2.9 per cent for

---

[1] Early indications of this possibility are found in statements such as these: "West Germany is becoming the third most important military power in the North Atlantic Treaty Organization, taking the place left vacant by France's troubles in Algeria and its disputes with its allies . . . By the end of next March, West Germany will have a 200,000-man force in the NATO defense line against any Soviet aggression, Herr Strauss said.

"A further indication of West Germany's emergence as the West's major continental military power was contained in the report that for the first time Germans will produce missiles. They will work with France and Italy on antiaircraft missiles which probably will be equipped eventually with nuclear warheads, informants said . . ." Associated Press, "Bonn Role in NATO Grows," *The Christian Science Monitor*, December 18, 1958, p. 9:6–8.

the United Kingdom. If one applies these rates to the dollar equivalents of the 1955 national incomes of these countries—estimated for that year at $51 billion, $45 billion, and $38 billion for the United Kingdom, France, and Western Germany, respectively—it appears that West Germany alone would overtake the United Kingdom, in regard to gross national product, by 1962, and similarly France by 1965. The predictive value of such exercises in projecting current trends into the future should certainly not be overestimated. But to statesmen who must think at least sometimes about the world of 1965, these figures may offer food for thought.[2]

Moreover, German power potential, economic and otherwise, is not exhausted by the capabilities of Western Germany. If reunification should come, at any time during the next ten or fifteen years, Germany would be a nation of 70 million, clearly overshadowing in industrial strength, at least for a time, all other countries except the United States and the Soviet Union. If German prosperity and prestige should attract once again a sufficient number of Austrians to revive the old sentiment for Austro-German union, the restored Greater Germany would soon comprise nearly 80 million people, and rank clearly as the third power in the world. None of these prospects is certain, but they represent real possibilities which exist for Germany and not, to any similar degree, for other powers. German policy is made inevitably against the background of this potential power.

The External Constraints

Germany's unusual potentialities are confronted by unusual restraints imposed upon her by the outside world. The country is divided; so is Berlin, her former capital. Eastern Germany is, in effect, under Soviet rule, and even the Federal Republic is required by treaties, as well as by the policies of her government, to have foreign troops on her soil. At least as much as other West European countries, the Federal Republic depends on United States military protection and political and economic good will, if no longer on outright economic aid. Such external constraints on the foreign policies of a country are not unique, but they are rare for a country of this size and degree of technological advancement; they have persisted for an unusually long time, and they seem likely to continue for some time in the future.

---

[2] The income estimates for 1955, computed in U.S. dollars at official rates of exchange, were taken from Research Center in Economic Development and Cultural Change of the University of Chicago, "The Role of Foreign Aid in the Development of Other Countries," in 85th U.S. Congress, 1st Session, Senate Document No. 52, *Foreign Aid Program: Compilation of Studies and Surveys* (Washington, D.C., U.S. Government Printing Office, July 1957), Appendix I, Table 1, p. 239. The rates of economic growth are given in United Nations, *Economic Survey of Europe in 1957* (Geneva, 1958), Chapter II, p. 3, Table 1.

Personal Uprootedness and the Lack of Acceptable Public Traditions

German foreign policy must be made under unusual conditions of psychological uprootedness. Most other countries have established national traditions to guide them. The members of their elites have a vast number of stable personal associations with places and people from their childhood, as well as with the values, beliefs, and traditions of their youth and early manhood. Individuals, groups, and nations all draw upon their past as a source of stability and guidance for the decisions of the present. But the German people and their leader cannot draw upon the memories of their homes and their past as freely and as often as other people can. Over one-fifth of them are expellees and refugees who may not see their former homes again. Additional numbers have been uprooted and displaced by the Second World War, and by the labor transfers, by the mass evacuations, sometimes by the political persecutions of the Nazi government, or by the allied bombings that leveled their cities and wiped out their former homes. In the stark physical sense, many millions of Germans cannot go home again to the places where they or their parents played as children.

What is true of their homes is even more true of their past. In the words of a distinguished observer:

> For the last ten years, Germans of all shades of opinion . . . have had to work together. . . . They have built a state and rebuilt an industrial economy. . . . Former resistance sympathizers and former [Nazi] party members . . . must now work . . . together. . . . But if such a group started to discuss the history of their country from 1933 to 1945, painful recollections would dominate the mood; discord would be certain to ensue. Necessary reticence in such gatherings has become a general reticence. In this sense . . . modern German history does begin in 1945.[3]

How tempting to pretend that all could be forgotten—that a poker-faced generation of amnesia cases could build a new German future by spreading clean new wallpaper over the family closets that contain too many skeletons! Indeed, they can be found—the smooth and evasive men of affairs, the elite members with the large gaps in their biographies—but how could they themselves forget what has happened? The American people have been unable to forget their own Civil War for what is now well-nigh a century. One can hardly expect the German people in the Old World to succeed in a feat of psychological suppression that has proved impossible in the New. To be sure, the feat of repression of recent history seems to have succeeded in part, on the surface, and in the short run. But the Germans' memories are here, as yet indigestible and incompatible, and they will have to be looked at and thought about if they are ever to be laid to rest. Until that time, however, they cannot be used as

[3] James B. Conant, *Germany and Freedom* (Cambridge, Harvard University Press, 1958), p. 18.

reliable and agreed-on guides to action. With their true and deep memories too deeply split, too often irreconcilable or intolerable, the German people and their leaders often have only artificial and shallow surface memories as guides to action.

Many surviving political symbols of the past appear now divisive—even Charlemagne appeals far more to Catholics than to Protestants—or else they appear as symbols of expediency and ambiguity. Does Bismarck's unparalleled popularity in the Federal Republic refer to the "Iron Chancellor" who united Germany by a "realistic" policy of blood and force, or does it refer to the prudent statesman who always avoided conflict with England and who maintained for so many years a secret agreement with Russia as a reinsurance for his dealings vis-à-vis the West? Does it refer to the victor over France, to the implacable enemy of the Poles, to the "honest broker" between Russia and England, or to the patient and persistent architect of ever greater German power? No other great nation has quite as many unresolved ambiguities in its image of its own past and of its desired future.

The Long Morning After: Consensus on Caution and Stability

Like other uprooted peoples after an epoch of war and revolution, many Germans of all ranks are longing above all for stability. Their private lives are filled with rebuilding of homes, of careers, of friendships—with the restoration or reconstruction of the whole fabric of private human relations that had been devastated or stunted by the uprootings of the past. Their politics are characterized by a broad pragmatic consensus on the need for order, security, and growth. Their mood has still something of the sober and disillusioned conservatism of a long morning after. It is a mood not wholly dissimilar to the one that once let diligence, craftsmanship, and *Hausmusik* flourish in Germany after the Thirty Years' War, or to the mood of the furniture- and family-conscious *Biedermeier* age after the Napoleonic upheavals.

German foreign policy can thus be based on an unusually broad basis of pragmatic agreement. It can count on a mood of conservatism, of disillusionment with ideologies, and of increased emphasis upon the private sphere of life which is highly compatible with an emphasis on competence, thrift, and productive effort, and thus eventually with a very large increase in the economic and administrative capabilities of the nation.

On this point German history could be instructive. The conservative Germany of the original Restoration and *Biedermeier* years of 1815–30 was also the Germany that saw the quiet drive for national economic unification which soon prevailed in Prussia and, by 1834, in most of Germany. These were also the years of the beginning Industrial Revolution in the Rhineland which eventually brought about a vast increase in German strength both in the economic and ultimately in the military field. To some future historian the new pragmatic conservatism of the Federal Republic in the years 1949 to 1958 may well appear as another epoch of rebuilding and increasing Germany's material capabilities for whatever policies the German people and its leaders may adopt at some future date if their mood should come to change. Until such a change, however, popular agreement to a foreign policy of cautious strengthening of German influence and power may well rely on unusually solid popular support.

The Limits of Agreement

Popular support for a moderate German foreign policy is remarkably dependable within a broad area of agreement, even though this area of agreement is confined by unusually sharp and critical limits.

Within the limits of consensus, however, the government and the ruling foreign policy elites of the Federal Republic have an unusually broad political mandate from the German people. It is a mandate compounded of relative apathy about the formation and content of policy and habitual efficiency and discipline in carrying it into effect, once it has been decided by the elites. Germans not only accepted various moderately unpopular policies of the Adenauer government with far less protest than Englishmen, Frenchmen, or Italians would have done, but they could also be depended upon to obey the laws and pay the taxes to carry these policies into effect. Within the limits acceptable for minimum concensus, the German elites have not only unusually wide leeway for decision, but also the likelihood of unusual effectiveness in execution, so far as mass compliance is concerned.

Agreement on foreign policy may prove limited, not only in substance but in time. German political consensus and stability appear markedly vulnerable to changes at home or abroad. Such changes could be economic, such as a major depression, or political, such as a major international crisis or substantial Soviet offer in regard to German reunification. Or they could be more gradual and cumulative in their impact, such as the change of political generations within Germany and perhaps the gnawing of sheer boredom.[4]

The foreign policy consensus is vulnerable to erosive changes over time, and its vulnerability is greatly increased by the conspicuously provisional character of the Federal Republic itself. Its people are being told daily by the authorities themselves that this "rump" state is not meant to last, that Bonn is only a provisional capital, that there is no German constitution but only a "Basic Law." Only a reunified Germany within her

---

[4] To some young Germans in the 1960's, Ludwig Erhard's reports of prosperity may ring as hollow as Louis Philippe's "Enrich yourselves, gentlemen!" did to the poet Lamartine who answered: "France is bored."

1937 frontiers is to be the true state, Berlin is to be the true capital, with the Bundestag already now periodically journeying to West Berlin in order to hold symbolic sessions. A real constitution is to be written only for this united Germany, by an all-German assembly, and all international alliances and agreements of the Federal Republic, such as its NATO membership, are to be reappraised and accepted or rejected by the all-German government and legislature. Pending this reunification, all political arrangements are to be provisional. Popular loyalties and sentiments are not to be given to the present West German state but only the future reunited Germany. There are only Germans, no "Federal Republicans." They sing as their anthem the traditional "Deutschland, Deutschland über alles," which refers to a united Germany. The same black, red, and gold flag is hoisted to the east and to the west of the line that is now dividing Germany. With a partly unacceptable past and an officially provisional present, the future of the German political consensus may well seem less than certain.

Time may destroy but it can also heal. It may set limits to the present consensus about German foreign policy but it may also consolidate gradually men's expectations of peace, constitutionalism, and democracy, and confirm their habits of behaving in accordence with these expectations. Time may thus bring a new and more fundamental consensus to German politics and foreign policy. It may wear away the one-eighth of the voters that today still profess clear-cut Nazi views and loyalties, and the one-fourth of voters who express anti-democratic and pro-Nazi views on many topics. It may strengthen the one-quarter or one-third of German voters who now profess all-weather support for democracy. It may enable Germans to look openly at their past, at all of it, and to see it more steadily in the light of a new period that no longer seems provisional but that has become securely established.

Until such a deeper and more fundamental political and moral stability is achieved, the makers of German foreign policy will have to play their roles against a background of continuing change and under conditions of unusual complexity and tension. As these conditions have changed in recent years, the patterns of influence in the formation and conduct of German foreign policy have changed with them. No change, however, has the force of fate. The actors in the foreign policy process have had real choices in responding to the impact of changes in the past, and they will have increasingly important choices in the future.

CHAPTER 16

Who prevailed:
The changing patterns of influence
in the German foreign policy process

In politics, no one is likely to win all the time. In the give and take among many domestic and foreign influences over foreign policy, no single group, individual, or government can always be expected to prevail. In the case of Germany, no foreign power—not even the United States— could completely dictate domestic decisions or override the consensus of mass opinion and elites. The external and the internal influences may go some way to balance each other; elites may balance or overbalance mass opinion; some elite groups may be counterpoised to others; and key individuals, such as the Chancellor, may try to shift the balance by their actions.

Nevertheless, some actors have tended to prevail far more often than others, or, at least, to find themselves more often on the winning side. Does this indicate that they had greater influence?

Judgments about Influence

On some particular issue, any group may embrace a distasteful policy in order to join the stronger battalions, or to rush to the assistance of the victors. But unless we assume a very unusual group indeed, we may expect that a group will tend to support in the long run such policies as appear rewarding to them. These policies might have prevailed, of course, without their help; but if their assistance were always useless, we might expect that in the long run such a group would cease to be taken seriously in politics. In short, if a group continues to be regarded as politically significant, and if the policies which it favors continue to prevail, then we may reasonably infer that it is more influential in politics than some other group for which these conditions do not hold, or hold only to a markedly lesser degree.

Influence is thus inferred provisionally from repeated association with prevailing policies, together with the continuing enjoyment of substantial status and prestige. It cannot well be inferred in this manner from any one decision, but only from several or many; and the inference should be tested and checked against other types of evidence.

In the end, the ascription of political influence to some person, group, or government is a matter of judgment. The use of operational definitions, quantitative codings, computations and the related apparatus of measurement at best can check and aid such judgments; it cannot replace them. Some charts and codings of this kind, concerning data about various policy decisions, will be presented later in this chapter. (See Tables 16.1 to 16.5.) None of these, however, are intended to represent anything more than aids to judgment, putting into more visible and systematic form some of the processes of surveying evidence which we are carrying out ordinarily, in our minds, with less formality, when we are forming our opinions about the relative influence of this or that group, agency, or politician.

A General Estimate of Influence

With these qualifications in mind, what can we say about the actors in the German foreign policy process?

The record of actual decisions between 1952 and 1958 confirms the intent of the Basic Law. The most influential single actor appears to have been the Chancellor, followed at a small distance by the cabinet and by the leadership group of the CDU and at another distance by the diplomatic elite.

All these are domestic actors. No foreign government, not even that of the United States, has matched the influence of the first three. The evidence suggests clearly that this leading constellation did not act like puppets of the United States; in several decisions they supported and carried policies very different from, and indeed partly opposed to, the policies preferred by the United States.

The United States, for its part, did exercise considerable influence over German foreign policy decisions—or, at least, such decisions more often than not had a way of yielding results closely in line with stated American policy preferences and objectives. No other foreign power approached this influence of the United States.

Of the other foreign powers, France had some influence on German policies; or, to put it differently, German policies were not infrequently so framed as to accord with the wishes and interests of France. The United Kingdom was markedly less often accommodated in this manner by German policy, and the Soviet Union had most of the time little or no direct influence, or a negative one, on the German policy decisions taken.

Associated with the leading domestic elite groups most influential in foreign policy—the cabinet, CDU leaders, and diplomats—are two other elites with a not dissimilar basic outlook. The Roman Catholic bishops and the high-level civil servants both appear to have some marked influence on, or reason for satisfaction with, the trend of foreign policy decisions. They are followed, at a distance, by the big business leaders—insofar as these cared to interest themselves in foreign policy matters—and by the press elite. The military had not yet appeared in sufficient strength to write a political record in the field of foreign policy for the Bonn Republic.

Finally, three elites—the Social Democratic leaders, the trade union leaders, and the bishops of the Evangelical Church—appeared to have had relatively the least influence over the making of foreign policy. These groups usually could expect to feel neutral or slightly negative about an "average" decision, or they might expect to have a policy decision favorable to their wishes balanced in short order by another decision carried despite their opposition. The Social Democrats and the trade union leaders showed interest in foreign policy issues, but had relatively few channels of access to the places where decisions were made. The Protestant bishops showed less interest in foreign policy, and their opportunities for access to decision making and decision makers were likewise limited. Both Labor and the Protestant Churches seemed unlikely to cooperate effectively in the near future, and they were handicapped by class and residential barriers to their political appeals. Social Democrats and trade unionists have persistently failed to win much middle-class support, or to make much headway among the rural population. The major Protestant churches, on the other hand, are predominantly middle-class and rural; the urban and industrial working class in considerable part has become estranged from them. The influence of these elites on foreign policy has been mainly indirect, and seems likely to remain so unless there should be some major change within one of them or in the general political situation.

The pattern of influence indicated thus an inside group of elites with marked influence: the politicians of the cabinet and CDU leadership; the administrative elite in diplomacy and the civil service, and the Roman Catholic bishops. In contrast to these, three elites seemed somewhat debarred from influence and access to policy decisions: the Socialist and trade union leaders and the Protestant bishops. Three intermediate elites showed a clear potential for increasing their influence; big business, the press leaders, and the military, and the influence of all three has been rising since 1955.

The distribution of influence has changed in time. Two stages or periods stand out in contrast. The first, preceding the granting of sovereignty to the Federal Republic, extends from 1949 to May 1955. The second, after sovereignty, extends from May 1955 to the time of writing, and quite possibly beyond. The two periods are distinct not only in legal form but in the substance of the policy decisions taken and in the considerable changes in regard to influence over the policy process.

Influence Patterns Before Sovereignty: 1949 to May 1955

The first stage in the political development of the Federal Republic was the period of occupation. It lasted from the formation of the Republic in September 1949 until its emancipation from the rule of the Allied High Commission in May 1955.

Throughout the period, German policy had to follow the lead of the allies, and in particular of the United States, in order to earn their confidence and win the next concessions from them on the road to sovereignty.

The five major German foreign policy decisions of the period, pertaining to the agreements on ECSC, EDC, Israeli reparations, the Saar, and NATO membership, respectively, were made in full accordance with known desires of the government of the United States. Britain and France, supporting the same policies, though not always with the same enthusiasm, shared this American success, and thus, presumably, had an only slightly lesser degree of influence. The Soviet Union was strongly opposed to the four policies which linked Germany more firmly to the Western bloc, and it was presumably at least mildly opposed to the fifth, the German-Israeli Reparations Agreement.[1] Soviet opposition, however, was ineffective in all cases; it produced no visible modifications in the outcome.

Within Germany, only Chancellor Adenauer had identified himself completely with policies that were adopted. German mass opinion was usually, on the average, lukewarm, divided, or indifferent. Among the German elites, the groups closest to the Chancellor—the cabinet, the leaders of his party, and the chief diplomats—gave substantial support to his foreign policy. Two other groups closely identified with his regime—the senior civil servants and the Roman Catholic hierarchy—supported the same policies but not always with equal consistency or vigor.

The main opposition to the four "Western bloc" policies came from the Social Democrats; but this produced no major changes in the decisions taken. It was the solid support of just this party, however, which enabled Adenauer to carry the fifth decision—the Israeli agreement—on which he was deserted by a substantial portion of his own party. Many of the Social Democratic views on these matters were shared, with a lesser degree of intensity, by the trade union leaders and possibly by the Protestant bishops. Though these groups were no more successful in modifying the policies of the government, they had been less strongly committed to any such endeavor.

The leaders of the business community were closely associated with many domestic policies of the government, but it seems that in this period they took far less interest in most foreign policy matters, or else they

---

[1] It will be recalled that the German Communist party opposed the agreement, and that the Soviet-controlled German Democratic Republic accepted no reparations obligations of this kind.

were divided, or even in some instances moderately opposed to the government's course.

The press elite was often noncommittal or divided, reflecting the coolness of mass opinion and the divisions among the political parties and major interest groups. Even the relatively most popular decisions of the government, those in favor of ECSC and of the Paris Agreements, were only mildly supported by the balance of the press. The military leaders, finally, were as yet not much in evidence. They seem to have made no concerted major effort to exert influence, nor are there any indications that they did so.

In sum, the main influence over German foreign policy between 1949 and May 1955 was exercised from abroad, by the United States and its main Western allies. There was relatively little spontaneous domestic support for the policies that emerged. For the most part they were accepted as means to an end—the removal of the occupation regime, the preservation of Western protection and support, and the restoration of Germany's national independence and international position. Chancellor Adenauer and his associates undertook to procure these ends by sponsoring the decisions required, but mass opinion and most of the elites remained more or less aloof from the highly circumscribed German foreign policies of the occupation era. With the coming of sovereignty, this situation was to change.

The Realignment of Influence: 1955 to 1958

The most striking fact about the foreign policy decisions of the sovereign Republic since mid-1955 is the shift of influence from the external to the internal actors in the policy process. The period since 1955 has been rich in foreign policy decisions. These decisions—listed in Table 16.1—did not support consistently the interests of any power except Germany.

The United States government was not enthusiastic about Germany's opening of diplomatic relations with the Soviet Union. Nor was it pleased with the decision to shorten the length of military training for conscripts to twelve months as against the eighteen months planned within Germany's NATO program, or indeed with the decision to cut back the scale and tempo of the German military build-up.

France and England would have preferred more "European" or "NATO" solidarity from Germany in their dealings with the Arab world, but Germany decided on a policy of Arab friendship, loans and trade, neutrality in the Suez war of 1956, and the conspicuous early recognition of the Iraqi revolutionary government in 1958.

Russia finally must continue to oppose the basic pro-Western trend of German policy and the continued emphasis on American friendship,

NATO alliance (including the acceptance of atomic weapons for the German army and the possibility of American missile bases on German soil), and efforts toward European integration in such decisions as the conclusion of the Euratom and Common Market Treaties.

Taken together, these policies were neither opportunistic nor chaotic. They were based on an estimate of self-interest, loyalty to explicit alliances and treaty obligations, and on a decent respect for the feelings of allies as well as for the feelings of Asian and African peoples. They involved an independent appraisal of German interests as well as of the interests of the non-Communist world. Vis-à-vis the West as a whole, Germany's policy was not that of a pupil or a puppet, but that of an ally.

It is not certain, however, whether this will make Germany more popular abroad. Foreign governments are not always more pleased with allies than with satellites. No foreign power has been able to dominate German foreign policy, and no foreign power has had cause to be more than mildly pleased—and sometimes even displeased—with the sum total of its course.

Compared to the pre-1955 period, United States influence has declined. Seen in international terms German foreign policy has become markedly more independent. It stands by its allies but it will now override their known wishes in regard to particular issues. As it pleases its allies somewhat less, it also is less consistent in displeasing their adversary. German policy is now less completely lined up with United States preferences, and less consistently resented by the Soviet Union.

The influence of France and the United Kingdom has fallen even more. Neither country can present any longer even the appearance of controlling, or substantially influencing the whole of German foreign policy, even though they may obtain accommodation on particular issues.

Of the two, France has been more successful in obtaining such concessions, particularly in regard to economic problems on the European continent, even if on other occasions German policy makers have preferred to cultivate Arab friendship, particularly in Egypt and Iraq, rather than defer to French wishes in those regions.

England, on the other hand, has found fewer accomodations from Germany, while feeling equally keenly German political and economic competition in the Arab world. On balance, England may well feel somewhat displeased with the trend of German policies since 1955, and embarrassingly unable to influence them with effect. The markedly cool attitude of a good deal of British opinion on the occasion of President Heuss's visit to England in the fall of 1958—despite the President's consistent democratic record and splendid human qualities—may be understood more readily against this background.

The shifts from the pre-1955 period were particularly drastic during the first two years of readjustment, from the winning of sovereignty in May 1955 to the Soviet intervention in the Hungarian uprising in October

1956. The mood of relaxation of international tensions after the Geneva Conference of 1955 between Russia, the United States, France, and Britain may have contributed to the markedly greater independence of German foreign policy in this period. It is possible, however, that some form of psychological rebound after the occupation years would have occurred in German politics and foreign policy even if current East-West tensions had remained unchanged. In any case, the relatively greater independence of German foreign policy has persisted, to some degree at last, even in the tense years after 1956; the early German recognition of the Iraqi revolutionists in 1958 may serve as an instance. An even more striking illustration is the ignoring of United States objections to the cutting of United States coal exports to Germany by a new German coal tariff in early 1959. An American newspaper report reflects eloquently the changed atmosphere in Bonn:

> The Bonn Government brushed aside a last-minute request of the United States for a sixty-day delay and the Bundestag approved a 10 per cent tariff today on foreign coal imports.
> The tariff is aimed at curbing the import of United States coal. It was approved by the Bundestag, the lower house of Parliament, by a substantial majority. Party discipline was imposed on reluctant Government Deputies to carry the bill against Socialist and Free Democratic opposition.
> Twelve hours earlier the Foreign Ministry advised the United States Embassy that it was too late to hold up the tariff measure, designed to overcome the overproduction crisis in the Ruhr coal industry.
> The Embassy had requested the sixty-day delay in imposing the tariff after it had become clear that the United States protest, delivered Tuesday, would be ignored . . .[2]

As the external influences on German foreign policy have declined, the internal ones have risen. Taking the average of eleven policy decisions in 1955–58, mass opinion has been moderately but markedly favorable to the general course adopted, even though particular decisions—such as the acceptance of atomic arms for German soldiers and the possible establishment of American missile bases on German soil—have remained unpopular.

With its greater freedom of maneuver, German foreign policy has increased its ability to accomodate domestic elite opinions and interest groups. All elites that were surveyed appear to have drawn more closely together, and they seem to have moved, on balance, toward a markedly greater support of, and satisfaction with, the foreign policies adopted.

Only the Chancellor's influence has declined somewhat. He could no longer point to the overwhelming need to adopt his policies in order to win critically needed concessions from the West. He had to modify his

---

[2] Arthur J. Olsen, "Bonn House Votes Coal Import Duty," *The New York Times*, January 31, 1959, p. 2:8.

position on the issues of the length of military service for conscripts in late 1955, and on the manpower levels of the armed forces in October 1956. Though less towering than before 1955, his over-all influence nevertheless remained high, and so did that of his close associates, the cabinet, the CDU leaders, and the high-ranking diplomats.

Another group, however, has now joined the ranks of those visibly influential in foreign policy matters. Big business now appears far more clearly in favor of the particular policies pursued than was the case before 1955. The more independent German policy after 1955, opening up additional opportunities and markets in areas outside the main Western countries, and often in competition with them, has been more in line with business interests. In the Near and Middle East, in Latin America, and even in Communist bloc countries the current German policies have helped German exports to reach third rank in world trade, reaching 8 per cent of the total in 1957. In the same year, nearly 18 per cent of the German national product went into exports, compared with hardly 10 per cent in 1936. In the 1957 exports, capital goods predominated heavily, particularly in the trade with underdeveloped countries, in contrast to the consumer goods emphasis of the 1930's.[3] These trade patterns imply the need for more trade with neutralists, more competition with other Western countries, and a more skillful and independent foreign policy. Since 1955, trends in German foreign policy have often been responsive to these needs.

Though overtaken by big business, the senior civil service and the Roman Catholic hierarchy have retained their inside position; German foreign policy continues to be markedly compatible with their views. The military leaders have gained in importance. Though their views have not always been heeded, they seem to be moving toward the status of insiders in the foreign policy process.

Even the opposition has abated. While it has remained intense on some issues, its views have been accommodated on others. The press elite, reflecting in part mass opinion, may find recent foreign policy more to its liking. The Social Democrats and trade union leaders, too, may feel at least mildly pleased, on balance, with the trend of many of the foreign policy decisions since mid-1955. Reflecting the reduced cleavage between the other elites, the balance of press opinion is now more often in favor of official foreign policies. Only the Protestant bishops seem still to be much of the time outside the circle of those whose views are heeded. Whether by choice and lack of interest, or because of political ineffectiveness, they still rank at the bottom of the foreign policy elites.

It should be recalled at this point that all that has been said so far in this chapter has been based on impressions. These impressions have been coded and arranged for convenient comparison in Tables 16.1 to 16.4,

[3] Wolf Dieter Lindner, "The Balance Sheet of German Foreign Trade," in *Meet Germany* (5th rev. ed., Hamburg, Atlantik-Brücke, May 1958), pp. 45–47.

and our over-all estimates of rank orders of influences have been made in their light. These estimates may prove fallible indeed. Is there any empirical evidence of elite attitudes than can be used to check them?

A sample survey of elite members in 1956 revealed their attitudes toward a number of 1952–55 policy decisions in regard to European integration.[4] The results are shown in Table 16.5.

While the selection of the surveyed does not make the results wholly comparable with other data, they reveal some interesting cleavages between elites and mass opinion and between different elites. All elites appeared more strongly in favor of European integration and of a military effort than was mass opinion, and they were far less indifferent. While the public was most strongly opposed to the military aspects of these pro-Western policies, the civil service, business, and military elites were relatively most opposed to any loss of sovereignty. All elites agreed with the public in giving most support and least opposition to relatively ambiguous and innocuous propositions, such as "Western European Union," with no clear-cut implications of new military efforts or new restraints on sovereignty.

Of all elites surveyed, the military—who included key officers engaged in organizing the new German army in association with Theodor Blank, the first Federal Minister of Defense—showed on the average the relatively lowest levels of support, and the highest levels of resistance, to all schemes of supranational integration. Among all elites, support fell off and opposition increased with extent of interference with national sovereignty implied by each scheme.

Together with our earlier findings, these data may suggest something about prospective elite attitudes and influence patterns in the future. As the internal setting becomes more important for foreign policy, and external influences decline, the influence of domestic elites, skeptical of supranational institutions, may increase. If these elites have their way, German military strength will be built up. To the extent that the military elite, in particular, gains in size and influence, the resistance to supranational integration may be expected to increase still further. An armed and sovereign nationalism might well be the outcome.

German opinion as presently constituted would oppose militarization; and if mass opinion should continue to gain weight in the policy process, it would slow down the trend to greater armaments but not necessarily the trend toward stronger assertion of national sovereignty. The preference of mass opinion in this respect are indicated by a comparison of poll results given in Table 16.6.

---

[4] This survey was carried out in 1956 by the University of Cologne for a research project under the direction of Professor Daniel Lerner at the Center for International Studies at the Massachusetts Institute of Technology. The data are given in Suzanne Keller, "Attitudes Toward European Integration of the German Elite" (Center for International Studies, Massachusetts Institute of Technology, October 1957, multigraphed), p. 26, Table 6.

TABLE 16.1

INTERRELATIONSHIP BETWEEN INTERNAL AND EXTERNAL COMPONENTS

Issue	1 ECSC Treaty Jan. 1952	2 Reparations Agreement with Israel March 1953	3 EDC Treaty May 1953	4 Paris Agreements Feb. 1955
Action proposed by Chancellor..	Parl. approval	Parl. approval	Parl. approval	Parl. approval
Alternative course of action.....	Reject treaty	Reject treaty	Reject treaty	Reject treaty
Internal Components	REACTION TO CHANCELLOR'S PROPOSED COURSE OF ACTION			
Political elites:				
Cabinet	3	1	3	3
CDU	3	00	3	3
SPD	—3	3	—3	—3
Administrative elites:				
Senior civil servants..........	3	1	2	2
Senior diplomats	—	1	2	3
Military leaders	—	—	—1	3
Economic elites:				
Big business	00	—2	—1	2
Trade unions	00	2	—3	—3
Religious elites:				
Roman Catholic church.......	3	1	2	0
Evangelical church	—1	1	—2	—2
Press	1	00	00	1
Aggregate elite score...........	9	8	2	9
Mass opinion	1	—2	—2	2
External Components[a]				
Western powers:				
U.S.[b]	6	6	6	6
U.K.	2	3	3	3
France	3	3	3	1
USSR	—3	—1	—3	—3
External aggregate	8	11	9	7
Summary				
External average	1.6	2.2	1.8	1.4
Mass opinion	1	—2	—2	2
Elite opinion (ave.)...........	1.0	0.8	0.18	0.82
Total (ave. of above 3 rows).....	1.2	0.33	—0.01	1.41
Course of action taken.........	Chancellor course	Chancellor course	Chancellor course	Chancellor course

Key: 3, very favorable; 2, mostly favorable; 1, mildly favorable; 0, indifferent; 00, divided; —1, mildly opposed; —2, opposed; —3, strongly opposed.

[a] Official reaction of government.

[b] U.S. reaction counted double; hence external average obtained by dividing external aggregate by 5.

IN 16 FOREIGN POLICY ISSUES, 1952–1958

Issue	5 Franco-German Saar Agreement May 1955	6 Diplo. Relations with Soviet Union Sept. 1955	7 Length of Milit. Conscrip. Serv. Dec. 1955	8 Size of Armed Forces May 1955– Oct. 1956
Action proposed by Chancellor..	Accept treaty	Estab. diplo. relations	18 mos.	500,000 men by 1960 as promised U.S. in 1955
Alternative course of action.....	Reject treaty	Do not estab. diplo. relat.	12 mos.	Slower build-up
		REACTION TO CHANCELLOR'S PROPOSED COURSE OF ACTION		
Internal Components				
Political elites:				
Cabinet	1	1	1	1
CDU	1	1	1	1
SPD	—3	3	—3	—3
Administrative elites:				
Senior civil servants..........	0	1	1	0
Senior diplomats	2	1	2	0
Military leaders	—2	1	2	3
Economic elites:				
Big business	—2	2	—2	—1
Trade unions	—2	3	—3	—3
Religious elites:				
Roman Catholic church.......	2	—1	0	0
Evangelical church	—2	3	0	0
Press	—2	2	—1	00
Aggregate elite score...........	—7	17	—2	—2
Mass opinion	—2	2	—3	—3
External Components[a]				
Western powers:				
U.S.[b]	6	—4	6	6
U.K.	3	—2	3	3
France	3	—2	3	1
USSR	—2	3	—3	—3
External aggregate	10	—5	9	7
Summary				
External average	2.0	—1.0	1.8	1.4
Mass opinion	—2	2	—3	—3
Elite opinion (ave.)...........	—0.64	1.55	—0.18	—0.18
Total (ave. of above 3 rows).....	—0.21	0.85	—0.46	—0.59
Course of action taken..........	Chancellor course	Chancellor course	Alternative to Chancellor course	Alternative to Chancellor course

Key: 3, very favorable; 2, mostly favorable; 1, mildly favorable; 0, indifferent; 00, divided; —1, mildly opposed; —2, opposed; —3, strongly opposed.

[a] Official reaction of government.

[b] U.S. reaction counted double; hence external average obtained by dividing external aggregate by 5.

TABLE 16.1

INTERRELATIONSHIP BETWEEN INTERNAL AND EXTERNAL COMPONENTS

Issue	9 Position in Suez War Nov. 1956	10 European Common Market Treaty July 1957	11 Euratom Treaty July 1957	12 Yugoslav Recognition of DDR Oct. 1957
Action proposed by Chancellor..	Neutrality	Parl. approval	Parl. approval	Sever diplo., not econ., rel. with Yugoslavia
Alternative course of action.....	Support or oppose Israeli French British attack	Reject treaty	Reject treaty	Do not sever relations
Internal Components	REACTION TO CHANCELLOR'S PROPOSED COURSE OF ACTION			
Political elites:				
Cabinet	2	3	3	1
CDU	2	2	3	1
SPD	1	2	3	—3
Administrative elites:				
Senior civil servants.........	1	3	3	0
Senior diplomats	2	3	3	1
Military leaders	00	00	2	1
Economic elites:				
Big business	2	2	3	—2
Trade unions	2	2	3	—2
Religious elites:				
Roman Catholic church.......	—1	3	3	3
Evangelical church	0	1	2	—1
Press	2	2	3	—2
Aggregate elite score...........	13	23	31	—3
Mass opinion	2	2	2	1
External Components[a]				
Western powers:				
U.S.[b]	6	4	6	6
U.K.	—1	—3	1	0
France	—1	3	3	0
USSR	—3	—3	—3	—3
External aggregate	1	1	7	3
Summary				
External average	0.2	0.2	1.4	0.6
Mass opinion	2	2	2	1
Elite opinion (ave.)...........	1.18	2.09	2.82	—0.27
Total (ave. of above 3 rows).....	1.13	1.43	2.07	0.44
Course of action taken..........	Chancellor course	Chancellor course	Chancellor course	Chancellor course

Key: 3, very favorable; 2, mostly favorable; 1, mildly favorable; 0, indifferent; 00, divided; —1, mildly opposed; —2, opposed; —3, strongly opposed.

[a] Official reaction of government.

[b] U.S. reaction counted double; hence external average obtained by dividing external aggregate by 5.

(*Continued*)

IN 16 FOREIGN POLICY ISSUES, 1952–1958

Issue	13 Rapacki Plan for Disengagement Feb. 1958	14 Equip Armed Force with Atomic Weapons March 1958	15 U.S. Missile Bases in Germany March 1958	16 Iraqi Revolution July 1958
Action proposed by Chancellor..	Reject proposal	Atomic arms	Permit bases	Immed. diplo. recog. (before U.S., Britain, and France)
Alternative course of action.....	Accept conditionally	No atomic arms	Forbid bases	Delay recog.
	REACTION TO CHANCELLOR'S PROPOSED COURSE OF ACTION			
Internal Components				
Political elites:				
Cabinet	3	3	1	2
CDU	3	2	1	2
SPD	—3	—3	—3	3
Administrative elites:				
Senior civil servants....	2	1	1	0
Senior diplomats	2	3	1	2
Military leaders	2	3	2	2
Economic elites:				
Big business	2	2	1	3
Trade unions	—2	—3	—3	3
Religious elites:				
Roman Catholic church.......	2	1	0	0
Evangelical church	—2	—2	—2	0
Press	00	—1	—2	2
Aggregate elite score...........	9	6	—3	19
Mass opinion	2	—3	—2	2
External Components[a]				
Western powers:				
U.S.[b]	6	6	6	—2
U.K.	3	1	3	—3
France	3	1	2	—3
USSR	—3	—3	—3	3
External aggregate	9	5	8	—5
Summary				
External average	1.8	1.0	1.6	—1.0
Mass opinion	2	—3	—2	2
Elite opinion (ave.)............	0.82	0.55	—0.27	1.73
Total (ave. of above 3 rows).....	1.54	—0.48	—0.22	0.91
Course of action taken..........	Chancellor course	Modified Chancellor course	Modified Chancellor course (permit bases if NATO requests them)	Chancellor course

Key: 3, very favorable; 2, mostly favorable; 1, mildly favorable; 0, indifferent; 00, divided; —1, mildly opposed; —2, opposed; —3, strongly opposed.
[a] Official reaction of government.
[b] U.S. reaction counted double; hence external average obtained by dividing external aggregate by 5.

TABLE 16.2

SATISFACTION SCORE
EX POST REACTION OF INTERNAL AND EXTERNAL COMPONENTS

Issue	1 ECSC Treaty Jan. 1952	2 Reparations Agreement with Israel March 1953	3 EDC Treaty May 1953	4 Paris Agreements Feb. 1955
Internal Components				
Political elites:				
Cabinet	3	1	3	3
CDU	3	00	3	3
SPD	—3	3	—3	—3
Administrative elites:				
Senior civil servants	3	1	2	2
Senior diplomats	—	1	2	3
Military leaders	—	—	—1	3
Economic elites:				
Big business	00	—2	—1	2
Trade unions	00	2	—3	—3
Religious elites:				
Roman Catholic church	3	0	2	0
Evangelical church	—1	1	—2	—2
Press	1	00	00	1
Aggregate elite score	9	7	2	9
Mass opinion	1	—2	—2	2
External Components[a]				
Western powers:				
U.S.[b]	6	6	6	6
U.K.	2	3	3	3
France	3	3	3	1
USSR	—3	—1	—3	—3
Aggregate external components	8	11	9	7
Summary				
Mass opinion score	1	—2	—2	2
Ave. of aggregate elites	1.0	0.7	0.18	0.82
Ave. of external components	1.6	2.2	1.8	1.4
Total (ave. of above 3 rows)	1.2	0.3	—0.01	1.41

Key: 3, very favorable; 2, mostly favorable; 1, mildly favorable; 0, indifferent; 00, divided; —1, mildly opposed; —2, opposed; —3, strongly opposed.

[a] Official reaction of government.

[b] U.S. reaction counted double; hence external average obtained by dividing external aggregate by 5.

IN FOREIGN POLICY PROCESS IN 16 FOREIGN POLICY ISSUES, 1952–1958

Issue	5 Saar Agreement May 1955	6 Diplo. Relations with Soviet Union Sept. 1955	7 12-Month Conscription Dec. 1955	8 Slower Army Build-up Oct. 1956
Internal Components				
Political elites:				
Cabinet	1	1	1	2
CDU	1	1	2	2
SPD	—3	3	2	2
Administrative elites:				
Senior civil servants	0	1	0	0
Senior diplomats	2	1	0	0
Military leaders	—2	1	—2	—2
Economic elites:				
Big business	—2	2	2	0
Trade unions	—2	3	2	2
Religious elites:				
Roman Catholic church	2	—1	0	0
Evangelical church	—2	3	0	0
Press	—2	2	2	2
Aggregate elite score	—7	17	9	8
Mass opinion	—2	2	2	3
External Components[a]				
Western powers:				
U.S.[b]	6	—4	—6	—6
U.K.	3	—2	—3	—3
France	3	—2	—3	—1
USSR	—2	3	3	3
Aggregate external components	10	—5	—9	—7
Summary				
Mass opinion score	—2	2	2	3
Ave. of aggregate elites	—0.64	1.55	0.82	0.73
Ave. of external components	2.0	—1.0	—1.8	—1.4
Total (ave. of above 3 rows)	—0.21	0.85	0.34	0.78

Key: 3, very favorable; 2, mostly favorable; 1, mildly favorable; 0, indifferent; 00, divided; —1, mildly opposed; —2, opposed; —3, strongly opposed.

[a] Official reaction of government.

[b] U.S. reaction counted double; hence external average obtained by dividing external aggregate by 5.

TABLE 16.2

SATISFACTION SCORE
EX POST REACTION OF INTERNAL AND EXTERNAL COMPONENTS

Issue	9 Neutrality in Suez War Nov. 1956	10 Common Market Treaty July 1957	11 Euratom Treaty July 1957	12 Break of Diplo. Rel. with Yugoslavia Oct. 1957
Internal Components				
Political elites:				
Cabinet	2	3	3	1
CDU	2	2	3	1
SPD	2	2	3	—3
Administrative elites:				
Senior civil servants	0	3	3	0
Senior diplomats	2	3	3	1
Military leaders	00	00	2	0
Economic elites:				
Big business	2	2	3	—2
Trade unions	2	2	3	—2
Religious elites:				
Roman Catholic church	0	3	3	3
Evangelical church	0	1	2	—1
Press	2	2	3	—2
Aggregate elite score	14	23	31	—4
Mass opinion	2	2	2	1
External Components[a]				
Western powers:				
U.S.[b]	6	4	6	6
U.K.	—1	—3	1	0
France	—1	3	3	0
USSR	—3	—3	—3	—3
Aggregate external components	1	1	7	3
Summary				
Mass opinion score	2	2	2	1
Ave. of aggregate elites	1.27	2.09	2.82	—0.36
Ave. of external components	0.2	0.2	1.4	0.6
Total (ave. of above 3 rows)	1.16	1.43	2.07	0.41

Key: 3, very favorable; 2, mostly favorable; 1, mildly favorable; 0, indifferent; 00, divided; —1, mildly opposed; —2, opposed; —3, strongly opposed.

[a] Official reaction of government.

[b] U.S. reaction counted double; hence external average obtained by dividing external aggregate by 5.

(*Continued*)

IN FOREIGN POLICY PROCESS IN 16 FOREIGN POLICY ISSUES, 1952–1958

Issue	13 Rejection of Rapacki Plan Feb. 1958	14 Atomic Arms for Army March 1958	15 U.S. Missile Bases March 1958	16 Recog. of Iraqi Regime July 1958
Internal Components				
Political elites:				
Cabinet	3	3	1	2
CDU	3	2	1	2
SPD	—3	—3	—3	3
Administrative elites:				
Senior civil servants....................	2	0	1	0
Senior diplomats.......................	2	3	1	2
Military leaders.......................	00	3	2	2
Economic elites:				
Big business..........................	2	1	1	3
Trade unions..........................	—2	—3	—3	3
Religious elites:				
Roman Catholic church.................	2	1	0	0
Evangelical church.....................	—2	—2	—2	0
Press	00	—1	—2	2
Aggregate elite score....................	7	4	—3	19
Mass opinion...........................	2	—3	—2	2
External Components[a]				
Western powers:				
U.S.[b]	6	6	6	—2
U.K.	3	1	3	—3
France	3	1	2	—3
USSR	—3	—3	—3	3
Aggregate external components...........	9	5	8	—5
Summary				
Mass opinion score......................	2	—3	—2	2
Ave. of aggregate elites.................	0.64	0.36	—0.27	1.73
Ave. of external components..............	1.8	1.0	1.6	—1.0
Total (ave. of above 3 rows)..............	1.48	—0.55	—0.22	0.91

Key: 3, very favorable; 2, mostly favorable; 1, mildly favorable; 0, indifferent; 00, divided; —1, mildly opposed; —2, opposed; —3, strongly opposed.

[a] Official reaction of government.

[b] U.S. reaction counted double; hence external average obtained by dividing external aggregate by 5.

TABLE 16.2 (*concluded*)

SATISFACTION SCORE

EX POST REACTION OF INTERNAL AND EXTERNAL COMPONENTS IN FOREIGN POLICY PROCESS
IN 16 FOREIGN POLICY ISSUES, 1952–1958

Issue	Total all issues/ Av. satis. score		Total Jan. 1952–May 1955 Av. satis. score		Total May 1955–July 1958 Av. satis. score	
	Total	Score	Total	Score	Total	Score
Internal Components						
Political elites:						
Cabinet	33	2.1	11	2.2	22	2.0
CDU	31	1.9	10	2	21	1.9
SPD	—4	—0.3	—9	—1.8	5	0.5
Administrative elites:						
Senior civil servants	18	1.1	8	1.6	10	0.9
Senior diplomats	26	1.7	8	2	18	1.6
Military leaders	6	0.4	0	0	6	0.6
Economic elites						
Big business	13	0.8	—3	—0.6	16	1.5
Trade unions	1	—0.1	—6	—1.2	9	0.6
Religious elites:						
Roman Catholic church	18	1.2	7	1.4	11	1
Evangelical church	—7	—0.4	—6	—1.2	—1	—0.1
Press	10	0.6	0	0	10	0.9
Aggregate elite score	145	0.91	20	4	125	11.4
Mass opinion	10	0.6	—3	—0.6	13	1.2
External Components[a]						
Western powers:						
U.S.[b]	52	3.3	30	6	22	2.0
U.K.	7	0.4	14	2.8	—7	—.6
France	15	0.9	13	2.6	2	.2
USSR	—21	—1.3	—12	—2.4	—9	—.8
Aggregate external components	53	3.3	45	9	8	.7
Summary						
Mass opinion score	11	0.6	—3	—0.6	13	1.2
Ave. of aggregate elites	13.44	0.84	2.06	0.41	11.38	1.03
Ave. of external components	10.6	0.66	9.0	1.8	1.6	0.1
Total (ave. of above 3 rows)	11.35	0.71	2.69	0.54	8.66	0.79

Key: 3, very favorable; 2, mostly favorable; 1, mildly favorable; 0, indifferent; 00, divided; —1, mildly opposed; —2, opposed; —3, strongly opposed.

[a] Official reaction of government.

[b] U.S. reaction counted double; hence external average obtained by dividing external aggregate by 5.

TABLE 16.3

THREE IMPLIED DECISIONS, 1956–1958 ISSUES THAT MAY HAVE BEEN OR MIGHT HAVE BEEN RAISED, CHANCELLOR ADENAUER'S PROBABLE POSITION AND PROBABLE SATISFACTION OF INTERNAL AND EXTERNAL COMPONENTS IN REGARD TO THE CHANCELLOR'S POSITION, AND THE PROBABLE OUTCOME

Issue	Sever All Relations, Incl. Econ., with Yugoslavia, Oct. 1957	Seek Treaty Amend. to Permit Production of ABC Weapons	Establish Diplo. Rel. with Com. China	Total	Ave.
Government policy (actual)	Sever only diplo. relations	Defer request	No diplo. relations		
Main alternative (hypothetical)	Sever all relations	Demand treaty revision	Est. diplo. relations		
Internal Components					
Political elites:					
Cabinet	1	2	2	5	1.67
CDU	—1	2	2	3	1
SPD	3	3	—2	4	1.33
Administrative elites:					
Senior civil servants.......	1	—1	0	0	0
Senior diplomats	1	—2	—1	—2	—0.67
Military leaders	—1	—3	0	—4	—1.33
Economic elites:					
Big business	3	—2	—2	—1	—0.33
Trade unions	3	3	—2	4	1.33
Religious elites:					
Roman Catholic church....	—2	0	2	0	0
Evangelical church	2	2	1	5	1.67
Press	2	2	1	5	1.67
Aggregate elite score........	12	6	1	19	6.33
Mass opinion	—1	3	1	3	1
External Components[a]					
Western powers:					
U.S.[b]	4	4	6	14	4.67
U.K.	0	2	—1	1	0.33
France	0	3	—1	2	0.67
USSR	—3	3	—3	—3	—1
Aggregate external components	1	12	1	14	4.67
Summary					
Average external components	0.2	2.4	0.2	2.8	0.93
Mass opinion	—1	3	1	3	1
Average elite opinion	1.09	0.55	0.09	1.73	0.58
Total (ave. of above 3 rows)..	0.10	1.98	0.43	2.51	0.84
		OUTCOME			
Outcome	Chancellor course	Chancellor course	Chancellor course		

Key: 3, very favorable; 2, mostly favorable; 1, mildly favorable; 0, indifferent; 00, divided; —1, mildly opposed; —2, opposed; —3, strongly opposed.

[a] Official reaction of government.

[b] U.S. reaction counted double; hence external average obtained by dividing external aggregate by 5.

TABLE 16.4

AVERAGE SATISFACTION SCORES FOR THE CHANCELLOR, 11 DOMESTIC ELITES,
AND 4 FOREIGN GOVERNMENTS

Score	5 Decisions 1952–May 1955				11 Decisions June 1955–1958			
	Internal		External		Internal		External	
3.0	Chancellor	3.0	United States	3.0				
2.8			United Kingdom	2.8				
2.6			France	2.6				
2.4					Chancellor	2.3		
2.2	Cabinet	2.2			Cabinet	2.0		
2.0	Diplo., CDU	2.0			CDU	1.9		
1.8					Diplomats	1.6		
1.6	Civil serv.	1.6			Business	1.5		
1.4	Rom. Cath.	1.4			Mass opinion	1.2		
1.2					Rom. Cath.,			
1.0					civil serv.	1.0	United States	1
0.8					Press	0.9		
					Trade union,			
0.6					military	0.6		
					SPD	0.5		
0.4								
0.2							France	0
0.0	Milit., press	0.0			Ev. Ch.	—0.1		
—0.2								
—0.4								
—0.6	Mass op., bus.	—0.6					United Kingdom	—0
—0.8							USSR	—0
—1.0								
—1.2	Trade union,							
	Ev. Ch.	—1.2						
—1.4								
—1.6								
—1.8	SPD	—1.8						
—2.0								
—2.2								
—2.4			USSR	—2.4				
—2.6								
—2.8								
—3.0								

TABLE 16.5

GERMAN ELITE ATTITUDES IN 1956 TO PAST POLICY DECISIONS CONCERNING
EUROPEAN INTEGRATION*

	Politicians	Civil Service	Big Business	Journalists	Military	Ave. 5 Elites (1956)	Mass Opinion (1954–56)
Western Eur. Union (1955)							
For	94	96	90	85	81	89	68
No opinion or no info.	0	0	5	3	0	2	25
Against	5	4	5	13	19	9	7[a]
Paris Agreements (1955)							
For	77	80	80	62	70	74	42
No opinion or no info.	4	0	15	10	10	8	34
Against	18	20	7	28	20	19	24
NATO (1955)							
For	78	79	78	67	69	74	29
No opinion or no info.	8	8	11	3	6	9	60
Against	13	13	9	31	25	18	11
ECSC (1952)							
For	81	79	68	74	50	70	10
No opinion or no info.	6	0	10	13	6	7	85
Against	13	21	22	13	44	23	5
EDC (1952)							
For	69	63	63	64	56	63	37
No opinion or no info.	5	8	13	0	6	6	34
Against	26	29	25	36	38	31	29
Average, 5 issues							
For	80	79	76	70	65	74	37
No opinion or no info.	5	3	11	6	6	6	48
Against	15	17	14	24	29	20	15

* Sources: Suzanne Keller, "Attitudes Toward European Integration of the German Elite," M.I.T., Center for International Studies, multigraphed (October 1957), p. 26; *Jahrbuch I*, pp. 343, 362, 365; *Jahrbuch II*, pp. 340, 349. A somewhat different tabulation for a larger number of elites, based on the same survey, is given in Table 12.1.

[a] In the poll of mass opinion, respondents were asked in September 1955, without details, whether they would vote for or against forming of a United States of Europe. This question is not exactly comparable to the one about elite attitudes to the somewhat more specific Western European Union agreement of 1955.

TABLE 16.6

POPULAR SUPPORT IN THE FEDERAL REPUBLIC FOR DIFFERENT FORMS OF LARGE-SCALE
POLITICAL INTEGRATION

Issue	Per Cent in Favor	Date of Poll
1. German reunification desired	90	1949–59
2. Return of Oder-Neisse territory	80	March 1951
3. United States of Europe	75	December 1956
*4. Close political cooperation with U.S.	69	April 1956
*5. Close economic cooperation with U.S.	69	April 1956
6. Reunification insisted on	65	September 1956
*7. Close political cooperation with England	49	April 1956
*8. Close political cooperation with France	43	April 1956
*9. Close economic cooperation with England	39	April 1956
10. EDC	37	September 1954
11. Reunification preferred to military alliance with West	36	December 1955
*12. Close economic cooperation with France	34	April 1956
13. Military alliance with West preferred to reunification	31	December 1955
14. NATO	29	September 1956
*15. Close economic cooperation with Russia	27	April 1956
*16. Close political cooperation with Russia	23	April 1956
*17. Close economic cooperation with Israel	12	April 1956
*18. Close political cooperation with Israel	10	April 1956
19. ECSC	10	April 1956

Sources: Line 1: Estimate; no direct poll questions found; line 2: *Jahrbuch I*, p. 13; lines 3–9; *Jahrbuch II*, pp. 316, 338, 342; line 10; *Jahrbuch I*, p. 362; lines 11–19; *Jahrbuch II*, pp. 324, 338, 340, 349. The poll results marked with an asterisk are based on a smaller sample (996 persons). Cf. *Jahrbuch II*, pp. xlv, 338.

If foreign policy decisions were mechanically determined by the relative weight of pressure groups, then German foreign policy could be expected to show in the future an increase in nationalism and an eventual abandonment of serious attempts at European integration. Foreign policy, however, is not thus mechanically made. Rather, it is largely shaped by a process of individual and group learning, and it can be greatly influenced by the effects of personality and the impact of events.

News of events change attitudes, even though they are screened at first by most men in terms of the attitudes which they already hold; if the new experience is sufficiently impressive, a net change results. But governments and leaders can make news. They can provide experiences, vicarious or actual, for elite members and for the rank and file of voters —experiences strong enough to produce changed attitudes. The results of foreign policy decisions taken at any one time can thus change the elite preferences and mass opinion which will influence the next foreign policy decisions.

The content and the results of a foreign policy decision can make or break the political fortunes of its makers. The last, but major, influence on the foreign policy process is thus the substance of foreign policy itself. It is to the content of the foreign policy decisions that are likely to face Germany in coming years that we must finally turn for the conclusion of our study.

CHAPTER 17

Germany rejoins the powers:
Policy choices and their implications

The kind of country that emerged in 1949 as the German Federal Republic determined the kind of German foreign policy that was to characterize much of the following decade. It was a state based on limitations and compromises, on the cautious regaining of strength, on the avoidance or postponement of intolerable choices. Within this limited area of agreement, as earlier sections of this study showed, effective political unity could be maintained. Beyond it lie substantial cleavages of attitude and interests, and the possibility of stubborn deadlocks.

Government, interest groups, and the general public all desire, by and large, a peaceful return of Germany to leadership and power in Europe—and through Europe, perhaps in a larger area of the world. A substantial majority want peace, freedom from Communist control, and economic and political links to the United States—and they do not want to have to choose between these aims.

Second to these primary goals comes German reunification as a long-range aim, but its importance may well be increasing, rather than diminishing, as time goes on. European integration comes only in third place. It is often seen as a road to German leadership, or to the attainment of other German goals, rather than as an end in itself. Among German elite members, as well as among the electorate, there are many who are likely to show little enthusiasm for remaining in any close European community which would prove unresponsive to German leadership or major influence. Other groups—though perhaps less strong—might be willing to accept a more modest role for Germany in a united Europe.

For a time, all these goals can be pursued at once; and any remaining cleavages can be bridged again for a time, by adroit formulations. Thus an official formulation of policy asserted in 1955: "In the foreground . . . there are three groups of tasks to be attained: the reunification of Germany, the problem of security, and European integration. All three . . . presuppose one another mutually: . . . no reunification without security, no security without reunification, no security without European integration."[1]

---

[1] Germany, Federal Republic, Presse- und Informationsamt der Bundesregierung, *Leistung und Erfolg 1955: Die Bundesregierung berichtet* (Bonn, n.p., n.d.), pp. 15–16.

By 1957, the assertion of the necessary interrelation of these three goal areas had become somewhat less emphatic. The report of the Minister of Foreign Affairs no longer occupied the first place in the government's review of its activities, as it had in previous years; it had yielded priority to that of the Minister of Economic Affairs who reported an "upward trend of the economy which had not been believed possible to this extent even by optimists . . ."[2] The foreign affairs report, now in second place, then simply stated: "The federal government pursued in 1957 the same goals in foreign policy as in the past years: restoration of the governmental unity of Germany . . . security . . . promotion of the further integration of Europe . . ."[3] References to the possibility of having to choose at some time between these objectives—or between any wider range of goals or policies—were avoided.

Yet, as time goes on, major policy choices may have to be made; and these choices, in turn, may remake Germany. Much as in the past the nature of the new state dictated much of its foreign policy, so now the policies chosen are determining in increasing measure the future character of the German nation. The foreign policy decisions which are pressing even now upon the Federal Republic and its Western allies may go far to shape the kind of Germany with which Europe and the world will have to live.

The End of an Era

The decisions to be faced now are falling due at the end of an era. It is the end of the era of obvious Western superiority in nuclear weapons and delivery systems over the Communist bloc: with the race for globe-girdling rockets and missiles a new age of uncertainty has dawned. It is the end of the era of optimistic popular confidence in democratic and constitutional pro-Western governments among the new nations of Asia and Africa: already by the late 1950's, military dictatorships were shooting up like mushrooms upon the ruins of recently drafted constitutions. It is the end of the era of full employment and untroubled prosperity in many countries, and notably in the United States: higher margins of unemployment now are putting American governments before the choice of tolerating a slowing down of economic growth, or even stagnation, and the involuntary idleness of larger numbers, or of permitting a more rapid progress of inflation, or of imposing a hitherto unpalatable level of government controls. And these hard choices must be faced in the United States and other Western nations at the very time that the forced-draft industrialization of the major Communist countries is hitting its full stride. In retrospect, it may well appear everywhere as the end of an era of relative comfort and security for Western policy makers after their military

[2] *Leistung und Erfolg, 1957*, p. 9.
[3] *Ibid.*, p. 23.

triumphs of 1945. In Germany, however, this end of a world-wide period of growing stabilization and relative stability may well coincide with the end of a not less well marked epoch in German politics. In one form or another, it will be the end of German powerlessness; and it will be, inevitably and necessarily, the end of the Adenauer era. What policy choices will be open to the successors of the old Chancellor, and what kind of Germany will develop from their decisions?

A Nation in Search of a Role

Earlier parts of this study have recounted to what extent the German people are looking upon foreign policy as something more than a mere instrument to secure specific goals. They look, it appears, upon foreign policy largely as a task to be chosen or a role to be played—a role in which they will then be seen by others as well as by themselves. It is their own public image and their self-image that are at stake in their basic foreign policy decisions, in addition to all the special interests of elites and pressure groups who may have particular stakes in the outcome. The international role chosen for the country as a whole will not only influence the distribution of material rewards among these domestic interest groups; it will influence also the specific role available to each particular elite within it, and thus its morale, its prestige, and its opportunities for action. What roles will be open for Germany in the early 1960's, and what possible gains or losses does each role promise to the main elites concerned?

Nine Roles to Choose From

Out of the many possible roles of German foreign policy, nine may be singled out here for at least brief examination. These possible roles for the German Federal Republic are:

1. The crusader for East German and for East European liberation
2. The confederate of the Communist-ruled German Democratic Republic
3. The wily small country playing its big neighbors off against each other
4. The chosen economic and military ally of the United States in the North Atlantic Treaty Organization
5. The strong neutral power
6. The strong uncommitted power, swinging the balance between East and West
7. The mainstay of Western European integration
8. The adviser and business partner of the ex-colonial countries in Asia and Africa
9. An important member of the United Nations

The first two of these roles may be dismissed quickly. After two lost World Wars, Germany is in no mood for crusading. Most of her elites, with the sole exception of the military, would have far more to lose than to gain from such a course, and her military men would take a dim professional view of the odds involved in such a course. The role of a partner of the Communist-ruled DDR in a Soviet-approved German confederation would be equally unattractive. Mass opinion, as well as most or all elites, would oppose it at this stage.

Both these policies imply hazardous and unpopular extreme commitments to either West or East; both offer only quite restricted opportunities for subsequent choices; and both seem sure to be rejected. More limited commitments, with fewer risks and greater freedom of further choices, are far more likely to find favor, or at least a measure of serious consideration.

The Player with Two Balls

The image of German diplomacy playing off East and West against each other, with no substantial German commitment in terms of power involved, has sometimes been the object of interested speculations.

In the later 1950's some journalists took an exuberant view of German opportunities in the near future. A popular weekly wrote in April 1957:

> If all goes according to plan, German foreign policy . . . will at last be able to play the diplomatic game with two balls: On the one hand, one will be able to negotiate with the Western powers about an initiative in the German question, and on the other hand with the Soviets about an improvement in relations, which is—according to the concurrent views of Konrad Adenauer and Nikolai Bulganin—the precondition for reunification.[4]

A respected review gave a more sober estimate:

> We have more of a bipartisan foreign policy than both (major) parties care to admit. . . . In foreign policy matters we are not independent, and it often smacks of phrase making to call here for German initiatives. It is rather in regard to our internal affairs that we are really sovereign.[5]

Both views just cited, the optimistic and the pessimistic one, agree in seeing German foreign policy as not backed by any substantial amount of German power. According to one view, this lack of power can—and, according to the other view, cannot—be compensated for by diplomatic skill. Most elites are unlikely to believe that this could be done, even though mass opinion and a few elite members, particularly among the Social Democrats, would like to believe it. The others—and they are apt to be a majority of the influential in the Federal Republic—may well be interested in a conspicuous alternative: to increase German power,

---

[4] *Der Spiegel*, April 3, 1957, p. 12.

[5] "Wo findet der Wahlkampf statt?" *Die Gegenwart*, 12:5 (March 9, 1957), pp. 1–2.

political, economic, and military, including the power of atomic weapons. The most prominent exponent of this view has been the energetic Federal Minister of Defense, Franz Josef Strauss.

The Indispensable Power

Faced by severe limitations upon what the Federal Republic can do at present in international affairs, and by a divided domestic opinion as to how its small present leeway for maneuvers should be used, some German statesmen in early 1957 again sought unity through ambiguity, by promising greater German power that would force concessions from other countries, yet not endanger peace beyond the limits of tolerable risk. The implications for foreign policy have been put illuminatingly in an article by Defense Minister Franz Josef Strauss:

> In the age of the *pax atomica* there are no military solutions. . . . The problem of reunification, too, must and can only be solved politically. . . . However one may regret it . . . the fact remains that position and influence of a people depend as well upon the strength and dependability of its allies as upon its own military power. . . . Those who ask us—quite rightly—to accept Soviet power as a reality, should after all not deny their own people the right and the opportunity to become likewise a reality. In all negotiations about reunification, risks and chances must be weighed against each other. The risks will diminish, the chances will improve, the more Germany herself has to throw into the scales. . . . A policy of strength in the age of the hydrogen bomb means in no case that one wants to use military pressure, with the risk of a third World War, in order to bring about some territorial changes, if necessary even by force. A policy of strength means rather that one's own freedom of decision cannot be influenced by pressure from hostile or unfriendly quarters . . . *Germany . . . must become so indispensable to her Western friends, and so respectable for her potential adversary, that both will value her presence in the negotiations.*[6]

In another formulation of his views, Herr Strauss was quoted as adding:

> . . . although there exists a preference . . . for a reunited Germany to belong to a military alliance with the West, the hard political requirements of the German people might cause them to make a decision according to the Austrian pattern (of neutralization between East and West). . . . Such a decision would have to rest on very sober political and military considerations. . . . *Without possessing potential power, Germany will never have a chance to be heard.*[7]

Such acquisition of military power by the Federal Republic, if it could be done gradually and at little risk, would be welcomed by most of the members of the dominant cluster of elites—the cabinet, the CDU

[6] Franz Josef Strauss, "Sicherheit und Wiedervereinigung," *Aussenpolitik*, 6:3 (March 1957), pp. 140–47. Italics added.

[7] M. S. Handler, "Key Aide in Bonn Offers Unity Idea: Defense Minister Suggests Use of Military Potential to Attain Objective," *The New York Times*, February 20, 1957. Italics added.

leaders, the civil servants, the diplomats, and, of course, the military. It might also be welcomed, albeit more cautiously, by most leaders of big business. The Roman Catholic hierarchy would have no objections, but would not be enthusiastic, and a majority of Protestant Church leaders might be even less so. The Social Democrats and the trade union leaders, on the other hand, are vehement in their opposition against such a course;[8] and the press is divided in its reactions.

There seems no doubt that the policy of enhancing the political and military power of the Bonn government is actively backed by some of its younger and more energetic members, who are at the same time serious contenders for national leadership in the post-Adenauer era. The two most aggressive personalities in the 1958 Cabinet, Franz Josef Strauss and Gerhard Schroeder—the latter a former member of the Nazi party—occupied the two most strategic posts in relation to the physical force of government, Strauss as Minister of Defense, and Schroeder as Minister of the Interior. In October 1958, Herr Schroeder was pressing for a highly controversial constitutional amendment to expand federal police powers. Deploring constitutional limitations on the federal government's powers in matters of subversion and other threats to the security of the state, Minister Schroeder coupled his call for wider police powers with a demand for the abolition of constitutional limitations on the government's powers to deal with subversion and internal disorder. His opponents saw in this proposal an attempt to revive Article 48 of the Weimar Constitution, which had been used by Hitler to institute his dictatorship under the cover of a "constitutional emergency."[9]

The pressures for a policy of greater national power are paralleled, and to some extent reinforced by pressures for more unfettered national sovereignty. As the German military machine increases, and with it the influence of the military elite, German willingness to restrict national sovereignty for the sake of further progress toward "Europeanization" seems likely to decline. The task of German diplomacy may then be to maintain the image and mood of international cooperation, while safeguarding in fact the largest possible national freedom of action.

Some of the policies of late 1958 gave perhaps a foretaste of future possibilities. A French leader like General de Gaulle, who is himself dedicated to preserving French national institutions against possible internationalization, may well continue to find German diplomatic support; his success in slowing or reversing the trend toward further restrictions on French sovereignty would necessarily serve to protect also the

---

[8] For a recent example of feeling in these circles, see *Protokoll der Verhandlungen des Parteitages der Sozialdemokratischen Partei Deutschlands vom 18. bis 23. Mai 1958 in Stuttgart* (Bonn, SPD, 1958), *passim.*

[9] "Schroeder verlangt eine Notstands-Gesetzgebung," *Frankfurter Allgemeine Zeitung,* October 31, 1958, p. 1. See also Arthur J. Olsen, "Germans in Clash on Police Powers," *The New York Times,* November 6, 1958, p. 14.

sovereignty of Germany and, with it, that of the German army. French claims to develop and possess nuclear weapons under her own national control will similarly appear as precedents for Germany. Thus a policy of growing German sovereignty and nuclear armament may proceed within the framework of temporary mutual diplomatic support between French and German right-of-center governments.

Yet the policies of Ministers Strauss and Schroeder, of building up the power of the German military and police, did not answer the question as to the specific foreign policies which this enhanced power is to serve. Among the nine major policies, listed earlier in this chapter, three seem to offer the most conspicuous courses to which German sovereign power could be committed.

The first of these roles would be that of a strong and favored ally of the United States, in the military context of the North Atlantic Treaty Organization as well as in matters of trade and investment. The second role would be that of a strong neutral power, resembling a huge Switzerland—too strong to be attacked or undermined by anyone, and too clearly neutral and nonaggressive to arouse serious fears abroad. The third role would be that of a strong uncommitted power, playing once again the "game with two balls" between East and West, but now strong enough to swing the balance of power against either side.

The first policy might attract support among business leaders and the military, but the opportunities for putting it into practice are sharply limited. Mass opinion has favored American friendship, but has rejected the acceptance of military NATO burdens at a level comparable to that of America's other major NATO partners, France and Britain. Any conspicuous German attempts to replace France and the United Kingdom in their present roles as the main allies of the United States, and as the principal Western powers beside it, would only provoke French and British resentment which could make itself felt quite effectively in many ways. American policy has encouraged German recovery, but does not want to become dependent upon Germany as its only strong partner in Europe or in the world at large. The Federal Republic is gaining already from the American and NATO alliance about as much as it is likely to gain. Therefore, any attempts to make the role of American ally even more predominant in German foreign policy would lead quickly to diminishing returns.

The second policy—that of Germany as a strong neutral power—has appealed in the past to Social Democrats, trade union leaders, perhaps a part of the Protestant Church leadership, and to a minority of middle-class politicians and perhaps a few businessmen. It would find some backing among mass opinion—but not necessarily a clear-cut majority, once its costs in terms of lost United States friendship and support would have become apparent. Neutrality as a policy is currently being rejected in emphatic terms by the ruling political elite in the CDU and in the cabinet, as well as by the high civil servants, the diplomats, the Roman Catholic hierarchy, most of big business, and a majority of the military. Despite its appeal to a part of labor and socialist opinion, it finds little overt press support and a great deal of outspoken opposition. Unless current conditions should change greatly, its chances for acceptance seem remote.

There remains the third of this group of possible policies: the image of a strong Germany which would not be neutral but rather uncommitted —and perhaps pointedly and ominously so. This might be a pleasant fantasy for a minority of Germans, but it would not arouse any enthusiasm among mass opinion, and it would repel most elite members as both dangerous and impractical. Such a policy would alienate the United States; it would preserve and increase the hostility and fear of the Soviet leaders, and add to it the fears and resentments of much of Western Europe. It would expose Germany to the risk of isolation, weigh it down with military burdens, and expose its commerce to the restrictions of hostile and fearful nations in many parts of the world. A few military men, politicians, perhaps even a few diplomats and writers might toy with the idea, but a majority of leaders in every elite group would probably oppose it.

There are less risky and more rewarding alternatives available to the leaders of German foreign policy. One of these safer and more rewarding courses is that chosen by Chancellor Adenauer throughout the last decade: to make Germany the main supporter and beneficiary of the movement toward European integration.

"The First Servant of Europe"

Whether as political and military kingpin of Europe, and as the most successful competitor and senior cartel partner in the European market, or in a more modest role within the European community, Germany has still much to gain from further steps toward European integration, particularly so long as these steps still permit her to preserve the mainsprings of her national sovereignty and military power. For the time being, the cleavage between those who want Germany to lead a Western European community and those who would want her merely to join it has been adroitly bridged by the formulation of a prominent CDU leader and former diplomat, the president of the Bundesrat, Kurt Sieveking:

> England and France . . . will always . . . be preoccupied by extra-European tasks. . . . Italy is . . . not yet developed to its full strength. From this it is evident that Germany will become ever more the natural nucleus of crystallization for Europe. . . . Above all it must be made absolutely clear that this German foreign policy is far from any thought of any hegemony over Europe and that Germany, according to a well-known saying, is "the first servant of Europe."[10]

[10] Kurt Sieveking, "Die europäische Aufgabe der deutschen Aussenpolitik," *Aussenpolitik*, 8:3 (March 1957), pp. 150–51.

The "well-known saying" recalled by Herr Sieveking is indeed well known to almost every educated German: it is the classic eighteenth-century phrase in which the absolute ruler of Prussia, King Frederick the Great, called himself "the first servant" of the State, and thus pictured his enlightened despotism as a matter not only of right but of duty. Nationalists may take heart from what they may well read as a broad hint of future aspirations, while more liberal-minded "Europeans" may take comfort from the explicit rejection of any thought of German hegemony, which prefaces it in the same sentence. Like many a present-day political leader, Herr Sieveking is raising here two sets of overtones and expectations in the same statement, and thus appealing at one and the same time to different sections of his variegated audience.

A moderate "European" policy will permit the continuing build-up of German national strength under a European shell, with continued American support, and without serious risk of any concerted French and English opposition. Indeed it may permit Germany to act as spokesman for continental Europe vis-à-vis England in economic matters, or else to act as an "honest broker" between British and French interests in such matters as tariffs, quotas, and the European Common Market.[11] Inside Germany, such a policy will neither frighten nor antagonize mass opinion, and it may expect to retain the support of most of the elites.

Yet even this policy has its price. It could be the price of the indefinite postponement of German reunification. The government of the Soviet Union has no motive, for the time being, for conceding German reunion on Western terms, and neither the Western powers nor the Federal Republic has any effective means of pressure to make the Soviet leaders change their minds. A reunified Germany within the Western alliance system would represent a major shift in the international balance of power which almost any Russian government could be expected to resist. In the decade since 1948, there has been no visible gain in the relative power of the West, relative to the power of the Soviet bloc, that would make it seem likely that the West could make its will prevail in the late 1950's on an issue on which it could not gain more than a stalemate a decade earlier. If anything, in the ten years between 1948 and 1958 Soviet power has grown somewhat faster than Western power, and the over-all rates of economic growth in both power blocs do not promise any startling improvements in the Western position for the near future.

At this point, German policy makers are facing the limitations of European integration, both in the past and for the future. While there has been substantial and gratifying economic growth not only in Western Germany, but in most of Western Europe, it has not been enough to

---

[11] For an example of Dr. Ludwig Erhard, German Minister of the Economy, going to London in a role of this kind, see Harry Gilroy, "Europeans Widen Tariff-Cut Scope," *The New York Times*, December 4, 1958, p. 20:3–4.

change in any substantial way the balance of East-West strength in Europe—something that had been sincerely expected and widely predicted by European and American publicists and statesmen in 1948. The limited steps toward European integration, taken since 1948, have disappointed the pessimists by proving practicable. But they have also disappointed the optimistic hopes of 1948, for they have failed to change the balance of power in Europe, much less in the world, so as to make German reunification on Western terms in any way more likely.

Nor are any of the steps toward further European integration, insofar as they are under serious discussion, any more likely during the next few years to shift the balance of power significantly in favor of the West. At best they may help the West, like Lewis Carroll's Red Queen, to keep running fast enough to stay in the same place relative to its Soviet challengers.

These limitations apply not only to the aggregate strength of Western Europe but also to its unity. Up to a point, this unity has grown: there are by now few, if any, areas of acute and overt disagreement between the six countries that make up the European Coal and Steel Community. In particular, the traditional French-German antagonism has all but disappeared from the stage, even though some version might reappear again some day from the wings on cue.

What has lagged has been the growth of a deeper European unity of daily living and of popular attitudes. Significant indications of this lag can be found in the development of German elite and popular attitudes toward the conflicts of West European powers with native independence movements in their colonies. A poll in November 1956 showed the complexity of some of these attitudes: 86 per cent of respondents expressed sympathy for the Hungarian rebels, as against only 1 per cent who sympathized with the Russians who had just intervened against them, and 13 per cent who were uninformed or undecided; but at the same time, a mapority of 56 per cent declared themselves on the side of Egypt in the Suez crisis, while only 10 per cent expressed sympathy for France and England, and 34 per cent were uninformed or undecided.[12] This large outpouring of popular sympathy for Egypt at a time when she defied the West and was in open conflict with France, Germany's major partner in European integration, showed little of the "European" solidarity which has often been a general theme in official German foreign policy pronouncements. German press opinion has tended to stress the inevitability and strength of Asian and African independence movements, and to rejoice in the favorable reception which German products and German

---

[12] Erich Peter Neumann, "Nützt Ungarn der CDU?" *Der Spiegel*, 11:2 (January 4, 1957), p. 13.

businessmen have found in many of the recently independent countries. No European economic or political union, it is held, could possibly reverse this trend: "Also the sum total of West European national states," wrote a recent contributor to *Aussenpolitik*, "will not be able to avoid the positive answer to the claim of colonial peoples for independence . . ."[13]

The Business Partner of the Uncommitted World

Germany, in short, is not a colonial power. Her interests are different from those of her European neighbors who still control colonies—and whose controls often have a way of keeping German exports partly or wholly out of their dependent territories. Sovereign countries, on the other hand, no matter how underdeveloped, usually have offered relatively better opportunities to German traders. The extent of this discrimination can be gauged from the data for 1954, which are presented in Table 17.1. There is little doubt that it is still substantial, and that Germany will continue to be interested not only in European solidarity but also in a more independent national policy toward the underdeveloped countries.

The foreign policy resulting from these interests might well be double in character. Besides the limited commitment to European solidarity and the Common Market, it might be a policy of encouraging the national independence of Asian and African countries now still under foreign rule. In the same vein, it would be a policy of strengthening German trade and business connections with countries which are already legally sovereign, such as the Arab states, but which are still engaged in loosening their ties to the old colonial or oil interests of the other Western powers.

This is a foreign policy role for Germany as the business partner of Islam and as an adviser, guide, and business associate of all underdeveloped countries. There are no serious international obstacles to such a course. To the United States government this policy can be justified— as it has been justified in the case of the quick German recognition of the anti-British Iraqi rebel government in 1958—on the grounds that German good will and influence among Arab nationalists should be preserved, in the common interest of all Western powers. German influence, it is argued, is the best practicable alternative to complete Soviet penetration of these areas. If Britain and France find it more difficult to appreciate this particular German contribution to the common cause, there is little they can do about it; and they, too, are more inclined to blame the Soviet Union for encouraging nationalism and anticolonialism in Asia and Africa than to blame Germany for taking some advantage of a situation

[13] W. W. Sch. (Wilhelm Wolfgang Schütz), "Mitspracherecht von Afro-Asien," *Aussenpolitik*, 8:3 (March 1957), p. 139.

TABLE 17.1

Per Cent Excess or Deficit in 1954 German Export Dollar Volume	Sovereign in 1938 and 1954	
	Per Capita G.N.P. Above $300, 1954	Per Capita G.N.P. Below $300, 1954
+30% and above	Austria .... 509 Switzerland .... 240 Sweden .... 199 Hungary .... 194 Denmark .... 185 Rumania .... 184 Norway .... 122 Netherlands .... 113 Belgium .... 108 Italy .... 87 Uruguay .... 43 Iceland .... 42 Costa Rica .... 40 Columbia 31	Bulgaria .... 201 Iran .... 188 Yugoslavia .... 148 Greece .... 136 Turkey .... 135 Portugal .... 119 China (mainland) ...... 87 Spain .... 78 Nicaragua .... 67 Chile .... 56 Ecuador .... 52 Honduras .... 46 Egypt .... 43 Paraguay .... 31 Brazil 30
+0.1 to 29%	Argentina .... 26 France .... 25 Poland 20	Iraq .... 20 Thailand .... 14 Guatemala .... 10 Bolivia .... 9 Peru .... 8 Saudi Arabia 5
	Finland 00	
−0.1 to 29%	Venezuela .... −6 Czechoslovakia .... −17 Union S. Africa .... −27	El Salvador .... −1
−30 to 100%	Ireland .... −40 Panama .... −46 Australia .... −49 Cuba .... −63 United States .... −65 USSR .... −67 New Zealand .... −68 United Kingdom .... −71 Canada .... −85	Dominican Rep. .... −37 Mexico .... −40 Haiti .... −51 Japan .... −70

The percentages represent deviations in the share of each country in reported German exports, above or below its share in the reported exports of the world outside Germany. The trade data are based on figures in United Nations, Statistical Papers, Series T, Vol. VI, No. 10, *Direction of International Trade* (New York, 1956), and on computations in Karl W. Deutsch and I. Richard Savage, *Regionalism, Trade, and International Community,*

CUSTOMERS FOR GERMAN EXPORTS, 1954

Dependent 1938, Sovereign 1954		Dependent in 1938 and 1954	
Per Capita G.N.P. Above $300, 1954	Per Capita G.N.P. Below $300, 1954	Per Capita G.N.P. Above $300, 1954	Per Capita G.N.P. Below $300, 1954
Israel 225			
			Angola 104
	Syria 74		
			Nigeria 48
	Ethiopia 25		
	Lebanon 15		Mozambique 1
	Indonesia 4		
	Pakistan 00		
	India .... —3		Belgian Congo ..... —5
	Burma .... —12		Ghana .... —21
			Sudan .... —29
			Fr. Morocco .... —37
		Cyprus .... —39	Fr. Cameroons ..... —39
			Hong Kong .... —44
			Tanganyika .... —48
			French W. Africa... —52
			Fr. Equat. Af....... —58
	South Korea.... —71	ᵃBr. Pers. G. Sts.... —70	Madagascar .... —72
	Philippines .... —72		Malaya & Sing...... —76
	Taiwan .... —74		Rhodesia & Nyas.... —85
	Ceylon .... —77		Tunisia .... —86
			Algeria .... —89
		ᵃNeth. Antilles .... —96	Indo-China .... —94
	Albania ....—100	Trinidad ....—100	South W. Africa...—100
			Uganda ....—100
			British Guiana .....—100
			Jamaica ....—100
			Sarawak ....—100
			Kenya ....—100
			Sierra Leone ....—100
			Mauritius ....—100

forthcoming. G.N.P. estimates from Research Center in Economic Development and Cultural Change of the University of Chicago, "The Role of Foreign Aid in the Development of Other Countries," in U.S., 85th Congress, 1st Session, Senate Document No. 52, *Foreign Aid Program: Compilation of Studies and Surveys* (Washington, D.C., U.S. Government Printing Office, July 1957), Appendix I, Table I, pp. 238–39.

    Small amounts of exports to some countries may have escaped separate report in the United Nations tables used.

ᵃ Indicates per capita G.N.P. is estimated.

TABLE 17.2

Per Cent Excess or Deficit in 1938 German Export Dollar Volume	Sovereign in 1938 and 1954			
	Per Capita Income $125 or Above, 1938		Per Capita Income Below $125, 1938	
+30% and above	Hungary	423	Bulgaria	439
	Yugoslavia	342	Turkey	369
	Switzerland	194	Rumania	341
	Chile	172	Greece	272
	Denmark	168	Guatemala	269
	Italy	160	Ecuador	230
	Spain	157	Uruguay	171
	Czechoslovakia	152	Poland	164
	Sweden	141	Brazil	142
	Finland	122	Peru	139
	Netherlands	109	Iran	136
	Norway	105	Columbia	107
	Venezuela	60	Portugal	77
	Argentina	40	Mexico	69
+0.1 to 29%	Belgium	15	China	18
−0.1 to 29%	Union S. Africa	−24	Egypt	−03
	France	−28		
−30 to 100%	Australia	−62	Japan	−30
	United Kingdom	−68	USSR	−49
	United States	−74	Cuba	−100
	New Zealand	−83	Costa Rica	−100
	Canada	−86	Iceland	−100
	Ireland	−100	Thailand	−100
	Panama	−100	Iraq	−100
			Saudi Arabia	−100
			Paraguay	−100
			Bolivia	−100
			Haiti	−100
			Dominican Rep.	−100
			Nicaragua	−100
			Honduras	−100
			El Salvador	−100

The percentages represent deviations in the share of each country in reported German exports, above or below its share in the reported exports of the world outside Germany. The data are based on figures in United Nations, Statistical Papers, Series T, Vol. VI, No. 10, *Direction of International Trade* (New York, 1956), and on computations in Karl W. Deutsch and I. Richard Savage, *Regionalism, Trade, and International Community,*

CUSTOMERS FOR GERMAN EXPORTS, 1938

Dependent 1938, Sovereign 1954		Dependent in 1938 and 1954	
Per Capita Income $125 or Above, 1938	Per Capita Income Below $125, 1938	Per Capita Income $125 or Above, 1938	Per Capita Income Below $125, 1938
	Indonesia ..... —1		
	India .... —18		
			Belgian Congo .... —46
	Burma .... —81		Malaya & Sing...... —81
	Ceylon .... —82		Algeria .... —89
	ᵃIsrael ....—100		Mozambique ......—100
	Albania ....—100		Angola ....—100
	Ethiopia ....—100		Fr. Equat. Af.......—100
	Philippines ....—100		Fr. Cameroons .....—100
	Korea ....—100		Fr. W. Africa .....—100
	Syria-Lebanon ..—100		Nigeria ....—100
			Ghana ....—100
			Tanganyika ....—100
			Kenya-Uganda .....—100
			N. Rhodesia ....—100
			S. Rhodesia ....—100
			Hong Kong ....—100
			Indo-China ....—100
			Fr. Morocco ....—100
			Tunisia ....—100
			Sudan ....—100
			British Guiana .....—100
			Jamaica ....—100
			Cyprus ....—100
			Trinidad ....—100
			Neth. Antilles......—100

forthcoming. Data on per capita national income from W. S. Woytinsky and E. S. Woytinsky, *World Population and Production*, Twentieth Century Fund (New York, 1953), p. 391.

Small amounts of exports to some countries may have escaped separate report in the United Nations tables used.

ᵃ 1938 data for "Israel" refer to Palestine.

not of her making. It may thus be possible for Germany to pursue this policy together with a policy of limited European cooperation with the same powers whose influence she would be in part displacing overseas,[14] and she could return to the Near East without risk of war.

In domestic politics, a policy of this kind should be popular with mass opinion and the press, as well as with most of the elites. It would represent a course on which businessmen and trade unionists, CDU and SPD supporters could agree. No significant elite group would oppose it.

Somewhat more controversial would be an extension of this policy of increased contacts from the neutralist to the Soviet bloc countries. Part of mass opinion, some CDU leaders, civil servants, and the Roman Catholic hierarchy might have serious misgivings about a policy of increasing trade with the Soviet bloc and of extending diplomatic recognition to all of its members, if this should lead to a serious weakening of the friendship with the Western countries and particularly with the United States. Some limited steps in this direction, however, are not unlikely, provided that they stop well short of any major reorientation of Germany's international alignments.

Under these conditions, much would depend on the possibility of finding a role for Germany in which she could broaden and develop her contacts to the underdeveloped countries, and even her opportunities for limited negotiations with Soviet bloc members, such as Poland, without antagonizing her Western friends and without giving the impression of any secret double dealing. There is one obvious possible role in which such broader contacts could be developed publicly and respectably, without creating any undesirable fears or expectations of Germany's alienation from the Western community. It is the role of Germany as a member of the United Nations.

---

[14] The following statement is typical: "During last year the Federal Republic intensified further its trade relations with the developing countries. As a highly industrialized country whose production potential particularly meets in its structure the needs and wishes of the economically less developed countries of the Middle East, Asia, and Africa, the Federal Republic could offer, and also supply the technical equipment and plans needed by these countries for the development of their own production capacity. Also in the planning and devising of many projects the West German industry could make important contributions to the economic development of the Afro-Asian countries, be it in a purely consulting capacity or in connection with the delivery of plants. . . . In addition to private industry, the Federal Government also participated widely in offering advice and training facilities in the scientific and technical sectors. . . . The first appropriation from public funds, viz. $12 million, was made available for this form of technical assistance during the 1956–1957 fiscal year. . . . Seen as a whole, organized assistance to the developing countries is still at its start, but there is no doubt that in the Federal Republic the urgent necessity is recognized to render the widest possible aid to the politically not very stable and economically backward countries in order not to let them become easy victims of Communism." Wolf Dieter Lindner, "The Balance Sheet of German Foreign Trade," *Meet Germany* (5th rev. ed., Hamburg, Atlantik Brücke, May 1958), p. 48.

Membership in the United Nations: A Dormant Theme in German Politics

When in 1926 Germany took her place as a member in the League of Nations, and as a Permanent Member of its Council, only eight years after her defeat in the First World War, this was widely regarded at home and abroad as a triumph of German foreign policy. By the end of 1958, nearly fourteen years after the end of the Second World War, Germany had not yet attained membership in the United Nations, much less a seat on the United Nations Security Council. The contrast is striking, and not less so for being the result of a deliberate policy of the Adenauer government and of its Western allies.

Of all major countries of the non-Communist world, Germany alone is thus excluded. Italy, Japan, and Generalissimo Francisco Franco's Spain all have become United Nations members. India, Pakistan, and Indonesia consider membership their right, and so does every newly fledged nation in Asia and Africa. What is it that keeps Germany apart?

The policy that has brought about this situation, and may well perpetuate it for some time to come, is of long standing. It stems from the first years of German reconstruction after World War II, when the Western allies developed their occupation zones of Germany step by step into what is now the Federal Republic, while the Soviet Union made its zone of occupation into the German Democratic Republic, and a series of tense and precarious compromises preserved the special status of West Berlin. Representing more than two-thirds of the population of Germany and basing itself on free elections, the Federal Republic has consistently refused to recognize the legal existence of the East German state with its much smaller population and obviously Communist-dominated political system. In this refusal of recognition, the Federal Republic has been backed—and sometimes strongly urged to firmness—by its allies, particularly by the United States.

The Bonn government and its allies have thus become committed to oppose the admission of the German Democratic Republic to the United Nations, while the Soviet Union made it plain that it would veto the admission of the Bonn Republic without its Soviet-sponsored counterpart. In the Soviet view, it has been a matter of "two Germanies or none" in the United Nations, and thus far the Federal Republic and its allies have chosen "none." The Bonn Republic, rather than its allies, has borne the direct diplomatic costs of this decision.

The matter has long seemed too difficult for simple diplomatic trading. Membership for the two Germanies could not be traded for each other, since the Bonn regime has committed itself to denying the legal existence of an East German state rather than merely the legitimacy of its current government. Nor does it seem easy to find a non-German state that could be admitted so as to balance the admission of the Federal Republic. True, such Western nations as Italy, Spain, and Ireland have been admitted to the United Nations with Soviet consent, in exchange for such Soviet bloc countries as Rumania, Bulgaria, and others. But there is no country in the Soviet bloc and outside the United Nations of sufficient size and importance so that its admission could be traded by the West for that of Western Germany—with one possible exception.

Communist China has been waiting for ten years outside the United Nations. China is a Permanent Member of the United Nations Security Council, but the United States has insisted that the only representative of China is the exiled government of Generalissimo Chiang Kai-shek on the island of Formosa or Taiwan. This United States insistence has not been shared by some other major Western countries, such as the United Kingdom, but it has marshaled enough support to bar until now the government of Communist mainland China from the United Nations.

Gradually, during the 1950's, the votes cast by United Nations members against the admission of Communist China have receded in number. Sooner or later, it is expected, they will no longer be sufficient, and the Chinese Communists some day may take their seats, as representatives either of a single state recognized henceforth as China, or under some compromise "two Chinas" policy. Some observers believe that a development of this sort seems so likely that there should be no reason for either Red China or the Soviet Union to trade now any concessions on their part for something that will come to them soon in any case. This, however, is not the only view than can be reasonably held. The leaders of Communist China are not less interested in international recognition and prestige than are their Russian counterparts, and their patience may be less than superhuman. Since they know that they cannot win recognition and U.N. membership by force, they may be willing to trade some specific concessions for it now, rather than wait passively for a more distant and uncertain future.

Could the admission of the German Federal Republic be so linked to the admission of China that both these substantial powers would enter the United Nations at the same time and with the same status as Permanent Members of the Security Council, while the question of admission of the German Democratic Republic would be put aside? Would such an arrangement be in the interests of the Federal Republic and of its Western allies? And would it be acceptable to Communist China and the USSR?

All these questions are speculative. It may be profitable, however, to pursue them at least briefly. To take the last one first: a Western proposal of this kind might put the Soviet government into something of a dilemma. Should it insist on the admission of the Grotewohl-Ulbricht government to the United Nations, at the price of publicly discountenancing Mao Tse Tung and Chou En Lai, and frustrating a prominent objective of their policy? Or should they agree to the proposal, so as to accommodate their Chinese partners, and thus publicly relegate the East German Communists to a back seat? It might not be an easy decision to make; and the Chinese Communists might make it difficult for their Russian partners to avoid it.

But would such a compromise, however embarrasing to the Soviet bloc, be in the interests of the West? The answer to this question depends upon several basic assumptions. Western leaders may believe that in the United Nations China would add more strength to the Communist bloc than Germany would to the democracies. They may also believe that they have no interest in making the United Nations stronger, and in raising its prestige, by making its membership more nearly universal. They may thus disagree with the explicit judgment of both Secretaries General of the United Nations, Trygve Lie and Dag Hammarskjold, each of whom recommended in his official reports universality of membership for the United Nations.[15]

This is indeed the negative belief which both Chancellor Adenauer and the late U.S. Secretary of State Dulles seem to have held, and which has characterized their policies for well-nigh a decade. It has been a policy of nonrecognition for the present, and of little confidence in diplomacy and in the effects of more communication in the United Nations. In its earlier years, this policy was coupled with strong hopes for armed liberation or at least a roll-back of Communist power in the near future. These positive hopes have abated, while the old distrust of diplomacy and of freer contacts in the United Nations has remained. The result has been a certain immobility of Western policies, but it is not certain that this immobility will last forever.

If a somewhat different policy should come to be adopted, it might well be one of greater confidence in the positive contributions which Western Germany could make in the United Nations. Germany is the only major Western power which is not embarrassed by colonial difficulties, or by the many delicate problems that come with maintaining military and naval bases on the soil of foreign countries. Her influence among the African and Asian nations, notably in the Arab world, could be significant. She could add vigor, competence, and the benefit of a somewhat different viewpoint to the democratic side in many United Nations deliberations and decisions.

[15] Trygve Lie, *Introduction to the Annual Report of the Secretary-General on the Work of the Organization, 1 July 1951–30 June 1952* (General Assembly, Official Records: Seventh Session, Supplement No. 1A; New York, United Nations, 1952), p. 3; Dag Hammarskjold, *Introduction to the Annual Report of the Secretary-General on the Work of the Organization, 16 June 1955–15 June 1956* (General Assembly, Official Records: Eleventh Session, Supplement No. 1A; New York, United Nations, 1956), p. 1.

These advantages to the Western alliance, as well as to the United Nations organization, would hold true, even if another kind of compromise should come to be accepted: a "two Germanies" policy of simultaneous admission of the Federal Republic and of the East German Communist regime, with the question of China perhaps left in abeyance. Such a solution might be more distasteful to West German opinion, but even there its advantages might come to be regarded as outweighing its drawbacks. The contribution of an East German delegation to the Soviet position in the United Nations should be small. The representatives of the Grotewohl-Ulbricht government would probably be looked upon much like those of the Kadar regime in Hungary. They should impress few except those who are already sympathizers of the Soviet bloc. The Federal Republic's contribution to the Western group in the United Nations would be far more substantial.

The presence of a U.N. delegation from the East German government would make more difficult a legal point thus far maintained strictly by the government in Bonn: that the Federal Republic is the only legally existing German state. But such sharp legal points, in the absence of sufficient power to impose them on others, tend to become blunted in international practice. If Germany can be reunited some day in the future, reunification could merge two legally existing states as easily as one legal and one *de facto* state. If there is no reunification, insistence on the legal nonexistence of the East German regime will offer scant comfort. Whatever the political and symbolic value accorded to the strictly legal argument, it is likely to be weighed sooner or later against the positive gains to Germany and to the West that could be reaped by the Federal Republic in the United Nations.

If Germany could do some things for the United Nations, membership in the United Nations could do a good deal for the future development of Germany. It could give Germany a stable self-image and an honorable role—the role of pillar of the world organization, and of a helper, guide, and counselor to its less developed members. The more limited roles of this kind played already by Canada, Australia, and the Scandinavian countries may suggest the possibilities available within the United Nations to a country of the size and capabilities of the Federal Republic.

It has been one of the major functions of the United Nations to provide attractive and practicable international roles for the many emerging new nations in the world. Haltingly but perceptibly, many new and old nations have learned a new regard for standards of political conduct, and a new sensitivity to international opinion. For governments, diplomats, and public opinion at home, membership in the United Nations has provided significant experiences in the art of international understanding. The strengthening of these experiences and traditions in Germany might make a significant contribution to the consolidation of democracy and of a farsighted democratic foreign policy in that country.

The end of the old policy of nonrecognition of the East German government seems likely to come in any case within the next few years. Thus far, many German and Western policy makers have seen in this above all a great danger. Dangers surely there will be, but so might there be opportunities. Not least among these opportunities may be those that should follow from German membership in the United Nations. Of the nine foreign policy roles discussed earlier, this one may well appear somewhat more interesting in the future.

There is no telling how soon considerations of this kind may be entertained seriously by the government in Bonn. Challenged by Russian pressure at Berlin, and in particular by the announced Soviet intention to turn over to the German Democratic Republic the control of all land transport routes to West Berlin, Chancellor Adenauer in late 1958 called upon the Social Democrats to support a united foreign policy. His appeal was turned down by the opposition party, on the grounds that it had contained no suggestion of any change in the foreign policies which the Chancellor had pursued thus far and which the Socialists had strongly opposed. While foreign and domestic conflicts or crises of this kind may come and go, they do highlight the potential need for new ideas and new methods in German foreign policy, and the growing possibilities of some limited departures from some of the more rigid positions of the past.

Under these conditions, German policy makers are likely to be reluctant to make any drastic or irrevocable changes in foreign policy, and interested in finding policies that would permit them many choices and many shades and combinations of emphasis. They may thus look at the nine foreign policy roles, surveyed earlier in this chapter, from still another aspect. Which of these roles would be most compatible with the more or less simultaneous pursuit of other courses?

Which Courses Can Be Pursued at the Same Time: The Mutual Compatibility of Roles

The less its compatibility with other policies, the fewer are the effective choices offered by a foreign policy role. Viewed in this aspect, the role of crusader once again is not likely to appear attractive to German policy makers; too few other roles could be combined with it. It might be compatible to a limited extent with German roles in NATO, in European integration, and as a preferred partner of the United States, but it would exclude the postures of the neutral, of the uncommitted power, of United Nations membership, of negotiations with Russia or Eastern Germany, and it would impair considerably the pursuit of closer business relations with the underdeveloped and uncommitted countries.

The role of a confederate of the German Democratic Republic in a Soviet-approved German confederation would be similarly incompatible with many other policies, particularly those involving friendship with the Western powers. It could be combined with a neutralist policy and with a trade drive toward the underdeveloped countries, and possibly with a minor role in the United Nations, if Western objections should not become too strong.

Any policy of "playing with two balls" between West and East would also be difficult to combine with the pursuit of other objectives. It could be combined with U.N. membership and closer ties to underdeveloped countries, and sporadically with promises of neutrality, but most other policies would be incompatible with it. A weak but openly unreliable Germany would not be trusted enough by other powers to become a successful partner in European integration, nor in NATO or any other alliance with the United States, nor in a German confederation or similar step toward reunification. Being weak, it could not pretend to any successful balance-of-power policy.

An alternative policy for Germany, to seek military strength in continuing close alliance with the United States, would prove hardly more flexible. It would accord well with a policy of militant crusading, if the United States should choose to support such a course. More peacefully and safely, it could be combined with a vigorous policy of Western European integration, provided that the necessary French and Italian cooperation for further steps to integration were forthcoming. For whatever they might be worth, it would sacrifice, however, the options of neutrality, negotiated confederation, or partial reunification, playing with two balls, or trying to manipulate the balance of power.

More widely compatible would be a neutralist foreign policy. It could be combined with a balance-of-power policy, with United Nations membership, with a drive for closer ties to the underdeveloped countries, and even with membership in a loose German confederacy, so as to appease popular desires for some steps toward reunification. To a lesser but significant extent, a neutralist Germany could still pursue an active European policy in cultural and economic matters, as Sweden and Austria have done successfully. To be workable, however, a neutralist policy would require a formal or informal United States guarantee vis-à-vis the Soviet Union. This guarantee might not be forthcoming, and the prospective loss of American friendship might be the main deterrent to any German policy of neutralism. A policy of manipulating the East-West balance of power by sovereign armed strength could be combined, at least temporarily, with several other strategies. It would exclude the policies of crusading, confederacy with the DDR, and loyal NATO membership. It could put power behind a diplomatic game with two balls, or behind a course of neutrality, or of European cooperation, of winning and utilizing membership in the United Nations, and of bidding for economic and political leadership among the underdeveloped countries.

A policy of European cooperation would be even more effective in avoiding undesirable choices. It would make difficult only two other policies: Soviet-blessed confederacy with East Germany and diplomatic vacillation between Europe and the East. It would be compatible with all other major courses, even with either crusading or neutralism, in the unlikely event that either of these courses should come to be accepted as a general West European policy.

Membership in the United Nations and greater attention to the underdeveloped countries are the two policies that stand at the top of the list, so far as flexibility and compatibility with other courses are concerned. Only militant crusading would be difficult to combine with them. Every other of the major policy alternatives surveyed would remain wide open, and any of these could be pursued in conjunction with those two, if Germany's leaders should so choose.

It is possible that the juridical and psychological barriers against seeking United Nations membership may prevail in the minds of her leaders. The price—recognition of the existence of the Communist dictatorship in the German Democratic Republic—many seem unbearable. Elite as well as mass opinion in the Bonn Republic has often appeared as highly pragmatic and resistant to ideological abstractions. It remains to be seen whether the foreign policy of the Federal Republic will prefer the practical and moral opportunties of United Nations membership to the cost of sacrificing wholly or partly its long-maintained juridical and ideological insistance on the nonrecognition of its Eastern rival.

Whatever their attractions, however, neither United Nations membership, nor West European cooperation, nor the closest political and business ties to the underdeveloped countries, nor any other of the nine policies surveyed, could in themselves provide answers to the two crucial unresolved problems of German foreign policy in the late 1950's: reunification and armament. Upon these two might hinge, in the not-too-distant future, the national identity of Germany and the peace of the world.

Of the two problems, reunification is not now under the control of the Bonn government and of its Western allies, but armament is. The decision about the size, speed, and character of West German armament is largely in the hands of the government and people of the Federal Republic; together with their allies, they control it entirely as a policy decision wholly within the power of the Western bloc. It is a continuing decision, as the stages of armament unfold, and it is the most fateful decision about Germany that German leaders and Western leaders are holding in their hands. In the years after 1959, growing West German armament could undermine the status quo in Europe as effectively as any Soviet move against West Berlin.

Germany's Greatest Potential Contribution to the West:
Military or Civilian?

On July 2, 1958, the Bundestag voted unanimously to ask the federal government to work in Washington, Moscow, London, and Paris—in furtherance of the restoration of German unity—toward the establishment of a four-power body, at least at the ambassadorial level, to work out joint proposals for a German settlement. Since the organs for three-power consultations between Washington, London, and Paris had long been in existence, the resolution of the Bundestag urged, in effect, the opening of four-power negotiations with the Soviet Union. While the federal government postponed the carrying out of this resolution to the fall, German domestic initiatives were raising once again the questions of German armament, alliances, and reunification.

In the lead article of a leading bipartisan journal in foreign affairs, *Aussenpolitik,* of October 1958, a SPD deputy to the Bundestag and former German Ambassador to India, Ernst Wilhelm Meyer, made a series of striking proposals.[16] Germany should maintain her economic and cultural links to the West, he proposed, but offer to give up her military ties in order to gain Soviet consent to reunification. Thus Germany should offer to leave NATO, to avoid all military alliances, and to limit herself to a "first-class conventional army" without any nuclear weapons, in exchange for rapid steps toward reunification in some form. For the purpose of negotiations, the Federal Republic should join the four great powers, and it should accept the presence of representatives of the German Democratic Republic in the same forum. Direct negotiations with the DDR should be carried on at present only at the technical level. In order to get four-power negotiations started, the former ambassador proposed that the federal government should "omit for 18 months all measures of nuclear armament, in order to permit in this time the creation of the diplomatic foundations for the solution of the German question. In that event, there will never be any atomic weapons on German soil."[17]

The arguments cited in favor of these proposals were illuminating. Germany must not wait fatalistically for a reunification for which the late United States Secretary of State John Foster Dulles seemed willing to wait, according to his quoted words, for 50 to 100 years.[18] Even the ten to fifteen years often mentioned in Germany would be too long: at the current rate of emigration from East Germany, irretrievable damage and loss of leadership would occur there long before that time.[19] Consultations be-

[16] E. W. Meyer, "Gedanken zur Politik der Wiedervereinigung," *Aussenpolitik,* 9:10 (October 1958), pp. 614–30.

[17] *Ibid.,* p. 630.

[18] *Ibid.,* p. 617. In the same context General de Gaulle was quoted as allegedly having said, "No excessive zeal for German reunification! . . . I have been saying this for a thousand years." *Ibid.* Cf. also p. 619.

[19] *Ibid.,* p. 616.

tween the Federal Republic and its Western allies were a delusion. No such consultations had taken place before the Suez war in 1956, or before the Anglo-American troop landings in Jordan and Lebanon in 1958, or before the Quemoy crisis in the same year, although each of these events had brought Germany close to war. In any question that seemed vital to itself, no great Western power would have changed its policies because of anything the Federal Republic could have said or done in such a consultation, even if it had been held.[20] Finally, the fate of Hungary in 1956 had revealed the futility of the hope that Western strength could force the Soviet Union to political concessions, for it had shown that "except by war, a great power cannot be forced to anything whatever."[21] Hence, according to the author, the need for trading military disengagement for reunification; this disengagement should be limited to Germany. Allied troops might well stay in France and England, and the withdrawal of Russian troops from other East European states should not be made a condition for agreement. Rather, a "little package" deal would be most likely to be found acceptable to both sides.[22]

Within a short time, the atmosphere for the contemplated "little package" deal had sharply altered. Russia, rather than Germany, had taken the initiative with Premier Khrushchev's announcement in November 1958 that the Soviet Union intended to end the four-power military occupation of Berlin, and that it would hand over to the German Democratic Republic the control of East Berlin, as well as of all surface access routes to West Berlin. This move, if carried out, would have forced the Federal Republic and the Western powers at the very least to recognize in effect the East German regime, and it would have put serious pressure on them to make more substantial concessions. Subsequently Premier Khrushchev announced a delay of six months in carrying out the Russian move, on the grounds of allowing time for negotiations. The Western powers rejected the time limit as an "ultimatum" but indicated their willingness to negotiate without it.

In the background of this exchange stood an ominous remark made in the official note of the Soviet government to the United States. The Western powers should remember, it said, that German armament in the 1930's had led to a German attack on the West.[23] To its Western recipients in

[20] *Ibid.*, pp. 621–22.

[21] *Ibid.*, p. 622.

[22] *Ibid.*, p. 628.

[23] "The legitimate question arises: Can the very inspirers of the present policy of the Western powers toward Germany guarantee that German militarism, which they have nurtured, will not attack its present partners again and that the American, British and French peoples will not have to pay with their blood for the violation by the Governments of the three Western powers of the Allied agreements on the development of Germany along a peace loving and democratic road? Hardly can anyone give such a guarantee . . ." ("Text of Soviet Government's Note to U.S. Urging Free-City Status for West Berlin," *The New York Times*, November 28, 1958, p. 8.)

1958 this was not an impressive threat. To its German readers, however, this position and the Soviet note seemed certain to recall the German-Soviet pact of 1939 which had reinsured Hitler's Germany against Soviet attack and left it free to move against the weaker targets in Western Europe and beyond. The Soviet government seemed to be serving notice, in effect, to the German military that if they should become strong enough, the Soviet Union would offer them the same cold-blooded reinsurance agreement which it had offered and kept to Hitler in 1939–41. Against Soviet resistance, the former East German territories could not be re-covered at the cost of a major war; but German nationalists are left free to ponder whether with Russian nonintervention Alsace-Lorraine might not be regained some day more easily. None of this was said explicitly, of course, but the historical precedents are clear enough for the German nationalists to read between the lines. At the moment, all this was at most a hint for the future: at present no German government had the military power to establish itself as potential partner for such a policy. But whether German military and nuclear power would again reach such a level might well be decided in the next few years.

By the end of 1958, another round of negotiations seemed in the offing. The German army was as yet well below the strength planned for it origi-nally by NATO, and it had as yet no nuclear weapons. As yet, no irre-trievable decision had been made as to whether Germany should become a nuclear power, but the decision could not be long delayed.

Would Germany consider seriously limiting her close ties to the West to the political, economic, and cultural fields, and trading her present mili-tary alliances and potential future nuclear strength for substantial progress toward reunification?

In the short run, this seems quite unlikely. Chancellor Adenauer has committed himself to a policy of military alliance with the West and of refusing anything less than complete reunification on purely Western terms.[24] In this attitude, he appears to have the backing of a majority of the leaders of his party, and probably of a majority of West German elite members. Important economic, psychological, and political interests, both in the Federal Republic and in the United States, have become wedded to the policy of all-out alliance and gradual but increasing German arma-ment. In the United States, the late Secretary of State Dulles and many leaders of the Republican administration had similar commitments. These commitments are shared, moreover, by the most prominent figures of the old Truman administration, notably ex-President Harry Truman himself and former Secretary of State Dean Acheson, during whose terms of office

---

[24] See Chapter 14 in this study. See also Lewis J. Edinger, *West German Armament*, pp. 127–28; Sidney Gruson, "Socialists Spurn Bid by Adenauer," *The New York Times*, December 4, 1958, p. 3: 1–3; Henry S. Hayward, "London Rift with Bonn Denied," *The Christian Science Monitor*, December 9, 1958, p. 6: 6–8; etc.

the policy of West German armament was initiated. Both these men condemned flatly in 1955 the proposal of a fellow Democrat, ex-Ambassador
George Kennan, for military disengagement in Germany and Central
Europe. The considerable influence still exercised by these distinguished
leaders within the Democratic party makes it likely that continued German armament, including the introduction of nuclear weapons, will be
backed by the government and a majority of the leaders of both major
parties in the United States.

Within a few years, this situation may well change. In Germany as
well as in the United States, men less completely committed to the policies
of the past may succeed to office. American military interest may shift to
intercontinental missiles and away from conventional airplanes and inter-
mediate-range ballistic weapons with their dependence upon forward bases.
Interest might thus develop conceivably in a "semineutral" arrangement
under which certain countries, such as Germany, would remain part of a
Western early-warning network, but would be kept free of all installations
for attack, such as nuclear weapons and missile bases. Alternatively, early-
warning networks in certain areas could be managed by the national governments in cooperation with appropriate organs of the United Nations.

There is at least an American minority opinion in favor of a German
policy characterized by a greater willingness to extend diplomatic recognition, to negotiate a mutual withdrawal of foreign troops, and to limit the
speed and scope of German armament. Expressions of this view have included the widely discussed BBC lectures by ex-Ambassador George F.
Kennan, discussed earlier in this study.[25] The whole matter was summed
up by Walter Lippmann in early December 1958:

... an Allied reply which took the line of a negotiation between the two Germanies
would pose the basic question as to what are the practical conditions of a negotiated
settlement—and what are the possibilities of an all-European security system.

I realize, of course, that a reply of this kind requires a serious modification of
Dr. Adenauer's policy of the non-recognition of the East German state. If he vetoes
such a reply, the United States cannot now go over his head. But nevertheless it is
a sound way to approach the German question, and it would have powerful support
in the Western World, including Western Germany itself.

Indeed, it is hard to see how there can be any successful approach which does
not begin with and recognize the facts of life—which are that there are now two
Germanies and two Berlins, and that only slowly over a long period of time, and in
the climate of national freedom after the foreign troops have departed, can the two
Germanies become integrated again.[26]

Mass opinion in Germany would be cool in all likelihood to any prospect of negotiations with the East German government, but it would clearly

[25] See p. 55.
[26] Walter Lippmann, "The Reply to the Soviets," *New York Herald Tribune*, December 4, 1958, p. 26. Cf. also Joseph C. Harsch, "Second Thoughts on Berlin," *The Christian
Science Monitor*, December 3, 1958, p. 1:7–8.

welcome any development that would maintain the political and economic alliance with the West while reducing military ties and burdens and fostering steps toward reunification.[27] Ten years since 1948 have not significantly reduced the unpopularity of militarism, and particularly of atomic weapons, in Germany, and they have increased rather than dimmed, it seems, the popular desire for reunification.

If the pace of German armament were slowed or halted now, or if at least no radical change would occur from the type of military establishment Germany had in the 1950's, some settlement along these lines might prove acceptable to all concerned at some time before 1965. But well before that date, an irreversible threshold may be crossed. Once Germany has a mass army, with all the economic, political, and social influence of the military elite which this implies, German politics will never again be what it was in the 1950's. Once this German army has nuclear weapons, the patterns of power and the level of potential threats against the East, but also eventually against the West, will have risen irrevocably.

This threat is likely to appear considerably magnified, of course, when seen from the Soviet Union. To most Soviet citizens and leaders, despite official propaganda, the United States appears at most as a theoretical threat—a threat deduced by Marxist theory from its alleged "capitalistic," "plutocratic," and "imperialistic" character. For most Russians, there is no living personal experience related to these claims. Far more Russians have experienced American aid in World War II than have suffered from the small and half-hearted American intervention against Bolshevism after World War I. But almost every family in Russia still has poignant memories of deaths, losses, and deprivations suffered as the result of German actions in World War II. Where the alleged American threat is apt to look to most Russians somewhat shadowy and flat, any German threat must appear to them three-dimensional and in full color.

The image of a Germany equipped once again with large forces and nuclear weapons seems certain, therefore, to touch raw nerves not only among the Soviet elite but among the mass of the Russian people. It can be a powerful instrument of pressure, if a political solution can be worked out that is genuinely acceptable to the Soviet Union as well as to the West. In the absence of such a solution, the threat of German nuclear armament may prove a fateful provocation, precipitating and accelerating a crisis before statesmanship has found means to contain it.

A slow pace of German armament, stopping short of crossing the nu-

---

[27] A similar basic attitude seems indicated by recurrent German suggestions for increased business relations with the Soviet Union and the opening of formal diplomatic relations with Poland despite the Polish recognition of the Democratic Republic, and despite the unresolved question of the Oder-Neisse territories. Cf., e.g., Carlo Schmid, "Untertöne eines Briefes," *Aussenpolitik*, 8:3, March 1957, p. 138, and Kurt Sieveking, "Die europäische Aufgabe der deutschen Aussenpolitik," *Aussenpolitik*, 8:3, March 1957, pp. 152–53.

clear threshold into the whole world of ABC weapons that lies beyond, may have made a useful, if limited, contribution to the bargaining power of the West in the 1950's. A faster pace of armament, a decisively larger scale of German forces, or the introduction of weapons of mass destruction into the equipment of German forces might have radically different effects. To continue the armament policy of the 1950's as if it could be pursued without change may prove under these conditions to pursue a policy of incalculable risk.

There are deeper reasons in the West, however, for insisting on a policy of German armament than the mere force of political inertia, the interests of special groups, and the commitments of eminent statesmen. In the United States, the prospect of German armament has served as a psychological crutch—as an imaginary offset to the partial decline of Western power in other areas, and as a substitute for a fundamental effort to raise American strength more fully to the level of American commitments. The prospect of German soldiers was to compensate for the unwillingness of American voters to see a larger part of the youth of their country conscripted for military service. Atomic rockets on German soil were to compensate for the psychological impact of Soviet Sputniks and military rocketry. Rapid German economic growth was to balance somehow the lagging growth rates of American production in the 1950's. German conventional and nuclear forces were to substitute eventually for the unwillingness of the American taxpayer to shoulder the full burden of maintaining both a nuclear and a conventional military establishment at levels adequate for the policy commitments to which American opinion had become accustomed in 1947 and 1948.

A very well-informed observer cites a German general on this topic. The atomic weapon, says Lieutenant General (Ret.) Helmut Staedtke, is "the Maginot line of the unwilling taxpayer . . . in which he seeks to take shelter in order to avoid sacrifices." The General continues:

> Despite its larger population, the West is incapable or at least believes itself incapable of mobilizing armed forces equaling in strength those of the East. The West fails to do so because its peoples lack the necessary will and its governments the necessary power. One prefers to live well and not to sacrifice too much time and money for his freedom. One is afraid that Bolshevism may enter through the back door if the standard of living is lowered in order to improve the defenses. . . . If we prepare voluntarily for a situation in which we can counter a nonatomic attack only with atomic weapons, because we lack adequate classical forces and have failed to prepare for civil war, we are already marked in the future annals of history as "atomic war criminals born of degeneracy." If the West shrinks in the last minute, however, from resorting to the suicidal atomic weapons, the only alternative that remains is capitulation.[28]

[28] Lieutenant General (Ret.) Helmut Staedtke before a membership meeting of the *Arbeitskreis für Wehrforschung*, Frankfurt, printed as manuscript, without date (1956). Cited in Hans Speier, *German Rearmament and Atomic War*, p. 244. Cf. also the impressive argument in Dean Acheson, *Power and Diplomacy*, pp. 29–68.

Promoting German armament has been a device for the West, and particularly for us in the United States, to postpone facing some of our own basic dilemmas. This device will not work very much longer, and if we cling to it too tightly, it may do us more harm than good.

The German government and parliament have been, on the whole, more moderate on this issue than some American civilian and military spokesmen. They limited the levels of German armament and slowed its pace. They have returned the question of atomic missiles on German soil to NATO for decision. And they have held German military spending down to the Scandinavian level of 4 per cent of national income. By so doing, they have not only avoided a sharpening of conflicts with the East —where every increase in German armament serves to drive Poland and Czechoslovakia closer into Russia's arms—but they have also avoided putting unnecessary strains upon the slowly growing fabric of democratic consensus within Germany. In so doing, they may have served the best interests of the Western community of nations.

To maintain itself in the world, the West needs first of all its own strength, unity, and determination. From the German Federal Republic the West needs stability, prosperity, democracy, and cultural and moral integration far more than it needs soldiers. If Germany were as firmly democratic, and as firmly linked to the West, as Sweden and Switzerland are, and if she remained in the economic and cultural institutions uniting Western Europe, then her membership or nonmembership in a Western military alliance might matter very little.

Perhaps in the past we have overestimated the military bonds, and underestimated the civilian bonds of economics, politics, culture, and religion that may make or break the community of Western peoples. A sound, growing, and stable economy, and a genuinely accepted and deeply rooted democratic tradition may be the best contributions which Germany could make now and in the next few years to the security of the United States and of the Western world.

To make these contributions, Germany will need time, as well as patience and understanding from her friends. Every day her government and people must still make decisions about their future political identity —about the kind of country, deep down, that Germany will be. Some of the most important of these decisions may still be those that bear upon the official and unofficial attitudes toward the remnants of Nazism and old-line militarism inside Germany. Any major crisis in foreign policy is likely to strain the limited consensus of the different ideological and interest groups that have been held together by the conditions of the Adenauer era. Under such strains, any major decision about German foreign policy may well become involved in a decision as to what kind of country Germany is to become and what groups and ideas are to lead her. Some decisions of this kind—on the attitudes to the Nazi past, to the war criminals, to authoritarianism—have been made, while others have been largely or partly shelved thus far. If the rest of the world remains stable for the next ten years, these delayed decisions, too, may be made or else outgrown, and Germany's moderate foreign policy and constitutional domestic evolution may well remain secure.

Americans and all friends of Germany might do well to look upon the continuing political, economic, and spiritual recovery of the German people in the Federal Republic with realism and compassion—as if upon the recovery of a close relative from a very grave illness. No nation in history has committed such vicious acts of slaughter and wanton cruelty and has come as close to suicidal fury as Germany did under the rule of Adolf Hitler. Today, less than fifteen years later, the picture appears strikingly changed for the better. On the surface, the German Federal Republic looks like a stable political community, whose leaders are pursuing a steadfast policy of national recovery within a Western alliance, and who are backed in this enterprise by a wide measure of solid political consensus among their people. More closely considered, the body politic of this Republic resembles rather a political and psychological convalescent. The political unity of her population still is precarious, and could easily break under strain. Any policy by other Western powers designed to make Germany bear the major burdens of maintaining Western power in Europe in periods of major stress might well prove hazardous in the extreme.

Under these conditions time, wisely used, might well work for the West. Any additional year of peace, prosperity, and confidence might aid in the consolidation of German democracy and help Germany to become a full member of the Western community of nations by inner conviction and tradition, rather than only by strategic association and expediency.

The great humanitarian and democratic traditions are alive in Germany today, and a constitutional system of government has had a few years' time to take root. Very much may depend on giving these traditions a chance to become stronger in the next few years in an international environment that is sufficiently peaceful to permit them to become more firmly and deeply established in the social fabric and the living memories of the German people.

A list of dates*

Background

843–1806   First German Empire ("Holy Roman Empire")

1815–66   German Confederation

1819–44   Economic unification of much of Germany through Zollverein

1867–71   North German Confederation

1871–1918 Second German Empire

1871   18 Jan. Empire established, with Bismarck as Chancellor

1871–83   Kulturkampf: official discrimination against Catholics

1878–90   18 Oct. 1878. Anti-Socialist Law passed; renewed periodically until 1890

1887–90   Secret "reinsurance treaty" with Russia

1890   18 Mar. Bismarck resigns on request of Wilhelm II

1914–18   World War I

1918   28 Oct. Navy mutinies at Kiel; revolution spreads throughout Germany; Emperor abdicates (9 Nov.) ; Republic proclaimed by Socialist Scheidemann (9 Nov.)

           Army returns in good order, with Allied permission

1919   5–15 Jan. Spartacist (Communist) revolt crushed in Berlin

1919–1933 Weimar Republic

1919   19 Jan. National Assembly elected

           11 Feb. Socialist Friedrich Ebert, former harness maker, elected President

* For more detailed chronologies, see the following. For the entire period of German history, see William L. Langer, compiler and editor, *An Encyclopedia of World History: Ancient, Medieval, and Modern, Chronologically Arranged* (rev. ed.; Boston, Houghton Mifflin Company, 1952). For the period from 1918 to 1945, see *The Annual Register of World Events: A Review of the Year*, volumes 160 to 187, edited by M. Epstein (London, New York, Toronto, Longmans, Green and Co.) ; John W. Wheeler-Bennett, *The Nemesis of Power: The German Army in Politics, 1918–1945* (London, Macmillan and Co. Ltd., 1953), pp. 756–66; and Walter Hofer, editor, *Der Nationalsozialismus: Documente, 1933–1945* (Frankfurt-am-Main, Fischer Buecherei K.G., 1957), pp. 368–72.

For the postwar period, see volumes 188 to 199 of *The Annual Register of World Events*, edited by H. T. Montague Bell (1946) and Ivison S. Macadam (1947–   ); on the Berlin Blockade, W. Phillips Davison, *The Berlin Blockade: A Study in Cold War Politics* (Princeton, New Jersey, Princeton University Press, 1958), pp. 387–89; and on East Germany, Bundesministerium für Gesamtdeutsche Fragen, *SBZ von 1945 bis 1954; Die Sowjetische Besatzungzone Deutschlands in den Jahren 1945–1954* (Bonn, 1956). For more recent periods and for a general chronology, see the annual issues of *The New York Times Index*. In cases where the sources differ as to the exact date assigned to an event, we used our judgment; but the reader is advised to consult the sources for details.

4 Apr.–1 May. Soviet republic suppressed in Bavaria

28 June. Versailles Peace Treaty signed; ratified by Germany, 7 July

31 July. Weimar Constitution adopted

1920   13–17 Mar. Right-wing Kapp Putsch defeated by government-backed general strike

19 Mar.–3 Apr. Left-wing rising suppressed in Ruhr area

1922   16 Apr. Rapallo Treaty of German-Soviet cooperation

1923   11 Jan. Ruhr occupied by French troops; French-supported separatist Rhineland Republic fails

Runaway inflation: $1 = 4,200 million Reichsmark

12 Aug. Stresemann forms cabinet after Cuno's resignation; includes Socialists

8–11 Nov. Hitler's Beer Hall Putsch in Munich fizzles

15 Nov. Rentenbank under Dr. Hjalmar Schacht starts to stabilize currency

23 Nov. Stresemann cabinet falls; Wilhelm Marx (Center party) forms new government; Socialists out of national government until 1928, although continuing in coalition with Center party; Socialists in power in Prussian state government

1924   Stabilization of German currency; large U.S. private credits begin

1925   26 Apr. Field Marshal Paul von Hindenburg elected President by plurality of voters

16 Oct. Locarno Treaties stabilize Germany's western borders

1926   8 Sept. Germany joins League of Nations with permanent seat on League Council

1928   20 May. Socialist and moderate parties increase power in Reichstag elections; Socialists included in national government for the first time since 1923

1929   6 Feb. Germany signs Kellogg-Briand Pact

9 July. Hugenberg's Nationalists and Nazis form alliance; Hugenberg's conservative mass-media chain supports Hitler

Sept.–June 1930. Rhineland evacuated by French

1930   14 Sept. Reichstag elections: Nazi party emerges with 107 of 600-odd deputy posts

1930–32   Minority governments of Brüning and von Papen rule by emergency decree under Art. 48 of Weimar constitution

1931   21 Mar. German-Austrian Customs Union proposed; abandoned after French and Czechoslovak protest

11 May. Austrian Credit-Anstalt fails, followed by widespread financial collapse in Central Europe

11 Oct. Meeting of Hitler, Hugenberg, Schacht, and number of German industrialists at Bad Harzburg; "Harzburger Front" of right-wing parties formed; oppose existing government

1932   Six million unemployed in Germany

13 Mar. Presidential election: no candidate receives majority

10 Apr. Second presidential election: Hindenburg, with Socialist support, beats Hitler

20 July. Chancellor von Papen ousts constitutional government of Prussia

31 July. Reichstag elections: Communists, with almost five million votes, win 89 seats; NSDAP, 230; Socialists, 133; Center party, 97; no majority possible

12 Sept. Reichstag dissolved

6 Nov. Reichstag elections: NSDAP loses 34 seats; deadlock persists

17 Nov. Von Papen resigns chancellorship; Hitler refuses post one week later (24 Nov.)

1933–1945 The Third Reich

1933   30 Jan. Hindenburg appoints Hitler chancellor

27 Feb. Reichstag fire set by Nazis

5 Mar. Elections held under terror, giving 44 per cent of the votes to the Nazis, signaling end of Weimar Republic

23 Mar. Dictatorship established under Hitler, after passage of Enabling Act

28 May. Nazis win elections in Danzig and take over control of government

14 Oct. Germany withdraws from League and Disarmament Conference

1934   30 June. Blood purge: deviant Nazi leaders and others shot

25 July. Austrian Chancellor Dollfuss shot by Nazis in Vienna Putsch

2 Aug. Hindenburg dies of old age

19 Aug. Plebiscite approves placement of sole executive power in Hitler's hands (88 per cent votes in favor)

1935   13 Jan. Saar plebiscite (under League) shows 90 per cent in favor of union with Germany

16 Mar. Conscription reintroduced; armaments sped up

18 June. Anglo-German naval agreement

15 Sept. Nürnberg Laws deprive Jews of citizenship and rights of intermarriage

1936   7 Mar. Reoccupation and remilitarization of Rhineland, nullifying Locarno Treaties

27 Oct.–17 Nov. Anti-Communist pact signed by Germany, Italy, and Japan

1938   12–13 Mar. Austria invaded and annexed

12–29 Sept. Hitler granted Sudetenland by Western powers at Munich

1939   21 Aug. German-Soviet nonaggression pact

1 Sept. World War II breaks out: Hitler overruns much of Poland; Soviet Union occupies rest

1939–45   World War II

1939–41   Germany occupies much of Western Europe and Balkans

1941   22 June. Germany attacks Soviet Union; high point of German power

          23 Sept. Extermination of Jews begins; first experimental gassings at
          Auschwitz; massacre of 34,000 Jews at Kiev, 28 Sept.

          11 Dec. Germany declares war on United States after Japanese attack
          Pearl Harbor (7 Dec.)

1942   14 Sept. Germans enter Stalingrad; Battle of Stalingrad begins

          23 Oct.–3 Nov. Rommel turned back at El Alamein

          8 Nov. Anglo-American landings in North Africa

1943   31 Jan. Stalingrad surrendered by Germans; German forces at Stalin-
          grad capitulate, 2 Feb.

          10 July. Allies invade Sicily

          28 Nov. Teheran Conference begins; Cairo Declaration issued, 1 Dec.;
          Conference ends, 12 Jan. 1944

1944   6 June. Western Allies invade Normandy; advance into Germany; Rus-
          sians approach German borders

          20 July. Bomb plot by German generals narrowly misses killing Hitler;
          leaders of plot executed

1945   7–12 Feb. Yalta Conference of Roosevelt, Churchill, and Stalin: agree
          on final plans for defeat of Germany, occupation, control, and reparations

          Most major German cities largely destroyed by bombing

          30 Apr. Hitler commits suicide; Admiral Doenitz establishes provisional
          government

          7 May. Final German capitulation signed: Germany occupied and di-
          vided into four occupation zones, as arranged under terms of Teheran
          and Yalta agreements

1945–1949 Allied Military Government

1945   2 Aug. Potsdam Agreement announced: Western Allies and Soviets
          agree to demilitarize, denazify, and democratize all of Germany

          30 Aug. Allied Control Council established to govern Germany

          20 Nov. Trial of major war criminals at Nürnberg begins

1946–48   Economic distress in the wake of war

          Growing conflicts between Russia and Western Allies

1946   27 Feb. Forcible union of Communist and Socialist parties in Soviet zone
          proclaimed; intention announced late in 1945

          5 Mar. Churchill, in speech at Fulton, Missouri, calls for firmness against
          USSR; later advocates German recovery, 5 June

          30 June. Soviet Union closes zonal boundaries between Soviet Zone and
          three Western Zones

          6 Sept. Secretary of State Byrnes, in Stuttgart address, calls for fusion
          of American and British Zones, American protection of Germany, firm-
          ness against Russia

          30 Sept. Nürnberg judgment on major war criminals

3 Dec. Agreement signed by American and British military governors to fuse two Zones ("Bi-zonia"), effective 1 Jan. 1947

1947   1 Jan. Bi-zonal fusion comes into force

12 Mar. Truman enunciates "Truman Doctrine"; policy of containment

5 June. Secretary of State Marshall, in speech at Harvard, calls for economic assistance for European recovery

12 July. Paris Conference on Marshall Plan aid opens; Report of Committee on European Economic Cooperation signed, 22 Sept.

19 Dec. Truman sends Economic Cooperation Act, enabling implementation of Marshall Plan, to Congress

1948   6 Feb. Bi-zonal Charter signed; effective 9 Feb.

18–25 Feb. Communist coup in Czechoslovakia; Constituent Assembly adopts new constitution, 9 May; new constitution effective, 9 June

14 Mar. Economic Cooperation Act passed by Senate

15 Mar. Second Conference of Marshall Plan countries opens; Bi-zonia and French Zone represented by Allied Military Government

17 Mar. Brussels Pact signed by Britain, France, Belgium, Netherlands, and Luxembourg; enables formation of Western European Union, mutual protection against Soviet Union

3 Apr. Congress passes Economic Cooperation Act (establishing Economic Recovery Program, or ERP); Truman signs

16 Apr. Sixteen member-states of Committee for European Economic Cooperation pledge cooperation for recovery through ERP; Organization for European Economic Cooperation (OEEC) created; Allied Military Government signs for Bi-zonia and French Zone

1 June. London Agreement signed: provides for international control of Ruhr, and closer economic and political coordination in Germany among three Western powers

16 June. Soviets walk out of Allied Kommandatura in Berlin

18 June. Currency reform in Bi-zonia and French Zone; not effective in West Berlin

18 June. Soviet Military Government announces decision to blockade Berlin, effective 19 June

23 June. Soviet Military Government announces new currency for Soviet Zone and West Berlin

24 June. Soviets stop railway traffic to West Berlin, starting Berlin Blockade; American Military Government announces that vital goods will be flown into West Berlin by air, 25 June

18 Aug. Travel restrictions and frontier controls abolished between Bizonia and French Zone, thereby creating a de facto "Tri-zonia"

1 Sept. West German Constituent Assembly meets in Bonn to draft constitution; result of London Conference of 1–2 June

6 Sept. East Berliners blockade Stadthaus in East Berlin; Suhr leads West Berlin government to Charlottenburger Rathaus; East Berlin sets up municipal government in Admiralpalast, 30 Nov.

18 Oct. Foreign trade agencies of three Western Zones merged

Economic revival in three Western Zones

1949   19 Mar. German People's Council in Soviet Zone adopts constitution; approved by German People's Congress, 30 May

4 Apr. Creation of North Atlantic Treaty Organization (NATO)

8 Apr. Occupation Statute signed in Washington: replaces Allied Military Government with Allied High Commission; limits German sovereignty along certain lines; effective 21 Sept.

5 May. Statute for Council of Europe signed

8 May. West German Constituent Assembly at Bonn adopts Basic Law (Grundgesetz) for West German constitution

12 May. Berlin Blockade ends

12 May. Western Military Governors approve Basic Law

23 May. Basic Law signed by West German government; Adenauer proclaims German Federal Republic; effective 24 May

21 June. West Germany opened to tourist travel

14 Aug. Bundestag elections: CDU-CSU, 31.0 per cent votes; SPD, 29.2 per cent; Free Democratic party (Liberals), 11.9 per cent

7 Sept. Bundestag and Bundesrat formally open in Bonn

15 Sept. Vote for Chancellor: Adenauer receives 202 out of 404 votes

20 Sept. Adenauer presents his government and policy

21 Sept. Occupation Statute goes into effect; West Germany receives limited sovereignty

1949–1955 Period of Continued Allied Military Occupation and Political Supervision

1949   29 Sept. New exchange rate established (1 DM = 23.81¢ U.S.); follows British devaluation of the pound, 18 Sept.

7 Oct. Founding of German Democratic Republic (GDR); National Front established; GDR constitution proclaimed; provisional government established

11 Oct. West Germany given right by High Commission to appoint delegate to OEEC

22 Nov. Petersberg Agreement signed by three Western powers and West Germany; gives broader powers to West German federal government

4 Dec. Adenauer advocates German components in some type of Western defense system; declares opposition to formation of separate German army; all parties in Bundestag endorse position, 16 Dec.

15 Dec. German-American treaty signed providing for West German participation in ERP; Germany gets Marshall Plan aid

1950   21 Mar. Adenauer proposes Franco-German economic union

9 May. French Foreign Minister Schuman proposes French-German coal and steel community

9 May. German Federal Republic decides to become associate member of Council of Europe; ratified by Bundestag, 15 June

6 June. East German Communist party chief Walter Ulbricht in Warsaw agrees to Oder-Neisse line as border between East Germany and Poland;

German Federal Republic declares agreement void, 9 June; GDR ratifies agreement, 28 Nov.

25 June. Outbreak of Korean war strengthens American demands for German military contribution to Western defense system

11 Aug. Churchill resolution calling for creation of European army adopted by Council of Europe

19 Sept. New York Conference: Western powers agree to permit West Germany to have 30,000-man security force; declare that attack against West Germany would constitute attack against themselves

1 Oct. New constitution of West Berlin goes into effect

24 Oct. Announcement of Pleven Plan in French Assembly, providing for European army including West German components as alternative to creation of separate West German army

1951   15 Feb. Negotiations begin in Paris for creation of European army

6 Mar. High Commission authorizes creation of Federal Ministry of Foreign Affairs

18 Apr. Schuman Plan for European Coal and Steel Community (ECSC) signed by Federal Republic and five other states

2 May. West Germany formally admitted to Council of Europe

16 May. West Germany admitted to membership in World Health Organization (WHO)

12 June. West Germany joins International Labor Organization (ILO)

21 June. West Germany joins UNESCO

9 July. Britain formally ends war with Germany

15 Aug. Clash between 12,000 Free German Youth members (East German Communist Youth organization) and West Berlin police

10–14 Sept. Three-Power Conference in Washington on German problems expresses desire to change Occupation Statute of 1949, to give greater degree of sovereignty to Federal Republic

27 Sept. Unanimous vote in Bundestag promises restitution to Jews; negotiations with Israel begin shortly after

19 Oct. Formal termination of war between United States and Germany

7 Nov. Paris Conference on European army announces plans for 1,290,000-man army by 1952

20 Nov. Federal Republic signs United Nations Convention on the Status of Refugees

31 Dec. Marshall Plan ends; Mutual Security Agency replaces Economic Cooperation Administration

1952   1 Feb. Bundesrat ratifies ECSC (first state to ratify)

26 May. Allied-German Contractual Agreement signed, providing for abolition of Occupation Statute of 1949 on coming into force of EDC

27 May. European Defense Community signed in Paris

24 June. Federal Republic announces intention to contribute 500,000-man force within five years to Western defense system

25 July. ECSC treaty enters into force

20 Aug. Kurt Schumacher, Socialist leader, dies

10 Sept. German-Israeli Reparations Agreement signed

23 Oct. Neo-Nazi Sozialistische Reichspartei (SRP) outlawed by Constitutional Court

1953   5 Mar. Stalin dies

19 Mar. Bundestag ratifies EDC agreement; ratified by Bundesrat, 15 May; constitutional amendment adopted enabling German adherence to EDC; re-ratified by Bundesrat, 19 Mar. 1954; signed by President Heuss, 26 Mar. 1954

20 Mar. Bundesrat ratifies German-Israeli Reparations Agreement, effective 27 Mar.

17 June. Strike by construction workers in East Berlin on previous day turns into popular uprising; martial law is proclaimed, ending in East Berlin on 11 July

6 Sept. Bundestag elections: Adenauer wins large plurality in elections for second Bundestag; CDU-CSU, 45.2 per cent; SPD, 28.8 per cent; FDP, 9.5 per cent

29 Sept. Ernst Reuter, Socialist Mayor of West Berlin, dies

1954   25 Jan.–18 Feb. Four-Power Conference in Berlin ends without result

30 Aug. French parliament rejects EDC

7 Oct. Bundestag approves of Adenauer's decision to contribute military forces to Western defense system

23 Oct. Paris Agreements signed: providing for end of occupation of Germany; creating the Western European Union (WEU); enabling Germany to join NATO; Franco-German agreement on Saar

26 Oct. Franco-German agreement on economic cooperation; conclusion of Franco-German cultural agreement

1955   25 Jan. Soviet Union formally decrees end of war with Germany

18 Mar. Bundesrat ratifies all Paris Agreements

3 May. Signature of Franco-Saar economic convention

5 May. Deposit of instruments of ratification of Paris Agreements: WEU created; German sovereignty recognized by Western powers and occupation ended; Western powers retain rights in Berlin; Western troops remain in Germany as allies; Germany enters NATO

1955– The Period of Sovereignty

1955   9 May. Formal admission of Federal Republic to NATO

14 May. Mutual defense agreement signed in Warsaw by USSR and seven satellite states, including East Germany

3 June. ECSC Foreign Ministers meeting at Messina, Sicily, set up Inter-Governmental Committee to work out agreements on European Common Market and Atomic Pooling Arrangement (Euratom)

6 June. Adenauer recommends appointment of Defense Commissioner Theodor Blank to rank of Defense Minister, thereby establishing the Federal Defense Ministry; President Heuss nominates Blank, 7 June

7 June. Soviet Union invites Adenauer to visit Moscow

30 June. Federal Republic signs German-American military aid agreement

4 Aug. Franco-German trade agreement signed

9–13 Sept. Adenauer visits Moscow; negotiates agreement to resume diplomatic relations with the USSR, 20 Sept.; approved unanimously by Bundestag, 23 Sept.

20 Sept. GDR-USSR treaty recognizes East German sovereignty

23 Oct. Saar Referendum: Saarlanders reject proposed Europeanization of Saar, 423,434 to 401,973

11 Nov. Volunteer Law passed, providing for army induction of volunteers

18 Dec. Saar Landtag elections: CDU, 25.4 per cent; Christian People's party, 21.8 per cent; Democratic party, 24.2 per cent; SPD, 14.2 per cent; Communists, 6.6 per cent; Saar Socialists, 5.8 per cent; three pro-German parties under CDU leadership form coalition

1956   1 Jan. Volunteer Law goes into effect, calling up first 6,000 volunteers

18 Jan. German Democratic Republic passes law regularizing National People's Army, formally recognizing existence of 80,000-member army

26 Jan. West German Atomic Energy Commission inaugurated; followed by agreement with U.S. to purchase uranium-235, and with British to purchase atomic reactors

8 Mar. Bundestag passes constitutional amendment (with SPD support) to enable the introduction of conscription

4 June. France and West Germany agree on political and economic future of Saar

12 July. USSR announces creation of Eastern Institute for Nuclear Research, with USSR, China, East Germany, and six other Eastern European satellite states as members

17 Aug. Federal Constitutional Court orders dissolution of Communist party in West Germany

Sept. (approx.). Goal of 500,000-man army by 1959 reduced to maximum of 400,000 by 1961

27 Sept. Blank announces that 500,000-man goal is impossible because Bundestag cut eighteen-month service for conscripts to twelve months in National Service Bill under consideration

16 Oct. Franz Josef Strauss appointed Defense Minister, replacing Theodor Blank

23 Oct. Mass demonstrations in Budapest of previous day turn into insurrection; Hungarian revolution crushed by Soviet intervention

27 Oct. France and West Germany sign four agreements on Saar; ratified by Bundesrat, 14 Dec.; providing for inclusion of Saar in Federal Republic as federal land

29 Oct. Israeli troops invade Sinai Peninsula; followed by Anglo-French intervention, 31 Oct.; Federal Republic follows neutral policy in Suez war; German press criticizes Britain

8 Nov. Strauss proposes 500,000-man army by 1959

21 Dec. Bundesrat passes National Service Bill, providing for conscrip-

tion for period of twelve months; original government plan had called for eighteen-month conscription service; effective 1 Apr. 1957

1957   1 Jan. Saar becomes federal land

24 Jan. Lt. Gen. Speidel appointed commander in chief of central sector of NATO ground forces in Europe

25 Mar. European Common Market and Euratom agreements signed; ratified 30 July

4 Apr. Adenauer asks for nuclear-equipped German Army

12 Apr. Eighteen West German scientists announce refusal to assist in production, testing, or use of atomic weapons

10 May. Bundestag passes resolution asking for abolition of nuclear weapons testing

20 June. In East Berlin, Gomulka and Ulbricht confirm finality of Oder-Neisse line as German-Polish boundary

2 July. Bundestag defeats Atom Law, providing for constitutional amendment to permit development and peaceful use of nuclear energy

15 Sept. Bundestag elections: Adenauer's Christian Democratic Union wins first absolute majority of votes in German history; CDU-CSU, 50.2 per cent; SPD, 31.8 per cent; FDP, 7.7 per cent

2 Oct. Polish Foreign Minister Rapacki announces plan for denuclearization of Central Europe at General Assembly meeting

15 Oct. Yugoslavia recognizes German Democratic Republic; Federal Republic breaks diplomatic relations with Yugoslavia, 19 Oct.; trade relations continued

13 Nov. Strauss reports plans to set up West German territorial militia outside of NATO

14 Nov. Strauss announces that West German army is not to be equipped with nuclear weapons in near future

16 Dec. German Democratic Republic begins operation of its first atomic reactor

1958   15 Jan. Adenauer rejects Rapacki Plan for denuclearization in Central Europe; rejects Soviet proposals for East German–West German conference; proposes summit meeting on German reunification

21 Jan. Tripartite agreement to standardize and pool armaments signed by France, Italy, and West Germany; Britain agrees to pact, 25 Mar.

26 Feb. Defense Ministry sources report decrease in military goal from 500,000 to 350,000 by 1961

4 Mar. Strauss announces intention to accept United States offer of Matador pilotless bombers; Bundestag approves resolution to purchase American missiles, 25 Mar.; SPD, in opposition, appeals to public opinion in Germany

8 Apr. Soviet-German agreement signed, providing for repatriation of German citizens detained in USSR and for trade relations

7 May. Agreement signed between Federal Republic and United Arab Republic (UAR); provides for creation of 400 million DM in industrial credits for UAR, for German technical assistance to UAR, and for return of sequestered German private property

19 June. Strauss announces plans for revision of army along American lines, with nuclear-equipped battle groups

30 July. Federal Republic recognizes Iraqi revolutionary regime before United States, Britain, and France do so

30 Oct. Interior Minister Schroeder demands increased police powers and provisions for emergency government

10 Nov. Khrushchev asks Western withdrawal from Berlin

27 Nov. Soviet note proposes to establish West Berlin as a demilitarized "free city"

13–18 Dec. NATO Council of Foreign Ministers meets in Paris; U.S., U.K., and French Foreign Ministers reject Khrushchev proposal of 27 Nov.; NATO Council of Foreign Ministers endorses this position

15 Dec. Gomulka and Ulbricht issue Warsaw communiqué terming Adenauer the chief threat to European peace

25 Dec. Gromyko warns that Western determination to retain troops in Berlin may lead to "big war"

31 Dec. Western powers offer to confer with USSR on Berlin and Germany, rejecting the "free city" proposal of 27 Nov.

1959

5 Jan. Bonn government rejects Soviet proposal of 27 Nov.

4–20 Jan. Mikoyan visits United States; confers with Dulles and Eisenhower; indicates Soviet willingness to negotiate with United States on wide range of problems; Bonn government sending federal press chief, Felix von Eckardt, and chief of the political division of the foreign office, Herbert Dittmann, to Washington for talks with German representatives and American officials

28 March. German army reportedly scheduled to reach 200,000 men

11 May. Geneva Conference of Foreign Ministers of U.S., U.K., France, and USSR meets on German problems; GFR and GDR representatives are admitted as "advisers"

APPENDIX II

Some data on German social structure
and mobility, 1938–1955

All of the following tables are taken from Morris Janowitz, "Social Stratification and Mobility in West Germany," *The American Journal of Sociology*, LXIV, No. 1 (July 1958), 6–24, except Table II.5, which has been adapted from Professor Janowitz' data, so as to bring out more clearly the difference between the West German and the United States samples.

From these tables it appears that there has been a good deal of social mobility in West Germany; that the West German upper middle class now includes a relatively large share of newcomers, mostly from the lower middle class; that religion

TABLE II.1

TRENDS IN OCCUPATIONAL STRATIFICATION IN WEST GERMANY

(Based on Sample Survey Data)

	Year	
	1955	1939
Non-manual:		
Self-employed:		
Entrepreneurs	10.7	10.9
Professionals	2.9	2.6
Total	13.6	13.5
Salaried:		
Officials, managerial, technical	9.4	9.9
Clerical, sales	9.4	9.4
Total	18.8	19.3
Total non-manual	32.4	32.8
Manual:		
Skilled	13.3	13.7
Semiskilled	30.8	29.9
Service	4.1	3.1
Total manual	48.2	46.7
Farmers:		
Owners	10.6	14.9
Laborers	3.8	3.9
Total farmers	14.4	18.8
Unclassifiable*	4.9	1.8
No. of cases	(3,385)	(3,385)

(Janowitz, *op. cit.*, p. 8, Table 1.)

* Includes those war and social pensioners to whom no occupational position could be meaningfully assigned.

has something to do with social mobility; that political preference is still partly related to social class; and that—in Professor Janowitz' view—the social scene in West Germany now has come to resemble in many ways that in the United States.

The latter finding contains a good deal of truth, but it should be interpreted with caution. While it appears that Professor Janowitz' German sample was large, and chosen by up-to-date methods of random sampling, he had to rely for his comparisons with United States data in part on earlier surveys, made by others and leaving some room for argument about their techniques of sampling and of coding occupations into social classes. Table 5 shows the considerable differences between West German and American social structure that emerge from a further analysis of Professor Janowitz' data. It leaves at least a question whether the American people are realistically represented by a sample of which 29 per cent consists of members of the upper middle class, and another question as to whether the American lower middle class is as small in the present, and was as infertile a generation ago, as the sample would suggest. Readers who wish to pursue these points should turn to Professor Janowitz' article, cited above.

Professor Janowitz' findings represent pioneering research of a high order which can do much to illuminate the social basis of German politics. They are reproduced here with his kind permission.

TABLE II.2

CROSS-NATIONAL COMPARISON OF OCCUPATIONAL STRATIFICATION,
WEST GERMANY AND THE UNITED STATES, 1954–1955

	West Germany 1955	United States 1954*
Non-manual:		
Self-employed:		
Entrepreneurs	10.7	6.0
Professionals	2.9	1.4
Total	13.6	7.4
Salaried:		
Officials, managerial, technical	9.4	11.3
Clerical, sales	9.4	19.5
Total	18.8	30.8
Total non-manual	32.4	38.2
Manual:		
Skilled	13.3	13.6
Semiskilled	30.8	27.0
Service	4.1	11.1
Total manual	48.2	51.7
Farmers:		
Owners	10.6	5.9
Laborers	3.8	4.1
Total farmers	14.4	10.0
Unclassifiable†	4.9	....
Total	100.0	100.0

(*Ibid.*, Table 2.)

* Adapted from *Current Population Reports*, Series P-50, No. 59 (April, 1955), Table III, p. 4.

† Includes those war and social pensioners to whom no occupational position could be meaningfully assigned.

TABLE II.3

SOCIAL STRATA IN WEST GERMANY, 1955

	Per Cent	
	Present Generation	Father's Generation
Upper-middle strata:		
Professionals, managers and proprietors of larger establishments, and upper civil servants	4.6	3.0
Lower-middle strata:		
Minor officials, clerical and sales persons, small businessmen, and independent artisans	28.0	24.6
Upper-lower strata:		
Skilled workers and employed artisans	13.3	12.4
Lower-lower strata:		
Semiskilled and unskilled workers	34.9	31.6
Farmers	10.6	22.0
Farm workers	3.7	4.6
Unclassifiable*	4.9	1.8
No. of cases	(3,385)	(3,385)

(Janowitz, *op. cit.*, p. 10, Table 3.)

* Includes those war and social security pensioners to whom no occupational position could be meaningfully assigned.

TABLE II.4

INTERGENERATIONAL SOCIAL MOBILITY, WEST GERMANY, 1955

(Comparison of Heads of Household: Father's Generation and Present Generation)

Social Strata— Father's Generation	Social Strata—Present Generation, 1955								
	Upper- Middle	Lower- Middle	Upper- Lower	Lower- Lower	Farm- owner	Farm Worker	Unclassi- fiable	Total (Per Cent)	Total No. of Cases
Upper-middle	50.6	27.1	9.4	4.7	2.4	...	5.8	100	(85)
Lower-middle	8.3	55.6	12.0	17.6	2.0	0.9	3.6	100	(845)
Upper-lower	3.6	32.9	31.5	21.5	3.1	1.7	5.7	100	(420)
Lower-lower	0.7	14.5	12.4	61.5	2.6	3.6	4.7	100	(1,065)
Farmowner	2.1	17.3	7.9	25.1	39.3	3.9	4.4	100	(747)
Farm worker	0.6	8.3	10.2	43.4	4.4	25.5	7.6	100	(158)
Unclassifiable	3.0	20.9	14.9	37.3	1.5	7.5	14.9	100	(65)
No. of cases	(155)	(941)	(458)	(1,181)	(361)	(125)	(164)		(3,385)

(*Ibid.*)

TABLE II.5

A Comparison of Intergenerational Social Mobility: Western Germany and the United States

| | Columns 1–6 Present Social Status | | | | | | | | | | | | | | | | |
| (Rounded Percentages) | 1 Upper-Middle | | 2 Lower-Middle | | 3 Upper-Lower | | 4 Lower-Lower | | 5 Farmers | | 6 Unclassifiable | | 7 Total No. Cases | | 8 Per Cent Recruitment of Present Total | |
	US	G	US	G	US	G	US	G	US	G	US	G	US	G	US	G
1. Number of cases	387	152	293	927	175	449	288	1,155	189	483	—	152	1,332	3,318	—	—
2. Present social composition, %	29	5	22	28	13	13	22	35	14	14	—	5	—	—	100	100
Rows 3–7: Recruitment from previous generation: Father's social status, in per cent of each present component:																
3. Upper-middle	40	28	32	3	10	2	14	*	4	*	—	3	315	85	24	3
4. Lower-middle	10	46	15	51	4	23	5	13	2	5	—	20	106	845	8	26
5. Upper-lower	16	10	21	15	30	29	17	8	3	4	—	16	231	419	17	13
6. Lower-lower	12	5	16	17	26	30	32	57	7	14	—	32	246	1,065	19	32
7. Farmers	22	11	16	15	29	17	33	22	84	76	—	29	434	904	33	27
8. Total present component	100	100	100	100	100	100	100	100	100	100	—	100	1,332	3,318	100	100

(Janowitz, op. cit., p. 12, Table 7.)

Despite the upheavals of total war, German society still seems more rigid than that of the United States. In Western Germany, three of the five social strata tabulated—lower-middle, lower-lower, and farmers—have a majority of second-generation members, as against only one such stratum in America, the farmers. In the American sample, the upper middle class is relatively strong, and the lower middle class weak; in the German sample, the opposite seems true.

The authors are indebted to Mr. William H. Flanigan for valuable help and suggestions for this table.

* Less than 0.5 per cent.

264

TABLE II.6

SOCIAL STRATIFICATION, SOCIAL MOBILITY, AND RELIGIOUS AFFILIATION, WEST GERMANY, 1955

Social Strata— Present Generation	Religious Affiliation (Per Cent)	
	Protestant	Catholic
Upper-middle	5.3	3.2
Lower-middle	29.8	25.8
Upper-lower	13.7	13.5
Lower-lower	32.1	37.3
Farmowner	10.1	11.9
Farm worker	4.0	3.6
Unclassifiable	5.0	4.6
No. of cases	(1,748)	(1,516)

Intergenerational Mobility	Per Cent				Total No. of Cases
	Protestant	Catholic	Other	None	
No mobility	55.7	56.4	41.7	39.8	(1,876)
Upward mobility	18.7	17.5	14.6	31.5	(622)
Downward mobility	19.2	19.6	29.2	23.3	(668)
Unclassifiable	6.4	6.5	14.5	5.4	(219)
No. of cases	(1,748)	(1,516)	(48)	(73)	(3,385)

(Janowitz, *op. cit.*, p. 15, Table 8.)

TABLE II.7

SOCIAL STRATIFICATION, SOCIAL MOBILITY, AND EDUCATION, WEST GERMANY, 1955

Social Strata— Present Generation	Education of Respondent (Per Cent)					
	Grammar School	"Middle School"	Abitur*	University	No Data	Total
Upper-middle	1.5	16.0	23.9	65.9	...	
Lower-middle	23.4	53.8	56.7	22.7		
Upper-lower	14.0	11.0	10.4	6.9		
Lower-lower	39.8	9.8	4.5	4.5		
Farmowner	12.0	4.0	3.0	....		
Farm worker	4.3	1.1	....	....		
Unclassifiable	5.0	4.3	1.5	....		
No. of cases	(2,845)	(426)	(67)	(44)	(3)	(3,385)

Intergenerational Mobility	Males Only (Per Cent)			
	Grammar School	"Middle School"	Abitur*	University
No mobility	61.4	58.7	45.2	38.9
Upward mobility	15.5	22.1	33.3	52.8
Downward mobility	19.9	16.3	21.5	8.3
Unclassifiable	3.2	2.9	....	....
No. of cases	(1,211)	(172)	(142)	(36)

(*Ibid.*, p. 16, Table 9.)

* College-preparatory high school.

TABLE II.8

SOCIAL CLASS SELF-IDENTIFICATION, WEST GERMANY AND THE UNITED STATES

	Per Cent	
	Germany* West	United States†
Upper class	1.9	3.0
Middle class	43.2	43.0
Working class	48.5	51.0
Lower class	5.3	1.0
No data	1.1	2.0
Total	100.0	100.0
No. of cases	(3,385)	(1,097)

(Janowitz, *op. cit.*, p. 21, Table 14.)

* "In welche von diesen Gesellschaftsklassen würden Sie sich einstufen?"

† Richard Centers, *The Psychology of Social Classes* (Princeton, N.J.: Princeton University Press, 1949), pp. 76–77.

TABLE II.9

SOCIAL CLASS SELF-IDENTIFICATION AND OBJECTIVE SOCIAL STRATA,
WEST GERMANY, 1955

Self- identification	Objective Social Strata (Per Cent)							
	Upper- Middle	Middle	Upper- Lower-	Lower- Lower	Farm- owner	Farm Laborer	Unclassi- fiable	Total
Upper class	18.7	1.9	0.6	0.2	2.8	0	1.2	1.9
Middle class	70.3	75.3	37.1	15.0	59.3	12.1	42.7	43.2
Working class	7.7	20.0	57.7	76.6	30.4	75.8	42.7	48.5
Lower class	1.9	1.6	3.3	7.3	5.8	11.3	13.4	5.3
No opinion; no data	1.4	1.2	1.3	0.9	1.7	0.8	0	1.1
Total	100	100	100	100	100	100	100	
No. of cases	(155)	(941)	(458)	(1,181)	(361)	(125)	(164)	(3,385)

(*Ibid.*, Table 15.)

TABLE II.10

POLITICAL PARTY PREFERENCE AND SOCIAL STRATA, WEST GERMANY, 1955

Social Strata	Socialist	Christian Democrats	Free Democrats	Right* Groups	Commu- nist†	Other†	None or No Opinion
Upper-middle	1.6	6.1	13.7	5.8	....	....	3.6
Lower-middle	18.4	33.2	46.0	26.6	....	....	26.2
Upper-lower	18.4	11.8	10.6	10.1	....	....	12.8
Lower-lower	50.8	26.9	13.7	31.7	....	....	35.6
Farmer	7.5	18.3	12.8	18.7	....	....	15.0
Unclassifiable	3.3	3.7	3.2	7.1	....	....	6.8
Total	100.0	100.0	100.0	100.0	....	....	100.0
No. of cases	(767)	(953)	(238)	(147)	(11)	(62)	(1,207)

Intergenerational Mobility	Socialist	Christian Democrats	Free Democrats	Right* Groups
No mobility	53.8	57.5	55.3	48.6
Upward mobility	18.6	18.4	24.1	15.5
Downward mobility	22.8	18.8	11.7	27.4
Unclassifiable	4.8	5.3	8.9	8.5
Totals	100.0	100.0	100.0	100.0
No. of cases	(767)	(953)	(238)	(147)

(Janowitz, *op. cit.*, p. 22, Table 16.)

* German party (DP), National German party (DRP), and Union of Refugees and Disenfranchised (BHE).

† Too few cases for statistical breakdown.

APPENDIX III

Close-up of an elite: Details on the foreign policy elite in Group A

The following pages present individual data for 250 members of German foreign policy elites, which are the elites included in Sample A of Tables 9.1–9.7 in Chapter 9. Summaries for the total and for a number of subgroups have been given in the main text in Tables 9.1–9.8 (pp. 133–40), together with a list of sources.

The individual data that follow will permit a greater number of possible correlations to be tested. For instance, were diplomats who did not serve the Nazi government in 1933–45 to be found less frequently at the head of main German embassies in Western Europe, while those diplomats who did serve the Nazis were placed mainly in the smaller embassies and in most overseas assignments? (Among six chiefs of diplomatic missions to the major countries of the West, none appear to have served the Hitler regime in a governmental or diplomatic position, while a majority of the chiefs of diplomatic posts outside Europe—seventeen out of twenty-nine—were listed as having been in the diplomatic service under the Third Reich.) Or, to take a quite different problem, is there a relatively high number of Protestant diplomats coming from predominantly Roman Catholic West Germany? (Of nineteen West German diplomats, eight listed themselves as Protestant, six did not list their religion, and only five listed themselves as Roman Catholic.) It is possible to ask many questions of this kind, and it seems clear that one can get more information from the individual data than from the aggregations given in the text.

Another advantage involves the acceptance of a risk: our tables may well contain mistakes, and by publishing the individual data on which our elite statistics are based we make it more likely that our faults will be found out. Incorrect attributions can thus be corrected, and missing information can be filled in when found, or when it becomes available. It will thus become obvious how much more thorough a job should have been done. Publishing only the statistical summaries, as is often done in such elite surveys, would have left them far more immune to specific criticism—but also more resistant to any chance of correction and improvement by subsequent workers in the field.

Finally, we have added to the 250 incumbents of elite positions for whom we found individual data also those incumbents of such elite positions for whom we found no information other than their names. These persons presumably are as relevant for the composition of the actual foreign policy elite—such as, for instance, the diplomats—as are their colleagues for whom we have more detailed data. While Tables 9.1–9.8 in the main text are based only on those incumbents of elite positions for whom we had data, readers can allow for the possible "dark horses" in the total—as well as in any particular subgroup—by consulting the tabulation by individuals that follows.

As in Tables 9.1–9.8, individuals have been listed as often as they held different elite positions. Thus, Chancellor Konrad Adenauer appears as a member of the cabinet of the Federal Republic, and again as a member of the executive committee of his party, the CDU/CSU.

Other conventions for the individual tabulations are given in the following key:

General

n.d.—No data available

0—None indicated (where other biographical data are given; this is usually a matter of discretion for the biographee)

Columns

Column 3: Decade of birth

−90	up to and including 1890
91–00	1891–1900
01–10	1901–1910
10–20	1910–1920
21–	1921 and after

Column 4: Geographic origin (for definitions of regions, see Table 9.2)

WestG—Western Germany, including Alsace and Saar

NorG—Northern Germany

SouG—Southern Germany

CEasG—Central and Eastern Germany, including "Volksdeutsche" but not Austria

Abr—Abroad

Column 5: Religious affiliation

Prot—Protestant

RCath—Roman Catholic

No other religious affiliations (e.g., Jewish, Old Catholic, etc.) were indicated by any elite member surveyed.

Column 6: Education (highest level attained)

Dr—Doctorate

Univ—attended university

Sec—attended secondary school (15–18 years of age)

Prim—attended primary school (6–14 years of age)

Column 7: Military service

WWI—World War I (1914–18)

WWII—World War II (1939–45)

WWI&II—both wars

Column 8: Anti-Nazi record (major)

Pris—arrest, imprisonment, or concentration camp

Exil—exile

Persec—reported minor persecution, such as dismissal from office, loss of job, police harassment, loss of pension, denial of promotion, etc.

Resis—reported participation in resistance activities against the Nazi regime

Note: Only major anti-Nazi records of individuals have been listed with any attempt at completeness.

Minor anti-Nazi records usually are not reported in current biographical sources, quite apart from their much greater difficulty of verification. Nevertheless, an effort has been made to include such minor anti-Nazi records of individuals as happened to come to our attention.

Columns 9–10: Party preference before 1933 and after 1945. This refers to reported political affiliation, usually connected with some political function or office.

Right—pre-1933 German Nationalist party
postwar Deutsche Partei
(No elite member reported any pre-1933 Nazi party affiliation.)
Moderate—pre-1933 German People's party
German Democratic party (Staatspartei 1930–33)
Center party
postwar CDU/CSU
FDP (Free Democratic party)
BHE (Bloc of expellees and dispossessed/all-German bloc)
SPD—Social Democratic party
CP—Communist party (this applies to the early affiliations of a very few elite members)

Columns 11–13:

Indus—employed in industry
Bus—business, including industry and banking (management)
Milit—military service
ManLab—manual laborer
Stud—student
SocSrv—social service work (including churches)
Eco—economist
Acad—academic position, including teacher below university level
TUFunc—trade union functionary
Clergy—ordained minister or priest
Journ—journalist, editor
Cleric—clerical worker
Misc—miscellaneous jobs
Publish—publisher
Dipl—diplomat
Eng—engineer
Church func—lay functionary of religious organization
Polit—political positions, including elective government and party offices
Law—independent lawyer
POW—prisoner of war
( )—occupation in exile

Asterisk in column 12 (1933–45 occupation) denotes unsuccessful application for Nazi party membership (e.g., W. Nöldeke; K. Schwendemann).

Dagger in same column indicates Nazi party member (e.g., W. Melchers, NSDAP No. 7 077 242; F. von Twardowski, NSDAP No. 7 550 829).

The indications of former Nazi affiliations are obviously incomplete. They are rarely, if ever, avowed, and none was found in the standard biographical sources used for this survey. The few cases indicated here are based on press references (e.g., *The New York Times*, January 12, 1954) and on data supplied by Professor Paul Seabury of the University of California at Berkeley.

TABLE III.1

INCUMBENTS OF GERMAN FOREIGN POLICY ELITE POSITIONS, 1954-1956

	1	2	3	4	5	6	7	8	9	10	11	12	13
									Party Preference		Previous Occupation		
	Category	Name	Decade Born	Geog. Orig.	Relig. Affil.	Educ. Att'd	Milit. Serv.	Anti-Nazi Record	-1933 Rep. I	1945- Postwar	-1933 (Weimar)	'33-'45 (Hitler)	1945- (Postwar)
ADMINISTRATIVE ELITES													
For Off (1954)													
State Sec'y	Hallstein, Walter		01-10	WestG	Prot	Dr	WWII	0	0	CDU	Acad	Acad	Acad
Chief, Pol Div	Blankenhorn, Herbert		01-10	WestG	RCath	Univ	0	Persec	0	0	Dipl	Dipl	0
Chief, Trade Pol Div	Maltzan, Frh.V.von		91-00	CEasG	Prot	Dr	0	0	0	0	Dipl	Dipl	0
Chief Dipl Repres in													
U.S.	Krekeler, Heinz		01-10	WestG	Prot	Dr	0	0	0	Moder	Stud	Indust	Polit
U.K.	Schlange-Schöningen, Hans		-90	CEasG	0	Univ	WWI	0	Right	Moder	Polit	0	Polit
France	Hausenstein, Wilhelm		-90	SouG	RCath	Dr	0	0	0	0	Acad	Acad	Acad
Italy	Brentano, Clemens von		-90	WestG	RCath	Univ	0	0	Moder	0	Dipl& Polit	0	0
Rest of ECSC, Switzerland & Roman Catholic Europe													
Vatican	Jaenicke, W.		-90	CEasG	Prot	Univ	WWI	0	0	0	Govt	0	Govt
Belgium	Pfeiffer, Anton		-90	WestG	0	Dr	0	0	Moder	Moder	Polit	0	Polit
Luxembourg	Wilde, Karl		n.d.	n.d.	n.d.	n.d.	n.d.	n.d.	n.d.	n.d.	n.d.	n.d.	n.d.

Netherlands	Muhlenfeld, Hans	01-10	NorG	Prot	Dr	0	0	0	Right	0	0	Polit
Switzerland	Holzapfel, Friedrich	91-00	WestG	Prot	Dr	0	Pris	0	Moder	Acad	Acad	Polit
Austria	Mueller-Graaf, Carl Hermann	01-10	CEasG	0	Dr	0	0	0	0	Stud	0	0
Spain	Bayern, A. Prinz von	-90	SouG	RCath	Dr	WWI&II	0	0	0	0	0	0
Portugal	Wohleb, Leo	-90	SouG	RCath	Univ	0	0	0	Moder	Acad	Acad	Polit
Ireland	Katzenberger, Hermann	91-00	WesG	RCath	Dr	0	0	0	Moder	Dipl	0	Polit
Other Europe												
Norway	Broich-Oppert, Georg	91-00	CEasG	Prot	Univ	0	0	0	Moder	Dipl	Dipl	Polit
Denmark	Nöldeke, Wilhelm	-90	CEasG	0	Dr	0	0	0	0	Dipl	Dipl*	0
Sweden	Haack	n.d.	n.d.	n.d.	n.d.	n.d.	n.d.	n.d.	n.d.	n.d.	n.d.	n.d.
Finland (Trade miss)	Koenning, Reinhold-Friedr	n.d.	n.d.	n.d.	n.d.	n.d.	n.d.	n.d.	n.d.	n.d.	n.d.	n.d.
Iceland	Oppler, Kurt	01-10	CEasG	RCath	Dr	0	Exil	0	0	Stud	(Acad)	0
Greece	Kordt, Theodore	91-00	WestG	0	Dr	0	Resis	0	0	Dipl	Dipl	0
Turkey	Haas, Wilhelm	91-00	NorG	Prot	Dr	0	Persec	0	0	Dipl	Dipl	0
Yugoslavia	Kroll, Hans	91-00	CEasG	RCath	Dr	0	0	0	0	Dipl	Dipl	0
Commonwealth outside Asia												
Canada	Dankwart, Werner	91-00	CEasG	Prot	Dr	0	0	0	0	Dipl	Dipl	0
Australia	Hess, Walther	91-00	WestG	Prot	Dr	0	0	0	0	Dipl	Dipl	0
New Zealand	Boltze, Erich	91-00	WestG	Prot	Dr	0	0	0	0	Dipl	Dipl	0
U of South Africa	Holzhausen, Rudolf	-90	WestG	0	Univ	WWI	0	0	0	Dipl	Dipl	0

TABLE III.1 (*Continued*)

Incumbents of German Foreign Policy Elite Positions, 1954–1956

1	2	3	4	5	6	7	8	Party Preference		Previous Occupation		
								9	10	11	12	13
Category	Name	Decade Born	Geog. Orig.	Relig. Affil.	Educ. Att'd	Milit. Serv.	Anti-Nazi Record	–1933 Rep. I	1945– Postwar	–1933 (Weimar)	'33–'45 (Hitler)	1945– (Postwar)
Afro-Asian countries												
Ethiopia	Bidder, Hans	91–00	CEasG	0	Dr	WWI	0	0	0	Dipl	Dipl	0
Liberia	Röhrecke, Hans-Felix	n.d.	n.d.	n.d.	n.d.	n.d.	n.d.	n.d.	n.d.	n.d.	n.d.	n.d.
Egypt	Pawelke, Gunther	91–00	CEasG	RCath	Dr	WWI&II	0	0	0	Dipl	Dipl	0
Syria	Esch, Hans von der	91–00	WesG	0	Sec	WWI	0	0	0	Bus	Bus	0
Lebanon	Nohring, Herbert	n.d.	n.d.	n.d.	n.d.	n.d.	n.d.	n.d.	n.d.	n.d.	n.d.	n.d.
Iraq	Melchers, Wilhelm	91–00	NorG	Prot	Dr	0	0	0	0	Dipl	Dipl†	0
Iran	Gielhammer, Lutz	91–00	NorG	0	Dr	WWI	0	0	0	Bus	Bus	Bus
Pakistan	Schmidt-Horiy	n.d.	n.d.	n.d.	n.d.	n.d.	n.d.	n.d.	n.d.	n.d.	n.d.	n.d.
India	Meyer, Ernst	91–00	CEasG	0	Dr	WWI	Exil	0	0	Dipl	(Acad)	(Acad)
Ceylon	Ahrens, Georg	–90	CEasG	0	Dr	0	0	0	0	Dipl	Dipl	0
Indonesia	Allardt, Helmut	01–10	CEasG	0	Dr	0	0	0	0	Stud	Dipl	0
Thailand	Kaufmann, Gottfried	91–00	CEasG	Prot	Dr	WWI	0	0	0	Bus	Bus	0
Japan	Northe, Heinrich	01–10	CEasG	Prot	Dr	0	0	0	0	Stud	Dipl	0
Latin America												
Argentina	Terdinge, Hermann	91–00	WesG	RCath	Dr	0	0	0	0	Dipl	Dipl	0

272

Brazil	Oellers, Fritz	01-10	WestG	0	Dr	0	0	0	Moder	Stud	0	Polit
Chile	Campe, Carl von	91-00	NorG	Prot	Dr	0	0	0	Right	Dipl	Dipl	Polit
Uruguay	Schwarz, Werner	n.d.	n.d.	n.d.	n.d.	n.d.	n.d.	n.d.	n.d.	n.d.	n.d.	n.d.
Paraguay	Borgs-Maciejewski, Julius	n.d.	n.d.	n.d.	n.d.	n.d.	n.d.	n.d.	n.d.	n.d.	n.d.	n.d.
Peru	Mackeben, Wilhelm	91-00	WestG	Prot	Univ	0	0	0	0	Dipl	Dipl	Bus
Colombia	Schwendemann, Karl	91-00	SouG	RCath	Dr	WWI	0	0	0	Dipl	Dipl*	0
Venezuela	Mohr, Ernst	01-00	WestG	Prot	Dr	0	0	0	0	Dipl	Dipl	0
Mexico	Twardowski, Fritz von	-90	WestG	Prot	Dr	WWI	0	0	0	Dipl	Dipl†	0
Cuba and Haiti	Suss, Theodor	91-00	WestG	0	Dr	0	0	0	0	Acad	Acad	Acad
Cent Am	Klee, Eugene	-90	WestG	RCath	Dr	0	0	0	0	Dipl	Dipl	0
Dominican Republic	Korth, Georg	n.d.	n.d.	n.d.	n.d.	n.d.	n.d.	n.d.	n.d.	n.d.	n.d.	n.d.
Civ serv elite-state sec'y (1956)												
Chancellor's Office	Globke, Hans	91-00	WestG	0	Dr	WWI	0	0	0	Govt	Govt	Govt
Foreign O	Hallstein, Walter	01-10	WestG	Prot	Dr	WWII	0	0	0	Acad	Acad	Acad
Defense	Rust, Josef	01-10	NorG	0	Dr	0	0	0	0	Law	Govt	0
Interior	Bleek, Karl-Theodor	91-00	WestG	0	Univ	WWI	0	0	Moder	Govt	Govt	Govt
Interior	Lex, Hans Ritter von	91-00	0	0	0	WWI	0	0	0	Govt	Govt	Govt
All-German Affairs	Thedieck, Franz	91-00	WestG	0	Univ	WWII	Persec	0	0	Govt	Govt	Govt
Finance	Hartmann, Alfred	91-00	WestG	0	Univ	0	0	0	0	Govt	Govt	Govt
Expellees Refugees	Nahm, Peter-Paul	01-10	0	RCath	Dr	0	0	0	0	Journ	Farm	Govt
Military elite (1956)												
Chief Arm Forces	Speidel, Hans	91-00	SouG	Prot	Dr	WWI&II	Pris	0	0	Milit	Milit	Acad
Chief Air Force	Kammhuber, Josef	91-00	SouG	0	Sec	WWI&II	Persec	0	0	Milit	Milit	0

273

TABLE III.1 (*Continued*)

INCUMBENTS OF GERMAN FOREIGN POLICY ELITE POSITIONS, 1954–1956

1	2	3	4	5	6	7	8	9	10	11	12	13
								Party Preference		Previous Occupation		
Category	Name	Decade Born	Geog. Orig.	Relig. Affil.	Educ. Att'd	Milit. Serv.	Anti-Nazi Record	–1933 Rep. I	1945– Postwar	–1933 (Weimar)	'33-'45 (Hitler)	1945– (Postwar)
Chief, Navy	Rouge, Friedrich	91–00	CEasG	0	Sec	WWI&II	0	0	0	Milit	Milit	Writer
Dep Chief, Navy	Wagner, Gerhard	91–00	CEasG	Prot	Univ	WWI&II	0	0	0	Milit	Milit	Writer
CIC Milit Dist II	Horn, Hans-Joachim	91–00	CEasG	Prot	Sec	WWI&II	0	0	0	Milit	Milit	Bus
CIC Milit Dist IV	Pemsel, Max Joseph	91–00	SouG	RCath	Sec	WWI&II	0	0	0	Milit	Milit	Bus
CIC Off Training	Gaedcke, Heinz	01–10	CEasG	Prot	Sec	WWII	0	0	0	Milit	Milit	Bus
Ch o St Arm Forces	Kusserow, Ernst	01–10	CEasG	Prot	Sec	WWII	0	0	0	Milit	Milit	Bus
Dep Div Ch Def Min	Schaefer, Otto	01–10	WestG	Prot	Sec	WWII	0	0	0	Milit	Milit	ManLab
Dep Comm Mil Dist V	Baumann, Hans	01–10	SouG	Prot	Sec	WWII	0	0	0	Milit	Milit	Bus
Col Def Min	Baer, Bern von	11–20	CEasG	Prot	Sec	WWII	0	0	0	Milit	Milit	Bus
Col Def Min	De Maizière, Ulrich	11–20	NorG	Prot	Sec	WWII	0	0	0	Milit	Milit	Bus
Col Def Min	Einem, Kurt von	01–10	WestG	Prot	Sec	WWII	0	0	0	Milit	Milit	Bus
Ch Milit Recept Cen	Laubereau, Hugo	01–10	SouG	Prot	Univ	WWII	0	0	0	Milit	Milit	Bus
Div Ch Def Min	Meyer-Welcker, Hans	01–10	SouG	Prot	Dr	WWII	0	0	0	Milit	Milit	Stud
Comm Milit Train Sch	Philipp, Ernst	11–20	CEasG	Prot	Sec	WWII	0	0	0	Milit	Milit	Bus
Ch Recruit Milit Dist IV	Rathmann, Erich	01–10	WestG	RCath	Sec	WWII	0	0	0	Police	Milit	Bus

274

Position	Name										
Col Def Min	Willemer, Wilhelm	01-10	CEasG	Prot	Sec	WWII	0	0	0	Milit	Milit	Bus
OIC Nav Train	Blanc, Adalbert	01-10	NorG	Prot	Sec	WWII	0	0	0	Milit	Milit	Milit (all Nav aux)
CIC Nav Cor Unit	Hartmann, Werner	01-10	CEasG	Prot	Sec	WWII	0	0	0	Milit	Milit	SocSrv
Div Chief Def Min	Kähler, Wolfgang	01-10	NorG	Prot	Sec	WWII	0	0	0	Milit	Milit	SocSrv
Chief Nav Recruit	Schmidt, Karl	01-10	WestG	Prot	Sec	WWII	0	0	0	Milit	Milit	Govt
CIC Nav Cor Unit	Klemm, Helmut	01-10	WestG	Prot	Sec	WWII	0	0	0	Milit	Milit	Bus
CIC Nav Cor Unit	Reschke, Franz-Georg	01-10	CEasG	Prot	Sec	WWII	0	0	0	Milit	Milit	Bus
Lt Col Def Min	Freigang, Heinz	11-20	CEasG	Prot	Sec	WWII	0	0	0	Milit	Milit	Bus
Lt Col Def Min	Ziegler, Werner	11-20	SouG	RCath	Sec	WWII	0	0	0	Stud	Milit	Bus
Maj Def Min	Bragard, Ludwig	11-20	WestG	RCath	Sec	WWII	0	0	0	Stud	Milit	Econ
Maj Def Min	Karst, Heinrich	11-20	WestG	RCath	Univ	WWII	0	0	0	Stud	Milit	Acad
Maj Def Min	Koch, Horst-Adalbert	11-20	CEasG	Prot	Sec	WWII	0	0	0	Stud	Milit	Milit (US Ord empl)
Maj Def Min	Keilig, Wolfgang	11-20	CEasG	Prot	Sec	WWII	0	0	0	Stud	Milit	0
Inst Army College	Wagemann, Eberhard	11-20	SouG	Prot	Dr	WWII	0	0	0	Stud	Milit	Acad
POLITICAL ELITES												
CDU/CSU (1956)												
Chairm CDU & Chanc	Adenauer, Konrad	-90	WestG	RCath	Univ	0	Pris	Moder	Moder	Govt	0	Govt & Polit
VChairm CDU	Arnold, Karl	01-10	SouG	RCath	Sec	0	Pris	Moder	Moder	TUFunc	Bus	TUFunc
VChairm CDU PM State Govt	Hassel, Kai Uwe von	11-20	Abr	Prot	Sec	WWII	0	0	Moder	Stud	Bus	Polit
VChairm CDU Pres Bundest	Gerstenmeier, Eugen	01-10	SouG	Prot	Dr	0	Pris	0	Moder	Stud	Acad	SocSrv

TABLE III.1 (*Continued*)

INCUMBENTS OF GERMAN FOREIGN POLICY ELITE POSITIONS, 1954-1956

1	2	3	4	5	6	7	8	Party Preference		Previous Occupation		
								9	10	11	12	13
Category	Name	Decade Born	Geog. Orig.	Relig. Affil.	Educ. Att'd	Milit. Serv.	Anti-Nazi Record	-1933 Rep. I	1945- Postwar	-1933 (Weimar)	'33-'45 (Hitler)	1945- (Postwar)
VChairm CDU& Fed Min	Kaiser, Jacob	-90	SouG	RCath	Prim	WWI	Pris	Moder	Moder	TUFunc	0	Polit
Fed Min	Blank, Theodor	01-10	WestG	RCath	Univ	WWII	0	0	Moder	TUFunc	Stud	TUFunc
Fed Min	Brentano, Heinrich von	01-10	WestG	RCath	Dr	0	0	0	Moder	Law	Law	Polit
Fed Min	Erhard, Ludwig	91-00	SouG	Prot	Dr	WWI	0	0	Moder	Econ	Econ	Polit
Fed Min	Lübke, Heinrich	91-00	WestG	RCath	Univ	WWI	Pris	Moder	Moder	FarmOrg func	Bus	Polit
Fed Min	Schäffer, Fritz	-90	SouG	RCath	Univ	WWI	0	Moder	Moder	Govt	Law	Polit
Fed Min	Schröder, Gerhard	01-10	WestG	Prot	Dr	WWII	0	0	Moder	Stud	Law†	Law
Fed Min	Storch, Anton	91-00	WestG	RCath	Prim	WWI	0	0	Moder	TUFunc	Bus	TUFunc
Fed Min & CSU Leader	Strauss, Franz Josef	11-20	SouG	RCath	Univ	WWII	0	0	Moder	Stud	Stud	Polit
Fed Min	Wuermeling, Franz Joseph	91-00	CEasG	RCath	Dr	WWI	0	0	Moder	Govt	Govt	Govt, Bus
Parliament Leader	Krone, Heinrich	91-00	WestG	RCath	Dr	0	Pris	Moder	Moder	Polit	Bus	Polit
Dep Parliament Leader	Albers, Johannes	-90	WestG	RCath	Prim	0	Pris	Moder	Moder	TUFunc	SocSrv	Polit
Dep Parliament Leader	Cillien, Adolf	91-00	WestG	Prot	Univ	WWI	0	0	Moder	Clergy	Clergy	Clergy
VP Bundestag Comm Chairm	Jaeger, Richard	11-20	SouG	RCath	Dr	WWII	0	0	Moder	Stud	Govt	Polit

Role	Name											
Parliament Comm Chairm	Kemper, Heinrich	-90	SouG	RCath	0	0	0	Moder	Moder	Bus	0	Polit
Parliament Comm Chairm	Kiesinger, Kurt Georg	01–10	SouG	RCath	Univ	0	0	0	Moder	Stud	Law	Law-Polit
Parliament Comm Chairm	Kunze, Johannes	91–00	WestG	Prot	Univ	WWI	0	0	Moder	Church func	Church func	Church func
Parliament Comm Chairm	Pünder, Hermann	-90	WestG	RCath	Dr	0	Pris	Moder	Moder	Govt	0	Bus
Dep Parliament Leader CSU Com Chairm	Stücklen, Richard	11–20	SouG	RCath	Prim	WWII	0	0	Moder	Electr	Electr	Eng

SPD Ex Com (1956)

Role	Name											
Chairman	Ollenhauer, Erich	01–10	CEasG	0	Prim	0	Exil	SPD	SPD	Polit	Polit	Polit
V Chairman	Mellies, Wilhelm	91–00	WestG	0	Univ	WWII	0	SPD	SPD	Acad	Bus	Polit
Salaried Member	Eichler, Willi	91–00	CEasG	0	Prim	WWI	Exil	SPD	SPD	Journ	Journ	Polit
Salaried Member	Gotthelf, Herta	01–10	CEasG	0	Sec	0	Exil	SPD	SPD	Journ	0	Polit
Salaried Member	Heine, Fritz	01–10	NorG	0	Prim	0	Exil	SPD	SPD	Polit	Polit	Polit
Salaried Member	Kukil, Max	0	0	0	0	0	0	0	0	0	0	0
Salaried Member	Nau, Alfred	01–10	WestG	0	Sec	0	Resis	SPD	SPD	Polit	0	Polit
Minister State Govt	Albertz, Heinrich	11–20	CEasG	Prot	Univ	WWII	Pris	0	SPD	Stud	Clergy	Polit
Parliament Leader	Albertz, Luise	01–10	WestG	0	Sec	0	0	SPD	SPD	Cleric	Cleric	Polit
Parliament Leader	Albrecht, Lisa	91–00	NorG	0	Sec	0	Pris	SPD	SPD	Acad	Acad	Polit
Parliament Leader	Arndt, Adolf	01–10	CEasG	0	Dr	0	0	0	SPD	Govt	Law	Polit
Parliament Deputy	Birkelbach, Willi	11–20	WestG	Prot	Sec	WWII	Pris	SPD	SPD	Stud	Pris-Milit-POW	TUFunc

TABLE III.1 (*Continued*)

INCUMBENTS OF GERMAN FOREIGN POLICY ELITE POSITIONS, 1954-1956

| 1 | 2 | 3 | 4 | 5 | 6 | 7 | 8 | Party Preference | | Previous Occupation | | |
| | | | | | | | | 9 | 10 | 11 | 12 | 13 |
Category	Name	Decade Born	Geog. Orig.	Relig. Affil.	Educ. Att'd	Milit. Serv.	Anti-Nazi Record	-1933 Rep. I	1945- Postwar	-1933 (Weimar)	'33-'45 (Hitler)	1945- (Postwar)
Regional Leader Palatinate	Bolger, Franz	01-10	WestG	0	Sec	0	Exil	SPD	SPD	Polit	Polit	Polit
Regional Leader Hamburg	Brauer, Max	-90	NorG	Prot	Prim	0	Exil	SPD	SPD	Govt	Polit	Govt
Nonsalaried Member	Conrad, Kurt	0	0	0	0	0	0	0	0	0	0	0
Parliament Leader	Erler, Fritz	11-20	CEasG	0	Univ	0	Pris	SPD	SPD	Stud	Ind empl	Polit
Nonsalaried member	Gross, Emil	01-10	WestG	Prot	Univ	0	Exil-Pris	SPD	SPD	Stud	Pris	Govt-Polit
Nonsalaried member	Gründer, Marianne	0	0	0	0	0	0	0	0	0	0	0
Regional Leader Berlin	Kay, Ella	91-00	CEasG	0	Sec	0	Persec	SPD	SPD	SocSrv	Misc	SocSrv
Regional Leader Bavaria	Knoeringen, Waldemar von	01-10	SouG	0	0	0	Exil	SPD	SPD	Libr	Polit	Polit
Parliament Leader	Menzel, Walter	01-10	CEasG	Prot	Dr	0	Persec	SPD	SPD	Govt	Law	Law-Polit
Regional Leader Berlin	Neumann, Franz	01-10	CEasG	0	Prim	0	Pris	0	SPD	SocSrv	ManLab	Polit
Parliament Leader, VP Bundt	Schmid, Carlo	91-00	Abr	0	Dr	WWII	0	0	SPD	Acad	Acad	Govt-Polit
Parliament Leader	Schoettle, Erwin	91-00	SouG	0	Sec	0	Exil	SPD	SPD	Polit	Polit	Polit
Regional Leader N Rhine W'phalia	Steinhoff, Fritz	91-00	WesG	Prot	Sec	0	Pris	SPD	SPD	Polit	Misc	Polit

		91-00	SouG	0	Dr	WWI	0	SPD	SPD	Law	Law	Govt-Polit
Regional Leader Baden	Veit, Hermann	91-00	SouG	0	Dr	0	0	SPD	SPD	Law	Polit	Govt-Polit
Parliament Leader	Wehner, Herbert	01-10	CEasG	Prot	Sec	0	Exil	CP	SPD	Journ	0	Polit
Parliament Leader	Welke, Erwin	01-10	WestG	Prot	Prim	WWII	Pris	SPD	SPD	Polit	0	Polit
Parliament Leader	Wenzel, Fritz	01-10	CEasG	Prot	Dr	0	Persec	SPD	SPD	Stud	Clergy	Clergy
PM&Regional Leader Hesse	Zinn, Georg August	01-10	WestG	0	Univ	WWII	0	SPD	SPD	Law	Law	Govt-Polit

Federal cabinet (1956)

		91-00	SouG	0	Dr	WWI	0	SPD	SPD	Law	Law	Govt-Polit
Chancellor	Adenauer, Konrad	–90	WestG	RCath	Univ	0	Pris	Moder	Moder	Govt	0	Govt-Polit
Deputy Chancellor	Blücher, Franz	91-00	WestG	RCath	Sec	WWI	0	0	Moder	Bus	Bus	Polit
Foreign Minister	Brentano, Heinrich von	01-10	WestG	RCath	Dr	0	0	0	Moder	Law	Law	Polit
Defense Minister	Blank, Theodor	01-10	WestG	RCath	Univ	WWII	0	0	Moder	TUFunc	Stud	TUFunc
Finance Minister	Schäffer, Fritz	–90	SouG	RCath	Univ	WWI	0	Moder	Moder	Govt	Law	Polit
Economic Minister	Erhard, Ludwig	91-00	SouG	Prot	Dr	WWI	0	0	Moder	Econ	Econ	Polit
Interior Minister	Schröder, Gerhard	01-10	WestG	Prot	Dr	WWII	0	0	Moder	Stud	Law†	Stud
Minister All-German Affairs	Kaiser, Jakob	–90	SouG	RCath	Prim	WWII	Pris	Moder	Moder	TUFunc	0	Polit
Minister Atomic Questions	Strauss, Franz-Josef	11-20	SouG	RCath	Univ	WWII	0	0	Moder	Stud	Stud	Polit
Minister for Refugees	Oberländer, Theodor	01-10	CEasG	Prot	Dr	WWII	0	0	Moder	Acad	Acad	Bus
Minister of Justice	Neumayer, Fritz	–90	WestG	Prot	Univ	0	0	0	Moder	Law	Law	Polit
Minister for Home Construct	Preusker, Viktor-Imanuel	11-20	CEasG	0	Dr	WWII	0	0	Moder	Econ	Econ†	Publish

TABLE III.1 (*Continued*)

INCUMBENTS OF GERMAN FOREIGN POLICY ELITE POSITIONS, 1954-1956

1	2	3	4	5	6	7	8	9	10	11	12	13
								Party Preference		Previous Occupation		
Category	Name	Decade Born	Geog. Orig.	Relig. Affil.	Educ. Att'd	Milit. Serv.	Anti-Nazi Record	-1933 Rep. I	1945- Postwar	-1933 (Weimar)	'33-'45 (Hitler)	1945- (Postwar)
Minister for Transport	Seebohm, Hans Cristoph	01-10	CEasG	Prot	Dr	0	0	0	Right	Govt	Bus	Polit
Minister for Bundesrat Affairs	Merkatz, Hans-Joachim von	01-10	CEasG	Prot	Dr	0	0	0	Right	Stud	Acad	Polit
Minister for Family Affairs	Wuermeling, Franz-Josef	91-00	CEasG	RCath	Dr	WWI	0	0	Moder	Govt	Govt-Bus	Govt-Bus
Minister of Labor	Storch, Anton	91-00	WestG	RCath	Prim	WWI	0	0	Moder	TUFunc	Bus	TUFunc
Minister of Food, Agric & Forestry	Lübke, Heinrich	91-00	WestG	RCath	Univ	WWI	Pris	Moder	Moder	FarmOrg func	Bus	Polit
Minister Mail & Communic	Balke, Siegfried	01-10	WestG	0	Univ	0	0	0	0	Chemist	Chemist	Chemist
Minister without Portfolio	Schäfer, Hermann	91-00	WestG	Prot	Dr	WWI	0	Moder	Moder	Polit	Bus	Polit
Minister without Portfolio	Kraft, Waldemar	91-00	CEasG	Prot	Sec	WWI	0	Right	Moder	FarmOrg func	Govt†	Polit
Legislative leadership (1954)												
Pres Bundestag	Gerstenmaier, Eugen	01-10	SouG	Prot	Dr	0	Pris	0	Moder	Stud	Acad	SocSrv-Polit
VP, BT	Jaeger, Richard	11-20	SouG	RCath	Dr	WWII	0	0	Moder	Stud	Govt	Polit
VP, BT	Schmid, Carlo	91-00	Abr	0	Dr	WWII	0	0	SPD	Acad	Acad	Govt-Polit
VP, BT	Schneider, Ludwig	91-00	WestG	0	Dr	0	0	0	Moder	Law	Law	Polit

280

Position	Name											
Leader CDU/CSU	Krone, Heinrich	91–00	WestG	RCath	Dr	0	Pris	Moder	Moder	Polit	Bus	Polit
Dep Leader CDU/CSU	Albers, Johannes	–90	WestG	RCath	Prim	0	Pris	Moder	Moder	TUFunc	SocSrv	Polit
Dep Leader CDU/CSU	Cillien, Adolf	91–00	WestG	Prot	Univ	WWI	0	0	Moder	Clergy	Clergy	Clergy
Dep Leader CDU/CSU	Stücklen, Richard	11–20	SouG	RCath	Prim	WWII	0	0	Moder	Electr	Electr	Eng
Leader SPD	Ollenhauer, Erich	01–10	CEasG	0	Prim	0	Exil	SPD	SPD	Polit	Polit	Polit
Dep Leader SPD	Mellies, Wilhelm	91–00	WestG	0	Univ	WWII	0	SPD	SPD	Acad	Bus	Polit
Dep Leader SPD	Schoettle, Erwin	91–00	SouG	0	Sec	0	Exil	SPD	SPD	Polit	Polit	Polit
Leader FDP	Dehler, Thomas	91–00	SouG	0	Dr	0	0	0	Moder	Law	Law	Polit
Dep Leader FDP	Euler, August-Martin	01–10	WestG	Prot	Univ	WWII	0	0	Moder	Stud	Law	Polit
Dep Leader FDP	Mende, Eric	11–20	CEasG	RCath	Dr	WWII	0	0	Moder	Stud	0	Stud-Polit
Chairman Foreign Aff Committee	Kiesinger, Kurt-Georg	01–10	SouG	RCath	Univ	0	0	0	Moder	Stud	Law	Law-Polit
Chairm Comm on Borderland Question	Kemper, Heinrich	–90	WestG	RCath	0	0	0	Moder	Moder	Bus	0	Polit
Chairm Comm on Economic Matters	Naegel, Wilhelm	01–10	WestG	RCath	Univ	0	0	0	Moder	Bus	Bus	Bus
Act Chairm Committee on Foreign Trade	Margulis, Robert	01–10	WestG	0	Sec	WWII	0	0	Moder	Bus	Bus	Bus
Chairman All German Affairs	Wehner, Herbert	01–10	CEasG	Prot	Sec	0	Exil	CP	SPD	Journ	Polit	Polit
Chairm Comm on Expellees	Kuntscher, Ernst	91–00	CEasG	RCath	Prim	WWI&II	0	Moder	Moder	TUFunc	Bus	Polit

TABLE III.1 (*Continued*)

INCUMBENTS OF GERMAN FOREIGN POLICY ELITE POSITIONS, 1954–1956

1	2	3	4	5	6	7	8	9 Party Preference	10	11 Previous Occupation	12	13
								–1933 Rep. I	1945– Postwar	–1933 (Weimar)	'33–'45 (Hitler)	1945– (Postwar)
Category	Name	Decade Born	Geog. Orig.	Relig. Affil.	Educ. Att'd	Milit. Serv.	Anti-Nazi Record					
Chairman War Victims Committee	Petersen, Helmut	01–10	CEasG	0	Univ	WWII	0	0	Moder	Govt	Govt	Law-Publish
Newspapers						PRESS ELITES (1956)						
Publisher *Bild Zeitung, Hamburg Abenblatt, Welt am Sonntag*	Springer, Axel	11–20	NorG	0	Sec	0	0	0	0	Stud	0	Journ
Ed *Bild Zeitung*	Michael, Rudolf	–90	NorG	Prot	Univ	0	0	0	0	Journ	Journ	Journ
Ed *Frnkf Allgem*	Dombrowski, Erich	–90	CEasG	Prot	Univ	0	0	0	0	Journ	Journ	Journ
Ed *Hamb Abendbl*	Siemer, Otto	91–00	0	0	Univ	0	0	0	0	Journ	0	Journ
Ed *Süddeutsche Zeitung*	Friedmann, Werner	01–10	CEasG	RCath	Univ	WWII	0	0	0	Journ	0	Journ
Ed *Schwäbisch Landes Zeitung*	Frenzel, Curt	91–00	CEasG	Prot	Sec	0	Pris	SPD	0	Journ	0	Journ
Ed *Westdeutsche Allgemeine*	Brost, Eric	01–10	CEasG	Prot	Sec	0	Exil	SPD	0	Journ	Journ	Journ
Periodicals												
Ed *Aussen-Politik*	Borch, Herbert von	01–10	Abr	0	Dr	0	0	0	0	Journ	Journ	Journ
Publ *Das Andere Deutschland*	Kuster, Fritz	–90	NorG	0	Univ	0	0	0	0	Journ	Journ	Journ

Table of elite data (continued). No column headers are printed on this page; values are given in their column positions.

Role / Publication / Name												
Ed *Christ & Welt* — Wirsing, Giselher	01–10	SouG	Prot	Dr	0	0	0	0	Journ	Journ	Journ	Journ
Pub *Deutsche Kommentare* — Silex, Karl H.	91–00	CEasG	Prot	Dr	WWII	0	0	0	Journ	Journ	Journ	Journ
Ed *Deutsche Rundschau* — Pechel, Rudolf	–90	CEasG	0	Dr	0	Pris	0	Moder	Journ	Journ	Journ	Journ
Ed *Deutsche Zeitung* — Cron, Helmut	91–00	SouG	Prot	Dr	0	0	0	0	Journ	0	Journ	Journ
Publ & CoEd *Frankf Hefte* — Dirks, Walter	01–10	WestG	RCath	Univ	0	Pris	0	0	Journ	Journ	0	Journ
Publ *Die Gegenwart* — Reifenberg, Benno	91–00	WestG	RCath	Univ	0	0	0	0	Journ	Journ	0	Journ
Ed *Die Kultur* — Hönscheid, Johannes M.	21–	WestG	0	0	0	0	0	0	0	0	0	0
Ed *Münchener Merkur* — Buttersack, Felix	91–00	SouG	0	Dr	WWII	0	0	0	Journ	Journ	Journ	Journ
Ed *Rheinischer Merkur* — Roegele, Otto B.	11–20	SouG	RCath	Dr	WWII	0	0	0	Stud	Stud	Stud	Phys
Publ *Der Spiegel* — Augstein, Rudolf	21–	NorG	0	0	0	0	0	0	0	0	0	0
Ed *Die Welt* — Zehrer, Hans	91–00	CEasG	Prot	Univ	0	0	0	0	Journ	Journ	Bus	Journ
Ed *Zeitschrift f Geopolitik* — Pfeffer, Karl Heinz	01–10	WestG	0	Dr	0	0	0	0	Stud	Stud	Acad	Acad

ECONOMIC INTEREST GROUP ELITES

Employers (1956)

Genl Mgr Assn of Germ Chambers of Ind & Commerce — Frentzel, Gerhard	91–00	CEasG	0	Dr	0	0	0	0	Bus	Bus	Bus	Bus
Pres Assn of Germ Chambers of Ind & Commerce — Hammerbacher, Hans-Leonard	91–00	SouG	0	Dr	0	0	0	0	Bus	Bus	Bus	Bus

TABLE III.1 *(Continued)*

INCUMBENTS OF GERMAN FOREIGN POLICY ELITE POSITIONS, 1954–1956

| 1 | 2 | 3 | 4 | 5 | 6 | 7 | 8 | Party Preference | | Previous Occupation | | |
Category	Name	Decade Born	Geog. Orig.	Relig. Affil.	Educ. Att'd	Milit. Serv.	Anti-Nazi Record	9 –1933 Rep. I	10 1945– Postwar	11 –1933 (Weimar)	12 '33–'45 (Hitler)	13 1945– (Postwar)
Pres Assn of Germ Industry	Berg, Fritz	01–10	WestG	0	Univ	0	0	0	0	Bus	Bus	Bus
Chm Bd Gen Assn Private Banking	Pferdmenges, Robert	–90	WestG	Prot	Univ	0	Pris	0	Moder	Bus	Bus	Bus
Gen Mgr Gen Assn Private Banking	Dermitzel, Günther Erwin	91–00	CEasG	Prot	Univ	0	0	0	0	Bus	Bus	Bus
Co-chm Assn of Germ Wholesalers & Exporters	Dietz, Fritz	01–10	WestG	Prot	Sec	0	0	0	0	Bus	Bus	Bus
Co-chm Assn of Germ Wholesalers & Exporters	Fricke, Otto	01–10	CEasG	0	Dr	0	0	0	Moder	Bus	Bus	Bus-Polit
Pres Centr Org of Germ Retailers	Schmitz, Hans	91–00	WestG	0	Prim	0	0	0	Moder	Bus	Bus	Bus-Polit
Pres Germ Sect Int'l C of C	Heyl, Ludwig C. Freiherr von	–90	WestG	Prot	Univ	WWI	0	0	0	Bus	Bus	Bus
Chm Bd Germ Shipowners' Assn	Riensberg, Heinrich	91–00	CEasG	Prot	Dr	0	0	0	0	Bus	Bus	Bus
Employees & Farm Org Functionaries (1956)												
Chm of Germ Conf of Trade Unions	Freitag, Walter	–90	WestG	0	Prim	0	Pris	SPD	SPD	TUFunc	0	TUFunc

285

RELIGIOUS ELITES

Position / Name											
Dep Chm of GCTU — Reuter, Georg	01–10	WestG	0	Prim	0	Pris	0	0	TUFunc	0	TUFunc
Dep Chm of GCTU — Focher, Matthias	–90	WestG	RCath	Prim	0	Persec	Moder	Moder	Church org	0	TUFunc
Co-Chm Metal Workers Union — Brümmer, Hans	–90	SouG	0	0	0	0	0	0	0	0	0
Chm Germ Employees U — Rettig, Fritz	01–10	NorG	0	Prim	WWII	0	0	0	BusEmpl	BusEmpl	TUFunc
Chm Germ Fed of Civil Servants — Karmel, Angelo	01–10	WestG	RCath	Univ	0	0	0	Moder	Law	Govt	Polit
Press Leag of Germ Artisans — Wild, Joseph	01–10	SouG	0	Sec	0	0	0	0	0	0	0
Pres Leag Germ Farmers Ex Com CDU, Fed Deputy — Bauknecht, Bernhard	91–00	SouG	RCath	Sec	0	0	Moder	Moder	FarmOrg func	0	Polit
Pres Cent Org Germ Agric Hon Pres Leag Germ Farmers — Hermes, Andreas	–90	WestG	RCath	Dr	0	Pris	Moder	Moder	Econ	Govt	Polit

Protestants (1956)

Position / Name											
Chm Council of Germ Evang Church (EKD) — Dibelius, Otto	–90	CEasG	Prot	Dr	0	Pris	0	0	Clergy	Clergy	Clergy
Chm Council EKD — Dietze, Constantin	91–00	CEasG	Prot	Dr	0	Pris	0	0	Acad	Acad	Clergy
Ch Foreign Of EKD — Niemöller, Martin	91–00	WestG	Prot	Univ	WWI	Pris	0	0	Clergy	Clergy	Acad
Rep of EKD to Fed Govt — Kunst, Hermann	01–10	NorG	Prot	Univ	0	Persec	0	0	Clergy	Clergy	Clergy
Pres Annual Rally Evang Church — Thadden-Trieglaff, Reinhold von	91–00	CEasG	Prot	Dr	WWII	Pris	0	0	ChurchOrg	ChurchOrg	ChurchOrg
Pres Leag Evang & Ref Churches — Kamlah, Theodor	–90	0	Prot	Univ	0	0	0	0	Clergy	Clergy	Clergy

TABLE III.1 (Concluded)

INCUMBENTS OF GERMAN FOREIGN POLICY ELITE POSITIONS, 1954–1956

1	2	3	4	5	6	7	8	Party Preference 9	10	Previous Occupation 11	12	13
Category	Name	Decade Born	Geog. Orig.	Relig. Affil.	Educ. Att'd	Milit. Serv.	Anti-Nazi Record	–1933 Rep. 1	1945– Postwar	–1933 (Weimar)	'33–'45 (Hitler)	1945– (Postwar)
Bish United Ev-Luth Ch (VELKD)	Lilje, Hanns	91–00	NorG	Prot	Dr	0	Pris	0	0	Stud	Clergy	Clergy
Bish (VELKD)	Dietzfeibinger, Hermann	01–10	SouG	Prot	Univ	0	0	0	0	Stud	Clergy	Clergy
Bish (VELKD)	Halfmann, Wilhelm	91–00	CEasG	Prot	Univ	0	Persec	0	0	Clergy	Clergy	Clergy
Bish (VELKD)	Henke, Wilhelm	91–00	NorG	Prot	Univ	0	0	0	0	Clergy	Clergy	Clergy
Bish (VELKD)	Erdmann, Martin	91–00	NorG	Prot	Univ	0	0	0	0	Clergy	Clergy	Clergy
Bish (VELKD)	Herntrich, Volkmer	01–10	NorG	Prot	Dr	0	Persec	0	0	Acad / Clergy	Acad / Clergy	Acad / Clergy
Head Evan Ch of the Union Rhineland	Held, Heinrich	91–00	WestG	Prot	Univ	0	0	0	0	Clergy	Clergy	Clergy
Head Evan Ch of Union W'phalia	Wilm, Ernst	01–10	CEasG	Prot	Univ	0	Pris	0	0	Clergy	Clergy	Clergy
Roman Catholics (1956)												
Chm Conf of Bishops & Archbishops Cologne	Frings, Joseph Cardinal	–90	WestG	RCath	Dr	0	0	0	0	Clergy	Clergy	Clergy
Archbishop Munich & Freising	Wendel, Joseph Cardinal	01–10	WestG	RCath	Univ	0	0	0	0	Clergy	Clergy	Clergy
Archbishop Regensburg	Buchberger, Michael	–90	SouG	RCath	Dr	0	Persec	0	0	Clergy	Clergy	Clergy
Archbishop Paderborn	Jaeger, Lorenz	91–00	CEasG	RCath	Univ	WWII	0	0	0	Clergy / Acad	Clergy / Acad	Clergy

Position	Name													
Archbishop Bamberg	Schneider, Josef	01-10	SouG	RCath	Dr	0	0	0	0	0	0	0	0	Clergy Acad
Archbishop Freiburg	Seiterich, Eugen	01-10	SouG	RCath	Dr	0	0	0	0	0	Clergy	Clergy	Clergy Acad	Clergy Acad
Bish Fulda	Dietz, Johannes	-90	SouG	RCath	Dr	0	0	0	0	0	Clergy	Clergy	Clergy	Clergy
Bishop Würzburg	Döpfner, Julius	11-20	SouG	RCath	Dr	0	0	0	0	0	Clergy	Stud	Clergy	Clergy
Bishop Speyer	Emanuel, Isidor	01-10	WestG	RCath	Dr	0	0	0	0	0	Clergy	Clergy	Clergy	Clergy
Bishop Munster	Keller, Michael	91-00	WestG	RCath	Dr	0	0	0	0	0	Clergy	Clergy	Clergy	Clergy
Bishop Limburg	Kempf, Wilhelm	01-10	WestG	RCath	Dr	0	0	0	0	0	Clergy	Clergy	Clergy	Clergy
Bishop Passau	Landersdorfer, Simon	-90	SouG	RCath	Dr	0	0	0	0	0	Clergy	Clergy	Clergy	Clergy
Bishop Rottenburg	Leiprecht, Carl Joseph	01-10	SouG	RCath	Dr	0	0	0	0	0	Clergy	Clergy	Clergy	Clergy
Bishop Hildesheim	Machens, Joseph	-90	NorG	RCath	Dr	0	0	0	0	0	Clergy Acad	Clergy Acad	Clergy	Clergy
Bishop Eichstätt	Schröffer, Joseph	01-10	SouG	RCath	Dr	0	0	0	0	0	Clergy Acad	Clergy Acad	Clergy Acad	Clergy
Bishop Mainz	Stohr, Albert	-90	WestG	RCath	Dr	0	0	0	Moder	0	Clergy Acad	Clergy Acad	Clergy Acad	Clergy Acad
Bishop Trier	Wehr, Matthias	91-00	WestG	RCath	Dr	0	0	0	0	0	Clergy Acad	Clergy Acad	Clergy Acad	Clergy Acad
Head RC Liaison Office to Fed Republic	Böhler, Wilhelm	91-00	WestG	RCath	Univ	0	0	0	0	0	Clergy	Clergy	Clergy	Clergy
Pres Cent Com of Germ Cath	Löwenstein, Fürst Karl zu	01-10	SouG	RCath	Univ	0	0	0	0	0	0	0	0	0
Pres Cath Labor Org CDU Leader	Gockelm, Joseph	91-00	WestG	RCath	Prim	WWII	0	Moder	0	0	0	TUFunc	0	Polit
Pres Cath Employers Fed	Greiss, Franz	01-10	WestG	RCath	0	0	0	0	0	0	Bus	Bus	Bus	Bus
Pres Assn of Cath Publicists	Jansen-Cron, Heinrich	91-00	WestG	RCath	Dr	0	0	0	0	0	Journ	Journ	Journ	Journ

United States dollar imports and the German balance of payments, 1950–1957

This Appendix shows the changing importance of American military spending to West Germany's balance of payments.

Table IV.1 shows the total balance of payments of the Federal Republic, with items affected by political factors marked by note *a*. A large and growing surplus on current account (goods, services, and donations) will be seen.

Table IV.2 compares certain aspects of the German international account with the accounts of two other European states, France and Sweden. Like Germany, France has a large number of foreign troops on its soil; Sweden, of course, has none. The table shows that:

1. Receipts from services, while an important element in West German trade receipts, are a smaller (but growing) part of the total than in either of the other two countries.

2. For both France and Germany, government receipts for services form a high proportion of total service receipts (37 per cent and 24 per cent for France and Germany, respectively, in 1956), while for Sweden such receipts are almost non-existent. German government receipts are exclusively for services rendered to foreign military agencies, and for France military receipts form an overwhelming proportion of government service receipts (92 per cent in 1956).

Table IV.3 shows that:

1. German government service receipts are made up *entirely* of military receipts. All but a small portion are contributed by the United States.

2. Foreign aid from the United States declined sharply from 1952 to 1957, and is now extremely small.

3. All political items—government service balance, foreign aid, and compensations—show a stable net surplus over the period, even with the decline in foreign aid.

4. The positive items are very largely the result of increasing United States military spending. The negative items are preponderantly compensations to countries other than the United States.

5. Even with the political items excepted, the Federal Republic has a large and growing balance of payments surplus over-all.

6. The political items, nevertheless, contribute heavily to the total surplus. American military purchases alone contribute currently more than one-third of the over-all surplus in Germany's foreign exchange account.

Note to Table IV.3: One item contributing to the sharp increase in government service receipts for foreign military purchases is the concurrent decline in occupation payments by the German government. In the year 1952 the Federal Republic paid approximately $1,800 million to the occupying powers to cover the costs of the

TABLE IV.1
GERMANY: BALANCE OF PAYMENTS*
(Millions of U.S. dollars)

	1950	1951	1952	1953	1954	1955	1956	1957
Goods and services	-623	144	557	983	948	701	1,309	1,834
Receipts	2,184	3,852	4,701	5,321	6,469	7,673	9,268	11,109
Payments	-2,807	-3,707	-4,144	-4,339	-5,521	-6,972	-7,959	-9,275
Services	-73	-221	23	91	-6	-111	-89	-15
Gov't (largely military receipts)[a]	50	88	199	248	217	258	371	564
Donations	498	438	125	-13	-93	-194	-263	-393
Receipts	552	439	129	75	91	49	46	31
Payments	-54	-1	-4	-88	-184	-242	-309	-424
FOA/ICA[a]	303	416	114	44	63	24	29	17
Compensations[a]	—	—	—	-42	-121	-171	-241	-357
Total, Goods and services and Donations	-126	583	683	970	855	507	1,046	1,441
Errors and omissions (largely unrequited capital imports)	34	67	-28	57	99	-54	-151	-400
Private capital	—	—	—	23	85	65	5	6
Banks and official	-160	516	710	891	671	496	1,191	1,835
Long-term lending & borrowing	-109	35	191	369	41	52	111	138
Assets	12	-12	110	292[b]	—	—	45	53
Liabilities	-121	47	81	78	41	52	66	85
Short-term lending & borrowing, excl. dollars	-118	238	280	-10	-130	63	105	937
EPU	-152	266	131	172	65	32	167	322
Payments agreements	34	-28	208	152	-181	9	21	72
IMF-IBRD	—	—	-59	-293[b]	48	5	15	23
Other	—	—	—	-41	-61	17	-98	520
Gold and dollar balances	66	243	239	532	762	381	975	760
U.S. & Canada dollar balances	—	215	127	346	462	87	401	-287
Gold	—	28	112	186	300	294	574	1,047

* Sources: International Monetary Fund, *Balance of Payments Yearbook, 1956–57*, Vol. 10 (Washington, D.C., 1958), Germany, Federal Republic, p. 1. *Ibid.*, 1955–56 Vol. 9, 1957 Germany, Federal Republic, p. 1. *Ibid.*, 1950–54 Vol. 8, 1957 p. 87. *Ibid.*, 1947–53 Vol. 5, 1954 Germany, Federal Republic, p. 1.
Data for 1953–57 are converted from DM figures at the rate $.238 = 1 DM.
Data cover Federal Republic and West Berlin's transactions with rest of world, except Soviet zone of Germany; exclude military imports under grants.
Government services receipts include receipts from exchange of DM ($255 for 1955 and $326 for 1956) and other receipts from foreign troops in Germany ($37 for 1955 and $92 for 1956).

Figures do not always add because of rounding.

General note: The German balance for services is in actuality much more favorable than it appears above. It is customary, in balance of payments accounts, to record *exports* of goods at *f.o.b.* prices and *imports* at *c.i.f.* prices. But in the German accounts, both those published by the Deutsche Bundesbank and those released to the International Monetary Fund, *exports and imports* have been recorded at *f.o.b.* prices since 1952. Thus the balance of payments for transportation and insurance seems much less favorable than is really the case. This keeps the addition of government services receipts from resulting in a high net surplus for *all* services in the payments accounts.

a Items influenced by political factors.
b IMF-IBRD subscription.

TABLE IV.2

GERMANY, FRANCE, AND SWEDEN—RECEIPTS FROM SERVICES, INCLUDING GOVERNMENT RECEIPTS, 1950–1957*

(Millions of U.S. dollars)

	1950	1951	1952	1953	1954	1955	1956	1957 (1st half)
Germany:								
Receipts from goods and services	2,184	3,852	4,701	5,321	6,469	7,673	9,268	5,305
Receipts from services only	210	389	704	895	1,124	1,415	1,765	1,048
Govt. receipts[a]	50	88	199	271	243	292	419	313
Govt. receipts as per cent of total *services*	24	23	28	30	22	21	24	30
Service receipts as per cent of total *trade receipts*	10	10	15	17	17	18	19	20
France:								
Receipts from goods and services	2,461	3,157	2,872	3,195	3,826	4,646	4,701	2,342
Receipts from services only	581	661	848	1,040	1,282	1,496	1,423	641
Govt. receipts[a]	11	79	264	479	582	655	532	210
Govt. receipts as per cent of total *services*	2	12	31	46	45	44	37	33
Service receipts as per cent of total *trade receipts*	24	21	30	33	34	32	30	27
Sweden:								
Receipts from goods and services	1,429	2,276	2,111	2,012	2,159	1,730	1,943	—
Receipts from services only	323	490	525	527	571	627	725	—
Govt. receipts	2	6	8	8	8	8	8	—
Govt. receipts as per cent of total *services*	1	1	2	2	1	1	1	—
Service receipt as per cent of total *trade receipts*	23	22	25	26	26	36	37	—

* Source: International Monetary Fund, *Balance of Payments Yearbook, 1955–56*, Vol. 9 (Washington, D.C., 1957), Germany, p. 1; France, p. 1; Sweden, pp. 1, 2. *Ibid, 1950–54*, Vol. 8, 1957, pp. 84, 87, 187.

a For Germany, all government receipts are for paid services to foreign military agencies (see Table A.3). For France, government receipts are preponderantly (92 per cent in 1956) for paid services to foreign military agencies.

Deutsche Mark figures converted at $.238 = 1 DM; Swedish kroner converted to dollars at the rate $.193 = 1 Km.

TABLE IV.3
GERMAN BALANCE OF PAYMENTS—ITEMS INFLUENCED BY POLITICAL FACTORS, 1952–1957*
(*Millions of U.S. dollars*)

	1952 U.S.A.	1952 All Others	1953 U.S.A.	1953 All Others	1954 U.S.A.	1954 All Others	1955 U.S.A.	1955 All Others	1956 U.S.A.	1956 All Others	1957 U.S.A.	1957 All Others
Services:												
Govt. receipts	199	3	263	9	233	10	273	19	381	38	540	93
Of which, paid services to foreign milit. agencies	199	3	263	9	233	10	273	19	381	38	540	93
Receipts from exchange of DM	164	3	206	9	211	10	236	19	288	38	373	93
Other receipts	35	0	58	0	22	0	37	0	92	0	168	0
Govt. expenditure	−2	−8	−3	−20	−4	−23	−4	−30	−5	−42	−17	−52
Net govt. services	197	−5	260	−11	229	−13	269	−11	376	−4	523	−41
Donations:												
Net foreign aid	98	0	63	0	69	0	31	0	30	0	17	0
Net compensations	−17	−30	−18	−74	−13	−108	−33	−138	−57	−184	−93	−264
To Israel	—	0	—	−42	—	−84	—	−88	—	−79	—	−78
Net political items:												
Govt. services, foreign aid, and compensations	278	−35	305	−84	285	−121	267	−149	349	−188	447	−223
All countries	243		220		164		118		161		224	
Net balance of payments for all goods, services & donations	603		923		855		509		1,045		1,440	
Without political items	360		703		691		391		884		1,216	
Per cent of U.S. milit. spending in total balance	33		28		27		54		36		38	
Per cent of balance of all polit. items in total balance	40		24		19		23		15		16	

* Source: *Monthly Report of the Deutsche Bundesbank*, Frankfurt-am-Main, September 1958, pp. 36–39. The authors are indebted to Professor Robert Triffin for the identification of the "political" items, and to Bruce M. Russett for the computations,
U.S.A. includes International Monetary Fund, International Bank, and International Finance Corporation.
DM figures converted to U.S. dollars at $.238 = 1 DM.

291

occupation.[1] Since these payments were made in Deutsche Mark and were spent in Germany, they do not appear in the international balance of payments accounts. But with the attainment of sovereignty they were called "support costs," and fell to an annual total of about $300 million in 1957. As these German payments decreased, allied expenditure of foreign exchange in the Federal Republic had to increase by an equivalent amount. In 1957, United States payments rose to $540 million, and British, French, and Canadian payments together rose to $92 million. Thus a substantial part of the increase in government receipts from 1952 to 1957 is due not to any increase in purchases, but to the sharp increase in the proportion of those allied purchases which brought foreign currency to Germany.

This situation is further complicated by the fact that in the early years not all the occupation payments made to the allies were spent at that time. They accumulated in a special fund at the Bank Deutscher Laender, amounting to about $750 million in January 1956.[2] Presumably these have since been spent, although the rate of spending is unknown. Certainly they enabled the allies to make many of their military purchases in 1956 and 1957 in DM rather than in dollars, sterling, or francs, but in 1958 and in later years additional sums of foreign currencies may have to be paid to Germany, unless other arrangements are made.

These occupation (support) payments are important in at least two respects. The delay in spending these DM funds reduced somewhat inflationary pressures on the German economy from 1950 to 1956. In addition, they sharply reduced the importance of allied troop spending to the German balance of payments. With their cessation, government service receipts will become an even greater proportion of the Federal Republic's total international receipts.

[1] Press and Information Office of the Federal German Government, *Germany Reports*, 1955, p. 198.
[2] *The New York Times*, February 4, 1956, 1:6.

Bibliography

Acheson, Dean, *Power and Diplomacy*. Cambridge, Harvard, 1958.

Adorno, Theodor W., *Betriebsklima: Eine industriesoziologische Untersuchung aus dem Ruhrgebiet*. Frankfurt, Europäische Verlagsanstalt, 1955.

Allemann, Fritz Rene, *Bonn ist nicht Weimar*. Köln-Berlin, Kiepenheuer und Witsch, 1956.

Almond, Gabriel A., *The American People and Foreign Policy*. New York, Harcourt, Brace, 1950.

——— ed., *The Struggle for Democracy in Germany*. Chapel Hill, University of North Carolina Press, 1949.

Arntz, Helmut, *Tatsachen über Deutschland*. Bonn, Presse- und Informationsamt der Bundesregierung, 1957.

Bathurst, M. E., and J. L. Simpson, *Germany and the North Atlantic Community: A Legal Survey*. London, Stevens and Sons, 1956.

Böhler, Prälat Wilhelm Johannes, *Katholische Kirche und Staat*. München, Isar, 1953.

Borch, Herbert von, "Haben die Vereinigten Staaten eine Aussenpolitik?" *Aussenpolitik*, 8:3 (March 1957), 159–74.

Borries, Kurt, "Die Grenzen von 1937," *Aussenpolitik*, 8:3 (March 1957), 155–58.

Breitling, Rupert, *Die Verbände in der Bundesrepublik: Ihre Arten und ihre politische Wirkungsweise*. Meisenheim, Anton Hain, 1955.

——— "Die Wählerschaft modelliert am Parteisystem," *Die Gegenwart*, 1 June 1957, pp. 332–34.

Bremme, Gabriele, *Die Politische Rolle der Frau in Deutschland*. Göttingen, Vandenhock & Ruprecht, 1956.

Buchanan, William, and Hadley Cantril, *How Nations See Each Other: A Study in Public Opinion*. Urbana, University of Illinois Press, 1953.

Craig, Gordon A., *From Bismarck to Adenauer: Aspects of German Statecraft*. Baltimore, Johns Hopkins Press, 1958.

——— *NATO and the New German Army*. Princeton, Princeton University Center of International Studies (Memo No. 8), 1955.

——— *The Politics of the Prussian Army, 1640–1945*. Oxford, Clarendon, 1955.

Dechamps, Bruno, *Macht und Arbeit der Ausschüsse*. Meisenheim am Glan, Westkulturverlag, 1954.

Deutsch, Karl W., "Joseph Schumpeter as an Analyst of Sociology and Economic History," *Journal of Economic History*, March 1956.

——— *Nationalism and Social Communication*. Cambridge and New York, M.I.T. Press and Wiley, 1953.

Deutsch, Karl W., S. A. Burrell, R. A. Kann, M. Lee, Jr., M. Lichterman, R. E. Lindgren, F. L. Loewenheim, and R. W. Van Wagenen, *Political Community and the North Atlantic Area*. Princeton, Princeton University Press, 1957.

Dicks, Henry V., "Some Psychological Studies of the German Character," in T. H. Pear, *Psychological Factors of Peace and War*. New York, Philosophical Library, 1950.

Edinger, Lewis J., *German Exile Politics*. Berkeley, University of California Press, 1956.

——— *West German Armament.* Research Studies Institute, Documentary Research Division, Air University, Maxwell Air Force Base, Ala., October 1955.

Ellwein, Thomas, *Klerikalismus in der deutschen Politik.* München, Isar, 1956.

Eschenburg, Theodor, *Herrschaft der Verbände?* Stuttgart, Deutsche Verlagsanstalt, 1955.

——— *Staat und Gesellschaft in Deutschland.* Stuttgart, Curt E. Schwab, 1956.

Eyck, Franz, "Tensions in Western Germany," *Contemporary Review,* No. 1098 (June 1957), pp. 325–28.

Flechtheim, Ossip K., *Die Deutschen Parteien seit 1945: Quellen und Auszüge.* Berlin, Carl Heymanns Verlag, 1955.

Fröhner, Rolf, *Wie stark sind die Halbstarken? Dritte Emnid Untersuchung zur Situation der deutschen Jugend.* Bielefeld, Stackelberg Verlag, 1956.

Germany, Federal Republic, Bundesministerium des Innern. *Handbuch für die Bundesrepublik Deutschland, 1953, 1954.* Köln-Berlin, Carl Heymanns, n.d.

——— Bundesministerium für den Marshallplan, *Fünfter und sechster Bericht der Deutschen Bundesregierung über die Durchführung des Marshallplanes, Oktober 1950–März 1951.*

——— Bundesministerium für wirtschaftliche Zusammenarbeit. *Der Europäische Wirtschaftsrat—OEEC: Handbuch, 1956.* Godesberg, Verlag für Publizistik, 1957.

——— Bundesminister für wirtschaftliche Zusammenarbeit. *Siebenter und achter Bericht der Deutschen Bundesregierung über die Fortführung der Amerikanischen Wirtschaftshilfe (FOA).* Bonn, 1954.

——— Bundestagsverwaltung. *Amtliches Handbuch des deutschen Bundestages, z. Wahlperiode 1953.* Darmstadt, Darmstädter Verlagsanstalt, 1954.

——— *Deutschland im Wiederaufbau: Tätigkeitsbericht der Bundesregierung für das Jahr 1952.* Bonn, Deutscher Bundesverlag, n.d. Also issues for 1953, 1954, 1955.

——— The Press and Information Office of the German Federal Government. *Germany Reports, 1953.*

——— *Statistisches Jahrbuch für die Bundesrepublik Deutschland.* 1951, 1952, 1953, 1954, 1955, 1956. Stuttgart, W. Kohlammer.

"Glossen," *Aussenpolitik,* 4 (1955), 477.

Grossmann, Kurt R., *Germany's Moral Debt: The German-Israel Agreement.* Washington, D.C., Public Affairs Press, 1954.

Haas, Ernst B., *The Uniting of Europe: Political, Social, and Economic Forces, 1950–1957.* Stanford, Stanford University Press, 1958.

Habel, Walter, ed., *Wer Ist Wer?* Berlin, Arani, 1955.

Hartmann, Heinz, "Authority and Organization in German Management." Unpublished Ph.D. dissertation, Princeton University, 1958.

Heidenheimer, A. J., "German Party Finance: The CDU," *American Political Science Review,* 51:2 (June 1957), 369–85.

Hellpach, Willy, *Der Deutsche Charakter.* Bonn, Athenäum, 1954.

Hirsch-Weber, Wolfgang, and Klaus Schütz, *Wähler und Gewählte: Eine Untersuchung der Bundestagswahlen 1953.* Berlin, Vahlen, 1957.

Horne, Alistair, *Return to Power: A Report on the New Germany.* New York, Praeger, 1956.

Institut für Publizistik der Freien Universität Berlin. *Die Deutsche Presse: Zeitungen und Zeitschriften.* Berlin, Duncker und Humblot, 1955, 1956.

International Press Institute, *The Flow of the News.* Zurich, I.P.I., 1953.

Kaiser, J. H., *Die Repräsentation organisierter Interessen.* Berlin, Duncker und Humblot, 1956.

Kecskemeti, Paul, and Nathan Leites, *Some Psychological Hypotheses on Nazi Germany*. Washington, D.C., Experimental Division for the Study of Wartime Communications, Library of Congress, 1945. (Also in *Journal of Social Psychology*, November 1947–August 1948.)

Kirchheimer, Otto, "The Political Scene in West Germany," *World Politics*, April 1957, pp. 433–45.

Kliemann, Horst G., and Stephen S. Taylor, eds., *Who's Who in Germany*. Munich, Intercontinental Book and Publishing Company, 1956.

Knight, Maxwell E., *The German Executive, 1890–1933*. Stanford, Stanford University Press, 1952.

Knoll, Joachim-Heinrich, "Die Elitebildung im Liberalismus des Kaiserreichs." Dissertation, Erlangen, Friedrich-Alexander-Universität, 1956.

———— *Führungsauslese in Liberalismus und Demokratie Zur politische Geistesgeschichte der letzten 100 Jahre*. Stuttgart, 1957.

Knorr, Klaus, *The War Potential of Nations*. Princeton, Princeton University Press, 1956.

Köhler, A., and K. Jansen, eds., *Die Bundesrepublik; Taschenbuch für Verwaltungsbeamte 1954/55, 1956/57*. Berlin, C. Heymann.

Kohn, Hans, *German History: Some New German Views*. Boston, Beacon Press, 1954.

Kracauer, Siegfried, *From Caligari to Hitler: A Psychological Study of the German Film*. New York, Noonday Press, 1959.

Krieger, Leonard, *The German Idea of Freedom: History of a Political Tradition*. Boston, Beacon Press, 1957.

Lange, Max Gustav, *et al.*, *Parteien in der Bundesrepublik. Studien zur Entwicklung der deutschen Parteien bis zur Bundestagswahl 1953*. Stuttgart und Düsseldorf, Ring, 1955.

Luther, Hans, *Weimar und Bonn*. München, Isar, 1951.

Mangoldt, Hermann von, *Das Bonner Grundgesetz*. Berlin and Frankfurt, Franz Vahlen, 1953.

Mason, Henry L., *The European Coal and Steel Community: Experiment in Supranationalism*. The Hague, Nijhoff, 1955.

Matthias, Erich, *Sozialdemokratie und Nation*. Stuttgart, Deutsche Verlagsanstalt, 1952.

Mehnert, Klaus, and Heinrich Schulte, eds., *Deutschland-Jahrbuch 1953*. Essen, Rheinisch-Westfälisches Verlags Kontor, 1953.

Mellen, Sydney L. W., "The German People and the Postwar World: A Study Based on Election Statistics, 1871–1933," *American Political Science Review*, 37:4 (August 1943), 601–25.

Mendershausen, Horst, *Two Postwar Recoveries of the German Economy*. Contributions to Economic Analysis, 8, Amsterdam, North-Holland Publishing Co., 1955.

Merkatz, Hans Joachim von, and Wolfgang Metzger, *Deutschland-Taschenbuch: Tatsachen und Zahlen*. Frankfurt and Berlin, Alfred Metzger Verlag, 1954.

Mommsen, Wilhelm, *Die Situation der deutschen Parteien: Eine historisch-politische Betrachtung*. München, Isar, 1953.

Montgomery, John D., *Forced to Be Free: The Artificial Revolution in Germany and Japan*. Chicago, University of Chicago Press, 1957.

Münch, Fritz, *Die Bundesregierung*. Frankfurt, Alfred Metner, 1954.

Neumann, Elisabeth Noelle, and Erich Peter Neumann, *Jahrbuch der öffentlichen Meinung, 1947–1955*. Allensbach, Verlag für Demoskopie, 1956.

———— *Jahrbuch der öffentlichen Meinung, 1957*. Allensbach Verlag für Demoskopie, 1957.

Neumann, Erich Peter, and Elisabeth Noelle Neumann. *Antworten: Politik in Kraftfeld der öffentlichen Meinung*. Allensbach, Verlag für Demoskopie, 1954.

Neumann, Erich Peter, "Nützt Ungarn der CDU?" *Der Spiegel*, 11:2 (January 4, 1957).

Neumann, Franz L., et al., *Die Grundrechte: Handbuch der Theorie und Praxis der Grundrechte*. Berlin, Duncker & Humblot, 1954.

Neumann, Sigmund, "Germany: Changing Patterns and Lasting Problems," in S. Neumann (ed.), *Modern Political Parties*. Chicago, University of Chicago Press, 1956.

Oeckl, Albert, and Rudolf Vogel, eds., *Taschenbuch des öffentlichen Lebens 1956*. Bonn, Festland Verlag, 1956.

"Ollenhausers Mannschaft," *Die Gegenwart*, July 28, 1956, pp. 464–66.

Onslow, C. G. D., "West German Armament," *World Politics*, 3:4 (July 1951).

Parsons, Talcott, "Democracy and Social Structure in Pre-Nazi Germany," in *Essays in Sociological Theory*. Rev. ed., Glencoe, Free Press, 1954, pp. 104–23.

———— "The Problem of Controlled Institutional Change," in *Essays in Sociological Theory*. Rev. ed., Glencoe, Free Press, 1954, pp. 238–74.

Peak, Helen, "Observations on the Characteristics and Distribution of German Nazis," *Psychological Monographs*, 59, 1–44 (No. 6, 1945; whole No. 276).

Pilgert, Henry P., *Press, Radio and Film in West Germany 1945–1953*. Historical Division, Office of the Executive Secretary, Office of the U.S. High Commissioner for Germany, 1953.

Podzun, Hans-Henning, *Das Wehrarchiv: Handbuch des Wehrwesens der Gegenwart*. Bad Nauheim, Podzun-Verlag, 1956.

Pollock, Friedrich, ed., *Gruppenexperiment: Ein Studienbericht*. Frankfurter Beiträge zur Soziologie, Band 2; Frankfurt, Europäische Verlagsanstalt, 1955.

Pollock, James Kerr, *Money and Politics Abroad*. Part III, "Germany," pp. 205–76. New York, Knopf, 1932.

Pollock, James Kerr, and Homer Thomas, *Germany in Power and Eclipse*. New York, Van Nostrand, 1952.

Press Office, German Diplomatic Mission, Washington. *Handbook of German Affairs*. Washington, D.C., 1954.

Price, Hoyt, and Carl E. Schorske, *The Problem of Germany*. New York, Council on Foreign Relations, 1947.

Pritzkoleit, Kurt, *Manner—Mächte—Monopols: Hinter den Türen der westdeutschen Wirtschaft*. Düsseldorf, Karl Rauch Verlag, 1953.

Ranke, Hansjürg, *Evangelische Kirche und Staat*. München, Isar, 1953.

Reigrotzki, Erich, *Soziale Verflechtungen in der Bundesrepublik: Elemente der sozialen Teilnahme in der Kirche, Organisation und Freizeit*. Tübingen, J. C. B. Mohr, 1956.

Russett, Bruce M., *Economic Impact of German Rearmament*. Williamstown, Mass., Williams College, 1957.

Schachtner, Richard, *Die deutschen Nachkriegswahlen: Wahlergebnisse in der Bundesrepublik Deutschland, in den deutschen Bundesländern, in West Berlin, im Saarland und in der Sowjetzone 1946 bis 1956*. München, Isar, 1956.

Schäfer, Hans, *Der Bundesrat*. Köln-Berlin, Carl Heymanns, 1955.

Schaffner, Bertram, *Father Land: A Study of Authoritarianism in the German Family*. New York, Columbia University Press, 1948.

Schmid, Carlo, "Untertöne eines Briefes," *Aussenpolitik*, 8:3 (March 1957).

Schuetz, Wilhelm Wolfgang, "Mitsprachrecht von Afro-Asien," *Aussenpolitik*, 8:3 (March 1957).

Schultes, Karl, "German Politics and Political Theory," *Political Quarterly*, 28:1 (January–March 1957), 40–48.

Schumpeter, Joseph A., *Aufsätze zur Soziologie.* Tübingen, Mohr, 1953.

Seabury, Paul, *The Wilhelmstrasse.* Berkeley, University of California Press, 1954.

Sieveking, Kurt, "Die europäische Aufgabe der deutschen Aussenpolitik," *Aussenpolitik,* 8:3 (March 1957), 147–54.

Snyder, Richard C., and Edgar S. Furniss, Jr., *American Foreign Policy.* New York, Rinehart, 1954.

Speier, Hans, *German Rearmament and Atomic War: The Views of German Military and Political Leaders.* Evanston, Row, Peterson and Co., 1957.

—— *Social Order and the Risks of War: Papers in Political Sociology.* New York, George W. Stewart, 1952.

Speier, Hans, and W. Phillips Davison, eds., *West German Leadership and Foreign Policy.* Evanston, Row, Peterson and Co., 1957.

Stackelberg, Karl-Georg von, ed., *Jugend zwischen 15 und 24: Eine Untersuchung zur Situation der Deutschen Jugend im Bundesgebiet.* Bielefeld, Emnid-Institut, 1954.

Strange, Susan, "The Schuman Plan," in *The Year Book of World Affairs.* London, Stevens, 1951.

Strauss, Franz-Josef, "Sicherheit und Wiedervereinigung," *Aussenpolitik,* 6:3 (March 1957), 140–47.

Taschenbuch für Wehrfragen 1956. Bonn, Festland Verlag, 1956.

Trossmann, Hans, *Aufgaben und Arbeitweise des deutschen Bundestages.* München, Isar, 1953.

—— *Der Zweite Deutsche Bundestag: Seine Vorgeschichte, sein Aufbau und sein Wirken.* Bonn, Verlag Bonner Universitäts-Buchdruckerei Gebr. Scheur, 1954.

Truman, David B., *The Governmental Process.* New York, Knopf, 1953.

Uhlig, A. W., *Hat die SPD noch eine Chance? Heisse Eisen,* Bd. 2. München, 1956.

United Nations, Department of Economic Affairs, Economic Commission for Europe, *Economic Survey of Europe in 1953.* Geneva, 1954.

—— Statistical Office. *Per Capita National Product of 55 Countries, 1952–54.* Statistical Papers, Series E, No. 4 (Sales No. 1957 XVII.2), New York, 1954.

—— Statistical Papers. *National and Per Capita Incomes of 70 Countries in 1949.* Statistical Papers, Series E, No. 1, New York, 1950.

United States, Department of Commerce, Office of Business Economics, *Foreign Grants and Credits by the United States Government.* December 1955 Quarter. Washington, D.C., April 1956.

—— International Cooperation Administration. *Operations Report, Data as of March 31, 1956.* Washington, D.C., 1956.

—— Office of the High Commissioner for Germany (HICOG), *Reports.* Listed in Bruce Lannes Smith and Chitra M. Smith, *International Communication and Political Opinion.* Princeton, Princeton University Press, 1957, pp. 205–12.

United States Congress, Senate. *Protocol on the Termination of the Occupation Regime in the Federal Republic of Germany and Protocol to the North Atlantic Treaty on the Accession of the Federal Republic of Germany.* 83rd Congress, 2d Session, Executives L and M, U.S. Government Printing Office, Washington, D.C., 1954.

—— *Foreign Aid Program: Compilation of Studies and Surveys.* 85th Congress, 1st Session, Document No. 52. U.S. Government Printing Office, Washington, D.C., 1957.

Wallenberg, Hans, *Report on Democratic Institutions in Germany.* New York, American Council on Germany, 1956.

Wallich, Henry C., *Mainsprings of the German Revival.* New Haven, Yale University Press, 1955.

Weymar, Paul, *Konrad Adenauer: Die autorisierte Biographie.* München, Kindler, 1955.

Wildenmann, Rudolf, *Partei und Fraktion. Ein Beitrag zur Analyse der Politischen Willensbildung und des Parteisystems in der Bundesrepublik.* Meisenheim, Westkulturverlag Anton Hain, 1954.

Wiskemann, Elisabeth, *Germany's Eastern Neighbors: Problems Relating to the Oder-Neisse Line and the Czech Frontier Regions.* Issued under the auspices of the Royal Institute of International Affairs. Oxford, London, New York, Oxford University Press, 1956.

"Wo findet der Wahlkampf statt?" *Die Gegenwart,* 12:5 (March 9, 1957), 1–2.

Wolff, Kurt H., "German Attempts at Picturing Germany: Texts," *Studies in German-American Postwar Problems,* No. 3. Columbus, Department of Sociology and Anthropology, Ohio State University, August 1955.

Zink, Harold, *The United States in Germany 1944–1955.* New York, Van Nostrand, 1957.

Index

For further names of authors see Bibliography. References apply to German Federal Republic unless otherwise specified.

Bavarian People's party, 67
Bayrischer Rundfunk, 120n
Belgian Congo, trade with, 229, 231
Belgium: and Brussels Pact, 253; Catholic hierarchy, 107; and ECSC, 156; and EDC, 164; and European integration, 156; trade with, 228, 230
Bell, H. T. Montague, 249n
Berelson, Bernard, ix n
Berlin, division of, 190; Four-Power Conference, 256; Four-Power occupation, 241; as symbol, 193
Berlin, East, 5, 241; and Oder-Neisse line, 258; riots, 255; rising (1953), 256
Berlin, West, 5, 141n; access to, 237, 241; aid to, 145–48; Bundestag meetings in, 193; and demilitarization, 259; negotiations on, 233; and occupying powers, 166, 256
Berlin Blockade, 55, 253–54
BHE. *See* Refugee party
Biedermeier age, 192
Bild-Zeitung of Hamburg, 114, 119n, 120n
Bismarck, 6, 18, 21, 249; after resignation, 81; as "honest broker" between Russia and England, 192; as symbol, 14, 192
Bi-zonia, bi-zonal, 253
Blank, Theodor, as defense minister, 203, 256, 257
Blankenhorn, Herbert, 156, 170, 173
Bloc, blocs, 46, 47
Boehm, Franz, 173
Böll, Heinrich, 16n
Bolivia, trade with, 228, 230
Bombing, World War II, 16, 191
Bonn: interest group liaison staff in, 93; as provisional capital, 193. *See also* German Federal Republic
Borch, Herbert von, 123
Bourgeois, 65, 71. *See also* Bürgerlich
Brandenburg-Prussia. *See* Prussia
Braunschweiger Zeitung, 120
Brazil, trade with, 228, 230
Breitling, Rupert, 92n, 94n
Bremen, 134
Brentano, Heinrich von, 55, 78, 185
Britain, British government. *See* United Kingdom
British Guiana, trade with, 229, 231
British Persian Gulf States, trade with, 229, 231
Brüning, Heinrich, 250
Brunswick, 134
Brussels Pact, 253
Buchanan, William, viii n, 34n
Buchenwald, 3
Budapest, demonstrations in, 257
Bulganin, Nikolai, 220

Bulgaria: trade with, 228, 230; and United Nations, 234
Bundesrat, 56, 254–59; president, 224; and Saar agreement, 257; and states in foreign policy, 51
Bundestag, lower house, parliament, x, 44, 52, 56, 57, 62, 193, 254–59; CDU majority in, 166; and chancellor, 52; and civil service, 82; dissolution, 57; and executive responsibility, 52; interest representation in, 91–92; members in cabinet, 77n; powers of, 57–59; president of, 78; right of investigation, 57
Bundestag committees, 57, 58, 62; chairmanships and vice-chairmanships, 78, 80, 92; class origins, 126; coordination, 92; and elite, 78; and foreign policy, 79; and interest groups, 92; members, 80
—All-German Affairs, 58, 126n; Budget, 58; Defense, 57; Economic Policy, 92; European Security, 58; Expellees, 58; Foreign Affairs, 57, 126n; Foreign Trade, 58, 92; Legal, 170; Money and Credit, 92; Nationalization, 92; Patents, 92; Refugee Affairs, 92; Transport, 92
Bundestag elite, 76, 78, 92, 140; Adenauer's leadership in, 76; and chancellor, 53; characteristics, 78; and generations, 129; influence, 80, 204–14; religious affiliation, 79; social origins, 126, 131; and West Germans, 127
Bundestag views and policies: armament, 246; coal tariff, 201; ECSC, 156, 158–59; EDC, 165; Israel, 170–76; reunification, 240
Bureaucratic elite. *See* Administrative elite
Bureaucracy, bureaucratic. *See* Administration
Bürgerlich, 64, 71
Burma, trade with, 229, 231
Business, businessmen, 71, 232; age, 127; conservatism, 64; in Federal Republic, 35; financial contributions, 93, 99; in German Party, 158; government control of, 157; influence, 214; interest groups, 91, 92, 100; and USSR, 244n
—views and policies: Adenauer, 181; Afro-Asian countries, 226; Arab world, 172; CDU, 93, 95; confidence in economy, 150; ECSC, 159–60; Israel, 171–72; neutralism, 223; reunification, 181
Business elite, big business, 97–101, 223; composition, 100; education, 102; and generations, 129; geographical representation, 102; influence, 98, 99, 197, 202, 204–14; interest in foreign policy, 101, 197–98; political irresponsibility, 101; religious preferences, 102

War crimes, criminals, attitude toward, 42,
246–47; convictions for, 105; Nürnberg,
252
Warsaw. *See* Poland
Warsaw Pact, 256
Weapons: ABC, 167, 213, 245; conventional,
243; limitations on, 167. *See also* Nuclear
weapons, Armament, Missiles
Wehrarchiv, Das, 85, 86, 133
Weimar Republic. *See* Republic, Weimar
Weisenborn, Günther, 138n
Weizmann, Dr. Chaim, 168
Welt, Die, 119n, 120
Welt am Sonntag, 119n, 120n
West, Western, Western world, 17, 23, 245;
alliance with (*see* Alliance, Western);
concessions from, 66; economic position,
225; Egyptian defiance of, 226; needs,
246; news of, 113; policies, 235; power,
225, 241, 245; security, contributions to,
246; threats to, 244; and U.N., 235; unity
of, 246
—ties to, 42, 46, 232; cultural, 240, 242;
economic, 240, 242; military, 240; political, 242
West Berlin. *See* Berlin, West
Westdeutsche Allgemeine Zeitung, 119n,
120n
Western Alliance. *See* Alliance with West
Western Allied forces, in Germany, 163, 165
Western Christendom, 11
Western Europe. *See* Europe
Western European integration. *See* Euro-
pean integration
Western European Union, 167, 253; attitudes
toward, 21n, 27–29, 166–67; Council of
Union, 167; creation, 256
Western powers, concessions from, 75; con-
cessions to GDR, 241; cooperation with,
64, 69, 70, 126, 155; influence, 204–14;
protection by, 199; and reunification, 74
Westfalenpost, 120n
Westfälische Rundschau, 120n
Weymar, Paul, 163n, 170n, 173n
Wheeler-Bennett, John W., 249n

Wiechert, Ernst, 16n
Wilhelm II, Emperor, 81, 249
Wiskemann, Elisabeth, 96n
Withdrawal, of foreign troops, 21, 243
Women, 35, 64; and army, 30; and democracy, 43; housewives, 43; and news, 113;
newspaper readers, 112; and SPD, 71;
and suppression of parties, 63
Work, work habits, 34, 150
Work week, 150
Workers, associations of, 101; and CDU, 95;
democratic opinions, 43; in elites, 126,
136n; organizations, 97; in population, 35,
126; salaried, 35; salaried organizations,
101–3; semiskilled, 36; skilled, 17, 36;
skilled, supply from East Germany and
Italy, 150; and SPD, 70, 71; unorganized,
71; unskilled, 36. *See also* Labor, Trade
unions
—white-collar, 37, 71; and army, 167; and
democracy, 43; and ECSC, 159; in population, 35
World Bank, 147
World Health Organization (WHO), 255
World Jewish Congress, 170
Woytinsky, E. S., 231
Woytinsky, W. S., 231
Writers, 16, 224

Yale University, xi
Yalta Conference, 252
Youth, young people, 20, 26, 30, 39, 40, 65;
and anti-Semitism, 41n, 42n; and army,
30; and military service, 44, 86; and
Nazis, 40, 43, 44, 86; in population, 35;
and prosperity, 45; among refugees, 104,
150, 179; among university rectors, 123
Yugoslavia: diplomatic relations with, 206,
210, 213, 258; neutrality, 47; recognition
of GDR, 258; trade with, 228, 230, 258

Zeit, Die, 115
Zeitblom, Serenus, 17
Zeitschrift für Geopolitik, 119n
Zollverein, 249